A Licence to Be Different

• • • •

First published in 2007 by the
British Film Institute
21 Stephen Street, London W1T 1LN

There's more to discover about film and television through the BFI. Our world-renowned archive, cinemas, festivals, films, publications and learning resources are here to inspire you.

Cover design: Eureka

Typeset by The Little Red Pen, Dublin
Printed in the UK by Cromwell Press, Trowbridge, Wiltshire

British Library Cataloguing in Publication Data
A catalogue record for this book is available from the British Library

ISBN 978-1-84457-204-5 (hbk)
ISBN 978-1-84457-205-2 (pbk)

Image credits: Photographs of Jeremy Isaacs and of Sir Richard Attenborough by Gemma Levine/Hulton Archive. Reproduced by kind permission of Getty Images. Photograph of Michael Grade by Keystone/Hulton Archive. Reproduced by kind permission of Getty Images. Photograph of opening-night script reproduced by kind permission of Paul Coia. Photographs of Jon Snow and Jim Gray and of Tim Gardam © Guardian News & Media Ltd 1999. Photograph of Michael Jackson © Guardian News & Media Ltd 2001. Photograph of Mark Thompson © Guardian News & Media Ltd 2003. Photograph of Luke Johnson © David Levene 2005. Photograph of Andy Duncan © Martin Godwin 2006. Photograph of Kevin Lygo © Felix Clay 2007.

A Licence to Be Different

The story of Channel 4

• • • •

Maggie Brown

To my parents, Marion and Cecil

Contents

● ● ● ●

Foreword

Channel 4 is a brilliant accident of history, and Britain's cultural life over the past quarter century has been all the richer for it. At its heart, the organisation exists to provide a forum for individual voices making one-off programmes that would otherwise never reach a national audience. And at its finest, Channel 4 can be sublime: stirring drama, riotous comedy, compelling documentaries, unbeatable current affairs. The BBC is a vast state-sponsored institution; ITV a huge commercial business. Channel 4 sits between these goliaths, a quirky amalgamation that aims to deliver public goods while retaining the verve of the private sector.

As this history shows, Channel 4 regularly supplies shock and awe to British citizens via the television – and not always in the way planned. It has an impressive capacity to infuriate – and inspire. It has always been the broadcaster most reliant on independent producers, so they have frequently brought their most extreme – and innovative – ideas to us. While this does not make for a peaceful existence, I suspect that Channel 4's integral policy of taking creative risks is the only way an artistic body can renew itself on a regular basis. Otherwise the schedule becomes clogged with long-running series and predictable formats, leaving no room for radical breakthroughs.

As a launch pad for new talent, Channel 4 has a remarkable track record. It has given early breaks to an astounding array of comedians, directors, writers, actors and presenters – and even television executives. Many have gone on to considerable fame and fortune, from Stephen Frears to Jonathan Ross. And it is surely no coincidence that the bosses of the two largest television broadcasters are also former Channel 4 chief executives.

The creative economy has also benefited enormously from the huge success of Channel 4. PricewaterhouseCoopers estimate the corporation's contribution at £2 billion a year, while its activities support 22,000 jobs. Its investment in British films and policy of regional production distinguish it from other broadcasters. It has achieved this without any direct cost to the taxpayer, save gifted spectrum. There can be no other part of the state that offers such enjoyment and value to the taxpayer for so little cost, while also boosting the economy.

In 1966 E.B. White wrote in an essay in support of public-service broadcasting:

> I think TV should be providing the visual counterpart of the literary
> essay, should arouse our dreams, satisfy our hunger for beauty, take us
> on journeys, enable us to participate in events, present great drama and
> must explore the sea and the sky and the wood and the hills [. . .] it
> should restate and clarify the social dilemma and the political pickle.

When it works, Channel 4 does all this and more. It can do this because it is independent: it sells its own advertising time to fund its programmes. Overall, I believe
Channel 4 provides more distinctive entertainment and enlightenment at less cost,
to more citizens, than any equivalent body in Britain today. And because Channel 4
generates its own revenues, it is independent from shareholders, independent from
in-house production, even independent from government – most of the time. This
allows Channel 4 to remain undeterred by controversy and still able to take risks. It
is not afraid to break taboos, expose hypocrisy and lead campaigns like that inspired
by *Jamie's School Dinners*. From time to time, it is almost deliberately obscure or
provocative. In a democracy the media is a vital forum for legitimate debate; only in
totalitarian regimes are contrary opinions forbidden.

Channel 4 faces challenges ahead, as do all the so-called 'legacy' media companies: newspaper and magazine publishers, radio and other television broadcasters.
The advent of digital television has led to an explosion of choice for the television
viewer, while the arrival of new competitors means the price of content such as imported shows has risen. Meanwhile, the online world is attracting an increasing share
of the advertising cake – and of viewers, especially younger audiences, traditionally
Channel 4's heartland.

But very few, if any, of these impressive new channels or websites are delivering
what might be called public-service broadcasting. Their objectives are purely commercial. By contrast, while Channel 4 is entrepreneurial and flexible, its overriding
purpose is to show diverse, experimental and educative television – original British
commissions from all over the country.

Moreover, Channel 4 is embracing the digital age and expanding its horizons beyond a single channel. It already has successful offshoots like E4 and More4, together
with Film4. It has a significant online presence and is about to launch a raft of DAB
radio stations. Further new media initiatives are planned. Long-term Channel 4 cannot rely on its core channel; it must diversify and broaden its appeal, as consumers
obtain information and entertainment from an ever wider array of platforms.

Maggie Brown's book paints a slightly mixed picture of Channel 4's first twenty-
five years. While I disagree with some of her interpretations, I think this is an important document, which is why I championed the project within Channel 4. She has
tried hard to reveal the truth, although inevitably elements of the story are subjective. Ultimately, she is a commentator on the outside, who is trying to create a dra-

matic narrative. She can never understand the complexities and subtleties of actually trying to balance the conflicting aims of a quirky, hybrid institution like Channel 4. Life is never as simple as books portray. Nevertheless, I salute her industry.

The principal message of the book must be this: Channel 4 has been a pioneer from the start and remains a huge force for good, despite its mistakes. It pushes the boundaries in every genre, from news, to documentaries, to comedy, to film, to reality television. It is staffed by many outstanding people and supplied by inspired programme-makers. It helps keep other public broadcasters up to the mark and generates enormous added value for the creative economy in Britain. I sincerely hope Channel 4 prospers and is around to celebrate its fiftieth anniversary with another history, listing many more great achievements.

Luke Johnson

Acknowledgements

The idea of writing the history of Channel 4 first came to me in September 1997, at a dinner party in Notting Hill. Another guest was the new Chief Executive of the channel, Michael Jackson. At the time, Jackson was at the start of a mission to reinvigorate the channel, a crusade that would result in stand-out programmes such as Sacha Baron Cohen's Ali G, and *Queer as Folk*.

Just two months earlier I had attended a farewell dinner for Jackson's predecessor Michael Grade, whose larger-than-life personality dominated the channel for ten years. That party had been held in the mirrored ballroom of the Dorchester Hotel. Guests started off by playing bingo, and by each place setting was a pair of Grade's trademark red socks, tied with golden string.

I was amazed that no one had seen the need to record this unique chapter in British broadcasting history, relying instead on Jeremy Isaacs' first-hand account of founding the channel, which went up only to 1987, when Isaacs left Channel 4. But Channel 4 never had much sense of its past: then, as now, it was always looking to the future.

While other projects took priority, the idea stayed with me, and I kept a beady eye on Channel 4 and watched as many of its programmes as life permitted. In 2005, with the channel's twenty-fifth anniversary looming, I raised the idea with Luke Johnson, the then newish Chairman of Channel 4, at the Edinburgh Television Festival. We talked it over on a coach to the conference centre, and by the time we arrived, I knew I had a deal. Johnson is a fast worker.

As an outsider to the channel and to television, Johnson grasped immediately the need for a history with a page-turning sense of narrative – as did Andy Duncan, Channel 4's Chief Executive. Both have played key parts as patrons to this history, and without them it could not have happened. Andy Duncan has been unstintingly kind and patient in providing access and supporting the project, as have others at Channel 4 – crucially David Scott, the former Deputy Chief Executive, who helped me write a detailed synopsis and facilitated access to Channel 4 boardroom minutes.

Channel 4 enabled the book to be written but with this important caveat: this is not an official history. Although I am the first outsider to be granted supervised access to its archive, the interpretation and organisation of this history is all mine. An approved version would read quite differently. I wanted it to be accessible, to wear its authority lightly so as to interest as many people as possible, not just media experts and policy wonks. Channel 4 exists for everyone.

Channel 4's archivists, led by Rosie Gleeson, deserve special thanks: they unearthed many gems, enabling some extra chapters, notably on the relationship between Michael Grade and the dramatists Alan Bleasdale and Dennis Potter, to come to life. Pamela Dear, the archivist of its public record, was another key person who kindly smoothed my path and looked out lost documents with a maternal affection for the channel. The *Guardian*'s own research team were helpful in digging up long forgotten articles. Within Channel 4, Claire Grimmond, who provided key information on programme performance and ratings, and Rosemary Newell, were stars. The Royal Television Society's Simon Albury offered advice and Archivist Clare Colvin mined the archive for conference reports and speeches. I was also warmly encouraged in the project by an industry contact since 1980, Sir George Russell, who devoted hours to briefing me, as did David Glencross, the former Chief Executive of the Independent Television Commission, who lent me key reading material.

The Chairmen, Richard Attenborough, Michael Bishop, Vanni Treves and Deputy Chairman Barry Cox all agreed to be interviewed, as did Jeremy Isaacs, Michael Jackson, Mark Thompson and Directors of Programmes, Liz Forgan, John Willis, Tim Gardam and Kevin Lygo. On the regulatory side, Ofcom was extremely helpful, with Stephen Carter and Richard Hooper providing key insights, while other Ofcom experts, led by Kate Stross and Mark Bunting, painstakingly took me through their financial review of Channel 4. Chris Smith, the former Secretary for Culture, Media and Sport helped me put the crucial 1997–2001 period into context. The one person who refused to be involved was Michael Grade. I managed without him.

The people I interviewed on the record are listed in the footnotes. I thank them all for their time and patience. They include Founders Anthony Smith, generous with encouragement and advice; Roger Graef; Justin Dukes; Paul Coia; Tim Simmons, who provided some wonderful videotapes of Jeremy Isaacs and his notes to staff; Pam Masters; Jo Wright, who first reminded me of the leading role a pot plant played in Channel 4's early presentation; Cecil Korer; Sue Stoessl; Mike Bolland and Sue Woodford. Nigel Stafford-Clark was a mine of information. John Morrison, a founder of *Channel 4 News* provided long-lost documents about the early disaster days, as did Peter Moore from the 1997 era.

None of this would have happened without the utter professionalism and steadfast support of my publisher, Rebecca Barden of the British Film Institute (BFI), who was a true midwife to the book. Michael Leapman, with whom I once job-shared on the *Independent*, also played a pivotal role, bringing all his experience and flair to patiently advising, editing and reading the script over a period of months. Liz O'Donnell project-managed the final stages with speed and accuracy. Richard Paterson at the BFI kindly read the completed book and advised, as did Corinna Honan, who provided encouragement and seasoned editing advice. Thanks also to Jan Tomalin at Channel 4 who rooted out the odd inaccuracy. Matt Wells, Media Editor of the *Guardian* patiently let me concentrate all my efforts on the history, rather than journalism, during the crucial months of 2007 when I was finalising the book.

This is the story of an amazing British experiment.

Enjoy.

Maggie Brown
September 2007

1

How Celebrity Big Brother
changed Channel 4

● ● ● ●

In the autumn of 2006, Channel 4 began to lay plans for its twenty-fifth anniversary on 2 November 2007. It should have been preparing a celebration. On launch in 1982 it was a tiny experimental station with burning ambitions and an independent spirit, determined to do things differently. By now it was a sleek media company headquartered in a palace of glass and stainless steel designed by Richard Rogers, with an annual turnover of almost £1 billion. The contrast was astonishing; but then, Britain, too, was a different and, in particular, a more prosperous place.

Though facing mounting accusations of betraying its mission, the mature channel was still basking in what was to be a final hour of Indian summer after a two-year period of sustained success.[1] For the past ten years, during the decade of Tony Blair, no one had seriously questioned Channel 4's unusual status, its privileges and independence. But, as August turned into September, the atmosphere changed, the mood music shifted from an upbeat major key to an ominous minor one.

Several forces were conspiring to bear down on this strange British experiment which had grown out of Margaret Thatcher's decision to shake up the television establishment by allowing the creation of a fourth channel, publishing programmes made by small independent producers and paid for, irony of ironies, by ITV. The mounting pressure on Channel 4 contributed to the most damaging episode in the company's history: the outburst of naked racism on *Celebrity Big Brother* in January 2007, which provoked an unprecedented level of complaints[2] and was deeply harmful to a broadcaster priding itself on catering to contemporary multicultural Britain.

Although the incident, principally involving the Bollywood actress Shilpa Shetty and, a former dental nurse whose celebrity status dated back to her role in the third series of *Big Brother*, appeared to blow up out of nothing – the cooking of a chicken, the waste of an Oxo cube – it was no storm in a casserole. The essential ingredients were all in place and had been simmering away since the series started. At some stage, over some issue, *Big Brother* was bound to overheat and, in the process, to shatter Channel 4's image. Even before the Jade Goody outburst, the show's producers and crew of more than 300 were struggling to keep hold of the show's audience, whose average age was climbing worryingly, and were resorting to ever more contrived antics and bizarre twists.

● ● ● ●

The defining moment of the channel's change in fortunes can be pinpointed with some accuracy: a meeting in the boardroom on Thursday, 21 September 2006. This was when the Director of Television, Kevin Lygo, in charge of the programme budget of £500,000 (more generous than BBC2's), called together his senior commissioners, mostly high-flyers in their thirties. The channel has always held programme reviews on Thursdays, and, in the early days, under Jeremy Isaacs, they were disputatious affairs, astounding newcomers with their frank exchanges of views. By now, they had matured into cooler, more scientific debates, with the ratings expert setting the scene by analysing the past week and the key demographics, examining whether enough of the right people were watching. The right people generally meant young adults – a narrow focus that was a measure of the journey the channel had travelled towards commercialism, abandoning Isaacs' ambition to be eclectic, to provide something for everyone some of the time.

This meeting, though, was different. Lygo, the cultured and witty son of an admiral and a collector of antique Tibetan bronzes,[3] called the meeting to raise the question overshadowing the channel: should we renew *Big Brother*? Has it been running too long? Can we manage without its extraordinary appeal to younger viewers? Can we imagine the channel without it? How quiet would it feel throughout the summer?

They were rhetorical questions. Lygo knew they had no choice but to renew, and in his presentation he spelt out the unassailable fact: the programme provided half the channel's profit. For some recent recruits, this scale of dependency was a shock, the first time they had looked up and seen the *Big Brother* sword of Damocles hanging over their heads. All the same, Lygo wanted to make sure of their support, and to his relief there were no dissenters. Most said they were still enamoured of *Big Brother*, they thought it continued to be ground-breaking and touched a national nerve: the critics, mostly middle-aged and above, could be shrugged off because the basis of their dislike of *Big Brother* was clearly their failure to understand young people.

The channel's problem was that *Big Brother* was a format invented by a supplier. Unlike other profitable programmes such as *Wife Swap* or *Hollyoaks*, it could easily be taken away and sold to a rival. Under a contract agreed in 2002 by Mark Thompson, who was now Director General of the BBC, *Big Brother* had become a multimedia event, and coverage had effectively doubled. It was expanded again when the deal was renewed in 2005 and would expire in 2007. Endemol, the producer, was using this break to bid up the price, which would eventually double to £40 million a year, with a big annual increment from 2008. In addition there was an extra £7-million bill for making *Celebrity Big Brother*, which was extended.

The issue was urgent because ITV had emerged as a rival suitor for *Big Brother*. It had courted the programme all year, hiring consultants and negotiating determinedly with the producers. This flirtation was already the talk of the glitzy programme market in Cannes in April 2006. ITV estimated that the summer's *Big Brother* was worth £88 million to Channel 4 in advertising, generating a surplus of £68 million.[4] That sum excluded sponsorship, spin-offs, E4 and *Celebrity Big Brother*. As Lygo admitted, 'Endemol had to some extent underpriced it. It was the channel's most profitable programme and probably the most profitable anywhere. It was a wonderful bargain.'[5]

When *Celebrity Big Brother* was added in, the two provided the main channel with 15 per cent of its income and the majority of the company's profit.[6] Even at a doubled price, it was still going to subsidise unprofitable news, current affairs and drama. And, apart from the financial considerations, Lygo simply could not stomach the idea of his most cherished programme turning up elsewhere.

ITV's wooing of *Big Brother* was partly tactical. In August, its outgoing Chief Executive, Charles Allen, had pilloried Channel 4 for seeking government handouts to underwrite its public-service future while at the same time pumping out ever more commercial programmes. In private conversations with the Culture Secretary, Tessa Jowell, he would point out that *Big Brother* was transmitted, on average, once every three nights during 2006; but in public he was careful not to attack the programme directly, because if he did so people would stop believing that he wanted to buy it.

He calculated that ITV would emerge the winner whatever happened. If he acquired *Big Brother*, Channel 4's balance sheet would be in tatters. If the clear signs of his interest forced a steep increase in the price – which is what happened – then the channel would be damaged also, if less severely. After all, ITV had a score to settle after Channel 4 had lured away Paul O'Grady, host of its successful 5 p.m. programme, early in 2006. Simon Shaps, ITV's Director of Television, was in truth uncertain about how long the *Big Brother* brand would remain strong and worried that, if it did move to his channel, it would unbalance the output. That was why ITV, after all the sniffing around, never put in a formal bid. Nor is it clear that Endemol would have wanted *Big Brother* switched to ITV.

There was, however, a further barrier to the renewal of the contract: the Channel 4 board was itself ambivalent, and would remain so. The first words the Deputy Chairman, Lord Puttnam, had exchanged with Andy Duncan, after he was appointed in

January 2006, had been: 'What shall we do with *Big Brother*?'[7] It was undermining political support for the channel, and its impact was overshadowing the much better programmes that formed the bulk of its output. He was concerned that the hunt for novelty and ratings would lead to places the channel should not and could not go.

The Board considered *Big Brother* twice that autumn, in September and October, before somewhat unhappily deciding that it would be financially irresponsible to do anything but renew, although they told Ofcom that they expected profits from the strand to be significantly lower from 2008 onwards, as the three-year contract with Endemol, if honoured, would cost in total £180 million. After the decision, the Chairman, Luke Johnson, commented,

> There was a consensus about renewing. Individually there were differences but if you saw the facts as presented to us there can be no doubt about it, it was the right thing to do. The deal is only for three years, which felt about right. The big issue is what to replace it with. How long will it last?[8]

This was a matter of great concern. Lygo and his colleagues had been hunting for prime-time hits and replacements for several years, to kick-start the channel's creative escape from *Big Brother*, but nothing had worked. They tried again in November and December with a reality show, *Unanimous*, in which a group of people argued unpleasantly over who should win £2 million, but the show caught nobody's imagination. The channel's former magic touch of coming up with a fresh hit when needed – *The Tube*, *The Big Breakfast*, *Grand Designs* – seemed to have deserted it, and there would be no let-up from the trend in the coming months, with flop following flop.[9]

There were two reasons for this. Since 1993, when it began to sell its own advertising time, the channel had been increasingly trapped by the iron rules of the marketplace, which laid emphasis on year-on-year comparisons, to such an extent that the schedulers could not afford a downwards dive from an experiment. Second, *Big Brother* and other long-running programmes such as *Wife Swap* were partly sapping the ability to innovate as they crowded out other things, soaked up programme funds and lessened pressure on the handful of dominant programme suppliers to Channel 4 to put their creative thinking caps on.

Big Brother, in short, was an extreme manifestation of the trap all television networks around the world are falling into: the biggest hits are a mixed blessing, because a channel becomes over-dependent on them. To be able to discard them painlessly requires the goose to lay more and more golden eggs, until exhaustion sets in. ABC experienced this in America with *Who Wants to Be a Millionaire?* which it ran five times a week. On ITV, *Coronation Street* and *Emmerdale* risk the same outcome. But, in a sense, Channel 4's dependence on *Big Brother* was worse because it went totally against the spirit of the channel Jeremy Isaacs had founded, where the schedule changed season by season. That was fine when there was a guaranteed income, but in the fierce commercial environment of 2006, such luxuries were unaffordable.

Isaacs rationed himself that autumn to an article in *Prospect* magazine, mourning the channel's loss of 'quiet seriousness'. Luke Johnson had no time for such pomposity. 'No one has to watch it', he snapped.[10]

Channel 4 was also heavily reliant on two other successful shows, which its rivals wanted and could easily take from it: *Deal or No Deal* and *Desperate Housewives*. During the summer, ITV bid for *Deal or No Deal*, another Endemol production whose round-the-year success had pepped up the channel's audience by the same amount as *Big Brother* when averaged out. Channel 4 held on to it, but the price went up 60 per cent.[11]

The battle to keep key American imports was tougher. The channel had a deal with Disney's Buena Vista that allowed it to pick two new series a year for a two-year span. In order to hold on to the third series of *Desperate Housewives*, it paid a staggering £950,000 per episode, more than it cost to make an original British drama such as *Shameless* and ten times the average price of bought-in US series. This was when it became evident that Channel 4 could no longer afford to sustain its boast as the home of the best American imports, as Lygo would confirm at the Edinburgh Television Festival in 2007. It was outbid by Sky for *Lost*.

There was also a three-cornered scrap with ITV and BBC1 over Gordon Ramsay. Peter Fincham, Controller of BBC1, fancied him as the new face of cooking and offered a deal that would extend to the chefs working in Ramsay's restaurants. But the former footballer stayed with Channel 4, striking a four-year deal worth an estimated £8.5 million. He explained that he liked the channel's style and its people:

> Channel 4 don't do here's one I made earlier, or cook along with Gordon
> – it's cutting edge. My relationship with them goes back a long way. Kevin
> Lygo without a shadow of doubt, has tenacity, and Sue Murphy [Head of
> Factual Features] has the most creative brain in television. Kevin and Sue,
> like tomato and basil, mango and passion fruit, both highly acidic, both
> full of vitamin C, explosive when combined together.[12]

At least Ramsay knew where he belonged, but the autumnal woes continued with a sudden decline in the advertising market as money was switched to the Internet. It was like the sun going behind a big black cloud. 'This channel becomes a very different place when the money stops flowing', Lygo mourned.[13] Drama was cut down to one new series a year in 2007, and a commitment to screen one expensive drama each month was chopped back from twelve to eight a year. Endemol also then succeeded in bringing the new *Big Brother* contract forward a year.

In this edgy, unhappy mood, with Andy Duncan, the Chief Executive, lobbying for government assistance, what Channel 4 needed above all was a quiet time, out of the limelight and free from controversy. *Celebrity Big Brother* loomed, and the instinct was to play safe. Lygo intervened in December to weed out two controversial housemates proposed by Endemol. The first was O.J. Simpson, the American football star who was acquitted of murdering his wife and a friend in the televised 'trial of the century' in 1995, although he was subsequently found liable in a civil court case. In 2006, his book *If I Did It*, a fictional account of the murder, was withdrawn from publication. 'They all really wanted him', Lygo recalled. 'I just thought you can't have someone who has been so closely involved in something like this.'[14]

The second rejected housemate was John Leslie, the former *Blue Peter* presenter who had been questioned over an alleged rape of Ulrika Jonsson. 'I rejected two dodgy characters', Lygo reflected wryly, 'then you end up with the most controversial *Big Brother* ever. It just goes to show – what do I know?'[15]

Lygo sympathised with a faction on the Board, led by Lord Puttnam, who argued that if they were stuck with *Big Brother* they should ensure that it was dominated by conversation and not crude antics or sex. He did not see a problem with Jade Goody: 'She hadn't been racist or violent. She'd been on loads of television.'[16] But the tension between Endemol and the channel, generated by the arguments over the participants, did not augur well for communication and trust.

Celebrity Big Brother, the fifth and longest series, made a fairly promising start on 3 January 2007. Donny Tourette, a minor pop star, went in the jacuzzi with his suit on and later escaped over the perimeter wall, then Leo Sayer, a singer and songwriter, walked out in a huff. The seventy-nine-year-old film-maker Ken Russell quit when Jade Goody's mother Jackiey and partner Jack Tweedy arrived: he called them 'the terrorists.' The foul-mouthed Jackiey lasted just a week before being voted out, having never managed to master the name of the Bollywood actress Shilpa Shetty, who at least brought some tone to the proceedings; she called her simply 'the Indian'.

Then came the explosion. Jade, along with Jack Tweedy, the model Danielle Lloyd and the singer Jo O'Meara, were accused of racism in their treatment of Shilpa and their language towards her. On Monday, 15 January, the *Daily Mirror* reported growing fears on internet sites that Shetty was being bullied and that the incidents might be racist in origin. It got worse when the following night's programme featured a row over Shilpa's cooking of a chicken and the use of a stock cube. There were also three conversations, not reported to Channel 4 by Endemol, which involved composing a limerick, on which the word 'Paki' was implied by the rhyme, but not spoken.

The next night's programme showed Jade ranting at Shilpa in a truly ugly scene. Calling her a loser and a liar, she shouted, 'Go to the slums.' When Shilpa begged her to shut up, Jade screamed: 'No you shut the fuck up. Who the fuck are you to tell me to shut up? You're not some Princess in Neverland . . . You're a normal housemate like everyone else. You need to come to terms with that. [. . .] Your head is so far up your fucking arse you can smell your own shit.'

Big Brother was now dubbed 'Bigot Brother', and the tabloids, led by the *Mirror*, were up in arms. Gordon Brown, the Chancellor of the Exchequer and prime-minister-in-waiting, happened to be in India when the story burst onto the front pages. When he was in Bangalore, effigies of *Big Brother*'s producers were burned by angry crowds, mortified at the treatment of the star actress. He made his displeasure clear: 'I want Britain to be seen as a country of fairness and tolerance.' On the same day Tony Blair answered questions about the programme in Parliament but Channel 4's executives kept quiet, hoping the row would blow over.

Housemates are kept insulated from the coverage given them by the press, so Jade had no way of knowing about the uproar she had provoked. When questioned about her behaviour in the Diary Room, she referred to the Indian actress as Shilpa Poppadom, a slur that the producers thought so significant they aired it twice. On the Thursday, Luke Johnson went on Radio 4's *Today* programme to discuss the BBC licence-fee settlement, due to be announced that morning. He refused five times to respond to questions about racism on *Big Brother*.

That same afternoon, Andy Duncan was addressing the Oxford Media Convention, the wild, stormy weather providing an appropriate backdrop to the gathering crisis. The row could not have come at a worse time for Duncan, who was at the conference to argue that Channel 4, as a beleaguered public-service broadcaster, needed help to overcome a looming future funding gap. He arrived early and agreed to hold an impromptu press conference. Wearing his trademark crumpled black polo shirt with horizontal stripes, with black rings around his eyes and beads of sweat on his forehead: he looked like he had not slept.

Shortly before he read out his press statement, the news broke that Carphone Warehouse had suspended its £3-million sponsorship deal with *Big Brother*. The firm's founder Charles Dunstone had watched the show the night before and decided his company should no longer be associated with it. The decision triggered other commercial disasters for those involved in the row: Jade's perfume brand, Shh..., was removed from the shelves, and Danielle Lloyd lost a £100,000 modelling contract.

Duncan's statement was a cack-handed attempt to take the sting out of the ugly exchanges and bullying by interpreting them high-mindedly as sobering evidence of a culture clash, a valuable lesson about racism still lurking just beneath the surface of British society. He said:

> The latest series of *Celebrity Big Brother* has strayed into particularly controversial territory – the issue of racism and whether or not it remains ingrained in British attitudes despite all the progress we have apparently made towards becoming a truly multicultural society. We

cannot say with certainty that the comments directed at Shilpa have been racially motivated or whether they stem from broader cultural and social differences.[17]

Producers had spoken to Jade and to Shilpa, who said she did not feel that behaviour towards her was racist.

Duncan was trying to play for time because he had been assured there would be a reconciliation between Jade and Shilpa. He had worked out a form of words that made it look as if he was absolving himself from responsibility. '*Big Brother*'s unique strength is that it is ultimately the public who will decide whether or not the behaviour of certain contestants has been unacceptable.'

It was an unconvincing performance. Duncan was the first non-broadcaster to head Channel 4, and his inexperience was cruelly exposed. Seen alongside Johnson's stubborn silence on the *Today* programme, it was evident that neither of the two men who ran the channel knew how to cope with such rapidly escalating political crises. As the channel's own review would later conclude, its executives appeared to be somehow condoning unacceptable behaviour by intervening either too late or not forcibly enough. It was left to Tessa Jowell, the Culture Secretary, to tell the conference that she had found the programme disgusting, 'racism masquerading as entertainment.'[18] A penitent Jade was ignominiously voted out of the house while Shilpa stayed on to win the contest.

The *Guardian*'s Media Editor Matt Wells weighed in on Monday, 22 January with a judgement that hit hard and reverberated around the channel: 'The events of the past week have served only to illustrate the desperate lack of creative, strategic and political leadership.' The Channel 4 Board met that day and finally issued a profound apology. The most critical director was reported to be vicious in condemning the executives: 'I don't understand how you let this happen.' The Board set up a review led by Tony Hall, a non-executive director and former Head of BBC News, and Rabinder Singh QC. In some ways, their report was more critical than that of Ofcom, which eventually found the channel guilty of failing to apply generally accepted standards on three counts.

On 25 January, when commissioning editors met at a programme review committee, their mood was angry and confused. Some agreed with Dorothy Byrne, the Head of News and Current Affairs, who said she felt embarrassed, upset and humiliated by a programme whose contract they had agreed to extend and by a set of people at the top who had not been able to see straight. Others thought the huge public row was a storm in a teacup and would blow over and were unable to see that the channel had managed to come across as cowardly and arrogant at the same time.

The atmosphere by April was febrile. *Celebrity Big Brother* had put Channel 4 in jeopardy, and there was the grim prospect of *Big Brother 8* on the horizon. 'If I asked that question now, should we renew *Big Brother*, I wouldn't get the same unanimous response',[19] Lygo observed in July, as *Big Brother 8* crawled uninspiringly through the summer, losing support fastest from the young adults it is designed for. At this stage, the channel decided that *Celebrity Big Brother* would not be coming back in January 2008. It was ironic that Jade Goody, the first celebrity created by *Big Brother*, should unwittingly have killed off its lucrative offshoot.

The row over *Celebrity Big Brother* exposed the delicate balancing act Channel 4 performs between commercial and public service, the key to its unique position as the Jekyll and Hyde of British television. Shine a light one way, and you reveal a cynical, ruthless commercial broadcaster. Turn the beam in the other direction, and you will find the surviving remnants of a benign, soft-centred institution regarded at its birth, a short twenty-five years ago, as a miracle of pragmatic Thatcherism.

2

The long and winding road

● ● ● ●

Television sets in the late 1960s came with four buttons. Three were for BBC1, BBC2 and ITV, but the fourth was blank, even though there was capacity for another service. It was known as the empty channel and became a growing source of vexation. For two decades, there was tortuous debate about what should happen to the tantalising spare frequencies. After the launch of ITV from 1955 onwards, as a commercial alternative to the BBC's then solitary television channel, the Independent Television Authority (ITA) spoke of the potential for a second ITV channel, a rival advertising-funded service. But governments were suspicious of too much television and, indeed, of broadcasting's power in general – an attitude that would hold back the introduction of commercial radio until the 1970s, when the pirate stations forced the issue.

In 1960, Harold Macmillan's Government set up the Pilkington Committee to inquire into broadcasting, including the possible allocation of a third new television channel. By then, ITV had grabbed 70 per cent of viewing, but the BBC, which had relaunched its pre-war television service in 1946, was starting the fight back with more adventurous programming. When Pilkington reported in 1962, it rounded on what it saw as ITV's vulgarity and populism and praised the BBC for its more responsible standards. That was why the third channel went to the BBC, as BBC2. After a shaky launch in 1964, it became a success under David Attenborough, and some in the independent sector began to campaign for a second ITV service, to level the playing field. But, in 1966 Harold Wilson's Government decided it would be too expensive, and in 1970 the ITA dropped the idea.

In 1968, a time of social and political ferment all across Europe, the Free Communications Group (FCG), a diverse collection of programme-makers and journalists, began to demand more outlets for expression and a television channel to accommodate them. Opposition to the war in Vietnam was at its height. Tensions between Government and broadcasters over Ireland was starting to mount, and politicians were determined to keep radio and television on a tight leash. Four years earlier, the political satire show, *That Was the Week That Was*, watched by 12 million people at its height, had been dropped by the BBC after thirteen months, ostensibly because it might be seen to influence the forthcoming General Election. In 1965, the BBC governors had refused to allow transmission of *The War Game*, a dramatic reconstruction of the aftermath of a hydrogen bomb dropped on Britain, showing a member of the armed forces shooting a civilian. Harold Wilson was openly hostile to the BBC, believing that it was biased against him, and he refused to increase the licence fee.

New ITV contractors went on air in 1968 with eight-year franchises, but from the beginning they were preoccupied with their battles against the industry's powerful trade unions. Thames, the new service for Londoners during the week, was launched on 29 July and immediately went dark for two hours. London Weekend Television (LWT) started on Friday 2 August, only to have the technicians' union black out the station's first show, *We Have Ways of Making You Laugh*. But when they did get on air, the programmes were disappointing. The FCG used its newsletter, *Open Secret*, to contrast the shoddy service LWT was offering with the high-minded programme promises it had made to secure the franchise, opening up legitimate questions about how effectively ITV was regulated and run. There was, too, discontent within the BBC, expressed in underground papers by anonymous authors with titles such as *Shit*, *The Brutish Empire* and *Burial*. Scurrilous mock-ups of *Radio Times* were passed from hand to hand, lampooning governors and the Director General. A growing number of disaffected young people working in television began to hatch schemes, their frustration heightened by the knowledge that there was an empty channel waiting to be filled.

But the rumblings of discontent did not come only from the lower depths of the industry. On 18 November 1969, an establishment lobbying group, the 76 Group, was launched in the House of Commons. At a meeting chaired by Brian Walden, then a Labour MP, the group, some of whose members were also involved with the FCG, pledged 'to represent the views of men and women professionals employed in television and radio united by a common concern over the future of broadcasting and dismay at recent events in both ITV and the BBC.' Its principal demand was for a new royal commission to look into the organisation of broadcasting after 1976, when the BBC Charter and the ITV Act were both due to expire. Along with another organisation, the Campaign for Better Broadcasting, the 76 Group placed an advertisement in the *Guardian* headed 'Crisis in Television and Radio: A Royal Commission Now!' It was signed by 102 distinguished names.

On 14 May 1970, the Government caved in and announced there would be an inquiry, led by Lord Annan, Provost of University College, London. Four days later,

Harold Wilson called a General Election for 18 June, which Labour lost. The Conservative Government, led by Edward Heath, saw no need for the Annan Inquiry, and Christopher Chataway, the new Minister of Posts and Telecommunications, announced that it would be postponed indefinitely. The campaigners for change were deeply frustrated, and their frustration turned to anger when it became apparent that the Conservatives, who had introduced commercial television fifteen years earlier, were thinking of handing over the new channel to the existing ITV companies, as ITV2. The advertising industry also sounded the alarm, stressing that to allow the present franchise-holders to operate the new channel would strengthen their tight monopoly on television advertising. Naturally enough, the ITV barons were delighted by the indications that the Government would see things their way, and the five largest companies drew up a schedule for ITV2 as complementary to the main channel, competing with BBC2 and eating into its ratings. If ITV1 was seen as the equivalent of the *Daily Express*, ITV2 would be the *Telegraph*.

In July 1971, the ITA invited views from people working in television but tried to avoid a public debate. This led to an alternative public debate organised by the FCG and *Time Out* – the first TV4 conference. It drew together a wide cross-section of interests beyond broadcasters, including members of the Conservative Bow Group, the National Union of Teachers and university academics; but none came up with a cogent proposal. The dominant note was one of protest, the insistence that Britain did not need more of the same. This public unease forced Chataway to concede that, in the face of that level of dissension, the channel could not be allocated. For the time being, the ITV companies had been faced down, but they continued to lobby discreetly, and in March 1973 Sir John Eden, who had replaced Chataway, declared that there was no need to put off a decision on the fourth channel any longer. He asked for submissions. This was the cue that a modest, soft-spoken former television executive, with a burning thirst for change, had been waiting for. His name was Anthony Smith, and he was about to demonstrate that the power of the press was mightier than the airwaves.

● ● ● ●

If you stand outside Fortnum & Mason in Piccadilly and look across to the Royal Academy, you will see a small turning next to it, with the word 'Private' written on the tarmac. Behind it, across a courtyard, sits an eighteenth-century mansion, withdrawn from the traffic, with chandeliers blazing day and night. This is the Albany, designed by William Chambers for the first Viscount Melbourne but converted in 1802 to provide elegant suites, known as sets, for gentlemen up from the shires. It is a fine establishment address, whose twentieth-century residents included such as Malcolm Muggeridge, Tony Armstrong-Jones, Graham Greene, J.B. Priestley and

Edward Heath. For the past thirty years, it has been the London home of the intellectual father of Channel 4, Anthony Smith, who on weekdays moves easily from his drawing room – all elegant sofas, Persian rugs and period green paint on the wall – to a library next door. He is a thinking man and a generous host, combining unobtrusive sharpness with dogged persistence. Between 1988 and 2006, he was President of Magdalen College, Oxford, and before that he ran the British Film Institute (BFI), proving a formidable fundraiser and networker at both.

People assume that Smith is a product of the wealthy Home Counties, as are so many of his former students and peers. In fact, he is the son of a poor mother and went to a now defunct grammar school in Harrow. From there he made his way to Brasenose College, Oxford, where he read English, then joined the BBC as a general trainee, producing current-affairs programmes. He was exceptionally talented but his own man and, therefore, distrusted by many of his superiors. When he resigned in 1971, so as to think and write about the future direction of broadcasting, he had been a member of the *Tonight* team and Editor of *24 Hours* – an admired precursor to *Newsnight* – for seven years. He had dealt with politicians of all hues in the ferment of the 1960s, sent news crews around the world and counted the investigative author Tom Bower among his protégés. A purer meritocrat would be hard to find.

He was also someone who placed his faith in independent institutions, because he knew from his own life experience that good ones could nurture people. He once said that if he had the money, he would found a well-endowed independent university college, outside of Oxford or Cambridge. 'I believe in autonomous institutions. People live in families, institutions and schools and they add a real richness to life. I believe in a collegiate system – Channel 4 as originally practised. I hate state control.'[1] After he resigned from the BBC, he became a research fellow at St Antony's College Oxford, and from here he campaigned to challenge the hold over the nation's broadcasting exerted by the BBC and ITV. On the face of it, he could be seen as part of the problem, one of the Oxbridge male elite who had, with input from show-business agents and impresarios such as Lew Grade and Cyril and Sidney Bernstein, shaped the system. He was, thus, perfectly camouflaged to act as a reformer.

After Smith's withdrawal from the hurly-burly of television, he worked on a study of the relationship between the audience, broadcaster and state, which later surfaced in his book, *The Shadow in the Cave*. He also joined in discussions with the Association of Broadcasting Staff (ABS), a union mainly composed of BBC employees, to respond to the request from the Minister of Posts and Telecommunications, Sir John Eden, for ideas about the fourth channel. There was a dragon to be slain. The ITV heavyweights were lobbying for control of any new channel.

It was while sitting in the ABS's Marylebone office that a new concept came to Smith.

> As we talked, the idea germinated in my mind of a formula for a television organisation that ran like an American foundation. It received applications, it gave out money. This one would give out the money and the broadcasting time. It would have a transmitter. I said, let's call it the Open Broadcasting Authority. The ABS let me write out the plan and use it as a possible option. In the context of the discussion of that time, there was no alternative.[2]

The ABS President, Tom Rhys, supported the idea in a letter to *The Times* in January 1972. Three months later, Smith fleshed out the proposal and exposed it to public debate through a 3,000-word article in the *Guardian*, published as part of its nascent media section. The *Guardian*, and its Media Editor Peter Fiddick, would act as facilitator of the fourth-channel debate, carrying other articles from Smith, refining the concept, during the 1970s.

Smith's first article began with the sonorous words: 'Once in a decade an opportunity arises in Britain for the creation of a new television channel.'[3] It should, he wrote, be run by a national television foundation – a more respectable, less anarchic name, he felt, than the Open Broadcasting Authority. It should be the responsibility of a body of trustees, appointed with the approval of the Minister of Posts and Telecommunications. They would have a very small staff, a central transmitting studio, but all the rest of the content would come from hired studios. The secretariat of the foundation would be responsible for processing applications for programmes and encouraging ideas from authors in society at large. He was trying to define an institution without grand designs for itself, more a broker and enabler. It would foster a new method of making programmes, commissioning from independent producers, thus breaking free from the large BBC and ITV programme departments where office politics was too often the factor determining which ideas and people were backed.

This thoughtful prospectus included some slightly odd elements. Smith maintained there was no need for regular schedules, since programmes could be arranged in 'festive seasons [. . .] with a tendency towards the ad hoc rather than continuous filling in with identical programmes.'[4] But it was essentially a well-considered article, destined to be much photocopied, handed around and discussed. It provoked a *Late Night Line Up* debate on BBC2 in which the charismatic former Director General of the BBC, Sir Hugh Carleton Greene, took part. He initially opposed the idea, but in a Granada Guildhall lecture the following October, he said, 'I suggest this should be set up more or less as proposed by Anthony Smith [. . .] as a centre for every type of experimental programming.'

Smith's case for the National Television Foundation in truth was rather incomplete. The weakest part of the proposal was how to finance the foundation in a way that allowed it freedom. Smith came up with a list of possibilities: sponsorship by large companies, unions and ministries; a government grant; advertising – not as traditional spot but in a large slab once a night; sales overseas; and a licence fee. His final option was that the existing broadcasting organisations might pay for experimental work. This is quite close to what happened in the first phase of Channel 4, when it lived off an annual subscription from ITV which, as a quid pro quo, sold its advertising. Smith's was a considered vision, put forward with sincerity and without apparent self-interest. Later, the campaigning became more commercially motivated when advertising agencies and a handful of large producers began to smell opportunities. One of the reasons the article had such an afterlife was that it talked about the point of the new channel, providing access to the airwaves for fresh voices, an escape from the so-called consensus and from the bias towards safe programming.

Smith argued that broadcasting, with only three channels, was restricted by the licensing regime with controls that ultimately chained it directly to the state, preventing society from properly informing itself. He gave a topical example. Britain had just experienced a miners' strike, and a hugely disruptive three-day week was about to be imposed. 'Few people in Britain had any idea of the determination of the miners to strike so long and so determinedly: the point could not be made satisfactorily in a programme or two on the BBC or ITV.'[5] And in a pitch that appealed directly to many of the younger campaigners and programme-makers, he noted,

> If you are outside the world of television it is difficult, to the point of being impossible, to introduce an idea into it. Something fundamental has to change in broadcasting if the closed world of programme makers is to open not merely its ranks, but its minds. The conditioning of fifty years of the BBC, and twenty of ITV, of whole working lives sheltered in large organisations, has to change. There are people who want to initiate programme ideas which could not be conceived within Television Centre or Granada or Thames. It cannot be that broadcast communication is intended by nature to be conducted in perpetuity inside large, single-minded corporations and programme companies exclusively.[6]

Though the concept of a separate foundation did not eventually win through, most of the ideas supporting it did. They became the seeds that grew into a fresh way of thinking about television. Other radically minded broadcasters – including John Birt, David Elstein and Jeremy Isaacs – also sent in suggestions to the Government which were close to the eventual deal struck over Channel 4, but most were reluctant to go public because they wanted to protect their jobs. Smith, freed of the daily grind of making programmes, focused on taking the campaign into the public arena rather than simply circulating his thoughts within the industry. He argued for a democratic opening up of the airwaves, an 'imp in the mechanism'. He caught the mood of dissatisfaction about the state of television which had been growing since the 1960s, in particular over the heavy regulation of political programmes. John Birt later wrote:

> I saw much broadcasting as clichéd and formulaic. I bridled increasingly at the prevailing notion of mass programming, of serving a homogeneous audience of people with uniform tastes. I felt this about my own generation, whose needs were rarely met by television. I also felt keenly that ethnic minorities, and other groups – like gay people – barely surfaced.[7]

Smith now says that to understand what Channel 4 was about you have to go behind the debates and the clamour from different pressure groups and 'look at the intellectual moment at which pressure for it began.'[8] There was no Internet, no mobile phones, no videos, DVD or multichannel television to act as outlets for frustrated communicators.

> You have to understand the role of the duopoly and why it became a tremendous vexation for thousands of people. The point was that society was no longer homogeneous. There were a great many different interest groups – the 1960s had shown that – but the screens were not catching up. People had begun making films and then videos in the 60s. There wasn't an easy domestic recording system as now, but there was a desire to use the moving image among people coming through the underground movements, and they had causes they wanted to express – everything from taking drugs, having sex, changing the laws about sex, the whole gay-rights thing, the homelessness issue, the beginning of the feminist movement. All these things were bubbling around here and abroad and at the same time the capacity to make messages was growing in the population. Meanwhile, we were all made to believe the broadcasting we were getting was very good. I suppose it was by international standards; but it was all in the hands of this rather well-paid, superior civil-service class. They drove around in big cars. They drank rather a lot and, like all drunks, they didn't listen. They couldn't hear, literally and metaphorically, what was going on around them, what demands were really being made – demands that their comfortable duopoly was able to frustrate.[9]

This view was echoed by Michael Darlow, a television producer since the early 1960s and a major campaigner for Channel 4, which he later meticulously chronicled. 'Increasingly we came to believe that the whole system of control and funding in film and television was inappropriate to the needs and aspirations of the new age.'[10] Meanwhile, as the 1970s advanced, there were more freelances and independent producers, often living hand to mouth, hungry for work. The top tier had a status quo to defend. They were comfortable, and they were aided and abetted by very powerful trade unions, the Association of Cinematography and Television Technicians (ACTT) and the Association of Broadcasting Staff. Certainly, ITV and the unions, in some ways, had a vested interest in collusion. The unions wanted wealthy monopolistic employers they could milk by threatening to pull the plugs and walk out – as the print unions were able to do with national newspapers. Smith's proposal was taken up by disparate lobbyists ranging from Mary Whitehouse's National Viewers' and Listeners' Association – whose campaigns to 'clean up' television had been initially ignored and then mocked by broadcasters – to trade unionists in other industries who felt their views were ignored or distorted.

In 1974, Smith wrote another article, this one of 6,000 words, and refined his thinking about funding and ranges of programmes. Labour had listened, and when it returned to power that year it set up a new Annan Committee, four years after the Conservatives had stood down the old one. Smith was approached to become a member, but his name was removed by Harold Wilson, because he had written to Wilson criticising his soft line on the Czech Government's suppression of the human-rights movement led by the playwright Václav Havel. Smith was replaced at the last minute by Anthony Jay, co-author of the comedy *Yes Prime Minister*, who had founded an independent production company in the mid-1960s. Smith's friend, the broadcaster-turned-Labour-MP Phillip Whitehead, was, however, a member of the committee, and Smith himself was able to exert a strong influence on it even without formal membership. Lord Annan wrote asking him to submit his National Television Foundation plan and to undertake research projects.

The committee had to sift through 750 submissions and held twenty-five days of hearings. The BBC, partly in order to head off ITV2, backed the National Television Foundation. When the report came out on 13 March 1977, it proposed an Open Broadcasting Authority, separate from the Independent Broadcasting Authority (IBA) and the BBC – a triumph for Smith, Phillip Whitehead and the programme-making lobby. According to the blueprint for Channel 4, it would have a prime duty to serve minorities as well as majorities, plugging the gaps in the BBC's output. It was to act as a publisher of other people's ideas. 'We attach particular importance to this third category as a force for diversity', said Annan. It was to aim at celebrating differences, rather than seeking consensus. The report even quoted Anthony Smith's borrowing from Rousseau: 'If I am free to say anything I want to say except the one thing I want to say, then I am not free.'[11] It attached particular importance to independent producers as programme suppliers as a force for new thinking. Programmes could also be offered by the ITV companies, whose frustrated programme-makers would

welcome new outlets and the chance to make use of idle studios. 'The younger generation of producers is bubbling over with ideas which are not allowed to surface',
Annan said.

'It had bought my whole bill of goods, all the notions of a plural system, and the
philosophical support for the broadcasting authority', Smith pointed out.[12] But still
nothing concrete would yet emerge. The Government, losing popularity and cling-
ing to office with a wafer-thin majority, was in no mood to take what was likely to be
a controversial initiative. So in January 1979, when it seemed to Smith that Margaret
Thatcher was going to sweep the Conservatives back to power, he went to see Sir
Keith Joseph, one of her most trusted and influential allies, who ran the Centre for
Policy Studies. Smith reasoned that he needed to depoliticise the Channel 4 proposal. Udi Eichler, a Thames Television producer and a member of a Conservative
think tank, arranged the introduction. 'I went to see Keith Joseph', Smith recalls.

> He was there with Norman Lamont, his new Parliamentary Private
> Secretary, a little bouncy thing. I explained this was a way of intro-
> ducing competition and enterprise into the broadcasting system but
> keeping the notion of public service dominant. Sir Keith listened very
> intelligently and asked intelligent questions – he's another intelligent
> Magdalen man. He said: 'Norman, this is very interesting. Why haven't
> we done anything about this?'.[13]

And in a further bid to implant the idea with the probable new regime, Smith
went to see Willie Whitelaw, the prospective Home Secretary, who would be the
pivotal figure in the debate. Shortly before the election, Whitelaw had opposed the
creation of an Open Broadcasting Authority and had endorsed the IBA, which had
replaced the ITA in 1971, as the body to handle changes.

In the General Election of 3 May 1979, Mrs Thatcher won a majority of forty-four
in a campaign fought on Labour's record on the economy, symbolised by the Saatchi
poster, 'Labour Isn't Working'. At first, the outlook for Channel 4 looked bleak, with
the big ITV companies able to exert more influence on the Conservatives than they
had on Labour. The Queen's speech of 15 May included a brief statement that the
life of the IBA would be extended and that it would be responsible for the fourth
television channel. By this time, though, a new alliance, the Channel 4 Group had
been formed to draw together campaigners under one banner for a final push. It
had a small office, a single employee – and a future to win or lose. Six months after
Anthony's Smith's meeting with Sir Keith Joseph, they were sitting in a dingy room
in Great Pulteney Street, Soho, when, as Michael Darlow described it, the penny
dropped. They were studying a copy of the Conservative manifesto, in particular the
section on encouraging small businesses and the thirst for enterprise. That was it!

They could rebrand themselves as part of the solution, a 'free market in ideas.' They sacked their organiser and recruited instead, for £30 a week, a thin, pale, intense young man called Michael Jackson, who had just graduated in media studies from the Central London Polytechnic but who had made a big impression on Sophie Balhetchet, a key campaign member. His professor, Nicholas Garnham, also a staunch advocate of Channel 4, said he was unique, very bright, more focused on his goals than any other student he had ever taught.

At this stage, the IBA was fostering the notion that independent producers could supply just 15 per cent of Channel 4's programmes, meaning that ITV would make the rest and thus be the dominant player. The Channel 4 Group decided to target the 1979 Edinburgh Television Festival that August and argue against such overwhelming ITV influence. They wanted at least half the programmes to come from independents and for the channel to have a programme controller with complete freedom. Jeremy Isaacs, who was to give the opening MacTaggart Lecture, would use his speech to stake his claim to found it. Each morning of the Festival, the whippet-thin and self-effacing Jackson would go to the Red Star parcels office to pick up a batch of leaflets sent up from London, and before each session, he and Balhetchet would dash in to place briefing sheets on the seats. No one would ever have expected that this underfed-looking youth with intense eyes would, eighteen years later, become Channel 4's third Chief Executive, with a chauffeur-driven Lexus and a salary of nearly £500,000.

3

Isaacs:
maverick founder

● ● ● ●

In August 1979, Jeremy Isaacs was like a proud stag driven out of his kingdom. He had 'resigned' from Thames Television where he had been an adventurous programme director and now, without a steady salaried job, had joined the ranks of freelancers – the grass roots of the movement to create a separate fourth channel. Prone to private bouts of insecurity, he was by no means confident that, a year later, he would win the glittering prize of founding Channel 4, not least because the proposal was still fluid and its supporters split into rival camps.

The World at War, his epic history of the Second World War, had been screened by ITV during 1973 and 1974 and had been acclaimed around the world. It had established his reputation as one of the best British television producers of his generation, but it had not protected him from being passed over when a fiery rival, Bryan Cowgill, the Controller of BBC1, was made Managing Director of Thames in 1977 – an appointment that Isaacs learned of from the press. The two men were as incompatible as oil and water. With typical directness, Isaacs had told Cowgill, now his boss, that he, Isaacs, ran the programming:

'Bryan . . . I want to make one thing clear. I am Director of Programmes at Thames, responsible for our programme department, for all our programmes and for the schedule. I need to know that you accept that.'

'That's right', Cowgill replied.

'In that case', Isaacs wondered, 'what will *you* do?'[1]

It was a deliberately provocative comment, and from that point, Isaacs, whose contract was due for renewal, was mentally steeling himself to leave. In the end, his departure, in 1978, was explosive. The terminal row was over his decision to allow the BBC to run unscreened material from *This Week*, the regular Thursday night Thames current-affairs programme, which he had once edited. *This Week* had made a string of well-researched programmes about Northern Ireland, critical of the Labour Government's policy. These had exasperated Roy Mason, Secretary of State for Northern Ireland, a combative ex-miner, who put pressure on the IBA to act. The authority's lay members had the legal power of publishers and could block any programme before transmission. The offending piece featured reports by Amnesty International of mistreatment of suspects by the Royal Ulster Constabulary at the Castlereagh Interrogation Centre and included interviews with members of the IRA. The IBA banned it – and, in protest, members of the ACTT union prevented a replacement programme being shown, which meant blank screens on ITV.

When the BBC asked the next morning if they could see the material, Isaacs, angry and rebellious, said: 'Give it to them.'[2] He was echoing an earlier decision made by Denis Forman at Granada over the first edition of *World in Action*, when he had allowed the BBC's *Nationwide* programme to use excerpts. Isaacs was called upstairs by the Thames Chairman, Howard Thomas, who accused him furiously of insubordination, adding that it was a sacking offence. Isaacs said he was resigning anyway.

This meant that by 1979, now aged forty-six, he was regarded as brilliant but a maverick, with a reputation for sticking up for programme-makers. This endeared him to radical producers and ensured loyalty from the ranks but played badly with those who might manage him or regulate his programmes in future. They viewed the *This Week* incident as a sign of immaturity and irresponsibility. Yet, his status among programme-makers ensured that he was asked to attend the Edinburgh Television Festival, founded in 1976 to debate such matters as the fourth television channel and chaired in 1979 by Paul Bonner, a benign BBC executive. Isaacs was invited to give the keynote MacTaggart Lecture, a signal honour and a marvellous opportunity for an ambitious man on the job market, at the height of his powers, fuelled by a sense of destiny.

Isaacs spent August at the family holiday home in Ceibwr, North Pembrokeshire, with his wife Tamara, composing his thoughts about what sort of fourth channel was wanted. He thought back to the 1973 submission he had made in confidence to the Minister of Posts and Telecommunications, which had proposed a separate channel under the control of the IBA rather than the ITV companies. Although ITV would fund the channel and sell its advertising, a separate programme controller would schedule it. On 27 August, relaxed but primed, he arrived at the George Hotel, in Edinburgh's elegant New Town, where delegates were congregating in the bar in an atmosphere more charged than anyone could have anticipated.

The lecture was given in the austere Georgian lecture hall of the Royal College of Physicians, a short walk from the hotel. The packed audience of around 200 included civil servants from the Home Office Broadcasting Department and a strong turn-out from the militant independent producers lobby. Isaacs, at his most bull-like, relished the moment and plunged into what was blatantly a public job application. A gifted orator, he fleshed out his vision of a distinctive channel, serving minorities, with conviction, while at the same time sounding grounded and realistic.

> We want a fourth channel which extends the choice available to viewers; which extends the range of ITV's programmes; which caters for substantial minorities presently neglected; which builds into its actuality programmes a complete spectrum of political attitude and opinion; which furthers [. . .] some broad educational purposes; which encourages worthwhile independent production; which allows the larger regional ITV companies to show what their programme-makers can do. We want a fourth channel that will neither simply compete with ITV1 nor merely be complementary to it. We want a fourth channel that everyone will watch some of the time and no one all of the time. We want a fourth channel that will, somehow, be different.[3]

He hoped to see more black Britons on the screen, more programmes made by women that men would watch, more programmes for the young. And he threw in what was designed to be a juicy bone for the campaigners: 'Up to now independent producers have had a raw deal because no one has needed their services. A fourth channel will suck in a new influx of programme-makers.'[4]

Yet, despite that pronouncement, his words did not wholly satisfy the Channel 4 Group – who had assiduously prepared a thirteen-page briefing pamphlet – because he contradicted their belief that any great new source of energy and ideas was out there among independent producers, waiting to be tapped. He said most such ideas were trapped within the BBC or ITV and suggested that independents would make only a modest contribution. He did not specifically endorse the IBA's assessment, made in a paper that summer, that a 15-per-cent share for independents would be realistic, but his thinking seemed to chime with their approach. He spoke honestly, based on his experience of working within ITV, rubbing shoulders with creative people who also felt frustrated.

The campaigners' doubts about him were strengthened the following day, when his speech was debated at the Festival. Isaacs then speculated that maybe only a 10-per-cent initial contribution from independent producers would be achieved. The reality was that he had not paid sufficient notice to the growing clamour for change within the nascent independent sector – he had been too busy making and overseeing ITV programmes. Asked to explain how a fourth channel could be different if the majority of its programmes came from the ITV companies, Isaacs replied that the fourth channel would be 'different, but not that different.' The much-quoted remark was aimed at appeasing the radicals while not doing anything to frighten the horses – in this case, the ministers who would make the final decisions on the new channel. Yet, the radicals were not appeased, in particular not Roger Graef, the Har-vard-educated documentary-maker who had created a distinctive niche and who would become a founding board member of Channel 4 in 1980, playing a key role in selecting its chief executive and driving its ethos. He was deeply irritated by Isaacs' limited expectations.[5]

The tension at Edinburgh between those who worked within ITV and the in-dependent producer lobbyists grew so heated that the Home Office civil servants billed to speak beat a hasty retreat. Further announcements would be left to Willie Whitelaw, the 'one nation' Home Secretary who was to speak in two weeks' time at the more sober, industry-based Cambridge Broadcasting Convention. Meanwhile, other would-be contenders to run Channel 4 entered the Edinburgh debate, includ-ing Anthony Smith and the ambitious thirty-four-year-old John Birt, who cam-paigned with the radical slogan, 'Let All Voices Be Heard.'

Isaacs, though, had laid down his marker. The lecture showed that he grasped what Channel 4 could be about and understood how it could be realised. Graef later admitted that on this point 'he absolutely got it.'[6] Although there would be many questions raised about his suitability, he was now the one to beat. In the meantime, he returned to programme-making. His television history of Ireland, made for the BBC and narrated by Robert Kee, won a BAFTA award for Best Factual Programme, enhancing his reputation. And in 1979, he also became a governor of the BFI. This taught him the value of independent film producers and led him to appreciate the value of community-based film-making and video workshops – all lessons he would take with him to Channel 4 . . . eventually.

How had this combative television producer been shaped? Where did his dar-ing, self-confidence and conviction come from? Isaacs' father was a jeweller and his mother a doctor, and he was their eldest son, raised in Bearsden, a comfortable middle-class suburb of Glasgow, populated by the professional classes. They were a prosperous but radically minded family, staunch Labour supporters. Born in Sep-tember 1932, Jeremy was old enough to experience living through the Second World War, while too young to be devoured or damaged by it. After the horrors of fascism, many middle-class people of Jewish descent turned to Communism and socialism. The *Manchester Guardian* and the *Glasgow Herald* were delivered daily to the Isaacs home, supplemented with a weekly Hansard ordered by his father in response to a comment by a primary-school teacher that one day the young lad could be Prime Minister. He duly pored over the parliamentary debates, questions and answers.

Family life included books, music, debate and attendance at the synagogue. There were numerous family connections with Israel. Jeremy's first visit was in 1955, and his youngest brother Michael, from whom he became estranged, emigrated there – he and his wife Rebecca were blown up by a Fatah bomb in Jerusalem in 1975, orphaning their two young children.

Jeremy and his brothers were educated at the fee-paying Glasgow Academy, where he was the only Labour supporter in his class, gleefully celebrating a series of by-election victories between 1945 and 1951. Lord Reith, the first Director General of the BBC, had also been a pupil at the Academy. Isaacs remembers him presiding over a prize-giving ceremony in June 1950 and offering the boys some characteristic advice: that when shaking hands they should always look people in the eyes.

Isaacs went on to read classics at Merton College, Oxford, where his debating skills led to his election as President of the Union and Chairman of the Labour Club and where he struck up an unlikely lifelong friendship with the Conservative politician Michael Heseltine. He then had to complete two years' national service at Maryhill Barracks, Glasgow, so it was not until 1957 that he arrived in London to seek his fortune, although the first thing he did was to attend the inaugural meeting of the Campaign for Nuclear Disarmament (CND) in Central Hall, Westminster. Like many Oxbridge arts graduates of the time, he applied for a traineeship at the BBC. The interviewer's note on him read: 'Small, dark Glaswegian Jew. Very much alive.'[7]

Unemployed, but shortly to marry his South African girlfriend, Tamara, he took advice from the rising young journalist Bernard Levin and also sought help from an unconventional source. The father of one of his schoolfriends was George Singleton, the owner of the Cosmo cinema in Rose Street, Glasgow, who was acquainted with Sidney and Cecil Bernstein, the owners of the Granada cinema chain and founders of Granada Television, launched in 1956 as the ITV franchisee in Manchester. Singleton wrote to the Bernsteins recommending Isaacs, and the letter was passed to Denis Forman, Granada's Managing Director, who offered him a job at £18 a week.

In Manchester, he worked for the legendary David Plowright, then Granada's News Editor, who was bent on taking the deference out of political reporting. Isaacs helped make Granada's election marathon, where all candidates in all the local constituencies were invited to present their case in two minutes sharp. He was then put in charge of the weekly press review, *What the Papers Say*, which he took from Manchester to Granada's offices in Golden Square, London, to be close to the pool of opinionated journalists from which the programme's presenters were drawn. It was a perfect grounding for a novice producer, giving him early experience of coping with the 1955 Broadcasting Act's insistence that every programme on an issue of industrial or political controversy must display due impartiality. Ensuring balance was a duty that would frequently cloud his career in broadcasting. The solution on *What the Papers Say* was to rotate presenters of contrasting political persuasions; but it would not always be that simple.

He also produced *All Our Yesterdays*, recalling the events of the week from twenty-five years ago, and made his first foray into historical documentaries. Denis Forman wrote, 'His quick wit, well-stocked mind and terrier-like aggression marked him as someone who would go places.'[8] The first place he went, after five years at Granada, was Associated Rediffusion, holder of the London weekday franchise, which ran what was then ITV's only true weekly current-affairs show, *This Week*, all fifty-two weeks of the year. He turned it from a hosted magazine into a single-subject format without a regular presenter, allowing his reporters the space to explore and illuminate controversial issues.

He believed in dramatic techniques for driving home the message of the programmes. One of them, screened close to Christmas, campaigned for tough drink-driving laws. The reporter, Desmond Wilcox, went to Jack Straw's Castle, a public house in Hampstead, to interview drivers on their way home after ten pints of beer. Isaacs lined up 120 volunteers to represent visually the number killed on the roads over the holiday period, then cut straight to a live interview with the Transport Minister. In 1965, the BBC poached him to ginger up their declining current-affairs flagship *Panorama*, presented by Richard Dimbleby, then dying of cancer. Trying to repeat his success with *This Week*, Isaacs turned it from a magazine to a single-subject programme. Some powerful people did not approve of the change, and he was unable to deal with the perpetually poisonous BBC politicking. His ten-week experiment ended in defeat, but he refused to reverse it, and in December 1966 he was fired.

He was quickly welcomed back to Rediffusion in a more senior role, as Head of Features, overseeing *This Week*. With him he brought a few refugees from *Panorama* who had supported his changes. In 1968, Rediffusion lost its franchise, but Isaacs stayed on with the new company, Thames, whose Programme Director, Brian Tesler, would become an important ally and constructive critic of Isaacs in Channel 4's early rocky days.

By 1971, the Conservative Government, reacting to disquiet about programme standards, suggested it would change from taxing ITV's revenue at source to taxing its profits. This concession did wonders for programme budgets, as the companies sought to cut their taxable profits by spending more on quality content. In this unusually expansive climate for programme-makers, Isaacs proposed *The World at War*. This stately, twenty-six-episode history of the Second World War, drawing on archive footage, took fifty people some three years to make, and each of the films had an individual producer. The one about the Battle of Britain was produced by David Elstein, who would later edit *This Week* and become an influential campaigner for Channel 4. The major achievement of the series was to break away from a British-centred view of the war and to fuse narrative with a sparing analysis. Composer Carl Davis wrote the music; Laurence Olivier was coaxed into narrating.

Isaacs later said that making *The World at War* was 'at least till Channel 4 came along – the defining experience of my working life'.[9] It remains an ITV landmark to stand alongside *The Jewel in the Crown* or *Brideshead Revisited*. The real cost was never worked out, but the series was sold to more than 100 countries and is still being repeated on specialist history channels and sold as a vintage DVD collection. On the strength of it, Isaacs was promoted to Director of Programmes at Thames, where he encouraged adventure and innovation in programmes as diverse as the crime series *The Sweeney* and *The Naked Civil Servant* (1975), the drama about the gay life of Quentin Crisp.

After the terminal dispute with Bryan Cowgill, Jeremy Isaacs Productions was launched at his large Victorian family house in Chiswick, west London. He was a kitchen-table independent producer, on the phone drumming up business – and learning at first hand the discouraging lesson that broadcasters then had little need of outside suppliers. But he filmed the story of the convicted murderer Jimmy Boyle, in *A Sense of Freedom* (1979) for ITV, before making *Ireland, A Television History*, for the BBC. It was here that he met the Oxford-educated historian John Ranelagh, then at Conservative Central Office, whose father had been on the rebel side in the 1916 Rising. Ranelagh became Isaacs' right-of-centre sparring partner and would go with him from the BBC to Channel 4, remaining a provocative confidant and challenging the liberal–left philosophy that characterised its early commissioning editors, including Liz Forgan.

On 14 September 1979, Willie Whitelaw arrived at the Babbage Lecture Hall in Cambridge for the Royal Television Society's biennial broadcasting convention, where ministers traditionally set out their thinking. Here he outlined to a startled audience how far he had progressed towards a fourth channel and what he meant by the 'strict safeguards' on content and standards on which the waverers were insisting.[10] His speech included much more detail than anyone expected and contained bombshells for ITV.

> I start from the position we are looking for a fourth channel offering a distinctive service of its own. [. . .] There must be programmes appealing to and, we hope, stimulating tastes and interests not adequately provided for on the existing channels. We would expect a news service. [. . .] This is clearly a job for ITN [Independent Television News] with its resources and admirable record. Next I think it would be right for room to be found for educational programmes of various kinds.
>
> Where will the programmes come from? Three main sources, the network of ITV companies, the regional ITV companies and independent producers, and there must be assured and adequate finance for the purchase and commissioning of programmes for the channel from independent producers. But the fourth channel should not be dominated by the network companies. The independent producers have a most important role to play.

Acquisition and scheduling [. . .] will need to be separate from that of ITV1. The budget for the fourth channel will not necessarily be governed by the revenue from advertisements shown on that channel.'[11]

The hall buzzed as Whitelaw sat down. There was real shock on the faces of ITV executives, who had not expected a rout on this scale. Suddenly, the debate over controlling the fourth channel was effectively over. The key decisions had been taken rapidly that summer, and ITV had lost out. They were not getting an ITV2 to battle with BBC2. The Channel 4 Group had won: the radicals, to their amazement, had carried the day with a Conservative Government. John Freeman, the statesmanlike Chairman of LWT, formally closing the session, could only warn that any failure to schedule ITV1 and the fourth channel jointly would be a 'recipe for muddle, friction and failure.'[12] Whitelaw's visionary decision would begin a process of transformation that is still in progress, by creating an outlet focused on commissioning programmes. Anthony Smith would later reflect: 'It is the only dialectical force in history that has taken a group of left-wing intellectuals and turned them into businessmen.'[13]

Behind the scenes, the IBA had been persistently lobbying and developing policy and continued to do so rapidly during the autumn. The speech pleased them, but even their officials were not fully prepared. Whitelaw had moved a long way from a cautious stance towards the Annan Committee's Open Broadcasting Authority in 1977 to embracing a fourth channel funded by a levy on ITV. Most observers had assumed the Conservatives would naturally favour the softer option of ITV2, with an input from independents to challenge the power of the unions. But advertisers had lobbied hard against extending ITV's power, and they had won the day. Above all, the unacceptability of more of the same was underscored by a disastrous ACTT strike that autumn, on top of previous blackouts. This further hardened attitudes within a government already decidedly unsympathetic to trade unions. The only way to weaken the unions' grip on ITV, they calculated, was to increase the power of the independents.

In November, the IBA published 'The Fourth Channel: The Authority's Proposals'.[14] The Authority would set up a separate non-profit-making company and would distance itself from it (because it also regulated the ITV companies) by instituting a board of twelve to fourteen people. ITV would have four members on the Board, with another five able to speak for other potential suppliers. So the fourth channel would have a considerable degree of independence. The funds would come from the ITV companies – though the exact formula was still to be worked out – via a fourth-channel subscription which was estimated at between £60 million and £80 million in the first year. The IBA added that 'we would not wish to see the fourth channel as a permanent pensioner.' A start date of autumn 1982 was set.

In December, the IBA followed up with the *Fourth Channel Policy Statement*, spelling out a requirement for 15-per-cent educational output and religious broadcasting of one hour a week and collaboration with ITV rather than competition on acquiring the rights to films, sports events and other programmes to prevent prices being driven up. ITV would lead the negotiations on rights, so, in a sense, the infant Channel 4, though largely autonomous and separately scheduled, would be protected by its older and much larger big brother. The real challenge ahead was a creative one.

On 6 February 1980, the Broadcasting Bill was published. The key clauses obliged the IBA to:

- ensure that the programmes contained a suitable proportion of matter calculated to appeal to tastes and interests not generally catered for by ITV;
- ensure that a suitable proportion of programmes were of an educational nature;
- encourage innovation and experiment in the form and content of programmes and generally give the Fourth Channel a distinctive character of its own;
- make sure that a substantial proportion of the programmes broadcast were supplied other than by persons namely a TV programme contractor and a body corporate under the control of a TV programme contractor.

For the shadow Labour spokesman, Merlyn Rees, it was all too permissive. 'Some clauses had the ring of an idealistic newspaper editorial – they read well but were surely too vague for anyone to put into practice.' During the Bill's rapid progress, the title of the new network was changed to 'the Fourth Channel' from ITV2. An attempt by the advertising industry to set up a separate sales force for the new channel, in the hope that competition would push down prices, failed to make any impact. All in all, this was a year of extraordinary activity after two decades of prevarication. Michael Jackson and Sophie Balhetchet lobbied like dervishes to the end. Lord Annan gave his reaction when the Bill reached the House of Lords on 14 July 1980:

> The Open Broadcasting Authority was born from an idea of Mr Tony Smith. It was he who talked about a foundation to run the fourth channel. Our committee took that piece of dough and began to bake it. I do not think that it got very far in the baking before we had to finish our report. The new channel is really the same loaf, only now it is done to a turn.[15]

And then the Bill was delayed. At the Cambridge conference, Whitelaw, so decisive over the fourth channel, had simultaneously retreated from an election-manifesto pledge to create a single Welsh-language television service. He offered the Welsh instead more language programmes on the BBC and HTV. This volte-face provoked a surge of Welsh nationalism, involving demonstrations and acts of defiance, and was a gift for Plaid Cymru, the nationalist party. Transmitters were raided; 2,000 people refused to pay their television licences; and then, in April 1980, Gwynfor Evans, the sixty-eight-year-old President of Plaid Cymru, declared he would begin a hunger strike on 1 October. No one doubted his word. So, in September, the Government backed down. 'We can't let poor Gwynfor die', said Whitelaw in a phone conversation with Brian Tesler.[16] There was a hurried political settlement. The Bill was already in the House of Lords when it was rapidly changed to include a new unique authority, the Welsh Fourth Channel, Sianel Pedwar Cymru (S4C), to replace Channel 4 in Wales. The finance was adjusted. Of the total advertising that ITV sold, there would be a three-way division, with 14 per cent for Channel 4 and 6 per cent for S4C. Unlike Channel 4, S4C would never aspire to be self-sufficient. Royal assent was delayed until 13 November, setting back Channel 4's incorporation.

During May, the IBA's Chairman, the educationalist Lady Bridget Plowden asked the gregarious and charming film actor and producer Sir Richard Attenborough to be Chairman of Channel 4. 'She said they were toying with the idea of breaking away from the establishment. I told her it was out of the question, I was making my film *Gandhi*', he recalled.[17] Attenborough, even then a show-business icon, indicated, however, that he was prepared to consider being Deputy Chairman. Plowden, together with her Director General Brian Young, a former Headmaster of Charterhouse School, cracked on with selecting nine consultants for the shadow Channel 4 Board. In June, Edmund Dell, a former Labour Secretary of State for Trade and Chief Executive of the Guinness Peat Group was made Chairman. He had a reputation for rectitude, for doing things properly, but he had no knowledge of the television industry, and his interpersonal skills were poor. The qualities he lacked were supplied in full measure by his deputy. Attenborough met him, and the two got on very well. 'I found him funny, witty, very tough and absolutely sure how the channel should be run. Either for good or evil, this had nothing to do with television'.[18] Attenborough laid down a condition, that the new channel would back British film-makers – it was his initiative that led to Film on Four.

The Board was composed of Anthony Smith, who had nursed but then abandoned hopes of running the channel and was now Director of the BFI; Sara Morrison, a director of the General Electric Company, married to a Conservative MP and landowner; Roger Graef; Anne Sofer, a member of the Inner London Education Authority; Dr Glyn Tegai Hughes, Warden of Grygnog College, Wales; and four ITV directors: Brian Tesler of LWT, Bill Brown of Scottish Television, David McCall of Anglia and Joyce Whitby, Head of Children's Programmes at Yorkshire. Tesler was the only representative of the 'big five' companies that effectively controlled the ITV network.

Despite careful selection to balance political affiliations, a curious thing would subsequently happen: the five independent directors and Dell and Attenborough all joined the Social Democratic Party (SDP) when it was formed in 1981. Anthony Smith remembers an incident at a subsequent meeting.

> Sara Morrison looked around the room and said, 'I know we are sup-posed to be representing different things, but we are really the same person. Look, everyone in this room is SDP.' And it was the case. In that week Dickie Attenborough was leaving the Labour Party, so was Anne Sofer, and I was going round with Shirley Williams. It was extraordi-nary. We realised we represented the chattering classes.[19]

The post of Chief Executive was advertised in July, and there were twenty-nine candidates. The consultants entered a period of intense debate. The early favourite was Brian Wenham, a former Controller of BBC2. A classic BBC mandarin, later ousted in the John Birt era, he declined to apply or put himself forward; but this was a job you had to be hungry for. Another early favourite, Charles Denton, had just been appointed to run programming at Central Television and felt he could not let the company down. Paul Bonner, Head of BBC Science and Features, was invited to apply by Graef.

In the end, the list was whittled down to two big rivals, Jeremy Isaacs and John Birt, and a compromise BBC executive, Paul Bonner. They approached the challenge completely differently. Birt was so passionate and zealous he submitted a fifty-page document with a fully worked-out schedule. He promised efficient organisation, certainly, but there was little evidence of the required creative streak. His Chan-nel 4 would cater to different interest groups: bird-watchers, motor-cyclists, anglers, gardeners and the like. He saw television as magazine publishing. Graef said, 'The Board's blood ran cold: it was so mechanistic, there was no room for experiment, for flexibility.'[20] Birt later acknowledged that at thirty-six he did not have the necessary expertise to start a new channel.[21] Even his greatest admirer, his boss Brian Tesler, was set back by his serious tone.

Isaacs, by contrast, sent a letter listing his nine priorities for the channel, based on the requirements of the Act but placing a high priority on the arts, especially film-making. He promised a flexible schedule for quick responses and provision for the 'widest range of opinion in utterance, discussion and debate.' He also knew how to organise it, with a small staff of commissioning editors to select programmes by subject area. The channel would respond to offers from programme-makers, with no specific quota for the independent sector. Attenborough, backed by Smith and Graef, thought Isaacs was the obvious choice. 'He had the talent, the guts, the experi-ence, the determination.'[22]

But doubts remained, and the Board hesitated. Isaacs seemed over-confident, convinced the job was his, surprised that he had to be called back for a second interview. Edmund Dell was the sticking point. He had never heard of Isaacs until this point, despite having a deep interest in history, perhaps because he had only bought a television set a year before – from the very first the two men did not get on. He told his fellow board members he feared Isaacs was too 'old Labour.' Dell was not a typical politician: with his logical, meticulous, somewhat dour cast of mind, he felt more at home in the corridors of Whitehall than the hurly-burly of Westminster. He was intelligent and could be interesting and supportive, but he had nothing that overlapped with Isaacs, who liked people who sparked back. 'Jeremy hates people who come from that official public world of Britain', Anthony Smith observed. 'He had troubles at Thames Television, troubles at the BBC editing *Panorama*, and at the BFI. Dell was precisely the sort of person Jeremy despised.'[23]

Dell had wanted John Birt.[24] Indeed, he wrote to Birt later to say he had not been impressed by Isaacs and that he, Birt, had been the outstanding candidate. At a seminar in 1992, Dell said he'd told Birt that he had handed his application document to the newly appointed Isaacs so that he could learn from it and had informed Isaacs that Channel 4 would have been a better channel if he had bothered to read it.[25] The Board were worried about Isaacs' uncertain control of detail and financial affairs.

But, eventually, Attenborough proposed that Isaacs be appointed, and the Chairman, finding himself isolated, reluctantly gave in, with bad grace, warning them they were making a terrible mistake. Isaacs was told he had the job on Friday 26 September, when he went to Dell's office at Guinness Peat's headquarters in the City. A salary of £35,000 was agreed, and a five-year contract. There was one condition: Dell asked Isaacs to appoint Paul Bonner as Channel Controller. Isaacs, though surprised, complied, and in the event Bonner would prove an ally, not a threat. Dell, being the man he was, and harbouring resentment, did not crack open a bottle of celebratory champagne. Instead, Isaacs went from the City straight to familiar television land, to the BBC's documentary empire at Shepherd's Bush, to break the news and celebrate.[26]

Dell believed Isaacs was foisted on him, and this became a central problem. Attenborough later reflected:

> I should have been more aware this would rankle. The manner in which the company was administered slowly divided it. It was inevitable there would be a point at which Edmund and Jeremy came almost to blows. It was overwhelmingly just personality. I don't think it was fundamental philosophy. I don't believe there was great intellectual wrestling going on. It was rather petty. They were two very self-opinionated people. They were immovable.[27]

The Board were still worried about Isaacs' management skills. Channel 4 would need a financial director fast. Edmund Dell rang the BBC's Michael Checkland on a Saturday morning to see if he was interested in joining, but he was rebuffed. An advertisement produced a sheaf of applicants, but Graef now made another important suggestion to bolster the top team. He had met an interesting manager, Justin Dukes, who was running the *Financial Times* at a grim time for the newspaper business, when militant trade unions threatened production on an almost daily basis. Dukes had worked on plans to reorganise the whole broadsheet national newspaper industry. 'Roger Graef and I talked about a fly-on-the-wall television programme. It didn't happen because Lord Hartwell, then owner of the *Telegraph*, wouldn't join the group.'[28]

Graef rang Dukes that autumn and asked if he would be interested in joining Channel 4. Dukes, looking for an exit from the *Financial Times*, persuaded the Board to make him Deputy Chief Executive. His special skill – one that Dell so notably lacked – was in knowing what makes creative people tick. 'One of the realities was that if you could not get on with Jeremy there was no point in applying', he said. 'I invited Jeremy to my house in Gibson Square, quite close to Fleet Street, and we polished off a quantity of whisky. I was a great admirer of his work, and he'd just made a very good series on Ireland.'[29] In short, they hit it off.

A background in newspapers rather than television proved important in devising the new publishing and business ethos of Channel 4. Dukes described his seven-year partnership with Isaacs as 'like being on a tandem, riding behind him, saying steady on, then pedalling hard.'[30] He developed the image: 'There was no doubt that Jeremy was in the front seat. Occasionally I would say, "Jeremy, do you know where we are going?" I had respect for Jeremy, but it doesn't mean you buy the person 100 per cent. But in programming, ideas and vision, it *was* 100 per cent.'[31]

From the start, Dukes also made it his business to hold off Dell, to defuse rows between him and Isaacs, who were often not on speaking terms. He stopped clashes spilling over into resignations and kept this fundamental tension away from the press. He also ensured that the new company was free of the corrupt ways of the old media. People were not employed through their companies – a system that could be used to dodge taxes – but were given personal contracts. As General Manager, he brought in Frank McGettigan, a former colleague from the *Financial Times*, who insisted that everything had to be above board so as not to attract the attentions of the Inland Revenue. 'Meanness gave us strength', said McGettigan. 'We were not going to run a TV company where everyone was wallowing in gold bars.'[32] It was comparatively easy, of course, to declare what Channel 4 was *not* going to be. To decide exactly what this new channel *would be* was rather more challenging – and the challenge had to be met by just one person: Jeremy Isaacs.

4

Godfather in the green Rolls Royce

• • • •

On the bitterly cold morning of 16 December 1980, a green Rolls Royce, with the number plate RA 111, glided down Charlotte Street, then a fairly shabby neighbourhood in London's West End. Parallel to Tottenham Court Road and north of the tatty bit of Oxford Street, the road was nowhere near as ostentatiously prosperous as it would become twenty years later, when bronzed film directors sipped skinny lattes at the Charlotte Street Hotel and Ricky Gervais made small talk with Ash Atalla, producer of his hit series *The Office*. Back in 1980, it was a place to come to smash a few plates on a Friday night in budget restaurants such as the Anemos, where houmous counted as an exotic starter, and you could dance on the table, if you dared, after a bottle or two of retsina. There were also respected family-run restaurants with a loyal clientele: L'Étoile, Bertorelli's and the Trattoria Pescatori. The culture of eating out in pricey restaurants run by celebrity chefs had not yet taken off.

Charlotte Street was the centre of Fitzrovia, a district that still retained a whiff of the Bohemian raffishness which, in the earlier years of the century, had attracted such literary and artistic celebrities as Dylan Thomas, Augustus John and George Orwell to its pubs and cheap restaurants. It was quite distinct from Soho, just across Oxford Street, which, apart from being the traditional hub of London's sex trade, accommodated advertising agencies, more stylish restaurants and the editing suites that would later support Channel 4's independent programme-makers. This north side of Oxford Street was gritty, with a high proportion of social and student housing. Real people bought essentials in old-fashioned corner shops. Dentures were made in the building that was later to become the Charlotte Street Hotel. But there was, too, just a hint that the area was on the verge of transformation. The lack of traffic and the convivial spirit of the place meant that its pubs and cafés were among the first in

London to sport tables and chairs on the pavement for al-fresco meetings, providing a splash of colour in the rather grim world where people were just starting to adjust to Margaret Thatcher. Already the Saatchi & Saatchi advertising agency, icon of the Thatcher age, had moved to new headquarters at Number 80.

Out of the chauffeured Rolls stepped Britain's best-loved actor, director and producer, Sir Richard 'Dickie' Attenborough. His long list of credits, stretching back nearly forty years, included *Brighton Rock* (1947), *The Angry Silence* (1960), *A Bridge Too Far* (1977) and *Oh! What a Lovely War* (1969). The Oscar-winning *Gandhi* (1982) was soon to be released, and *Cry Freedom* (1987), his great statement about South African apartheid, lay ahead, as did a cameo role as the mad zoologist in *Jurassic Park* (1993). His public performances, though, are the tip of the iceberg for Attenborough. He is a man of organised flair and, by 1980, was active on numerous committees and boards. In the pocket of his dark businessman's coat was a little card detailing his appointments for the day, all meticulously kept. He would flash in and out of Channel 4's history for twelve years and more, acting as its godfather, guiding the channel longer than any other non-executive director or chief executive, as one of its most important founders.

Much later, when Sir Michael Bishop, a tough businessman, joined the Board in 1992, he found little as he had expected; but the biggest eye-opener was Attenborough. He had imagined what cynics call a luvvie, someone totally wrapped in the world of film and theatre and absorbed by his contribution to it. Instead, he found a man who got through more business in a day than he did.

Attenborough was Channel 4's Deputy Chairman. That morning, he was to join the Chairman, Edmund Dell, and Jeremy Isaacs. Dell and Isaacs barely spoke that morning. Dell had not wanted Isaacs as Chief Executive. He had reluctantly caved in only on meeting a wall of resistance from the rest of the directors, led by Attenborough.

The meeting was to decide on a headquarters for the nascent Channel 4. Wrested from the grasp of ITV after a series of campaigns and bitter fights stretching over two decades, the new channel had received its royal assent in November. The Government expected it to be on air by November 1982, nearly two years away. There was nothing prepared, no template for what was to be a startling experiment. Britain, with only three television channels, was way behind America, where the first rolling news channel, CNN, had just been launched. Since the introduction of commercial television in 1955, there was no indigenous tradition of starting new national television companies.

Attenborough, at least, had bid successfully in 1973 for the Capital Radio franchise, one of the first big commercial licences to challenge the BBC. Behind his showbiz charm and his much-satirised habit of calling everyone 'darling' lay guile and cunning. His ability to be organised, to charm, to make a dramatic entrance and exit, would prove vital in ensuring that he got his way. In the next few years, those qualities would prevent the rows between Isaacs and Dell from tearing the young company apart and becoming public. In due course, he would be instrumental in replacing Isaacs with Michael Grade and, through lobbying Margaret Thatcher's cabinet, in heading off privatisation.

These three men, accompanied by Isaacs' deputy Paul Bonner, a concession won by Dell, stood with their backs to the charming but down-at-heel five-storey Georgian townhouses that typified the area. They looked up at an ugly 1960s office building built by National Car Parks. It was a strange shape. The first two stories were broad, like a mini-plateau, and from them rose a small six-storey tower, oddly angled so that the council flats behind had some light.

At the time, and for much of the next year, the skeleton of what would become Channel 4's 215-strong team was camping in rooms at the headquarters of the IBA, the channel's regulator, in Knightsbridge. Isaacs now desperately needed his own place, to give some concrete shape to what was still a chaotic formula. The Channel 4 Board, all deeply opinionated people, had their own views. American-born Roger Graef, a well-regarded independent documentary-maker, said Channel 4 should be housed in a warehouse in King's Cross, in an experimental space with public access, so as to make direct connections with the audience as well as helping to regenerate that depressed area.

Fellow directors had mocked Graef's idea, wondering whether he wanted to furnish his people's palace with orange boxes. Edmund Dell's suspicion of television and media types ran deep, and he favoured a vacated British Steel research centre in Battersea, where the chief transport link was the dilapidated local rail station at Queenstown Road. It was certainly cheap, but when a survey showed that the building had been contaminated during its previous occupancy, the other board members sighed with relief.

So, it was Attenborough who would have the final say. 'I was mad about it, it had all the right associations, it was bohemian', he recalled.[1] Number 60 Charlotte Street was alongside Scala Street, named after the old Scala Theatre, where generations of children had seen Peter Pan fly over the front stalls in the annual Christmas production of J.M. Barrie's classic story. Number 60 had been developed in the 1970s as part of an undistinguished office block with a basement cinema. Isaacs said, 'To anyone else it was just a site, a forbidding and miserable place, where we met in freezing weather in overcoats. To Dickie, it was the Scala. He saw a tradition, an association. We are, as he would memorably say later, in show business.'[2] Isaacs wanted Charlotte Street too. For him, it was a concrete expression of his vision of the new channel as being connected with the mainstream but distinct from it. Other ITV companies were scattered in other parts of the West End while the BBC's Broadcasting House, that symbol of the media establishment, was a ten-minute walk to the west.

Dell was eventually won over by something more prosaic. The building was close to the Post Office Tower, which would relay Channel 4's signals to the transmitter network for broadcast. The proximity cut costs. The landlords were pleased to have them as tenants, too – so pleased that the rent was negotiated downwards and other tenants moved out.

For another influential board member, Anthony Smith, it also passed muster.

> You have to remember Charlotte Street wasn't as it is now. The important thing was that we were going beyond Soho. It needed either to be there or Shoreditch. We needed to be where ordinary people could be seen, or at least some of them, leading ordinary lives. Anyway, we had to find a building quick.[3]

Next day, at a board meeting, it was formally agreed that 60 Charlotte Street would be the first headquarters of Channel 4.

The building was fitted out during 1981, with a boardroom on the ground floor behind the modest reception area, through which hundreds of hopeful new television producers would troop in search of commissions. The old cinema became a small television studio, with the green room, make-up and transmission suite attached. When the cameras were finally wheeled into position, it was discovered the floor was not level, so they slid about.

Despite Isaacs' opposition, the Chairman had his own office next to the boardroom. It would enter Channel 4 folklore as the place which got wrecked by a frightened tiger cub, closeted there before being taken for filming.

The hippy, leftish spirit, which would characterise most of Channel 4's commissioners, thrived in Charlotte Street and survived almost intact until the channel left in 1994 for purpose-built premises in Westminster. Peter Moore, responsible for the successful documentary strand, *Cutting Edge*, controlled the key to the first-aid room on the top floor. He was persuaded to hand it out for private trysts when a prominent commissioner fell for another member of staff. The neighbouring restaurants played their part in shaping the culture. *The Tube* was commissioned in the Pescatori, almost directly opposite. Four years later, a young hopeful called Jonathan Ross and his television partner Alan Marke would wander up Charlotte Street on Friday mornings, bearing coffee and doughnuts for the Controller of Entertainment, in a successful campaign to launch *The Last Resort*, the breakthrough that led to *The Jonathan Ross Show*.

Roger Graef helped to wean his colleagues from stuffy boardroom practices to match the new channel. At his suggestion, they ditched the expensive and lavish board lunches in favour of a pre-board dinner, with a different set of programme commissioners each time.

I felt Tony [Smith] and I were champions of the ethos. How innocent and pure it was. Because we won, we good guys won. Jeremy was a good guy. No one ground axes: here were good people given the chance to create something from scratch. It was like being on a spaceship, with people asking, 'What do you need to get this thing launched?' This is not the way people begin channels now. Television lives in a zone of its own creation, recycles its own formats, it is very internalised. The more television there is, the more samey it becomes. Jeremy decisively broke with this, to the derision of a lot of people.[4]

5

Miss No One from Nowhere
joins Channel 4

● ● ● ●

On Monday, 1 December 1980, the *Guardian*'s women's page started a new series called 'Women and the Media Men', which asked, 'What do television, newspapers and radio make of women?' Liz Forgan, thirty-six, who had been editing the page since 1978, had decided to kick off the debate by interviewing Jeremy Isaacs, just starting to set up Channel 4. She noted approvingly in the article that he had once won a battle over a programme on the daring subject of premenstrual tension and, as Chairman of the BFI's production board, had dealt sympathetically with Marxist feminist film-makers.

Isaacs regarded the *Guardian*'s women's page as lively and unstridently provoking, but he had only met its editor once, at a party. In the interview, he told her there were far too few opportunities for women in television and that they would get a sympathetic hearing from him. 'I don't see why my weekly current affairs programme shouldn't be produced by women', he observed.[1] Forgan solemnly took notes and asked all the appropriate questions, but before the interview ended, it became apparent to both of them that an extra, quite unexpected item had been added to the agenda. This is how Isaacs described the encounter:

> A brisk, cheerful, plump [. . .] businesslike person introduced herself. I said I would answer her questions if, at the end, she would answer a question of mine. I asked her if she might be interested in taking charge of all Channel 4's news and current affairs output, its journalism. A couple of days later we had another brief chat in a pub. 'You are serious about this, are you?' she asked. She accepted.[2]

Eloquent and confident, Forgan was educated at Benenden, the girls' public school in Kent, then Oxford. Her journalistic experience included the *Hampstead and Highgate Express* and London's *Evening Standard*, where she had been a leader writer. She was brisk and clever without being intimidating and had a knack of appealing to powerful men without threatening them. She warned the impulsive Isaacs, 'Do you realise I don't like television? I never watch it. I hate and fear it like all newspaper journalists. I am the wrong person.' He replied, 'Just what we want. Perfect.'[3]

This unorthodox method of recruitment played badly with Channel 4's directors. Even the staunchest of Isaacs' supporters were furious when he broke the news at the first formal board meeting on 17 December, following royal assent to the Bill establishing the channel. The meeting had started happily enough. The registration of the company on 10 December was noted, along with the issue of 100 Channel 4 shares, owned on behalf of the public by the IBA. Sir Richard Attenborough was absent, but the previous day he had been on the site visit that settled on the 60 Charlotte Street headquarters.

Then Jeremy Isaacs spoke. He had, he said, hired three of the most senior and important commissioners already: Liz Forgan, Head of News and Current Affairs; David Rose, Head of Fiction; and Naomi Sargant to run education. The Board was shocked, for two important reasons. First, this was a public body, and there had been no open advertisement or consultation. Second, they had expected to be brought into the process of making appointments to such powerful positions. This was just the kind of maverick behaviour by their new Chief Executive that they had been warned about and dreaded.

Isaacs argued that time was of the essence. The independent sector was an unknown quantity, and some programmes needed to be commissioned early to be ready for the launch in November 1982. Education required lengthy negotiations with the Regulator. Films took time to make. The least controversial of the three appointments was David Rose, from the BBC, who had run a distinguished drama department in Birmingham. Rose would found Film on Four, one of the most enduring of Channel 4's strands. The directors from ITV knew he was a catch, and they made little fuss. Just four months later, on 2 April 1981, the first Film on Four was commissioned: *Angel*, by the Irish writer Neil Jordan, produced by John Boorman with a budget of just £300,000.

But the other two appointments were a different matter. For Dell, hiring Forgan was like waving a red rag at a bull. News and current affairs were his major concern. The *Guardian*'s women's page had been at the heart of the debate about feminism and sexual liberation in the 1960s and 1970s, and, although it had moved away from radicalism in recent years, some critics still saw it as representing a feminist, left-of-centre view of the world. That view was certainly distant from Dell's, and some board members felt that the impetuous Isaacs might have been motivated in part by a mischievous desire to rile the Chairman. He would write later, 'Edmund Dell, whose idea of the person to take charge of the channel's journalism would have been somewhere between a Harvard professor of economics and the editor of the *Financial Times*, was particularly put out.'[4] Isaacs stood firm, and the Board finally agreed to confirm the hirings but ruled that in future it should approve all appointments of commissioning editors and any others with a salary of over £17,500. Isaacs acquiesced, but he had succeeded in making the point that he, and he alone, ran the programming. Behind his back, one director would start referring to him as 'the Big I'.

Forgan was aware of the problem that had been caused by the unconventional style of her appointment.

> I think the whole industry was surprised and shocked. Who is this Miss No one from Nowhere? Edmund Dell made his views very clear to me and hated me from that moment on. What was odd was that Edmund decided early that I was a dangerous leftie, plying some left-wing agenda. He thought I was insufficiently heavyweight for the kind of journalism he had in mind. And I realised I was never going to convince him otherwise.[5]

Her arrival would trigger six years of battles over bias in the channel's current-affairs programming, until Dell stood down as Chairman.

For David Glencross, Deputy Director of Television at the IBA, it seemed clear that Forgan did not yet appreciate the difference between newspapers and television. Print was free within the law of the land to speak its mind. Television, on the other hand, was bound, rightly or wrongly, by a duty to treat politics and major public issues with due impartiality. This obligation was carefully policed by the IBA, although it was prepared to allow Channel 4 some leeway to experiment. Dell would take a stricter line, observing that where Isaacs thought he was creating a culture that was letting in fresh thinking, in fact almost everyone he appointed shared a homogeneous, left-of-centre worldview. Yet, even the liberal-minded documentary-maker Roger Graef, who contributed to the *Guardian* from time to time, thought that transplanting an editor without experience of television was risky. In the event, Forgan would show that running a powerful newspaper section, with articles from contributors, was in some respects good training for her new role, even though the costs and technical disciplines of television were so different.

'In retrospect', says Forgan,

> in some ways my lack of knowledge about television was a huge handicap. But I could see eventually what Jeremy was up to. He'd decided in his mind something I thought was absolutely right. In fact, this was my

message to the commissioning editors who joined us later. I said that we will make terrible mistakes, but people will forgive us anything except wasting this unbelievable opportunity to be different. They'll forgive us crap programmes. They will not forgive us for playing safe.

And of course there was a price to pay for it [. . .] But the great thing about Jeremy was that he had the courage of his convictions. Edmund thought Jeremy and I were doing violence to something he cared about, which was really well-considered journalism and political analysis. We kept trying to explain to him how that was not the whole story, how he had to try to understand what Channel 4 was about, that we were not just throwing away the toys, or breaking things for fun. He never ever understood it. Edmund Dell was in many ways a very disappointed man. He was a brilliant man, a successful politician, but he had the evil luck of reaching his pinnacle as Labour lost power. There he was, stuck with this funny television channel. He wasn't interested in this game of daring inventiveness. It wasn't his bag.[6]

There was also unease on the Board about the appointment of Naomi Sargant, a lifelong socialist and a leading Labour member of Haringey Council in north London. Here, Isaacs was laying himself open to a charge not just of political bias but also cronyism, for she was the wife of one of his oldest friends, Andrew McIntosh, briefly Labour leader of the Greater London Council before being deposed by supporters of Ken Livingstone. (He was subsequently made a Labour peer and served as Broadcasting Minister in the Blair Government.) Sargant had trained as a market researcher, been in on the birth of the Open University and was now its Pro-Vice-Chancellor, overseeing relations with students. Isaacs, with his wife Tamara, took Sargant and McIntosh out to dinner at the noisy Balzac restaurant, close to the BBC in Wood Lane, west London, that December. He asked her to come to Channel 4 and take charge of educational programmes, and she agreed.[7]

'I needed to recruit someone to put into practice the mandated educational remit', Isaacs said later. 'It could have been a triumph or a disaster.'[8] She had never done anything remotely like it before. At Channel 4 she would have the task of overseeing 15 per cent of output, or 400 hours a year of programmes, represented over the years by 238 separate series – and for the first two years she worked entirely on her own. Another potential hazard was that the two principal regulators, Sir Brian Young and Lady Bridget Plowden, were both deeply interested in education.

Her first task was to convince sceptical commissioning editors and schedulers that her output was worth screening in prime time. In the event, the consumer programme *For What It's Worth* became a hit and, almost accidentally, she pioneered the kind of lifestyle programmes that within a few years would spread to other channels. These ranged from the first television series on wine to off-beat gardening, such as *Plants for Free*. 'Some of her work was prophetic and far ahead of its time', said Isaacs.[9]

> In the early days I ran into Norman Tebbit who said he hadn't expected
> Channel 4 to be all about gays and Northern Ireland [which was how
> parts of the media were then caricaturing it] but about golf and yacht-
> ing. I told him to look at what Naomi Sargant was doing.[10]

But she was an emotionally vulnerable woman, prone to tears, unsure of herself in the strange world of television. Like Isaacs, she shared a vision, to make the world a better place.[11] But it would be a stressful experience.

● ● ● ●

The embryonic team settled into a suite of cramped offices in the IBA's building at 70 Brompton Road, opposite Harrods while the Charlotte Street building was being adapted for them. Justin Dukes, Managing Director of the *Financial Times*, virtually co-opted himself to the project as Managing Director and Deputy Chief Executive. Though not formally confirmed until May 1981, he was around long before that and attending board meetings. He became Isaacs' deputy in all matters except program-ming, and the two men found a modus vivendi. Dukes understood clearly that he must not seek to have an editorial voice. He was in his element, essentially inventing from scratch a television publishing company. In the start-up period, the IBA was handling the routine payment of salaries and tax, but unsolicited programme propos-als were starting to rain in, and nobody had yet devised a way of dealing with them.

'I found no organisation of any type I could see', Dukes recalls.

> There was no money – they hadn't thought about it. Jeremy was already
> busy buying things without any money, but we did not even have a list
> of things we were buying. This was an entirely creative engine, without
> regard to anything else. It was a case of Jeremy saying: 'I like that; yes,
> I'd like that. Come and have lunch.' After three weeks I went to Ed-
> mund Dell with a list of what had been promised already. I told him
> that unless I could have £12.5 million in the next seven days I thought
> we should have to declare Channel 4 insolvent. I had the money in 24
> hours. The dear old IBA had been sitting on it![12]

He rang the accountants Peat Marwick Mitchell and told them he needed some-one urgently to provide some financial management. They provided David Scott, a twenty-seven-year-old former public schoolboy. Unflappable and utterly loyal, Scott became a key member of the efficient 'officer class' posted around Isaacs to import some sense of order into his impulsive management style. He was to work with Channel 4 for twenty-five years, rising from Finance Director to Deputy Chief Executive, and came to represent the history and organisational backbone of the channel.

Dukes started to put together a team to look at all the business and contractual issues, ensuring that from the early days there was separation between the creative commissioning of programmes and the business side. That, at least, was the theory.

As crates started to fill with programme proposals from hungry would-be independents, Isaacs held an open meeting for them at the Royal Institution on 16 January 1981 – the day when it became clear that the commissioning team was going to be swamped by a tidal wave of proposals. Some 600 independents turned up, spilling out of the hall into the lobby outside the lecture theatre. Isaacs, in a thrilling speech, told them what he was looking for: programmes for young people, in a tone of voice they find congenial; programmes that show women as they are; programmes that explain the world and reflect a multicultural society; programmes to debate the great questions of the day – and lastly, as an afterthought, programmes to entertain.

Isaacs told the independents to send in ideas no earlier than 1 April 1981, because the commissioners were not in place to receive them, but no later than 1 June – after which he envisaged 'a rolling process'. He also committed the channel to dealing with the emerging Independent Programme Producers Association (IPPA), with whom it would work out payments and contracts, the terms of trade. The subscription to fund the project, worth £18.2 million to March 1982 and £85.4 million from April 1982 to 1983, would allow an average programme price of only £30,000 an hour, he warned. This was low considering that, eleven months later, the ITV companies would say they could not provide anything for less than £100,000 an hour. Already the new television channel was introducing change, setting programme budgets that undercut the grossly inefficient ITV. By March, Isaacs was warning the Board of 'the need to rely for an appreciable part of the time on programmes costing £10–15,000 an hour.'[13] Of the sixty hours a week Channel 4 would broadcast from the start, a quarter would be cheap films.

The January board meeting had considered a staff-structure paper, which proposed that the channel could be run by 130 people. The wise ITV heads said that would be too few. From Thames, the company hired Ellis Griffiths as Chief Engineer. A driven, efficient but gruff character with little small talk, he was trusted by Isaacs and had helped set up a modern system for South Africa's SABC. He would install the first fully computerised system of broadcasting in Britain, buying £2.6 million of equipment from America. An advertisement in January for commissioning editors produced 6,000 replies, despite the insecurity. Jobs were offered on contracts of three years only. This was probably too short, but the Board wanted to create perpetual change. Graef later said that five years would have been more sensible, given the time it takes to make certain programmes. But the atmosphere of constant insecurity meant that Isaacs, on a five-year contract (later extended to seven) would keep the whip hand. The areas he cared about most had been assigned to people not versed in the arts of television, from Liz Forgan to Michael Kustow, the first Arts Commissioner, a theatre director who had run the Institute of Contemporary Arts (ICA).

In April, after Forgan had been at Channel 4 for a few weeks and was starting to buckle under the torrent of ideas and people hawking them, she said to Isaacs,

> Look, there is a real problem here, I haven't a clue whether the next one through the door is the Rembrandt of British broadcasting, who has made genius programmes for the past forty years, or someone last seen selling villas in Lanzarote. Why don't I come in with a list of people who are coming in today and you can tell me whether he's a genius or a shyster – because you know.[14]

Isaacs would have none of it: 'Certainly not. If I do that, what's the point of hiring you? I specifically want someone who doesn't know that, who can start again, listen to them with completely fresh ears.'[15] As a result, her first commissions were a mixed bunch.

> I managed to hire quite a few 'villas in Lanzarote' types, but one or two geniuses. On the whole that was the price for freshness. It isn't always the way to do it. Sometimes you get innovation most easily from people who know most about it; but Jeremy mixed the two up. I am sure I paid far too much attention to people who were effectively reinventing wheels: it was *all* new to me.[16]

Nothing like it would happen in television again. There was a pent-up flood of people with ideas who had been longing for just the outlet and funding that Channel 4 was now providing. Whether this is what the Home Secretary Willie Whitelaw had intended or not, it was if someone had opened up a safety valve to take the pressure off. Many hopeful producers had been nurturing unfulfilled dream projects since the 1960s, especially women and groups such as gay lobbyists.

In June, the Trades Union Congress asked Isaacs and Dell to commission programmes from the unions and producers who represented their point of view and for an industrial-affairs advisory unit to vet all programmes dealing with unions.[17] That latter request was denied, but the pressure did result in a programme called *Union World*. And it was one reason why the agenda of some of the channel's early output seemed a little like a rehash of the concerns of the 1960s, rather than dealing directly with the bitter conflicts played out during the 1980s between free-market Thatcherism and unfashionable Old Labour.

● ● ● ●

In April 1981, an ambitious young director and producer of television commercials called Nigel Stafford-Clark was seeking to make his mark in television and film through the new channel. He had played no personal role in lobbying for Channel 4, but his wealthy boss, Mike Luckwell, a hard-bitten entrepreneur who owned the Moving Picture Company (MPC), had helped bankroll the Channel 4 Group in the hope of moving his company into the production of programmes as well as commercials. He was a tough taskmaster, demanding that every shoot was completed on time and on budget, on pain of dismissal. That insistence on discipline and quality had propelled MPC to the top, as the leading British maker of commercials. (It was subsequently bought by Michael Green to create Carlton Television.) Luckwell told a surprised Stafford-Clark to get himself commissioned by Channel 4. 'You can be Head of Programmes', he insisted. 'I'm telling you, I'm not asking you, to get in there. We are going to look foolish, after all this lobbying, if we've not got a single commission from Channel 4.'

'I went to the building they were squatting in', Stafford-Clark recalls.

> I could barely see David Rose and Naomi Sargant for the piles of scripts around them in their cubby-holes. As soon as they announced they were open for business they'd just been inundated with all this stuff, most of it probably best left in the boxes. It was absurd, so weird. They were peering around an avalanche of material. I didn't know anybody in television at all and I wasn't making any impression. I could see the hackles going up – someone from commercials was the antichrist.[18]

Everyone knew, once they set foot in the offices, that the tiny team of fourteen commissioners had far more proposals than could ever be turned into programmes. It would be a real dogfight. But those who failed to get a commission would be shut out for a whole year, perhaps for ever. That was why a lot of black propaganda was being spread among the rival contenders. 'People like me were saying BBC freelances wouldn't know a budget if it bit them on the backside. And they said that people like us, who made commercials, got a lavish budget and a week to shoot 45 seconds – it would all be too glossy.'[19]

Stafford-Clark decided that the only solution was to go back with a strong slate of programme proposals and see Isaacs in person. Convincing *him* was the key. 'I did get a meeting with him, and it changed my life in a funny way. He was intrigued at a commercials company trying to muscle in.'[20]

He recalls the meeting vividly. As he entered the room, Isaacs barked, 'So who are you? What do you think you have to offer?' Stafford-Clark began his pitch, explaining that in the first year the channel would need people who understood what a budget was. 'Only people who have made stuff with a commercials company know how to come in on budget.' Isaacs was getting exasperated. He did not want to be told by this young advertising man how to run his business. 'Get on with it', he snapped. So Stafford-Clark began to list his specific ideas. The first was for a series on painters by Tom Keating, the master forger who had also been Anthony Blunt's picture restorer. This clearly went down well, encouraging him to proceed to *Stand Your Ground*, a women's self-defence series, and *Mothers by Daughters*, which grew into *Fathers by Sons*. Two promising producers came with the package: Jenny Wilkes, who had worked on *The Naked Civil Servant*, and Britt Allcroft (later to become a multimillionaire with *Thomas the Tank Engine*). He also had three interesting film proposals.

After the forty-minute meeting, it was clear that Isaacs had taken a shine to him, accepting several of his proposals and referring him to the relevant departments.

> I went out of the room and stood by the door and thought: did that just happen? We were a major supplier to Channel 4 from nowhere. Jeremy was decisive and quite scary but the thing about him was that once he said yes he would defend you and it to everyone. You never had to watch your back. He was motivational. I cannot imagine anyone else getting that channel off the ground. He was the perfect person in the perfect job at the perfect time. He was a maverick. He had terrific energy. People tingled when they met him.[21]

The commissioners, though, were different, in that most of them had virtually no experience in television. They were going to make all their mistakes on the job. Budgets and programme ambitions were often ill matched, and they had to trust people to make the programme as commissioned, even if they had no track record in the business.

David Scott had already devised a payment system for programme suppliers, which rewarded those who underspent their budgets, and by July the terms of trade were agreed. For a programme in which Channel 4 paid for everything, it would have ownership. If it was then sold abroad, 70 per cent of the proceeds went to Channel 4. The commissioners would identify the programmes to be made, although any expenditure over £500,000 had to be referred to the Board. Then the Acquisition Department – headed by Colin Leventhal, a former BBC Head of Copyright – took over and negotiated the terms with the supplier. Often they coached independent producers into setting up a company.

A Programme Finance Committee, chaired by Dukes, would give final approval to the 'deal' memo. This too was designed to instil discipline, to keep track of things. David Scott's finance side allocated the money once agreed: there was a fee for directors and producers, plus a percentage for the production company. This was pioneering stuff. Claudia Milne, negotiating to make a series of current-affairs programmes, recalled that the only thing questioned in her production budget was money for mealtimes. The Channel 4 negotiator had previously worked for Wimpy. Completed programmes were passed to the Presentation Department, who would decide where the commercial breaks fell. Transmission was handled by Ellis Griffiths and team.

The Head of Marketing was Sue Stoessl, though she had no control over advertising, which was handled by the fifteen ITV companies. She had pioneered the art of using audience research to schedule programmes more scientifically and had helped John Birt write his detailed application to run Channel 4. Isaacs hired her after he and Bonner heard her talk at the London Business School. However, the first programmes were ordered and made long before a clear schedule was ever worked out. The very first project – Contract No. 00001 –was to turn the Royal Shakespeare Company's *Nicholas Nickleby* into a television event. The second was a recording of the comedian Max Wall, made in March as he was performing a one-man show at the Garrick Theatre in London's West End.

In June, more commissioning editors arrived. Alan Fountain from the BFI's Production Board was given £650,000 to drum up video programmes from twenty existing workshops around the country. Carol Haslam, a forceful BBC Open University producer, would run documentary series and those designated as educational. An experienced BBC hand, Cecil Korer, nearing retirement, who had made the popular *Ask the Family*, was handed light entertainment. Music was put under the control of Andy Park, who had been Programme Controller of Radio Clyde and was recommended by Gillian Reynolds, a radio critic. Sue Woodford, a sparky former *World in Action* reporter, was to run multicultural programmes. The wife of the millionaire investment banker Clive (later Lord) Hollick, she was the only one of the fourteen commissioners who was of mixed race, and one of only four women.

Providing programmes for Asian and black Britons in a protected slot was a major commitment. Woodford learnt how serious Channel 4 was about this when sitting on a beach in Tobago with her family in January.

> Rifling through the papers I saw this advert for commissioning editors, and there was one for multicultural programmes. I had previously tried to persuade LWT to do a news magazine programme for ethnic-minority viewers. They were doing *Skin*, a single-issue programme, and I felt strongly that it only ever concentrated on problems. It was a little ghetto area and it struck me as tokenism: it never showed the depth and diversity of other communities.[22]

She was about to give birth to her third child when invited to an interview by Jeremy Isaacs and Paul Bonner, at which she was offered the job.

> I was amazed. I took the baby to my first meeting of commissioning editors, with my mother-in-law, who was a midwife. I had pretty much a blank sheet of paper – blank only so far as I had to get stuff on screen. I wouldn't say I did what Jeremy wanted. What I put forward met with Jeremy's agreement. [. . .] As far as I could see, we'd have programmes for particular communities, made by people from them or close to them, and I wanted them to be visible on screen.
>
> I argued that it shouldn't just be me, doing programmes for black people and Asians – if that was the case the channel wouldn't be fulfilling its remit. The whole feel of the channel would come through other commissioners joining in. And I tried to get it written into contracts that programme-makers were required to address the cultural component of their workforce.[23]

In the end, Woodford commissioned LWT to make the programmes. She was criticised for not going to new independent producers, but she judged it too early to try to set up an independent production company staffed with people who did not have the background or the resources. 'We were taking chances anyway, with presenters who had never presented before. We had a new vision: we weren't playing totally safe.'[24] LWT came up with *Black on Black* and *Eastern Eye*, alternating from week to week. Trevor Phillips became the producer of *Black on Black* while Samir Shah made *Eastern Eye*.

'It had to happen', says Woodford. 'There was nothing for those audiences. From a business point of view it was also obvious there was an emerging middle class with nothing for them to relate to on British television. There was a lot of talent wasted and excluded.'[25] She also commissioned *No Problem*, a comedy that rejected stereotyping black people, as an antidote to *Love Thy Neighbour*. At the same time, the National Film and Television School started to devise short courses specifically for black and ethnic-minority workers, which Channel 4 sponsored.

At a July programme-policy weekend, Jeremy Isaacs assured his colleagues that there would be no wallowing in explicit sex or bad language for their own sake or shock effect.[26] But, during the year, negotiations advanced on a project called *Meadowcroft*, later renamed *Brookside*, which embraced plenty of both. Phil Redmond, who had created *Grange Hill* for the BBC, won Isaacs' support for hefty set-up costs, £3.6 million in the first year, plus a £2 million a year contract to create the twice-weekly soap devoted to tough social issues. Channel 4 bought the cul-de-sac in the outskirts of Liverpool. When the BBC saw it, they began planning *EastEnders*.

Mike Bolland, a former colleague of Paul Bonner who had been running a BBC2 youth show called *Something Else*, joined the team in October to commission youth programmes, even though Isaacs thought him a bit old at thirty-four and dubbed him 'the not-so-young Mike Bolland.' His task was to fill Fridays between 5.15 and 7 p.m., plus an hour on Mondays at 10 p.m., within a budget of £35,000 an hour. The first thing he commissioned was *The Comic Strip Presents . . . Five Go Mad in Dorset*, a parody of an Enid Blyton story, at £140,000 an hour. Dawn French, Jennifer Saunders, Adrian Edmondson and Peter Richardson shuffled into his temporary office. Isaacs loved the show, which played on the channel's debut night and led to a series of films.

Six months before launch, going through the tea chests full of discarded submissions, Bolland found what was to become *The Tube*. Andrea Wonfor, a Tyne Tees executive whose work he admired, had sent in a proposal for six half-hour rock shows with the title *Jamming*. Andy Park, the Music Commissioner, had turned it down, but Bolland thought, 'What if, for six months, we went live?'[27] Isaacs approved, and Bolland invited Wonfor to discuss it over lunch at the Pescatori. She said she wanted to involve a colleague from Tyne Tees, Malcolm Gerrie, a former teacher then working on children's and youth programmes. He had made his name by producing a live performance of *Tommy* in 1976, as a result of which David Puttnam, the film producer, advised him to go into television. As Wonfor and Bolland were lunching in Charlotte Street, Gerrie was in Stockholm overseeing a performance by Abba for a Tyne Tees youth show. Wonfor phoned him, 'The bad news is that they have passed on *Jamming*. The good news is they want twenty shows of 1 hour 45 minutes, live, from 5 November. Get on a plane tonight, to meet Jeremy tomorrow.'[28]

Gerrie rushed back to London, where the meeting had been arranged in another restaurant in Charlotte Street. Wonfor was waiting for him there, but after half an hour there was no sign of Isaacs, so they plodded through the meal. They were just getting the bill when the door crashed open, and there stood Isaacs, in a billowing black raincoat. Recalls Gerrie, 'He picked up my wine and downed it in one. He said he was really sorry. Mike Bolland had said this show would be a *Ready Steady Go* for the 1980s. "Make it live," he roared. "Give it balls. I've got to go." And off he rushed. I fell in love with Jeremy then.'[29]

● ● ● ●

In the autumn of 1981, a Head of Presentation had joined from the BBC and began the unglamorous but crucial work on how the channel would look on air. Pam Masters was nicknamed 'The Headmistress'. Her first task was to devise a logo, and she insisted that the task was handed to a young jeans-clad designer called Martin Lambie-Nairn, who had worked on branding such ITV programmes as LWT's *Weekend*

World and Thames's *This Week* – and who was, in fact, the only person with broadcast experience who had pitched for the job. He pondered how to get away from the floating globe of BBC1 and the skyline of Thames. He came up with the flying yellow, red, blue, green and purple matchsticks, forming the number 4 – a trademark that would last for fifteen years.

He explained how he had arrived at it: 'I thought of those wooden puzzles which fit together to create a number or letter . . . Channel 4 didn't make programmes, it just commissioned them, so the identity expressed the idea of different elements coming together.'[30] Masters insisted it appeared on screen as a three-dimensional image. When she received the test version in the summer of 1982, she judged it as soft, lacking impact. The solution was to dash to Los Angeles and use computer animation, then in its infancy and not yet introduced in Europe. They went to Bo Gehring Aviation, which had worked with another firm, Information International, on complex computer animation for a film called *Tron* (1982). This was the only combination that could provide the solid modelling with highlights, glossy surfaces and shadows that Masters wanted. They had two months to get it ready, including tying it in with David Dundas's music.

When that was done, a new crisis loomed for Masters. She and her team approached the launch date of 2 November with the sinking realisation that the computerised system to log programmes and play out the schedule was not working properly. They would have to cue in programmes manually, the old-fashioned way – but they had not been given enough staff to do this for an extended period. It took six months to work out the computer problems – six months of ill-tempered rows and fractious meetings with technicians.[31] At the same time, she had to work with largely hostile and unhelpful ITV executives to settle the cross-promotion trails and common junctions – having the principal programmes on both channels starting at the same time. Meanwhile, as programmes were delivered to her department, she realised that the commissioners placed a low priority on presentation.

> There was no discipline. Commissioning editors – very outspoken, wonderful as they were – had no idea about running times or credits at the end. We had programmes arriving at any length. What did it matter, they asked, if it over-ran, or didn't run to time? We even had some that we didn't have the rights for: I took it on myself, in the very early days, to go through the schedule checking, to protect us . . . It was chaos.[32]

It was also rather surprising, and for a significant reason. Everyone had assumed that most of the programmes would come from the ITV companies, and surely *their* producers knew all about such disciplines. Well, yes, they did – but when people began to do their sums, a startling fact emerged: independent producers, some of them effectively novices, had grabbed 61 per cent of the commissions as the channel approached its launch – four times as much as had been anticipated. On the production front, at least, ITV had been routed.

By September 1982, the practical issue of how to fill the airtime on a modest budget still remained unresolved. One ruse was to pad the schedule with cheap American series. Leslie Halliwell, a film buff who worked for Granada, was the expert buyer for ITV and was deputed to buy old American favourites – such as *I Love Lucy* – and films for Channel 4. Isaacs didn't want to have to bid against ITV and drive up prices – a self-denying ordinance that initially meant he could only have what ITV didn't want. He was supposed to check with Halliwell before bidding on anything, in case ITV was interested.

But the crafty veteran Cecil Korer, competitive to his fingertips, did not let this gentlemen's agreement cramp his style. Having gone on a buying trip to Los Angeles with Halliwell, he returned in September to scout on his own. There he was tipped off about *Cheers*, the popular comedy set in a Boston bar. He immediately made an offer, and it was accepted. The agreed protocol had been breached, and Colin Leventhal, who had to draw up the deal documents, sensed that it would cause a problem with ITV.[33] Very soon a pained letter from Halliwell was on his desk: 'Dear Cecil, can we please try to keep our channels straight?' He said that *Cheers* had been under consideration by ITV. 'That's the way civil wars start.'[34]

Korer refused to take complete responsibility for upsetting ITV with his coup. On 14 September, he replied to Halliwell: '*Cheers*, I thought, was right for our channel, and I spoke to my chief executive who told me to proceed.' Isaacs also wrote to Halliwell: 'Although Cecil has my support, I agree we agreed he would check with you.'[35] It was, in any case, a fait accompli. *Cheers*, which cost just £5,000 an episode, became Channel 4's banker hit for the next decade and established the channel in the public mind as the place for the freshest American comedy.

The tension was palpable in the boardroom. The Board was told in September that when adding in the £50 million that had been paid for altering the transmitter network, along with other borrowings and loans, it had cost £200 million to get Channel 4 and S4C on air, for which ITV was basically responsible. When people later spoke of the miracle that Channel 4 represented, this financial assistance, foisted by an Act of Parliament onto an unwilling ITV, was a huge but largely unsung element in it. Brian Tesler warned the Board that Isaacs' schedule meant that the channel would take longer to earn its keep than had been envisaged – so ITV would be saddled with its losses for a while yet. In October, the grim mood was made still grimmer when Isaacs reported the bugs in the computer system. Even worse, the Institute of Practitioners in Advertising (IPA), representing advertising agencies, had chosen this moment to pick a devastating fight with Equity, the actors' union. The IPA wanted to cut repeat fees to actors used in commercials by basing payments on audience size.

Equity – supported by Richard Attenborough, among others – said no, it would only reduce the fee by 25 per cent.[36] The dispute, which was to last for two years, meant that most of the advertising breaks were empty, or filled with public announcements, programme trailers or irrelevant time-wasting images such as a potter's wheel. It made the new channel look amateur and, at times, unwatchable.

Stafford-Clark's abiding memories of the countdown before launch are overwhelmingly horrific – producers staggering grey-faced from edit suites, some with their budgets out of control, shows breaking down in the middle.

> It was this wonderful British affair, people running around, bumping into each other, falling over, permanent panic. This date was looming and already you could see the media circling. The people at Channel 4 could see what was coming – they knew there was going to be a storm of criticism and controversy when they launched.[37]

Willie Whitelaw sent a personal letter to Jeremy Isaacs on the morning of 2 November. 'I send to you and all at Channel 4, from all of us concerned with broadcasting at the Home Office, warm good wishes for the success of an exciting new venture.'[38] Isaacs would need all his confidence and leadership skills to hold it all together. They were not ready, not by a long way; but they had to go.

6

Launch:
a white-knuckle ride

• • • •

One golden rule of the media is that new launches never go according to plan, and on Tuesday, 2 November 1982, Channel 4 proved no exception. It was a traumatic birth, for three principal reasons. First, the programmes were of variable quality and length, lacking any consistency. Second, the computer-aided transmission system that was supposed to organise the output was not working properly, so there was a danger that at any moment the service might vanish into the ether. Third, there were not enough advertisements to fill the commercial breaks so that in some parts of the country viewers were obliged to stare at blank screens for three minutes, while others were forced to endure the same handful of commercials again and again. For instance, the ad for the Portuguese sparkling wine Mateus Rosé – one of the few that were transmitted – began to seem distinctly flat at the umpteenth repetition. No wonder so many viewers switched back to the established channels.

The problem of uneven programming was of the channel's own making. At the beginning, its commissioners and supervisors were too conscious of the fact that it was to be a new kind of television station, that they were to play the role merely of publishers, leaving the programmes' independent producers primarily responsible for content, so they allowed themselves insufficient time for checking and editing. As for the computerised transmission system, they had been too confident in the technology and too mean with staffing, so that there was inadequate human back-up when the computers developed glitches. The lack of advertising was caused by a devastating third-party dispute over repeat fees between the advertising agencies and Equity, which meant that only commercials without British actors could be used. This had no direct financial bearing on Channel 4, because the funding formula guaranteed its income, but it added to the tension of its difficult relationship with the

ITV network. If the new channel had been forced to live off its advertising, it would have run out of money and shut down – or, more likely, the dispute would have been sorted out more swiftly.

When Isaacs was signed up as Chief Executive in December 1980, the challenge he faced was creative, not financial. The launch was already fixed for November 1982, so he had just under two years to organise a roster of programmes. The date had been carefully selected by the IBA, as protective of its baby as any new mother. People watch more television as the evenings draw in, and advertising is normally at its most plentiful in the run-up to Christmas. The IBA also ensured that Channel 4 had a three-month start on TV-am, the other new commercial channel due to debut the following February. Before the Channel 4 launch, the consensus, backed up by research from the London Business School,[1] was that it would gain a 10-per-cent audience share within three years – enough to make it mass market but small enough to do minority-interest programmes. It was also predicted that it would attract enough upmarket and young viewers to allow advertising to be sold eventually at a modest premium.

Had a keen observer – perhaps an insomniac – been walking down Charlotte Street as a foggy dawn broke that Tuesday, he or she would have observed through the angular windows of Number 60 scores of figures already hard at work. Nearly all the 215 staff had come to work on launch day in the small hours: some had booked into Bloomsbury hotels and others had been in the office all night. One overworked editor had already fallen asleep at the wheel of his car and nearly killed himself. Yet, they knew that however many hours they put in at this late stage would not be enough and that the first new channel to launch since BBC2, eighteen years earlier, would take to the air before it was really ready.

The first programme, *Countdown*, was due to start at 4.45 p.m., and the verdict from viewers would be delivered soon afterwards. It was different from BBC2, which only a small proportion of the country could watch at first. Channel 4 could reach 87 per cent of viewers from the very start, and 71 per cent had expectantly tuned their televisions to the test signal in response to a £2-million publicity campaign of billboards, press, cinema and television advertisements featuring celebrities such as Adam Faith and Alan Freeman. One had the madcap Keith Allen snatching a woman's lapdog on a train as he exhorted everyone to watch.

A botched launch would create negative publicity for a channel with grand plans but unfamiliar programmes. The tension was felt most by those in the gallery and in the Presentation Department, the engine room where the programme tapes were played out and linked by announcers going live. This team included five former BBC people who recalled that the BBC2 launch had been spoilt by a massive power cut. While they prayed that nothing like that would happen, they knew from the dummy runs that the nagging problem with the computer software for automatic transmission, which linked to an internal system called Captain, was not working properly. The Chief Engineer, Ellis Griffiths, and his Deputy, John Haselwood, had spent hours trying to iron out the problems. When Griffiths had shown a visitor from ITV around a few weeks earlier, he was asked where the crew were. In theory, when the fully computerised system was in full working order, it could be run by one person. The visitor could not believe such minimal staffing was possible, and, indeed, given the computer failure, it was not. When the channel went on air, the transmission system was operated manually, although with insufficient staff to keep it up for long. It was a recipe for a shambles. Cueing in tapes without a big team provided unlimited scope for mistakes: a lapse of concentration could result in too early a shift to a commercial break, potentially ruining a programme.

So they continued to rehearse all through Tuesday. Tim Simmons, Deputy Head of Presentation, who would carry much of the burden, recalled: 'I knew at the end of the day we had people who could push buttons on the machines manually. We knew we could get on air. The question was staying on air, day after day. It was like a bad dream: we were in a state of desperation in the end.'[2] It was more problematic than running BBC1 or BBC2 because of the commercial-break patterns, but, on the plus side, Channel 4 did not have that many live programmes, apart from the news. That was why there was emphasis on lively, informal presentation between the programmes, to inject some immediacy; but it was essential that the links should be cued in smoothly, otherwise immediacy would quickly turn into chaos.

There was, too, a nagging threat of industrial action. The signal played out from Channel 4 went via the British Telecom Tower to all the ITV regions through a special black box. A series of pips and pulses warned of the upcoming advertising break, but it relied on ITV companies to have cued up commercials – assuming there were any. Nobody expected ITV to be overly helpful in a crisis, in part because the technicians' union, the ACTT, had a firm grip over it. Some regional companies were still in dispute over manning levels in their new Channel 4 control rooms as the launch countdown began.

Paul Coia, the first voice on air, had a tense twenty-four hours, as a fierce debate raged about how to open the channel. The Scottish-born former radio DJ had handwritten his script: 'Good afternoon, it's a pleasure to be able to welcome you at last to Channel 4.'[3] But the words 'at last' implied a desperate struggle – too close to the truth for comfort – so they were crossed out. Then it was decided to abandon the live opening and record Coia's words, in case he had a fit of nerves: 'Good Afternoon, it's a pleasure to be able to say to you, welcome to Channel 4.'[4]

While that discussion rumbled on, Cecil Korer, the Entertainment Commissioner, decided that the opening programme, *Countdown*, was unsatisfactory, and he sent it back to Yorkshire Television for last-minute editing. Then there was a late legal challenge to the comedy, *The Comic Strip Presents . . . Five Go Mad in Dorset*, a spoof on

Enid Blyton's Famous Five novels starring the then unknown Dawn French, Jennifer Saunders, Adrian Edmondson and Peter Richardson, with Robbie Coltrane as a mad shopkeeper. This was the start of a sporadic series, curtailed when the BBC snatched the performers to make *The Young Ones*. The previous evening, the Enid Blyton Estate and her publisher suddenly demanded to see it, and the threat of an injunction loomed. The Blyton camp were worried that satirising Famous Five values might harm the brand, especially when they learned that the comedy ended with Uncle Quentin being arrested, thanks to a Famous Five tip-off, because he was a homosexual.[5] Enid Blyton's niece and four lawyers packed into a small room at the channel: space was so tight that Mike Bolland, who had commissioned the programme, stayed outside. 'I looked in', he remembers, 'and saw this young woman solicitor starting to shake, then the whole room erupted in laughter.'[6] It was all right.

The channel was also locked in debate with the Regulator over a campaigning film about cruelty to animals, *The Animals*, narrated by Julie Christie and scheduled for Thursday, 4 November. It included footage of battery birds being de-beaked, cattle fed on cement dust and excrement and shackled calves trying to eat iron bars. The IBA objected to a murky piece of film of a raid by animal liberationists on vivisectionists, construing it as an incitement to violence. Victor Schonfeld, the producer, resisted any censorship, and Isaacs, too, was instinctively in favour of keeping the film intact but eventually accepted cuts to comply with the law. John Ranelagh, Isaacs' Special Assistant – a rarity at the channel for his conservative views – supported the cuts and found his Kennington house had broken windows when he eventually went home.

Isaacs had decided against a traditional opening ceremony, such as ITV's inaugural festivity at the Guildhall in 1955; nor did he want a gala night of special programmes and events. He decided instead to start in a low key, as if it was a run-of-the-mill night, although he had chosen a schedule that would make a statement about what viewers could expect from the new channel. The mix of programmes was his choice alone, with no input from the influential Head of Marketing Sue Stoessl. He hoped that during the opening week (which included 5 November), he 'would set off some fireworks to get viewers to visit us' while familiarising them with what would become signature programmes, such as *Brookside*.[7] 'Not for us the viewer who tuned in and then stayed tuned as habit-forming favourites succeeded each other', he wrote. 'We would be a channel for the choosy viewer, selecting a particular chocolate from the box, leaving the rest to others.'[8]

Several of his subordinates, including Ranelagh, begged him not to run a strong-ish drama called *Walter*, about a young man with profound learning disabilities, as the opening Film on Four. In the film, Walter's life goes to pieces after his parents die and he is stripped first of his job then his flock of pigeons and, finally, placed in a mental home. It was grim and demanding, but Isaacs stood his ground, and *Walter*, directed by Stephen Frears and starring Ian McKellen, provoked debate and won critical support, as well as the biggest audience of the night. 'We thought it was sending out the wrong message, yet it turned out to be the right one', Ranelagh conceded.[9]

During launch day, Isaacs made himself as visible as possible, buzzing around the building, exhorting, encouraging and thanking the troops. Perhaps inspired by all those history documentaries he had made, he adopted the posture of the belligerent French Marshal Foch, holding off the Germans at the Battle of the Marne in 1914, a vital victory at the start of the First World War: 'My centre is giving way, my right is in retreat; situation excellent, I am attacking.' He was to reach for this quote many, many times over the coming months and years. He radiated certainty, leadership, courage in the face of fire – qualities that won him the admiration of Sir Richard Attenborough, among others. More sceptical board members, though, questioned whether such qualities would have been needed if the launch had been planned with a little more discipline and foresight.

'Telegrams, messages, bouquets, champagne by the bottle, the magnum, the jeroboam, were delivered', Isaacs wrote. 'As the minutes ticked away I sat, glass in hand, with Edmund Dell, in my office overlooking Charlotte Street.'[10] The diligent Bonner stationed himself in the Presentation Department downstairs. Here, he agreed that instead of the standard two seconds of blank screen between fading the test card and running the dazzling 4 logo, they would leave *ten* seconds, to heighten the drama and the expectation. Nobody thought to tell Isaacs, though, and at 4.41 p.m., as the landscape test pictures faded to black, a hush fell over the entire building as Isaacs sat through the longest ten seconds of his life until eventually the logo, the glowing matchsticks in their five vivid colours forming a 4, came up with the channel's call sign of four distinct chords. 'My heart lurched – the test card was replaced not by our ident but by black. A black hole: black night. Then from the black came our logo, call sign, an announcer's voice, a seductive montage of promotional images, our signature music over. We were on air.'[11]

The opening sequence, this brilliantly coloured 4 emerging from black, would remain with viewers long after memories of the first rather inadequate programmes faded. Next came a reassuring preview tape, a shy deer, a line of dancing girls, frogs croaking in time to the theme music, a conductor's hands, red lips. The message was: try us. The commissioning team gathered at the back of the first floor watching it all on a large screen. 'A big roar went up', said Bolland. 'We were a bunch of quite sophisticated people, but then we were like kids. We started drinking champagne.'[12] Dell and Isaacs shook hands, a rare moment of shared achievement and goodwill, soon to evaporate. Isaacs picked up the phone and thanked Thames Television's Head of Advertising for managing to sell some commercial spots despite the crisis caused by the Equity dispute. He was told plainly that thanks were premature, that there was no sign the dispute would end soon.

Then it was into the first programme, *Countdown*. The quiz was the fruit of a decision to offer an alternative to children's programming, the only kind on BBC1 and ITV at that time of the afternoon. An adaptation of a French format, *Des chiffres et des lettres* (*Numbers and Letters*), it mixed the challenge of assembling the longest words possible out of nine letters with mental arithmetic and an anagram. The letters of the alphabet were printed on homely linoleum tiles. Korer, a veteran of *It's a Knockout*, had seen it and was attracted in some measure by its bargain price: £7,500 an episode. Isaacs detected in it a folksy, brain-teasing charm. Its presenter Richard Whiteley, the first face on Channel 4, told viewers: 'As the countdown to the start of a brand new channel ends, a brand new *Countdown* begins.' From the start, though, despite Korer's last-minute changes, it looked amateurish, and Whiteley, in a demure blue suit and pale blue tie – a far cry from his flamboyant later image – seemed tense. In Charlotte Street, jaws dropped. 'We hadn't seen it, and there had been a lot of anxiety about it', said Coia. 'It was horrendous. Naff. We knew we had *Walter*, this very good drama, coming up; we just hoped someone would still be around to watch it.'[13]

The first programme looked like the pilot it was, and the first-night audience of 3.5 million evaporated to 800,000 the following day. Whiteley, in his autobiography,[14] acknowledged that the first programme was not a success, but it could not be replaced by a later episode as they had to be run sequentially, with successful contestants competing again next time. Whiteley made matters worse with some appalling jokes that fell flat. 'He's got the nous to buy a scouse house', he said of one contestant, who lived in Manchester but wanted to move to Liverpool. The quip was received in complete silence by the studio audience, who remained unresponsive when, explaining the rules of the game, he said, 'It's what the post office have been doing for years – they get a lot of letters, then decide what to do with them.'

Even Carol Vorderman, whose remarkable powers of mental arithmetic would help her become a big name on television, looked dowdy on this her first appearance, in a mustard-yellow top and bright red lipstick. Ted Moult, a former farmer and a veteran media personality, ran the dictionary corner to check the words. To barely suppressed groans, Whiteley assured viewers he knew his onions from his potatoes – and when the hapless presenter turned up at the channel's launch party later that week, the trendy metropolitan guests ignored him pointedly.

At 5.15, *Preview*, a regular Saturday and Monday event, screened samples of new programmes, linked by Coia and the blonde announcer Olga Hubicka. This first edition included clips from *Walter* and an interview with the director Stephen Frears and highlighted *Tom Keating on Painters*, in which the noted art forger showed viewers how to paint themselves a Titian or a Monet. Also featured was *The Tube*, launching that Friday with The Jam, Pete Townshend and a Sting interview. At 5.30, *Pre-*

view gave way to *The Body Show*, 'safe exercises for people at home', demonstrated by Yvonne Ocampo, a slender ex-Bluebell girl sporting a Lycra leotard. One of a number of regular tutors for what would be a weekly slot, she took five people through gentle movements, set to quiet music, in a studio with a mirrored wall. Viewers could send a stamped-addressed envelope for a free leaflet listing keep-fit and dance places around Britain. As an example of consumer television, *The Body Show* was well-meaning but deadly dull. Its broader significance lay in its being the channel's first programme made by an independent production company: 51 Per Cent Productions, run by a group of five women.

Following it, competing with ITV's *Six O'Clock News*, was *People's Court*, a cheap buy-in from America, featuring Judge Joseph A. Wapner adjudicating on minor disputes: the first one covered a $70 deal for two tyres that went wrong and a pair of roller skates confiscated from a young African-American at a rink on suspicion of being stolen. A subsequent episode would settle who benefited after a male poodle was invited to sire puppies with a poodle bitch. This popular programme (Yorkshire TV would eventually make a British version) was the first on-screen evidence of Channel 4's need to stretch budgets with cheap imports, which would encompass Latin-American novellas and obscure foreign-language films as well as American shows. The new channel's income, about one-sixth of ITV's at this point, was much too low to allow the commissioning of original work for all slots, so from the beginning it was setting out its stall as a showcase for external acquisitions and independent production.

At 6.30 came *Book Four*, from Melvyn Bragg's LWT arts team. The presenter was Hermione Lee, an academic from York University, matched with three well-known authors – Len Deighton, William Boyd and Fay Weldon – discussing how they treated the subject of war in their novels. At one point, Lee underlined her credentials for this politicised channel by chiding Deighton for appearing to support the concept of war rather than deploring it. This strand was a product of Isaacs' generous view that Channel 4 must support those artistic endeavours apparently threatened by television. (Richard & Judy's Book Club is a descendant, but totally different in tone.)

Channel 4 News, at 7 p.m., was having difficulties with autocues and graphics. The presenter, Peter Sissons, held the show together, while the Economics Editor, Sarah Hogg, in a matronly pin-tucked white shirt, kicked off with a nervous explanation of how the Government was clamping down on public spending. Then came a report on the previous night's violence in Brixton, seemingly less grave than the riots of 1981. The bulk of the hour, though, went to the American mid-term elections, a significant test of President Ronald Reagan's standing. Godfrey Hodgson's tour of a number of key states was far from compelling, but Trevor McDonald did better with a crisp interview with Reagan's political adviser, James Baker.

Channel 4 News had promised that its coverage of the arts would be more than jeering at piles of bricks in the Tate, so it had a story about the discovery of a lost ending to Puccini's opera *Turandot* – making the assumption that a sizeable slice of its viewers knew the opera, knew the current ending and knew why a longer version would be more fitting. Then it was time for *Comment* – in essence a secular version of Radio 4's *Thought for the Day* – in which people with something to say were given airtime. This debut spot was handed to a distinguished former journalist, David Watt, then running the Royal Institute of International Affairs at Chatham House. He used his two and a half minutes to tell viewers, 'They're scared to give us more time than this, in case experts bore you.' In other words, in a nihilistic gesture of the kind that people would come to associate with the channel, his *Comment* was challenging the very validity of such comment pieces. Isaacs had wanted Watt to edit *Channel 4 News*, and on this evidence both sides had a lucky escape. All in all, this was a shaky start for a news programme promising to be 'not just the longest, but the best.' It looked terrible: the set was covered in yellow carpet, with dingy mustard panels on the studio walls. Isaacs later wrote: 'The wrong set, presenters ill at ease; no need to despair.'[15]

Then, at 8 o'clock, it was into *Brookside*, with a lengthy opening sequence featuring a milk float delivering to a number of the new houses set in a (deceptively) quiet, leafy close. When the new families started to interact, it was hard to follow and made no easier by a problem with the sound recording that ought to have been picked up before transmission. It was audible enough, though, for viewers to complain about six 'bloodies', one 'Christ', one 'piss off', one 'frigging hell', two 'dickheads', two 'pissings', a 'bugger' and a 'bollocks.' But, regardless of the crudity of the dialogue, it was clear from the first episode, which introduced topics such as vandalism and problems in the workplace, that this would make a gritty contrast to ITV's anaemic *Crossroads* and that the Grant couple, played by Ricky Tomlinson and Sue Johnston, would be worth watching.

At 8.30 came another economical import, *The Paul Hogan Show*, bought by Korer for £5,300. This was before the Australian shot to stardom in the *Crocodile Dundee* movies, when he was still best known here for his commercials for Foster's lager. The former Sydney Harbour Bridge rigger played a range of comic Aussie characters including Pot Belly the Pool Player, Perce the Wino and Sergeant Donger the Aussie Policeman. This was specially scheduled for launch night outside of what was to become its regular slot on Fridays at 10 p.m., where it helped establish Friday as the channel's entertainment night.

Walter came next and then, at 10.15 p.m., the most accessible show of the night, the Famous Five spoof in *The Comic Strip Presents*. The final programme, at 10.45 p.m., was Isaacs' personal favourite and involved another big shift of gear. The Raving Beauties' *In the Pink* was a tough feminist revue celebrating women's lives and disappointments, devised and performed by three actresses: Anna Carteret, Sue Jones-Davies and Fanny Viner. It combined recitations of poetry from Sylvia Plath, Stevie Smith and Dorothy Parker, mixed with popular songs such as 'I Want to Be Bobbie's Girl', 'Isn't She Lovely?' and 'I Will Survive'. David Rose, the Fiction Commissioner, had tipped off Isaacs after seeing it at Riverside Studios, Hammersmith, where it was recorded. One striking sequence involved a description of a woman stabbing her husband to death. It was certainly different.

Now, though, the team in Presentation faced a fresh problem: how to bring to an end to this white-knuckle ride of an evening. In the panic to get the channel on air, nobody had given any proper thought to a fitting finale. Tim Simmons suddenly remembered that his daughter Hannah had given him a good-luck candle shaped as the number 4 – the sort you put on a birthday cake. 'I'd taken it into work, so I stood it on a table next to the pot plant we'd taken from the first floor to liven up Presentation, and I lit it. That was the wonderful thing about Channel 4, it was improvisation.' Off screen, after the last of the day's images had faded shortly before midnight, the candle was gently blown out.

But it was not the end of the night for some. Ellis Griffiths and the Opera Consultant, Gillian Widdicombe – later to become Isaacs' second wife – stayed up. The channel was starting an opera series that Sunday with a three-hour telecast from the Metropolitan Opera House in New York of Mozart's *Idomeneo*, with Luciano Pavarotti in the lead. Because of the computer problems, they were having to find a way to do the screen subtitles manually. For everyone involved in the hair-raising launch, sleep came low on the list of priorities. 'We got to the stage we were so tired you couldn't drink, you would have keeled over', Pam Masters reflected.[16]

Despite all that effort, the first-night ratings were disappointing, given the level of advance publicity.

- 4.45 p.m.   *Countdown*   3.6 million viewers
- 5.15 p.m.   *Preview*   2.7 million viewers
- 5.30 p.m.   *The Body Show*   2.1 million viewers
- 6.00 p.m.   *People's Court*   1.5 million viewers
- 6.30 p.m.   *Book Four*   1.0 million viewers
- 7.00 p.m.   *Channel 4 News*   1.2 million viewers
- 8.00 p.m.   *Brookside*   2.8 million viewers
- 8.30 p.m.   *The Paul Hogan Show*   3.4 million viewers
- 9.00 p.m.   *Film on Four: Walter*   3.7 million viewers
- 10.15 p.m.   *The Comic Strip Presents* 3.3 million viewers
- 10.45 p.m.   *In the Pink*   1.0 million viewers

And what did the critics think of that first night? For the most part, the newspaper reviewers were relatively benign. The *Guardian*'s Nancy Banks-Smith pronounced

Channel 4 'trendy enough to make your teeth peel.' Chris Dunkley, the incisive *Financial Times* critic, attacked 'the feminist fanaticism of *In the Pink* and its un-healthy odour of hatred' – the start of a lengthy campaign against Isaacs' consciously gender-balancing programming. The *Sun*'s Charlie Catchpole gave it '4 out of Ten', while in *The Times*, Peter Ackroyd wrote magisterially, 'There is a tendency, perhaps, to excessive wind. [Channel 4 is] the SDP of television.' Hilary Kingsley in the *Mirror* thought *Countdown* the 'crummiest quiz ever seen on TV', while Herbert Kretzmer of the *Daily Mail* was more positive: 'A lusty, noisy and decidedly provoking infant . . . good luck to the brat.'

On everyone's desk on the morning after was a thank-you card from Jeremy. It was the first of his notes to 'All on Four' that would become part of the channel's culture – inevitably revolving around him, their leader. On Valentine's Day, he went round with red roses and Smarties. He could be hard, resolute, tough and ill-tempered – especially when someone dared park their car in his allocated space – but he led his disputatious band by creating a feeling of belonging to a huge quasi-family. Call it a cult of person-ality if you like, but they believed in him and stayed loyal to him, even as Channel 4 almost immediately came under attack.

The opening night had been a mixed bag, but then there was no intention to create a flowing schedule. Some programmes, like *Countdown* and *Book Four*, were essen-tially traditional, but although poorly executed in their different ways they amount-ed to a clear signal that Channel 4 was scheduling to complement ITV rather than compete with it. The news, scheduled for when the BBC and ITV were running soap operas and other entertainment, was clearly a big disappointment (see Chapter 7). The 6 p.m. slot became the home of mainly American buy-ins, with *I Love Lucy* join-ing *People's Court* there. There were palpable hits, led by *The Comic Strip Presents*, and the drama looked promising, while *Brookside* was a soap with potential.

As the schedule rolled out over the first week, the mix included more of the vaunt-ed niche programmes, targeted at minorities and the 'light viewer.' After *Brookside* on the Wednesday came the first current-affairs programme by a women's team, *Twenty Twenty Vision*, reporting on concerns surrounding the chemical 245 T. The 9 p.m. film was *P'tang Yang Kipperbang*, about a fourteen-year-old boy's loss of innocence, writ-ten by Jack Rosenthal, directed by Michael Apted and produced by David Puttnam as part of a Young Love season. It was followed by *Voices*, a weekly discussion on cultural issues chaired by the poet and critic Al Alvarez, which would have worked well on Radio 4. It was followed by *Sleevenotes*, an overview of world music.

On Thursday, after *People's Court* and *Tom Keating on Painters*, the first weekly *Family Special* was screened, designed for parents and their children. Later in the evening came the film about cruelty to animals which had provoked such concern at the IBA. Fridays were aimed at young people: *The Tube*, between 5.15 and 7 p.m., became the channel's first cult hit, routinely switched on in student unions across the land, although its measurable audience ratings were never much more than 1 million. Tim Simmons recalls Isaacs striding around the first floor as *The Tube* was on, proclaiming, 'Isn't it wonderful?!'[17] After the news, shortened to half an hour on Fridays, came *The Friday Alternative*, the most radical of news programmes, with such a left-leaning agenda that it triggered immediate special monitoring by the Regulator and was to be a source of huge friction. It was followed by *Deep Roots*, a story of reggae, and *Pleasure Palaces*, a series about the early cinema seen through the eyes and habits of working-class people, not Hollywood.

The policy of screening movies against Saturday-afternoon sport on ITV and BBC came into effect in that first week, followed by an omnibus of *Brookside* at 5 p.m. and then *Union World*, fronted by Gus Macdonald, a former producer of Granada's *World in Action* who later became a Labour life peer. This round-up of topics concerning trade unions quickly gained a reputation as one of the channel's most boring programmes: Arthur Scargill, the miners' leader, said he would rather watch the test card. Partly this was because its focus was too narrow. Dorothy Byrne, who worked on the programme, maintains that she was never allowed to interview employers: 'They'd ring up offering to put their point of view in a dispute, and we'd say no, we don't interview employers.'[18] Saturday was also the night for *A Week in Politics*, produced by Anne Lapping, formerly Economics Editor of *The Economist*. To screen political programmes on the night that is traditionally the time for letting your hair down seemed perverse to many, including Roger Graef and other board members, who criticised it severely a year later.[19]

When entertainment was finally admitted to that first Saturday schedule, at 7.15 p.m., it was of a decidedly distinctive kind, a performance special featuring the athletic dancer Mikhail Baryshnikov on Broadway, followed by a solo turn by the former music-hall comedian Max Wall. Other pairings that autumn included a dance version of Lorca's *Blood Wedding* and a Geordie comic, Bobby Thompson. Saturday evenings usually closed with a movie – Sidney Lumet's *Network* (1976) in the first week. On Sunday, *Matinée at the Met*, the Mozart opera from New York, was followed by *Face the Press*, where journalists posed sharp, incisive questions to politicians. That led into coverage of American football, independently produced by Cheerleader Productions, which would also cover basketball: these two sports, although mainstream in the USA, had only a minority following in Britain. After Part I of a filmed performance of *Nicholas Nickleby*, by the Royal Shakespeare Company, came a balancing discussion of Thursday's controversial diatribe about cruelty to animals, followed by *Scarface*, a 1932 black-and-white classic movie.

Mondays featured *Coping* – advice on how to deal with life crises – and live basketball, followed by *Opinions*, a half-hour scripted lecture delivered direct to camera that, for Isaacs, marked a return to the format pioneered in the early days of ITV by the historian A.J.P. Taylor. Isaacs had personally chosen as the first lecturer Professor E.P. Thompson, the left-wing social historian and anti-nuclear campaigner, whose invitation to give the BBC's Dimbleby Lecture had recently been withdrawn because of reservations about his politics. He spoke on the evil of the two dominant power blocs, the USSR and the USA. *Opinions* paid its lecturers £750 and would run for eight years, during which time it would provide a platform for people of all political persuasions and, despite the choice of the inaugural speaker, would help moderate the channel's image as haven of radical socialism. Early contributors included Bernard Williams, Karen Armstrong, Anthony Sampson, Salman Rushdie, Paul Johnson and Enoch Powell.

The programme's first producer was Nick Fraser, through the independent company, Panoptic Pictures, which he had helped to set up. Fraser was an accomplished print and television journalist who knew little about the technical side of television. According to Fraser, Peter Bazalgette said to him, 'It's very simple, use an autocue.' Fraser said that Bazalgette then went to Channel 4 and told them that there was this lunatic Nick Fraser who didn't even know what an autocue was – and did they want him, Peter, to do the show instead of him?[20]

Monday evening also had a distinctive Bolland show, *Whatever You Want*, hosted by the maverick Keith Allen from a bunker called the Zig Zag Club. It was a mouthy, opinionated magazine in the format that came to be known as access television. Allen was talented but difficult to control, and the programme was placed under review. Isaacs packed ten well-chosen films or dramas into the first ten days to tell viewers this was a key component of his channel's offering, and Film on Four was to become one of the trusted legs of the stool. It was a sign of the pre-launch pressure that one of the first films – *Semi-Tough* (1977), starring Burt Reynolds – was broadcast before the 9 p.m. watershed without anyone checking it for bad language. This provided an early opportunity for an assault by the National Viewers' and Listeners' Association, run by the clean-up-television campaigner Mary Whitehouse. With the arrival of Channel 4, Mrs Whitehouse's workload increased exponentially.

Stephen Lambert, a research student at Nuffield College, Oxford, and later one of Britain's leading producers, wrote a scholarly account of setting up Channel 4, published just before it went on air. He concluded:

> The one group who have not notably featured in the story of Channel 4 are the people who will now judge its performance – the television viewing public. Despite attempts to excite public interest in the subject, there has been no widespread demand for a fourth channel, and the long debate has been conducted almost solely by professional broadcasters and film-makers, politicans and civil servants, advertisers and academics.[21]

Ratings for the first six days show that the channel won an audience share of 6.6 per cent, which would have been acceptable had it then stabilised. Instead, audiences went on sliding gently but inexorably down to 3.5 per cent by Christmas, and 3.33 per cent in February 1983. An important factor in driving viewers away, easy to overlook in retrospect, was that many of the ambitious and challenging programmes were surrounded by blank commercial breaks or repetitious adverts. 'At times, Channel 4 was virtually unwatchable', acknowledged Sue Stoessl.[22] Nigel Stafford-Clark, who was there for the launch, recalled, 'It looked like amateur broadcasting, devastating. It was the worst possible thing. Commercials have fantastically high production values. Not till the dispute was resolved could they could become what they aspired to be.'[23]

For the opening night and the days immediately afterwards, only a tiny repertoire of commercials could be mustered. London viewers could count them on the fingers of two hands. They were Vauxhall Cavalier (highlighting the car's electric windows), the Alliance Building Society (text only), Alberto Jojoba hair conditioner, Young's seafood (showing a boat coming into harbour), Gypsy underwear from Berlei, the courier service TNT, Texas Home Care, Mateus Rosé and a few nannyish government warnings, mostly about looking after your purse. Some areas – such as Grampian, Ulster and Scotland – had no advertising at all. Even the best programmes were undermined.

The channel would eventually devise stratagems to cope with this, the longest-ever industrial dispute in television. It produced a short, soothing image of a potter's wheel and some seductive pictures of landscapes, but viewers soon found these boring too. It was in no position to make hours of short films to fill the commercial breaks, nor could it scrap them because of the ITV scheduling link. So, the duty log filled with complaints and irritation, especially from callers outside London. This problem came to dominate discussions in the weekly programme reviews during the next twelve weeks, when the actual content of the programmes was examined only sporadically. There was much more concern about the basic housekeeping: the lack of standard programme credits, the delivery of programmes late and of the wrong length to fit the running order. Some new independents, learning on the job, paid little regard to technical standards, to delivery deadlines or even to using cameras fit for broadcast.

Commissioning editors, many lacking experience of programme-making themselves, had been overworked and overwhelmed. One independent in the north-west received £93,000 for a programme it had not made and would never make. Two per cent of programmes delivered in that first year were so bad they could not be broadcast. Pam Masters said, 'It really hurt. A lot of it didn't work but Jeremy tried to make it work. It was trying to be too ambitious at the beginning – it didn't know what it wanted to be. I don't blame Jeremy for this lack of professionalism. He had huge faults, but he was a leader.'[24]

The strength of Channel 4's schedule was that it presented a different face to different people at different points of the week and the day. This mix would stand it in good stead later, as digital expansion offered the opportunity to launch dedicated film, youth and documentary channels. Already its penchant for one-off programmes, such as the drama *Walter*, rather than overloading the schedule with predictable series and serials, was helping the publicity, as newspaper previewers recommended them as picks of the day. The warm reaction to *The Comic Strip Presents* showed there was a real appetite for alternative comedy, but this was not fully reflected in the early schedules – evidence that Isaacs and his senior colleagues needed constant reminding that television is primarily an entertainment medium, at its most memorable when it gets close to the action – as with the bands on *The Tube* – rather than from earnest, grey, talking heads. For potential viewers, their fingers hovering over the remote control, the Channel 4 offer was at best promising rather than inviting, its defining characteristic a well-intentioned gravity interspersed with technical incompetence.

The announcers in presentation, when all went wrong around them, became accustomed to grabbing the *Radio Times* and talking about what was coming up. The pot plant, enlisted to make Presentation more interesting, became a star in its own right and even received fan mail. It was dressed up with Christmas lights and tinsel, and lonely plants around the country wrote it love letters: 'I'm a lonely Ficus in Barnstable, pining for you.'[25]

At the first board meeting after the launch, Jeremy Isaacs noted that press comment 'is mixed but widespread,' and he characterised the first audience figures as 'a bit disappointing, not disheartening.'[26] He added that *Channel 4 News* was disappointing and showed technical incompetence, while *The Friday Alternative*, the one programme the IBA had so far called to Channel 4's attention, was under review. Any early goodwill of viewers and television critics soon evaporated, though. On Saturday, 20 November, the *Daily Mail* ran a letter with the deadly headline, 'Channel Bore', a description that struck a chord and proved hard to live down. The *Sun*, meanwhile, began counting the number of swear words, and on 1 December dubbed it 'Channel Swore'. The more thoughtful Chris Dunkley found the consistency with which the programmes voiced the late 1960s attitudes of the *Guardian* women's page deeply ominous and detected a 'new fascism' in their espousal of multiculturalism and ultra-liberalism.

As Christmas drew near, the shortcomings became more apparent. The balance and mix were clearly wrong, with too strong an emphasis on factual programmes, many of them too politically committed and too strident, and too little entertainment, which had scarcely registered on Isaacs' radar. Early in December, a storm broke over a new late-night entertainment show for gay people called *One in Five* – the title based on the incorrect assumption that one in five people in Britain are gay. John Carlisle, the Conservative MP for Luton West, told the *Daily Mail* that the channel should be banned from the airwaves immediately. By mid-December, with the audience down to 4.2 per cent, the mood became more critical and Isaacs more chastened, although he started a board report by saying he had 'no regrets so far in the mix or quality of programmes.'[27]

This apparent complacency triggered a stinging riposte from Brian Tesler of LWT, the most senior ITV man on the Board. He said:

> Channel 4 needs to attract wider audiences. It needs more popular pro-grammes and popular series. It is important to ease the tone, to make the audience understand that minorities are not always earnest and de-pressed. A wider appeal is needed, a more varied schedule without too many long programmes in one evening. Act quickly before the image is set.[28]

Anthony Smith agreed, adding that viewing Channel 4 gave him the feeling of watching a series of videotapes. Isaacs responded that the channel's various goals pulled against each other: it was a balance of practicalities and ideals. He conceded, though, that a shift was needed along Tesler's lines, a move towards higher ratings, and he would consider alterations to presentation. He would try to make the channel more popular but was anxious that it remained distinctive.

Around this time, he hosted a drinks party for the band of independents who had done most of the work so far. Stafford-Clark went along. 'We were saying to each other that we'd been through fire, we were the companies who'd survived. He was Robin Hood, we were the Merry Men. We thought he'd come out and thank us for a great first contribution and maybe offer a more intimate relationship.'[29] They were soon disabused of that optimistic assumption. Isaacs, under pressure from above, used the event to crush any illusions. Under the remit, he reminded the producers they were only as good as the ideas they came up with. 'The idea was that once you finished a show you went back and joined the queue'[30] – a glimpse of harsh reality that would fuel the growing demands for guaranteed access for independents to the promised land of commissions from the BBC and ITV.

Ann Harris, working in Programme Acquisitions, remembers in the days before Christmas going to parties with her husband and begging him not to say where she worked. 'Channel 4 had raised a lot of hopes among ordinary people. Cab drivers in particular slagged you off. There was quite a degree of confusion at Charlotte Street.'[31] The week of 26 December saw the audience fall to 2.8 per cent, at the most competi-tive time of the year. Yet, Channel 4 also screened one of its loveliest programmes, *The Snowman*, for the first of many times. It started *Treasure Hunt*, casting Anneka Rice as a sky runner in a helicopter, being directed across Britain by contestants to find a treasure. The festive season also saw the debut of *The Irish RM*, a rustic comedy.

On Boxing Day, the *Star* ran a story saying that ITV chiefs, at a secret conference, had decided that Isaacs must go, that minority programmes had to be cut back, *Brookside* scrapped and a new schedule drawn up. The *Sun*, *Daily Mail* and most of Fleet Street weighed in. Sir Richard Attenborough made worried but supportive calls to Isaacs.

This story was strenuously denied and was not strictly true: there is no evidence of such a plot in the board minutes. But there is not usually smoke without fire, and, according to John Ranelagh, who doubled as Secretary to the Board, there was around this time an unminuted and informal debate amongst board members about what to do, of which no trace remains in the archive. Most of the board members may have been at the IBA for a regular consultation. Ranelagh says they asked to be left alone and had a long private meeting about the schedule, without Isaacs. They were prepared to fire him if they had to.

> Was Jeremy in danger of losing his job? Yes, he was. I was there. I was Secretary to the Board. I started packing up, but Edmund Dell asked me to stay but not to make any notes. They discussed Jeremy and the way the programming was going. It was not a case of 'Jeremy you will be fired', but 'Jeremy, you really are on notice, you have got to do something.'
>
> I was delegated to tell Jeremy this, and I was very worried about being the messenger. I didn't want to exaggerate, but not to underemphasise it either. It was important to get it right. It was extremely fortunate that I met Jeremy in the lift with another board member, Bill Brown of Scottish Television. Jeremy and Bill got on well. I saw nothing wrong in telling Jeremy in front of Bill – I was extremely glad he was there.
>
> So I said, 'Something's got to give, Jeremy.' My clear understanding was that this was a first unofficial warning. Bill Brown then told him to calm down: 'We're not going to fire you, but we are not afraid to if it comes to it.' Jeremy's face was frozen in a furious grimace. I was also present when he later had a conversation with Tony Smith and said 'I will do what I'm told.'[32]

Isaacs was sharp, streetwise and, by now, seasoned. This was his dream job. It was an open secret at Channel 4 around this time that his tenure was threatened, and loyal staff drew their wagons around him ever more protectively. The fact is that even if the ITV directors had wanted him to go, they were not in a majority on the Board. The independent directors, Smith and Graef, backed him, as did Attenborough. Said Graef, 'We were made into ogres when we were in fact supporters. I wish we had had the chance to talk about policy more.'[33] The IBA also knew that these were early days and that Isaacs needed time. All the same, at the January board meeting, the tone was as icy as the weather. The lack of advertising was seen as creating a disastrous situation. Tesler talked of shortening the hours Channel 4 broadcast, to save £7 million a year. Isaacs said this would be extremely damaging.

It was the criticism of programmes that hurt most. Dell said that while many of them were excellent, some were not and that there was a political imbalance.[34] Isaacs replied that he planned to strengthen the winter schedules and had started on presentation urgently: it would continue to be live, but properly scripted. He agreed that it was a matter of major concern that Channel 4 displayed a left-wing bias. He was mending fences in the light of a wave of criticism from Conservative MPs and was shortly to lunch with Willie Whitelaw. He had sent a copy of an *Opinions* lecture by the right-wing commentator Paul Johnson to Margaret Thatcher, and Number 10 told him she had enjoyed it very much. *Brookside*'s anti-capitalist stance was exasperating, and talks were under way about *The Friday Alternative*. As Isaacs later said, there was not a lot he could have done to fix the short-term weaknesses: the money was spent, the programmes had been ordered, they had to be played out.[35] The issue for the future was to make changes while staying true to the vision. He took up an offer from ITV to repeat the much-lauded serials *Brideshead Revisited* and *The Jewel in the Crown*, familiar mainstream programming. During February, there was frantic re-editing of programmes, so at least they ran at more conventional hour and half-hour lengths.

Soon after that bleak meeting, the Board called a conference at Berystede, Ascot, on 28 and 29 January to discuss changes and how to allocate the next year's budget. To prepare, Bonner went to see Tesler at LWT for advice about changing the schedule, and each of the commissioners drew up papers. The programmes that scored 1 million viewers were principally series and ranged from *The Sixties* – Michael Jackson's first commission – and *Tom Keating on Painters* to *The Tube* and, surprisingly to the high-brow commissioners, the consumer programmes, *For What It's Worth* and *Well Being*. Missing from the list was *Brookside*, which had shed 2 million viewers and was about to fall to a low point of 697,000 during February. David Rose said its 'enormous potential has not yet been reached',[36] but the producer had been told to moderate the language.

Mike Bolland proposed another twenty-six episodes of *The Tube* and six more *The Comic Strip Presents*. He acknowledged that Keith Allen's troublesome *Whatever You Want* was for the axe.

> It has arguably unearthed the most interesting but unmanageable presenter on Channel 4. Ultimately this programme is inconsistent, badly shaped and underscripted and cannot hold a regular audience. The producer and research team were ill-prepared for leaving institutional broadcasting. The programme looks like it comes from a garage underneath County Hall and just isn't good enough. I am increasingly

convinced this sort of magazine mix is not what young people want to see in 1983.[37]

It was laid to rest on 21 February after a spectacular row over an untransmitted item in which Allen stood outside Harrods in Knightsbridge and said that British soldiers were being recruited to defend the sort of people who shopped there. Cecil Korer, struggling with an inadequate budget of £7 million a year, spoke his mind: 'All channels, not least Channel 4, need laughter and enjoyment. Any shopkeeper has to have some downmarket product to attract passing trade.'[38]

While journalists lurked outside the Berystede meeting, convinced that Isaacs was doomed, inside Tesler launched a tirade. 'I found myself saying, for the first and only time in my life, we're in the Last Chance Saloon', he recalled later.[39] He said some of the programme ideas were barking mad, perversely oriented towards minorities. The schedule lacked fixed points, so viewers did not know what to expect, and Channel 4 was so determined to be different that it failed to make use of common junctions with ITV. Isaacs, his back to the wall, said he would make concessions but would not abandon the notion of trying to be distinctive.

Soon the changes started to flow. The spring schedule represented a major attempt to revamp the channel's image. Isaacs said that there would be a deliberate shift of re-sources to light entertainment, and he asked the Educational Department to down-play programmes about current affairs and to put more stress on consumer ones.[40] He diverted more funds to youth programmes and entertainment, while drama was cut. A two-year stock of documentaries was being accumulated. The February board meeting was told that the populist Cecil Korer was to be promoted to Senior Commissioning Editor from 1 April – but that was before he made what was to prove a terminal misjudgement.

On 8 February, the channel started one of its most notorious programmes, *Mini Pops*, a contest in which children under ten were dressed up and made up in adult fashion and sang and danced their way through suggestive pop songs. The worst example was a little girl performing 'Nine to Five', dressed in a white dressing gown and negligée. At the words 'when we make love', she took off her dressing gown. At a stage in television history when routines by Hot Gossip were seen as risqué and the extremes of teeny pop videos were a decade away, the series was slated as an encour-agement to child abuse, a paedophile's dream. On *Points of View*, a child psycholo-gist attacked it for sexualising children and predicted problems in the future for the children. The *Observer*'s television critic, Julian Barnes, denounced it as a 'repellent series . . . in which pre-pubescent children grimace and shimmy their way through show business routines.'

Complaints poured in from viewers, attacking the 'ghastly, disgusting show' and asking, 'Mini whores, are you out of your mind?' The series has remained so notorious that in 2006 it was voted the second-worst-ever television programme in a *Radio Times* poll. The irony was that, billed as a children's entertainment show, it attracted nearly 2 million viewers: a storming success in Channel 4 terms.

If they had taken care not to make up the children, stuck to innocuous songs and killed the suggestive dance routines, that might have drawn the sting. As it was, Korer was forced to confess that he had been naive and that the show had been recorded during a hurried week the previous August when he was on holiday. A second series was axed, and Korer's position was undermined. Mike Bolland became the Senior Commissioning Editor instead, and Korer left when his initial three-year term expired. But the channel received a temporary respite from further press assaults by virtue of another seminal television event. TV-am had been launched on 1 February and, true to the golden rule of new media projects, quickly found itself in much worse trouble than Channel 4. The spotlight shifted.

7

Disaster! Channel 4 News

• • • •

Channel 4's founders had very definite views about the sort of news programme they wanted. Analysis and issues were the watchwords. They were aiming at serious people and thought that if more than 1 million watched, then it would probably be the wrong sort of news. The daily programme would last an hour – double the usual length of the principal bulletins on other channels – with no frivolity, no royal-tour stories, no sport, no car crashes, no routine crime. It would concentrate on the things that really mattered: the economy, world events, American elections, energy, business, science, the arts. It was a high-fibre diet that valued expert discussion and explanation. Thoughtful, with liberal overtones, it was news by exclusion. Like muesli without sugar, it would need careful mixing to be palatable.

For a sense of what that recipe meant in practice, one heated debate in the channel's first year, in October 1983, was illuminating. It revolved around a key presenter and executive Sarah Hogg, who argued at the morning meeting – in what was to be her last month with the company – that it was not news that Cecil Parkinson, Chairman of the Conservative Party, was having an affair with his pregnant secretary, Sarah Keays. Trevor McDonald, another staffer at the table, observed that she made a devastating if misguided case but lost the argument. (As the wife of a Conservative cabinet minister, she might, of course, have had a vested interest in the outcome.) Much later, there was to be a stand-up row between Deputy Editor David Mannion and Peter Sissons – who emerged from the early mess to become the well-regarded main anchor – over whether the 1987 Hungerford massacre was a suitable lead story for a channel that did not do crime.

In 1981, though, as Channel 4 was preparing to launch, the first question was not what would be included in the news but who would supply it. The person whose job it was to sort it out was, ostensibly, Liz Forgan, whom Isaacs had hired from the

Guardian to be Commissioner of News and Current Affairs Programmes. Isaacs, though, would clearly have a major input, and the Chairman, Edmund Dell, had decided views of his own: he wanted news and current affairs to aim for the authority of the *Financial Times*, with a dash of *The Economist*. Some thought that the debate was academic anyway, because both the IBA and Willie Whitelaw, the Home Secretary, were on record as saying that the contract should go to ITN, the provider for the ITV network.

David Nicholas, the Welsh-born Editor of ITN, who could be passionate in defence of his territory, told his board in 1981 that 'any train that leaves the station, I want to be on it.'[1] But Forgan commented, 'Quite a lot of people thought *Channel 4 News* was a done deal with ITN before I arrived. If it was, I didn't know. I thought it was a genuinely open issue.'[2]

The truth was that neither Forgan nor Isaacs were sure ITN could provide something sufficiently different from *News at Ten*, their successful bulletin for the ITV network. ITN represented tabloid news. They were royalty mad. When Lady Diana Spencer exposed a nipple walking upstairs at the Royal Opera House, the ITN news team zoomed in and circled the spot. Channel 4 would not have gone within a mile of that story, and Forgan did not have high hopes for Nicholas and his team. 'They were frankly in a very well-designed, wonderful and extremely professional rut with *News at Ten*. They knew exactly how to do it, they churned it out every night, but they were not breaking new ground.'[3]

Edward Stourton, then a graduate trainee at ITN, sympathised with that analysis. He thought that *News at Ten*, even though it knocked spots off the BBC with its snappy packaged reports and gutsy approach, had become a nest of 'aged revolutionaries.'[4]

So there was a contest, of sorts. LWT's Director of Programmes, John Birt, and his associate Barry Cox came close to grabbing the prize from ITN by putting forward a painstakingly researched proposal for a short news segment followed by a daily dose of analysis. It was pitched with the authority of LWT's thoughtful Sunday-morning political programme, *Weekend World*. Birt had earlier led a reaction against sensationalism and picture-led tabloid news on the small screen. In 1975, he and Peter Jay, then the Economics Editor of *The Times*, wrote two widely debated articles about what they termed 'the bias against understanding' inherent in traditional television news programmes.[5] Because television demanded news you could see, it emphasised the 'what' rather than the 'why'. 'They took immense trouble; they had done more profound thinking about this than anyone else in the industry', Forgan recalled. 'It [their proposal] was brilliant and serious. In the end, I just decided it was a better risk to persuade ITN to put their energy at the service of a more ambitious news programme than to persuade John and Barry to undo the corsets: their approach would have strangled the life out of the programme, having analysis every day.'[6]

In any event, it is hard to imagine Isaacs wanting to give the contract to Birt, who had been Dell's choice for his own job. 'We knew that to give this one major contract to ITN was to risk running counter to the whole pluralistic purpose of the channel', he later wrote, 'but it seemed like the best hope.'[7] The decision, grudgingly agreed by the Channel 4 Board in August 1981, was consolation for ITN, who had just failed with their bid for the breakfast-television franchise. They threw themselves at this new challenge, but in a cack-handed way, not helped by a cut in the initial budget of £6.722 million, which ITN had anyway thought sparse.

Nicholas and ITN's top newscaster, Alastair Burnet, had several meetings with Isaacs to talk about the agenda. Forgan then met the Board of ITN.

> I outlined what we wanted: no sport, no royal stories, no plane crashes and lashings of foreign news. There was silence. One crusty director said to me: 'Well my dear, there's just one thing you have to understand: the news is the news is the news.' I said if there is a single sentence that sums up what we don't want, that is it.[8]

ITN was conventional, brilliant at what it did, but quite narrow in its established grammar. It soon became apparent that it was not planning to do anything radically different for Channel 4.

> One of the things that really endeared me to John Birt – John and Barry were thunderstruck by the news – was that shortly after the decision John rang up and asked if we could have lunch. So, I thought I had better take my medicine. But John was fabulous, he took me to L'Étoile. He said, 'I think you have completely made the wrong decision, but you have made it. I think Channel 4 is probably the most important event in my television lifetime, so despite all of this I have forgotten all about it. We will do everything we can to help you make it a success.' I thought that was fine.[9]

ITN thought Channel 4 would be dazzled when it offered their top anchor, Alastair Burnet, to launch their news hour. It was the ultimate sacrifice. He was seasoned, telegenic, immensely knowledgeable, poised. He had launched *News at Ten* while editing *The Economist*. ITN had used Burnet in making pilots for the programme, sending the message that they were devoting their most treasured resources to the task. Surely even Dell would be impressed? It was, however, a serious misjudgement. For the iconoclasts at Channel 4, Burnet was old news. 'I suspect that pilot was disregarded because of Alastair's presence', said Stewart Purvis, then a senior ITN producer. 'Word had got around that he wasn't wanted. So he stomped on set and behaved like the grumpiest boy I have ever seen.'[10] Forgan and Isaacs said, 'No, thank you'. It was a sign of the mutual incomprehension that initially dogged the relationship between the two broadcasters.

From that moment, Burnet, though to become a director of ITN, ignored *Channel 4 News*, its early struggles and later success. 'He didn't take it well', said Forgan. 'He is a brilliant newscaster but was completely identified with *News at Ten*. We were making a statement of doing something different. It would have been twenty times more difficult with Alastair. If he had never done a news broadcast before, he would have been a brilliant idea. But the moment someone switched on to us and saw Alastair, they would have thought of ITN.'[11]

There were, too, suspicions about his politics. Burnet, to be knighted in 1984, was already known as Thatcher's favourite newscaster. Channel 4 made it plain they wanted Trevor McDonald, the Trinidad-born reporter, who became their Roving Diplomatic Editor. He fitted them exactly – or so they thought: McDonald himself had reservations but kept them concealed.

In another sign of the way minds did not meet, David Nicholas wanted to call it *The News at Seven*, to identify it with ITN's flagship and to make it clear that *Channel 4 News* was part of the same family. Forgan said a very sharp no. 'The funny thing is', she recalls, 'we fought like anything to get them to give us the news at ten, but they wouldn't move. It was like asking the Queen to move Buckingham Palace. Much later, of course, they would have loved to have moved ITV news to 7 p.m., to free up the evening.'[12] The contract took six months to negotiate, and in October 1981, ITN was persuaded to accept a cut in the fee from the original £6.722 million to £5.43 million.

David Nicholas, anxious to protect ITN's reputation, was adamant that the editor of the news should be his choice. Channel 4 insisted on consultation, and Isaacs said the editor should come from outside ITN, as should some of the staff. ITN refused to let Isaacs have his first choice, David Watt, a former Political Editor of the *Financial Times*, and put forward Derrik Mercer, Managing Editor of the *Sunday Times*, a charming, thoughtful journalist but not a television professional. Isaacs allowed himself to be half-convinced. From Channel 4's perspective, he was at least a broadsheet journalist and a serious person, untainted by the dreaded culture of fast-moving tabloid news. If Forgan, who had been the *Guardian*'s Women's Editor, could switch to television commissioning, why shouldn't he make a similar transformation?

Mercer brought with him the sensibility of a newspaperman and tried to learn about television. He hired an impressive-looking team. The main on-screen face would be Peter Sissons, aged forty and an ITN graduate trainee, with a background in foreign and industrial reporting and presenting. Godfrey Hodgson, who had worked on the *Sunday Times* and the *Observer* and had some television experience, was Presenting Editor for Foreign Affairs. Sarah Hogg had come via *The Economist* and *Sunday Times*, and, although she had limited television experience, her political contacts were impeccable. As the launch neared, the staff expanded. Michael Crick, an ITN graduate trainee and a former President of the Oxford Union, was on the team and so was the young Edward Stourton. Other members included Damian Green, an economics specialist (later a Conservative MP); Lawrence McGinty, the former News Editor of *New Scientist*; Elinor Goodman from the *Financial Times*; Jane Corbin, who came from Thames; and Ian Ross, an experienced industrial reporter and television journalist. Half came from outside ITN, and some really struggled. Goodman had endless trouble with the technology; Stourton had to help her work a stopwatch to time her sound bites.

With the contract finally agreed, the studio was established within ITN's Wells Street headquarters, just north of Oxford Street and several hundred yards from Channel 4. Then detailed planning started – and with it came further heated disagreements. Channel 4 was violently opposed to the colour blue, so all the surfaces on its set had to be covered in custard-coloured carpet. The planning document for the opening titles broke with the tradition of starting with the headlines, led by the big story of the day and the relevant pictures. *Channel 4 News* would start with a spinning globe which would be transformed into a pie chart, flipped on edge, from which, through the magic of computer graphics, a piece of pie would drop down. John Morrison, one of the three Programme Editors, explained the thinking behind it.

> It might have written on it, 'The end of the world, what does it really mean?' Then that slice would go back into the pie and the next slice come down. If you're not interested in the end of the world, maybe you are interested in the state of the arts. All in all, it didn't signal that this was going to be an engaging experience.[13]

Studio presentation was even worse. A normal news programme had desks, but this one aspired to be casual, so desks were out. That imposed its own problems. The script can be put on a desk, and an hour's programme requires a thick script. There was a lot of on-screen peering, putting on and taking off spectacles and shuffling paper. Four main presenters meant a lot of people popping up, and this revealed an immediate, glaring problem: two of the main presenters, Hodgson and Hogg, were not great broadcasters. 'It just went wrong right from the start', said John Morrison. 'An unmitigated disaster', was Peter Sissons' verdict. He counted his first six months on *Channel 4 News* as utterly demoralising.

The first night, 2 November, was dreadful.

'Just terror', said Morrison. 'Scary. You could see it in front of you; very inexperienced people on screen, not doing it very well. We were making it up as we went along and it did look like that: it looked terrible.'[14] Mercer, in the space of a few weeks, was to become an isolated figure, as it became clear very quickly that he was not best suited to the job. He tried, without success, to graft himself onto the very definite ITN culture. 'Derrik's failure was not a very edifying sight', said McDonald. 'He was a nice, charming man, who embraced this rather vague idea, but he struggled in the post.'[15]

He soon learned that a lot of things that make sense in a newspaper do not make sense on television. One of the first things he did was to buy the television rights to Jimmy Carter's memoirs for $50,000. Peter Sissons crossed the Atlantic to record this with one of the Programme Editors, Peter Bluff, and Channel 4 ran enormous slabs of it when it launched. The trouble was that Carter was not Nixon. He was a one-term president, no longer controversial and, though worthy, not very illuminating. 'We had set out to do something ambitious and difficult', said Forgan, summing up the first terrible weeks. 'To do that with a bunch of amateurs was not very sensible. However clever we all were, we were amateurs at television news.'[16]

Those ITN staffers required to work across the two very different bulletins for ITV, and the new channel did not comprehend the Channel 4 agenda. ITN had specialised in crisp one- to two-minute news items, whereas the skills of making five- to twenty-minute films are quite different. Even such experienced journalists as Trevor McDonald had never done this. They thought all they had to do was copy *Newsnight* – launched on BBC2 in 1980 – but it meant that in practice the early films were poor. Jon Snow, later to step into Sissons' role, was in El Salvador for *News at Ten* when *Channel 4 News* began. He was asked to make ten-minute packages, but they were a disaster because he was given no cogent guidance. Everyone had to learn on the job. The audience noticed that something was amiss and deserted in droves.

After watching a Godfrey Hodgson film on touring America, McDonald thought, 'I have seen the new age of television. In which case it is the end of mine.'[17] He now says,

> With 20/20 hindsight it felt like you were watching a truck rushing downhill and you knew you should get out of the way. But nothing happened: everyone just stood there. It was so painful that a five-year-old would have known it was wrong. Yet, they let it happen. In the desire to be radical, they had thrown out not just the baby and the bathwater but the bath itself. It was almost as though the people at the top had washed their hands of it.[18]

Stewart Purvis, an up-and-coming young producer, was watching from the wings. He had known from the pilots that things were wrong. He realised that despite Mercer's formidable reputation it was clear he did not know about television, and nobody felt able to tell him what to do. 'Sitting on *News at Ten* I said I wasn't sure how we should handle this. We would be seen as whingers if we offered criticism. People said they should sit down with us and talk, but it was difficult. They were separate.'[19] And they wanted to stay that way.

The brief of the programme was difficult, in some ways ahead of its time. By January 1983, the audience had dropped to a meagre 250,000, meaning they scored a nil rating on the Broadcasters' Audience Research Board (BARB) measurement system. Forgan remembers:

> January 1983 was a terrible moment. We were derided and the ratings were tiny . . . The whole industry was dying for it to be a disaster because we had been very snooty by making the news last twice as long. Everyone was highly delighted with these awful moments. I had to go to the Board and say: 'Please keep the faith.'[20]

On 28 January, at Berystede, Ascot, Forgan gave the Board this assessment:

> I am aware members of the Board have strongly critical views about *Channel 4 News*. The present performance of this central programme represents a serious and urgent problem. The first, urgent priority is to get the news right. Already in hand; the structure is being simplified, signposting improved, news summaries expanded, a new set for February. I remain concerned about certain specific weaknesses, occasionally questionable news judgements, and about the air of languid monotony which sometimes characterises the programme.[21]

She felt the hour was worth persevering with, even though the opportunity it presented had not yet been exploited.

There was a smell of failure about it, and people began to think of leaving. Rumours of a putsch against Mercer circulated, and the staff started plotting. Crick said, 'In my years in the business, the politicking was on a level I've never experienced since. Everyone was nasty to Godfrey, who was difficult to get on with . . . Sarah was incredibly political, a plotter.'[22]

McDonald, at a lunch with Isaacs around this time, urged him to be more ecumenical. Maybe, he mused, they should stop insisting on the gold standard and try to attract more viewers. Isaacs told him he was too concerned about numbers, that Channel 4 was different, that it didn't mind small audiences. 'I said that the word "broadcast" implies spreading news. And I thought, Christ, I've ended up in the wrong place.'[23] That conviction was confirmed by an encounter at a party in Charlotte Street after one of the early news programmes. He spoke to a woman who thought that when they did foreign reports she would like to hear the person being interviewed, say in French or German, without being voiced over in English. 'I put my glass down and said, I'm leaving right now. It was just so bizarre.'[24]

In February, some changes were introduced. Desks came in. There was a longer opening news bulletin, up to ten minutes, before the in-depth segments began. The viewing figures perked up to more than 400,000 in February and March, but April and May were bleak, with ten nights of zero ratings. Sissons quipped that it would be cheaper to send viewers video recordings, and Isaacs began pressing for a new editor.

The crunch came with the General Election of June 1983. Mercer knew that the knives were out for him and decided to take a lead. He hired a room over the Gay Hussar in Soho, long a haunt of left-wing journalists, for a brainstorming meeting. His plans were intelligent but probably overambitious. He wrote that for *Channel 4 News* the election was an 'unparalleled opportunity to establish itself as a distinctive news service . . . We will do more than simply record the ACTIVITIES of the campaign.'[25] His aims included analysing the promises of the rival parties against past performance, providing a foreign perspective and running live speeches at 7.30 p.m. Twice a week they would stage three-way debates of up to fifteen minutes, set up with explanatory packages. Crick and Stourton would play active roles in planning it. They doubled the size of crews and went on air six nights a week. Damian Green was to prepare packages on unemployment and privatisation, while Green and Hogg would examine the macroeconomic record. Mark Webster and Ian Ross would cover the unions; Jane Corbin, immigration.[26]

Despite all that planning, the election coverage met nobody's expectations, and very soon things came to a head. Peter Sissons led a small delegation to make their views known to David Nicholas. Staff journalists spent hours plotting in a local wine bar, where they served an Italian wine labelled Machiavelli. ITN's Chairman Lord Buxton was worried that the news bulletin was becoming the scapegoat for Channel 4's other failures. Isaacs was in a rage and was heavily critical of ITN at a board meeting on 15 June. 'We insist on a more radical shift in their thinking and practice than has yet been evinced. We insist on an editor of our choice and then we give them a year to sort it out.'[27] If that did not happen, they would switch to a half-hour news programme and go to a different provider. Around ten days later, Stourton and McDonald went off to Beirut, and before they went, Mercer assured them he had the complete confidence of the management. By the time they were reporting from the Beka Valley, the news came that he had been fired. He made a bitter farewell speech to his staff – 'I'd like to thank all of you for your hard work and some of you for your loyalty'[28] – before retreating to his home in Barnes and a career in publishing.

Paul McKee, ITN's technical expert, who had handled most of the negotiations with Channel 4 over the contract, took over as temporary editor and started to steady the ship.

Although the relationship with Channel 4 remained fairly fraught, he appeared to have a better understanding of their needs than Mercer. As Crick wrote in a generous obituary of McKee: 'From his first team talk, *Channel 4 News* never looked back.' Meanwhile, changes were afoot at ITN that would have an impact on Channel 4. Alastair Burnet was to be made Editor of *News at Ten* as well as its anchor. It was the job that the ambitious Purvis had been angling for, and it was an open secret that Purvis and Burnet were not natural soulmates. Purvis began to distance himself from *News at Ten* by agreeing to produce some segments for *Channel 4 News*.

Purvis had a dazzling record as a *News at Ten* producer. He had been on duty in 1980 when the Iranian Embassy siege was ended by the SAS, and his coverage won three industry awards. But Channel 4 executives had never really regarded him as one of them. He was, they felt, too wedded to hard news and gossip, especially royal gossip. He it was to whom Prince Charles confided that he talked to his plants. He had organised coverage of the Prince's wedding and had masterminded several stories about Princess Diana. Asked why he had a copy of *Woman's Own* on his desk, he explained, 'It's the best royal coverage there is.'[29] Said Forgan, 'My doubt about him was the same as about Alastair. He was a brilliant Duty Editor on *News at Ten*, but would he bring any heart, any love to this idea of ours, which was so different?'[30] But *Channel 4 News* was in crisis, and it was time to set such doubts aside. The good news was that they were finally about to let in an executive who knew about television news and how to use the technology to bring stories alive.

Purvis arrived in July and was shocked by what he found.

> It was being run like a daily newspaper. All the decisions were made too late and the production schedule was all wrong. I just couldn't believe the show got on air some days. The morning meeting would discuss what we'd do, but the editors didn't assign stories till just before lunch. Then they went off for lunch and started work at 3 p.m. – far too late. With their weird philosophy of being different, they ignored the footage of the news of the day shot by ITN crews. They didn't want to use it. They talked about it being the wrong kind of video, just footage of people walking in and out of doors. But then they didn't have the resources to do their own stuff . . . David Nicholas tried to warn me off, in the nicest possible way, saying that good people were being sucked in and reputations lost.[31]

But Purvis ignored that advice and agreed to take charge for the time being.

He had the kind of experience that Mercer had lacked. He was a television animal, a very good journalist and technician, tough but usually fair. One of the things he did was introduce a post-mortem after each news programme, picking out one report and analysing how it could have been done better. He was hypercritical, and eve-ryone worked hard to make sure their reports were not the ones picked on. Purvis worked on the theory that journalists are good copycats, once they have been shown what is needed. He demonstrated he could do a professional job that conformed to the Channel 4 agenda.

But he still had to be approved by the Channel's powers-that-be, who remained insistent on a broadsheet-newspaper approach. In September 1983, he was sum-moned to lunch at the White Tower, a long established restaurant in Percy Street, facing north up Charlotte Street. At the table were Isaacs, Dell and Attenborough. Purvis immediately sensed the tension between Isaacs and Dell, who did most of the talking as the others chewed on their expensive kebabs. Dell was an intellectual who had run the Department of Trade and Industry and who had been thought of as a potential Labour chancellor, but he never made it because Labour lost power while he was in his prime. He cross-examined Purvis on the public-sector borrow-ing requirement, the International Monetary Fund and opera. 'I was bluffing my way through', Purvis recalled. 'Jeremy said a few things, but I was essentially being vetted by Dell.'[32] Finally, as the awkward meal neared its end, Attenborough, who had been mostly silent, leaned forward. 'Can I ask your views on female newsreaders?' Purvis said he was in favour. 'Oh good', said Attenborough. 'Darling, we are all, you know, in show business. Never forget that, will you?' Dell glowered.[33]

What Purvis did not know, until he formally took up the job on 17 October, was that he was sitting on a precipice. After a highly charged September meeting, the Channel 4 Board had sent a letter to ITN, setting out three conditions. Purvis could have the job for a year but had to reach a nightly audience of 750,000. He had to include items of identifiable analysis as well as weekly reports on industry, the economy, world affairs from a foreign perspective, science, new technology and the arts. And he must strengthen the editorial team. In other words, it was ITN's last chance.

'Channel 4 were astute', says Purvis. 'They let me have a go. If they had forced someone else on ITN, it would have been their fault. I hardly had any more guidance from Jeremy, just one of his customary notes: Dear Stewart, you know what we want, now do it.'[34]

Purvis and his team had discussions with Forgan about the element of their brief that they were most worried about: identifiable analysis. Purvis saw his skill as slip-ping analysis into news reports. What Forgan wanted was talking heads, discussing the issues, but he told her that analysis could be merged with narrative. He drew up a complete redesign for the first anniversary, with a conventional news round-up at the top, so that people did not feel they needed to listen to another bulletin to be properly informed. It would be built around Peter Sissons, with a junior presenter for the second slot.

One of the first victims of the new regime was Sarah Hogg. Purvis had heard complaints about her but thought she just needed a better producer, so he went off to make some films with her. He found she had few of the instincts of normal news reporters. She was married to a cabinet minister, Douglas Hogg, and must have had access to many real inside stories, but neither she nor *Channel 4 News* knew how to take advantage of that privileged access, and she resigned in November. Jeremy Isaacs went to the first night of the new programme on 2 November. When it was over, he clambered onto a table so that he could be seen by everyone and said, 'We are completely behind Stewart. Keep it going.'[35] It was a turning point, though Purvis for a long time felt he was operating in alien territory, with Channel 4 on one side and a suspicious staff on the other. He nearly had a breakdown and had to take days off for stress.

Then the year-long miners' strike came along and, just as the Falklands War had established the reputation of BBC2's *Newsnight* in 1982, this was the period that turned *Channel 4 News* into a national asset as the struggle between Thatcher and organised Old Labour was played out. It was here that the extra time in the bulletin was used to its greatest advantage. Reporters went out to interview both working and striking miners and broke stories about the true level of coal stocks. Night after night the team, led by the Industrial Correspondent Ian Ross, got close to the miners and inside their communities. The programme went on the road: on one occasion, Peter Sissons and Michael Crick were still were hunting for a place to present it from at 4 p.m. in the afternoon. Purvis got Arthur Scargill, the miners' leader, and Ian MacGregor, the Head of the National Coal Board, to make ten-minute films, and on 22 August they debated live on air – a coup in such a bitter dispute. He commissioned a poll showing that if Scargill had held an official ballot for strike action he would have won it, thus making it harder for the Nottinghamshire miners to go back to work – the event that heralded the collapse of the strike.

Crick thinks the programme may have been biased towards the striking miners.

> We were nearly all left of centre, we were greatly influenced by the Glasgow Media Group. Some people who worked for Channel 4 saw it as their job to back Neil Kinnock [. . .] The miners liked us, they thought we were the only crews sympathetic to them. We had C4 stickers, a logo on the cameras, and other ITN crews acquired some so that they could get the same access.[36]

Jane Corbin won a Royal Television Society award with a report from Shirebrook, a Derbyshire village, where she recounted how the wives and children of strikers and non-strikers heckled and swore at each other. It ran for twenty-four minutes, and Margaret Thatcher was said to have been moved.

By the time the strike was over, Channel 4 had become established as a major news provider. Research conducted in 1984 found that, compared with 1983, attitudes had improved. Nearly 13 million people watched *Channel 4 News* compared with 10 million previously. 'A majority feel it is different from other news programmes and compares favourably with them', though one-fifth still felt it was not as good as its rivals.[37] Viewers liked the weekly coverage of science but wanted more consumer information. The Channel 4 presenters were not at all well known. Three-quarters of viewers could not mention a single name, not even Trevor McDonald or Peter Sissons. It was watched by a good cross-section of ages and social classes: two-thirds married, just under half middle class and under forty-five. On the appreciation index, it scored 69 out of 100, up from the previous May, when it stood at 66. Viewers understood that it covered subjects in greater depth than other channels and liked it for that. The doubters on the programme cheered up. It seemed that at last they had found a successful formula – so successful that although it would be tweaked in future revamps, it would not fundamentally change.

8

Two tigers at the table

• • • •

During 1983, the crisis over Channel 4's news was overshadowed by rows about current affairs, which set Jeremy Isaacs and the unyielding Edmund Dell on a collision course. Their profound differences dominated boardroom discussions month after month and threatened to destabilise the company. Senior colleagues and other board members worked hard to keep the conflict under wraps, away from the press, and to avoid a showdown that could have led to resignations. They were particularly concerned to protect Liz Forgan from being drawn into the dispute and made the sacrificial lamb. At the Edinburgh Television Festival that August, Isaacs and Dell drank tea together, to put on a display of unity for the benefit of the press. But just three weeks later, matters came to a head and Isaacs' position was in real jeopardy.

The root of the conflict lay in his determination that his current-affairs programmes – or at least some of them – should embrace lively, opinionated journalism, making them the television equivalent of comment pages in the newspapers. In addition, he wanted them to be made by fresh people with interests that stretched beyond the narrow range of topics he thought the BBC and ITV had settled on. Yet, this was Thatcher's Britain, a time when protest and reporting on social issues was being marginalised by a prevailing ethos of 'I'm all right, Jack', and when a confident, strident government was becoming increasingly uninhibited in its criticism of broadcasters whose sympathies appeared to challenge its own.

As part of their hunt for new voices – which in some cases would sound to some like rather old voices – Isaacs and Forgan sought out alternative sources for current affairs. They commissioned programmes from two groups of women-only producers, science features with an axe to grind, campaigning films from radical directors such as Ken Loach and videos from workshops around the country, including Derry in Northern Ireland – usually run at 11 p.m., in the *Eleventh Hour* slot. The ap-

Above: Jeremy Isaacs, Channel 4 founder and Chief Executive, 1982–7.

Below: Sir Richard Attenborough, Channel 4 Deputy Chairman, 1982–7 and Chairman, 1987–92.

Above left: The opening-night script with announcer Paul Coia's handwritten amendments.
Above right: The original and still best-known Channel 4 ident.

Below: Carol Vorderman does her sums in the early days of *Countdown* (1982–).

Above: Barry Grant (played by Paul Usher) enjoys a cup of tea and a sit-down with father Bobby (Ricky Tomlinson) in *Brookside* (1982–2003).

Below: Ian McKellen in *Walter* (Stephen Frears, 1982), a Film on Four production, broadcast on launch night.

Above: Robbie Coltrane in *The Comic Strip Presents . . . Five Go Mad in Dorset* (1982), the first of a successful series for Channel 4.

Below: *Minipops* (1983), a short-lived and, to contemporary eyes, rebarbative feature of the early schedule.

Above: The original *Channel 4 News* (1982–) ident.

Below: Jools Holland and Paula Yates on *The Tube* (1982–7).

Above: *Desmond's* (1989–94), Channel 4's
innovative soap.

Left: Johnny (Daniel Day Lewis) and Omar
(Gordon Warnecke) outside the eponymous *My
Beautiful Laundrette* (Stephen Frears, 1985), a
success for Film on Four.

Above left: Oliver Reed stumbles off the set of *After Dark* (1987–91) after a confrontation with the feminist writer Kate Millett. Above right: *The Big Breakfast*'s (1992–2002) most successful pairing: Chris Evans and Gaby Roslin.

Below: Michael Grade, Chief Executive, 1988–97.

Robert Lindsay as council leader Michael Murray and Julie Walters as his mother in Alan Bleasdale's *GBH* (1991).

Dennis Potter in a moving last interview with Melvyn Bragg (1994).

Below: Chris Morris on *Brass Eye* (1997).

pointment of the inexperienced Forgan to oversee news and current affairs was in itself part and parcel of this approach. And for many campaigning groups and film-makers, it provided thrilling and novel opportunities that summed up what Channel 4 was there to do.

As Forgan later reflected,

> I think if the channel had been launched in the 1960s it would have been the same. It wasn't so much that it was breaking new ground as that, all around British television, society had been changing. So when Channel 4 said here's the door, it's open, there was just this whoosh of people coming in. We didn't invent them.[1]

The problem – a predictable one – was that a fair proportion of the programmes from newly independent producers were flawed in several respects. They tended to be shrill and to take a left-of-centre political position, violating television's legal duty to be impartial. The 1980s were politically volatile: there were real differences and battles fought between the parties and power blocs over a range of issues including the privatisation of public services, council-house sales and the influence of the trade unions. British forces were deployed in Northern Ireland, convulsed in a quasi-civil war, and the IRA was committing terrorist acts in mainland Britain.

The prevailing philosophy at Channel 4 was that its mission to innovate and inform ought to let it off the hook in terms of the traditional rules about political coverage, taste and decency. But the Broadcasting Act allowed no leeway for that kind of amnesty, and the IBA was, in law, still the broadcaster and publisher.[2] The IBA in truth found itself somewhere in the middle. Paradoxically, it took a less hard line than Dell, the channel's Chairman, and was more tolerant of early exuberance and mistakes. But the principle of due impartiality was crucially important, and, ultimately, the IBA was not prepared to stand by and allow broadcasting to follow the press into the realm of political partisanship. After all, were it to allow Channel 4 to pursue a left-wing agenda, it would have to extend this tolerance to other broadcasters coming from the opposite direction. Mrs Thatcher and many in her Government were already convinced that the BBC and now Channel 4 had an overwhelming bias towards the left, and in the case of Channel 4 that it was the natural instinct of most of its staff. They saw themselves as the opposition, since Labour was so ineffectual, while Thatcher's decade-long battle with the BBC was well under way. David Glencross, the IBA's Director of Television, would later remark that when the Government heard the word 'culture' it reached not for its revolver but its dictionary.

The most controversial strand, a source of continuous friction, was *The Friday Alternative*, which ran after the Friday's shortened *Channel 4 News* at 7.30 p.m. and took an opinionated alternative view of the week's news – which, in practice, meant that it set itself to oppose the Government on a broad range of issues. It also commented critically on media coverage and delighted in exposing the workings of television, not shrinking from criticising and embarrassing ITN, the makers of *Channel 4 News*. There was no better way to make implacable enemies.

The Board decided early on that the programme's critique of the media 'appeared consistently to present only one viewpoint, that of the left.'[3] Indeed, the show's first outing, on 5 November, grated even with the tolerant Isaacs. 'On day one it knocked off an item on the House of Lords, and knocked off the Lords in sixty seconds. You can't do that sort of thing for an easy laugh in a programme the rest of whose utterance you hope will be taken seriously', he wrote.[4] 'Juvenile skittishness and spite' was the reaction of the hawkish ITV director Brian Tesler, who had no time for it.[5] Forgan, who was hauled in to account for things later, recalled, 'Edmund [Dell] thought it was a complete, scandalous outrage. He could not understand why it was there. He thought we were being feckless with something he cared about.'[6]

The Friday Alternative was made by about twenty or so young, relatively inexperienced staff to a format created by David Graham, a seasoned and canny ex-*Panorama* producer. Sidelined by the BBC, he had been on the independent steering group campaigning for Channel 4 in the run-up to launch. He was a serious, independent-minded man with a reputation for digging behind the façade of sound bites and picture opportunities to look at facts and reality. 'I had grown dissatisfied with the traditional method of debating news – it was often lazy', he said.[7] He had done a stream of well-regarded programmes for *Panorama*, including one on the real unemployed, in which he combined academic data and analysis with reportage lasting six weeks on the Cambuslang estate in Scotland. His approach was, 'Find out more: don't simply stage a debate between people who represent consensual thinking.'[8]

This greatly appealed to Isaacs, who approached Graham in 1981 and invited him to lunch with him and Forgan. Channel 4 gave him a year's contract worth £1 million, and, with a partner, Peter Donebauer, he set up Diverse Productions in an old public washhouse in Fulham. Channel 4 financed the investment in state-of-the-art editing and production equipment, being one of the first producers to harness computers to cut production costs and make for slicker editing. At that time, when the BBC wanted to do graphics in current affairs, it pointed a camera at a sheet of paper. Diverse did instant green, black and red computer graphics, as well as cartoons, accompanied by noisy metallic music. This inventive and free use of graphics was much admired and would eventually become standard in the industry.

On the basis of his initial contract from Channel 4, Graham created a small media business, using a publishing model akin to a *Time Out* or *City Limits* (now defunct) collective, rather than *Panorama*. He hired young people with a radical bent: they had enthusiasm, they were cheaper and they were available. Anna Coote was a programme editor, and among other talented staffers was Steve Hewlett, later the Editor of *Panorama* when it landed its astonishing interview with Princess Diana. *The Friday Alternative* had no presenters (another saving) and could make programmes for around £20,000 each. The editorial approach was to be part of Friday youth nights, following the cultural tone of *The Tube* at the start of the evening. Graham reasoned that the one group of people who did not watch current-affairs programmes were the young. To address this, 'I thought it needed to be scurrilous.'[9]

From the very first show, as we have seen, it raised hackles in powerful places. It was uneven, reckless and immature and was prone to leaving out inconvenient bits of an argument. But it also ran some items unlike anything else on television at the time, and which certainly rattled the bars of the BBC and ITN. For example, on 7 January, a year after the Falklands War, when emotions still ran high, it focused on the way the British media had reported it, using internal BBC editorial news and current-affairs minutes leaked to Hewlett.[10] These showed how BBC local radio stations were prevented from using interviews with the widows of Falklands soldiers and questioned the language used in the reporting of the sinking of the *Belgrano*, the Argentine warship heading away from the exclusion zone when attacked. When BBC executives reacted by saying in private that these practices would have been at home in Goebbels' Germany, their remarks were also leaked and were reported gleefully on the following week's programme.

It returned to the subject the following month, broadcasting a tape of a conversation between the Prime Minister's combative Press Secretary Bernard Ingham and the BBC's Assistant Director General, Alan Protheroe, who liaised with the Ministry of Defence. This was technically a breach of the 1949 Telegraphy Act, and the Home Office put pressure on the IBA's new Director General, John Whitney: but the channel's lawyers had cleared it for broadcast because of the public interest.

In the 1983 General Election, *The Friday Alternative* mischievously filmed only the mouths of politicians making speeches, asking people to guess to which party they belonged. The programme also raised questions about the cost of maintaining the royal family, challenging their lifestyle as well as that of top BBC executives, whose lavish homes were photographed and shown on screen. 'We saw ourselves as consensus-busters', said Hewlett. 'We did not set out just to be opinionated. Some of us never bought the idea of opinion. We thought original journalism was the answer.'[11]

Support for the series started to ebb away, though. As early as December 1982, the IBA's chairman, Lord Thomson, had received a letter of concern from the Home Secretary, Willie Whitelaw, about political bias at Channel 4. Thomson also reported that at a liaison meeting with Dell and Jeremy Isaacs the authority sought changes to *The Friday Alternative*. Colin Shaw, the IBA's Director of Television, had forewarned Isaacs and provided him with a list of criticisms of the early programmes. In January, the Board had a long debate about political bias and the attacks from Conservative MPs. Dell wrote to Isaacs, 'This programme was appalling once more and some discipline must be exerted over these people very quickly.'[12] Isaacs told the Board that he agreed it was a matter of major concern.

During the early months of 1983, the producers worked to rectify problems with Forgan and Isaacs, who had certainly not given up on the programme. Graham was visited by Edmund Dell at the former washhouse.

> He made his views clear without being horrible. He said this is something I don't support – I want something like the *Financial Times*, something that does a thorough job. David Glencross at the IBA sent for me and said *The Friday Alternative* was in breach of the Broadcasting Act [Glencross disputed this] and that I was going to have to take a different course.[13]

Other programmes added to the pressure on Isaacs, including *Crucible*, an early series from Central Television aimed at supplying a different kind of science coverage from *Horizon* on the BBC. One programme, about the undemocratic nature of a public inquiry into building a nuclear power station at Sizewell, attracted fierce criticism from Dell. Then a film on funfairs, supposed to be about how people handle their fear mechanisms, turned into a diatribe about the way capitalist theme parks control their visitors. 'This is the last straw', Liz Forgan wrote to Central. She informed the Channel 4 Board in January 1983 that she would not recommission *Crucible* because 'efforts to ensure some control over production have failed'. She added that it had become 'a repetitive and simplistic political statement about science and scientists'.[14] The series ended after ten programmes.

Edmund Dell was now on a crusade. Justin Dukes observed that he would choose his battleground carefully, then grimly go to war. His next concern was a trade-union series by Ken Loach, also from Central Television, which eventually, to Forgan's chagrin, was returned unscreened. 'Loach made this brilliant series', she recalls.

> It depicted trade-union life in all its dinginess. All the programmes were designed to reach the same conclusion, that the trade-union leaders were selling out the rank and file. When Central delivered it to us, Edmund Dell was horrified – and so was I, but I really wanted to transmit it, it was so beautifully done. Solution: we needed a balancing discussion programme. So I went to the Trades Union Congress and drank more whisky than I ever drunk in my life, tickling them to take part. The one who wouldn't was Frank Chapple. I had three of the four big trade-union leaders on board, though.[15]

With the issue deadlocked, Dukes went with Forgan to Dell's house in Hampstead Garden Suburb in a bid to ensure his support, or at least a gracious truce. It was not to be. Unknown to Forgan, the issue was resolved when the Channel 4 Board was told that the series had been withdrawn by Central. Meanwhile, Loach's children wrote her letters, asking plaintively, 'Why have you banned my Daddy's programme?' She believes that Dell's reaction was that of someone who had no experience of journalism.

> Edmund didn't have this gene that said there is something shocking about not transmitting a piece of work – you really have to have overwhelming reasons for doing that. He had no idea. The rug was pulled completely out from under my feet. I was appalled. Everyone behaved badly except Jeremy and me.[16]

Most interesting, and of its time, was the experiment with women-only programmes. It had been argued for years that television current affairs was dominated by men, and if women made them it would be different. Would it? Forgan thought there was only one way to find out, and that was to try it.

> We had two very different attitudes. We had Twenty Twenty, run by Claudia Milne, who had worked for *World in Action*. She said she was not having any nonsense about gynaecology and feminism but would do the best story of the week, the best way she knew. 'We will knock the spots off *World in Action*.'
>
> Then there was Broadside, a women's collective, which said: 'We are women, we will see the world from the other end of the telescope.' Both of them made some wonderful programmes, but if you asked me what it proved about women making programmes that were different from men, I'd say very little. There was some evidence, especially from Broadside: they did do womanly things that would never stand a chance with *World in Action*. Second, they chose different witnesses, quite often women. They didn't choose identikit middle-aged men in suits. Third thing, it became quite clear that powerful men talking about serious subjects to a woman reporter did it in a different way. In one scene in a Broadside programme, the reporter was interviewing an MP outside Parliament. He'd been opposing the party on a policy, but when it came to the crunch he'd voted with his party, as they always do. She pointed out that sixteen times he had said he was against this and asked him: 'Why vote like that?' There was a pause, and he said, 'Oh, don't look at me like that.' Instead of being combative, he treated her like a human being.[17]

Broadside was a group of talented women producers, directors, camera operators and reporters including Holly Aylett, Sarah Boston, Sue Lloyd-Roberts, Dianne Tammes and Sarah Kennedy. The first programme in a ten-week run in early 1983 sympathetically profiled women protesters at Greenham Common. Edmund Dell objected to it as a crusading, anti-nuclear piece, and the IBA's Director General John Whitney once more complained. In a second and final series that summer, Sarah Kennedy talked to wives and widows of injured and slain Falklands soldiers, while Sue Lloyd-Roberts made a programme from Skinningrove, where unemployment was 60 per cent, the highest of any town, and encouraged the women to tell their experiences in prose and poetry.

By February, even the tolerant Anthony Smith was arguing that Broadside 'did not seem to understand proper journalism and had instead adopted a propagandist approach.'[18] In the run-up to an election, he felt the channel was in danger: Parliament and the IBA were watching closely.[19] But Broadside, if it was a problem, self-combusted, increasingly paralysed by a long and complicated falling out. By July 1983, the split was so severe that they could not continue to work together, and a third series was out of the question, though the individual programme-makers continued to make challenging work.

In late June, Graham and Isaacs were at the Banff Television Festival in the Canadian Rockies. They drove out to Lake Louisa together, and, as they walked around it, Isaacs said he was going to have to drop *The Friday Alternative*. Yet, on 20 July, more as a statement of his position than as a viable proposal, he presented the Board with a plan to recommission the programme after its contract ended that November. His plan for a five-month extension, following a six-week summer break, was supported by a written submission from Forgan; but he knew the initiative was doomed and he later admitted his heart was not in the defence.[20] The baffling conundrum of how to make current affairs appeal to teenagers and young adults remained unsolved, as was revealed by a simple statistic: the audience had collapsed from 671,000 in November 1982 to 188,000 in July 1983.

That July also saw the final *The Friday Alternative*, featuring Steve Hewlett in a bear suit, asking MPs questions, with a second item criticising Channel 4's output. This exasperated Liz Forgan, who had had quite enough. She decided *The Friday Alternative* was too anarchic and getting out of control. Typically, too, there was a final cock-up. A driver appeared at Diverse for the programme tape, but it did not arrive at Channel 4 and missed its slot. It was found later at the BBC, where the driver had mistakenly delivered it. It was retrieved and screened later.

Anthony Smith and Sara Morrison were lone voices of support on the Board, while Dell was uncompromising. He maintained that the programme contained superficial analyses of complex issues on the basis of inadequate research and that it had harmed Channel 4. It had started as an undiluted left-wing programme and had now become a left-wing programme striving to be balanced. 'The Chairman considered that certain public perceptions about the channel needed to be changed and it would be wise to sacrifice the programme.'[21] Brian Tesler reinforced Dell's point, asserting that *The Friday Alternative* was not a credit to Channel 4. It was duly axed.

Forgan and Isaacs were less dismayed about the loss of that one troublesome programme than by the incontrovertible fact that editorial control had been hijacked from them by the Board, but, in truth, the Board, and certainly the Chairman, had been very involved in editorial policy matters for months. Dell saw the cancellation as proof of an institutional failure to monitor the channel's output. In effect, he had called Isaacs to heel – at least for the moment.

● ● ● ●

Isaacs did not accept this as the end of the matter, and during the summer break he wrote two board papers. The first explained his philosophy of programming in terms of political impartiality and risk.

> My paper (Programmes, My First Year, and After: A Review) reaffirmed a positive commitment to representing all views to our audiences, not promoting any one view. But I pointed out that in the attempt to allow able and intelligent people to report on the world and express feelings, there was always going to be a risk that something in the channel's output would demand an answer.[22]

In short, he was not going to back down on his original approach of airing an array of different viewpoints.

This was the pivotal section of the paper:

> If programmes express no opinion there is no apparent problem. If, however, it is agreed that programmes or even series or strands may exhibit a particular view of the world, then immediately a real set of problems is presented, a consequence of a commitment to pluralism [. . .] What we have to do is to find and agree on ways of maintaining variety [. . .] while conforming with an obligation [. . .] not to allow the Channel to be used for the expression of any preponderant view.

It sounded innocuous enough, but when Dell read it over the weekend before the board meeting on 21 September, he saw red. In his view, Isaacs was merely restating a position he was all too familiar with, without providing a solution to the consequent problem of too many left-wing viewpoints. He wrote a diametrically opposed paper.

At this point, Deputy Chairman Richard Attenborough made one of his occasional but crucial interventions. He arranged a dinner the night before the board meeting at the White House, just north of Marylebone Road, a discreet restaurant well off the media industry's map. He booked a private room, without a closing time and ordered a huge buffet.

> I was trying to act between battling forces. The dinner wasn't a get together and have a chat, it was, please let's get together, just the two of you with me, at least get your bloody cards on the table and be prepared to make concessions. Because without that you are tearing the Board apart, putting the channel in danger. It was a potential disaster.
>
> They were like two tigers at the table. Fierce. The confrontation was so overt. My concern at this point was to save Jeremy, it had to be. Everyone in the company knew either one or the other faced having to leave the Board. The last thing I wanted was to do the chairmanship. [. . .]
>
> To put it crudely, it was a matter of pride as far as Edmund was concerned. The subject matter of the rows was irrelevant, he had this burning anger, we'd made a mistake with Isaacs, and he was being proven right by his intractable behaviour.[23]

Isaacs recalled a dinner from Hell:

> Edmund still attempted to be a domineering chairman. His idea of chairing a serious issue was to introduce the item by making a long utterance himself. That may be what chairmen of the politburo do, but it is not what chairmen of responsible creative bodies do! And at that dinner, he did exactly that. He said, 'Here is a paper I propose to table tomorrow in response to the Chief Executive's paper.' He intended to distribute it the following day.[24]

Dell handed the paper to Attenborough and Isaacs to read over dinner. The key point was a plan to introduce an independent method of assessment for the channel's troublesome current affairs. The subtext was that he was saying Isaacs was wrong. 'He might have got rid of me, who knows?' the intended victim reflected later.[25] At the board meeting the next day, Isaacs' paper was the first item and debated thoroughly. Attenborough reminded everyone that the channel was there to provide new opportunities. The crucial point was that Dell, aware from the White House dinner that he did not have Attenborough's support, let the debate flow and did not produce his paper as an alternative, provoking a vote of confidence. The reaction from the rest of the Board must have made it clear to him that he would have been isolated had he done so.

Attenborough had forced Dell to back off.

> I believed as far as Jeremy was concerned that without his inspiration the channel could suffer considerably. And although it would be very sad if Edmund went because of his passionate commitment to it, we could manage if he did go. I made Jeremy back down a bit, to ameliorate things. I succeeded, but I felt rather awful.[26]

The second, more emollient paper from Isaacs was on the commissioning process, supporting the view that things had to change and that editorial controls needed tightening. It emerged that ten of the commissioning editors would now report direct to Paul Bonner to ensure that nothing in the schedule was not capable of being transmitted under the Broadcasting Act. Isaacs would retain responsibility for actuality (news and current affairs), fiction and the arts.

However, that meeting was most remarkable for a potentially dramatic development that did not occur. For it also emerged that Dell had gone on his own to the IBA the previous afternoon to ensure that Bonner could be appointed alongside Isaacs to the Board next day. 'The hole in the corner manner of this one was curious to say the least, and the motivation fishy', Isaacs later wrote.[27]

> The point is Edmund had gone to make this suggestion to the IBA. He'd told them that there is this paper, the Board are very concerned about it, it is possible that by the end of tomorrow Jeremy will have left, and we absolutely must have somebody [from the programming side] on the Board.[28]

Dell, though, later maintained that during one heated debate about impartiality Isaacs asked him whether he was seeking his resignation. 'I replied I was not. The problem as I saw it was to correct the channel's political steer, to raise the quality of its current affairs output, not to sack the chief executive.'[29]

Isaacs, who saw Bonner as a colleague and not a rival, put it this way:

> I think he was preparing for me to leave. That's what I guess. It was also a terrible shock and insult to my deputy, Justin Dukes. Justin only heard about this just before the board meeting. It was a scandal. Edmund had no sensitivity towards people.
>
> Edmund did not threaten to dismiss me: no, certainly not, but he gave me a pain in the bum, going on about matters in dispute between

us, taking up far too much of my time and the Board's time by discussing them. Boards don't do that in television companies that are banging
out sixty hours a week. He could have said: 'I am making my feelings
clear, think about it', but he didn't. He went on and on, niggling.

I think it was pathetic; but the niggles got to me slightly more than
they should have done because we had had two years of strenuous activity in getting the channel on air in the time allowed us. There was all
that tension and responding to the reception to the channel – part heart-
ening, part critical. It might have been quite nice if Edmund had said,
'What a terrific job you are doing. I am so proud to be the Chairman. I
just wish you wouldn't let these do-gooders loose on aid policies!'[30]

The point was that, in public, Isaacs had already agreed in many places and fo-
rums that there were too many left-wing programmes on Channel 4 and that he
would try to find some right-wing programmes. What he did not want were bland
programmes that did not say anything. In the July issue of *Marxism Today* he had
conceded, 'I think the Channel has been perceived to be biased towards the left in
the totality of its programmes. I do think that that criticism is to some extent justified.' He added that the broadcasting institutions up to now had attempted to be fair,
objective, with varied viewpoints, proper political debate. But, despite that,

for years you got a very liberal suppression of racist opinions in this country. You equally get a suppression of the left-wing point of view on nuclear
issues or on fundamental questions of how society should be organised.
Although Channel 4 cannot be perceived as being politically biased I do
believe it is the role of broadcasting [. . .] to give some preponderance to
the voice and weight of opinion of critics in a society in order that the
power of those who control [. . .] power may be held in check.

On the charge of amateurish standards, he replied:

I think in some ways that is unfair and unjustified. Amateurish has almost exactly the wrong connotation for the work I am thinking about.
I'm thinking about letting new working-class voices through on to television without expecting them automatically to use the codes of language
and practice that are developed and smoothed and fine-honed inside
years of broadcasting institutions.

He could have added that he had built in *Right to Reply* from the word go. No
other channel had a programme that would, for example, allow trade unionists to say

they were fed up with the way their affairs were reported, despite the fact it also ran a sympathetic programme in *Union World*.

David Graham, chastened by *The Friday Alternative* experiment, put forward a new programme model that would meet Broadcasting Act requirements but still be spiky. It would do longer pieces but would have more experienced programme staffers working with guest editors such as Paul Johnson and Ken Loach, to make committed pieces. This time, Graham would make sure that the journalism was sound and that there were proper interviews, not rants. Steve Hewlett was retained as producer, with Alex Graham brought in to edit it, along with Christopher Hird and Peter Clarke, who came from the BBC. In January 1984, Channel 4 put it back in a prime slot in the schedule in its new form, with a different name, *Diverse Reports*. It ran for three years until the last programme in July 1987, an investigation of Israel's arms trade with embargoed South Africa.

David Graham, meanwhile, became a convinced free-marketeer and influential thinker about broadcasting and went on to produce an acclaimed series on the ideology of the right, called *The New Enlightenment*. He later argued that Channel 4 should sell its own advertising and compete with ITV, which put him in the same camp as Dell, who argued for this just before he stood down as Chairman in 1987.

To correct the channel from listing too far to the left, Isaacs turned to his Special Assistant John Ranelagh and gave him a duty to commission programmes from other parts of the political spectrum (i.e., the right). Yet, one of the fiercest controversies came from a seemingly safe and standard three-part history series made by TVS, the ITV contractor for southern England. *Greece: The Hidden War* was about the resistance at the end of the Second World War that led to the withdrawal of the Germans and the subsequent struggle for power. This had involved the cream of British Special Forces, charged with ensuring that the cradle of democracy did not fall to the Communists. It soon became clear that the channel had walked into a minefield. There were accusations that the completed trilogy was not balanced and that it gave undue weight and credibility to the communist partisans.

Peter Williams, the veteran documentary producer, reflected later, 'In this case we weren't trying to rewrite history, we were trying to make a series of acceptable films. But it was like witnesses to a street accident: no two eyewitness accounts matched. I really think these things mattered more in the 1980s.'[31] That observation provides a clue to the number and ferocity of all the arguments that raged around Channel 4 in its early years. People took television more seriously twenty years ago than they do today, because there was such a restricted choice. With only four channels, each one was under constant scrutiny. People got passionate, hurt and upset about television programmes to an extent that in most cases looks excessive from the viewpoint of the early twenty-first century.

Not all Channel 4's political and current-affairs programmes were inflammatory. The schedule included safer, more conventional strands, notably *A Week in Politics*, from Brook Productions, produced by Anne Lapping and David Elstein, from Granada and Thames respectively, both well experienced in current affairs. Vivian White was a correspondent, and Anthony King, Professor of Government at Essex University, provided sober analysis. An ambitious politician named Michael Portillo, then aged thirty, was, briefly, a researcher. Peter Jay became presenter in the autumn of 1983, adding gravitas and providing the channel with credibility at Westminster. This version lasted till 1986, when Vincent Hanna took over as presenter, aided by a witty, gossipy commentary from the *Guardian*'s Andrew Rawnsley.

After Broadside collapsed, Claudia Milne's company, Twenty Twenty Vision, expanded into its slot. Andy Harries, who later went on to run ITV's drama production and to produce the movie *The Queen*, was an early producer/director as the unit dropped its women-only rule. By nailing its colours to good journalism, irrespective of gender and avoiding the temptations dangled by Channel 4's experimentation, it grew into a successful company. 'I believe opinion journalism is never as strong as factual journalism', reflects its founder, Claudia Milne, echoing Steve Hewlett's view. 'I was always annoying Channel 4's commissioners. We ran in a more traditional way.'[32]

The first year's series looked at the abuse of psychiatry by the Soviet Union to detain dissidents and the abnormal cancer rates near Windscale (later Sellafield). By 1984, *Twenty Twenty* was an admired component of the channel's current-affairs output. It took risks, but it was thorough – and through Forgan it kept the commissioners informed of what it was planning. This open relationship stood the company and the channel in good stead in November 1984 when they first started to discuss with the IBA a special programme on the abuses of MI5, Britain's domestic-security service. Nobody was quite sure where, under the Official Secrets Act, the line could be drawn between national security and rightful disclosure, following the 1984 prosecution of Sarah Tisdall, a Ministry of Defence clerk who leaked documents concerning Greenham Common to the *Guardian*.

The Channel 4 programme depended on information from a former MI5 operative, Cathy Massiter, about how it used telephone-tapping surveillance against trade unionists and supporters of CND. Every word was, technically, in breach of the Official Secrets Act. By 28 January, a fine cut was available, and barrister Jonathan Caplan required some fifteen minutes to be excised. David Kemp QC then advised the IBA that transmission would be a criminal act and that the IBA, as a statutory body, should not knowingly break the law. At a meeting on 20 February, the IBA Board viewed the programme and barred transmission. Dell was alarmed, and the channel decided to return the programme to its makers. Isaacs argued that it was comparable to the Tisdall case, where secret documents leaked to the *Guardian* had been subpoenaed for her prosecution.

Claudia Milne bought the rights to the programme back from the channel for £1, then spent about £20,000 screening it to MPs and the media – already in a state of excitement over the acquittal of Clive Ponting, another civil servant, charged under the Official Secrets Act for leaking documents about the sinking of the *Belgrano* to the MP Tam Dalyell. The programme was shown at the Commons on 20 February, the day it was banned, and sparked heated debate. Within two weeks of the Westminster screening, the Attorney General announced that no prosecution would take place if the programme were broadcast. So the IBA was able to reverse its decision, and Channel 4 ran its programme, in a blaze of righteous publicity, on 8 March – after Milne had made sure that the channel reimbursed her expenses first.

The outcome was that MI5 had to re-examine its procedures and Parliament tried to make the security services more accountable, while the Government sought to make it harder for people like Massiter to speak out. As for Channel 4, it had covered itself in glory, if belatedly. '*MI5's Official Secrets* became that rare exception in current affairs . . . a programme that made a difference', wrote Isaacs.[33]

Meanwhile, the trial of Clive Ponting had led to another breakthrough for the channel. The independent producer Dennis Woolf suggested that the daily events could be transcribed and spoken, as live, by actors late each evening. The trial judge, who read about the idea in the press, ruled against it on the grounds that it might influence the jury.

But the channel took advice from an Australian lawyer, Geoffrey Robertson, who had made a name for himself on human-rights and press-freedom issues. He suggested reporting the case verbatim, but with the words spoken by reporters rather than actors. This would count as news coverage, which was allowable. Isaacs decided to go ahead on that basis and informed the IBA on the opening day of the trial that coverage would begin that night. The judge next day said that in its revised form the programme was not a threat to a fair trial, and it went out nightly till 11 February, when Ponting was acquitted.

Later, in 1988, Woolf and *Twenty Twenty* produced a dramatised version of the Government's attempt to suppress the book *Spycatcher*, by the renegade MI5 man Peter Wright. The method established then has been used many times since, both by Channel 4 and other broadcasters. It was a real innovation, of the kind that Isaacs and the other founders had in mind when the channel was launched. At last, Channel 4 was being taken seriously.

9

Calmer waters

• • • •

In May 1983, the humorist Miles Kington wrote in his column in *The Times* that Channel 4 was being replaced as a national joke by TV-am, the disastrous new breakfast channel. 'But surely you may ask, if Channel 4 is now getting praised, it must have been quite good to begin with. Why all the flak and criticism at the start? How can a national joke be so soon accepted as something quite good?' His theory was that the British have a curious habit of setting up Aunt Sallies, in order *not* to knock them down. Channel 4's fate was to be pelted with custard pies and rotten tomatoes until the next Aunt Sally came along. He predicted that it would soon become a much-loved part of the English scene.

Kington was getting a little ahead of events, but he was echoing what an optimistic Jeremy Isaacs wrote in another missive – a note to 'All at 4' – at that time:

> 'Six months young next week, going on nicely.
> New programmes this Spring.
> Viewers take time to find them.
> It is, as it was always going to be, a long, slow haul.
> But we are on the up.'[1]

The omens were better. Though the internal tensions over bias and the news would never quite blow themselves out, pragmatic changes to the programme schedule were under way, as the channel tried to reach out to more viewers by softening its image as a highbrow station overly concerned with championing oppressed minorities. It was, too, just starting to exploit its relationship with ITV, which had agreed that the pick of its programmes could be promoted regularly on the network. Used properly, this would provide millions of pounds' worth of free publicity, with access at any

Calmer waters ● ● ● ●   99

one time to around half the viewers in the land. Over Easter, ITV ran an evening of Channel 4 that attracted an audience of 19 million.

Although the channel's constantly changing schedule made it virtually impossible to memorise it and make appointments to view, it was providing something new to talk about. Programme standards were mixed, as they always would be, but hindsight suggests that they were not always as weird as the critics made out. One of the most mocked early films, *Quilts in Women's Lives*, was portrayed as a prototypical feminist manifesto but was actually rather touching. It depicted six women across America who turned to quilting as a means of comfort and self-expression. And while zero ratings were definitely not a thing of the past, on 12 May 1983 Channel 4 scored its highest audience to date for a Film on Four, *Secrets*, by Gavin Miller.

Agitprop elements were being toned down or phased out. Isaacs and his colleagues appeared to be taking the advice of the advertising industry magazine *Stills*, 'When it comes to some of the more gratuitously controversial material, it might be safer at this stage to trade provocativeness for pragmatism. Channel 4's laudable attempts at mischief should not become self-destructive; we are no longer living in the 1960s.'

The June General Election marked the last outing of the untameable Keith Allen as a comedian. He was chosen for a live election-night broadcast at 11.45 p.m. and assumed the character of an ex-miner turned security guard, watching the election results with a dog called Rinka – a reference to Jeremy Thorpe's relationship with Norman Scott, whose dog Rinka had died in suspicious circumstances. Mike Bolland, who was directing him from the Channel 4 studio, recalled, 'Just before we went on air, Justin Dukes, the Managing Director, came down and said, "I want you to know I really don't approve of this, that as far as I am concerned your neck is on the block for this".'[2]

As Dukes left, Allen pulled the earpiece out of his ear and threw it on the floor, signalling that he was not taking any instruction from the gallery. 'All we did was listen. We didn't have anything else cued up. We would just have to crash off air if necessary. As it turned out it was a really good performance. There were no complaints – probably no one was watching.'[3] But it was a relief to get to the safety of the late-night film, *Room at the Top* (1959).

Allen would write and act in many future Channel 4 dramas and films, notably *Shallow Grave* (1994) and *Trainspotting* (1996), and go on to play a villainous Sheriff of Nottingham in the BBC's revival of *Robin Hood*. But he never became one of the channel's stars, as Jonathan Ross did a few years later with *The Last Resort*.

As for the core schedule, the initially dreary *Countdown* was given the benefit of the doubt with a longer run. After some more wobbles, and the departure of its champion Cecil Korer, it started to climb into the channel's top ten programmes. In February 1984, its future was secured as a regular feature stripped across half the year, and later, under Michael Grade, it was extended through the whole year. At their monthly meetings, the channel's directors expressed acute concern over performance and audience share. All the same, the changes to the schedule in early 1983 were not crude plastic surgery, transforming it beyond recognition, as some critics had predicted. It was more a question of adjustment within the overall requirement to be different and distinctive. Several new drama purchases for the future, such as *The Far Pavilions* and *A Woman of Substance*, were safe and mainstream, while cheap American imports became more prominent.

Dukes later reflected that the changes 'were a matter of what works and what doesn't work.'[4] The trick was to persuade the feisty commissioning editors, who had been actively encouraged by Isaacs not to look at programme ratings, to give up things that did not work. But Roger Graef, the documentary producer on the Board, felt frustrated that for the first two to three years the channel's 'amazing gem-like programmes', largely went unwatched and unappreciated. 'They didn't try hard enough. It was like a secret. There was a sense that it was infra dig to sell programmes too hard. The impression was that the channel was too laid back, take us or leave us.'[5] As a consequence, many of the early programmes are now largely forgotten. Apart from *The Tube*, they had simply not been assimilated into popular everyday culture.

In a bid to reduce the number of dud programmes reaching the production stage, a new rule was introduced in early 1983 that nothing could be commissioned until it had been to the Programme Finance Committee, which included Justin Dukes and Jeremy Isaacs. Says Dukes:

> Jeremy and his commissioning editors had a slightly bad habit of saying yes to ideas when they should have said no. The result was that when programmes came in . . . well, I called it making programmes for the vaults. The acid test for how sloppy our decision-making process was came when the vaults stock rose above a certain level. I would ask what we were going to do about it. That was a discipline. It is extremely tempting for commissioning editors meeting people with strong views. They were persuadable. If they said yes, that meant we were building up assets we were not using, a gross waste of money to most sensible people. My job was to balance the regulatory requirement to make things, without finishing up with mounds of rubbish. At one point, there were sixty-five hours of documentaries we had not shown, paid for two years earlier.
>
> Jeremy Isaacs was fine if you gave him a framework to operate within. I went to dinner with him once. I said, 'You do know the vaults are full of opera, Jeremy' – this was just as he had cleared the commissioning of another opera series. The tradeoff was not to destroy flexibility and creativity.[6]

After the schedule changes and the tightening-up of the commissioning process, the 'long, slow haul' as Isaacs had described it, continued with the revamp of presentation in spring 1983. Regional and ethnic accents were out; announcers spoke scripted links in clear English, live but off camera. The rubber plant was returned to the first floor. Pam Masters easily won the argument that, since the programmes themselves were unfamiliar, Channel 4 must not drive viewers away with anything unconventional. Brian Tesler's proposals for more and better entertainment, shorter programmes running at conventional lengths and for some familiar repeats had been largely accepted. Tesler now was realistic. At the June board meeting, he said that the channel should be content for the moment with a 5 per cent share of audiences – half its ambitious original target – during the tough autumn ahead.

Throughout the year and beyond, executives cannily wooed newspaper journalists who wrote about television, conducting skilful public relations through generous hospitality. Clare Latimer, the caterer to 10 Downing Street, provided upmarket snacks at programme screenings. Commissioning editors lunched and wined and dined the channel's critics, doing wonders for the restaurant trade in Charlotte Street and nearby Soho. Isaacs also took advice from professional external publicists, Theo Cowan and Laurie Bellew, who had worked for Peter Sellers and a number of American stars in Britain.

The key public-relations objective during 1983 was to stem the hostile column inches, and in this they largely succeeded. By the time of the first anniversary party in November 1983, the hail of rotten tomatoes had largely stopped, as Kington had predicted. The rows between Isaacs and Dell were successfully hidden from the press. Sue Stoessl, Head of Marketing, said that Cowan was the wisest person she had ever met. 'However bad the headlines, Theo was there at 8 a.m., saying to Jeremy, "We're not going to respond, are we?" Jeremy listened to Theo. They were wonderful, they played an enormous part, they just loved the work, and they were dirt cheap.'[7]

Phil Redmond's biggest change was to cut out the swearing in *Brookside*. From November 1982 to July 1983, the soap's audience declined from 4.2 million to a little over 500,000, and research showed that bad language was the big turn-off. Once it was excised, the audience climbed steadily.[8] *Brookside* was renewed for another year that summer, then again and again until a three-year deal in 1985. There was no change in the gritty storylines. Dukes managed to get Redmond's production fee, a 10 per cent flat rate of the cost of the 104 episodes, cut from £360,000 a year to £290,000.

The more didactic educational programmes were moved. Instead, American imports were placed in the 5.30–6.30 p.m. zone, leading up to the news, a formula that Channel 4 would revive twenty years later with *The Simpsons*, as it constructed a new 'happy hour'. More old American comedies were bought in to join *I Love Lucy*: *The Munsters*, *Mary Tyler Moore*, *St Elsewhere* and *Bewitched*. The issue of

American programming was a sensitive one for Channel 4 from the start. But the channel's fiction budget of £20 million a year meant it could afford only one or two original dramas or mini-series a year, alongside Film on Four, even when the funds were eked out with canny finance deals.

Cheers had its first outing on Friday, 4 February 1983, attracting 1.5 million viewers, and from the start it was rarely out of the top five Channel 4 programmes. It became a cornerstone of Friday-night entertainment and was joined by another import, *Hill Street Blues*, then *Roseanne*; setting the pattern for Fridays until *Friends* and *Frasier* came along. The success of *Tom Keating on Painters* led to a repeat during 1983 and a second series, *Tom Keating on Impressionists*, in 1984, which drew 1.3 million, silencing those critics who had tut-tutted about him at first. *Years Ahead*, a series for older people presented by Robert Dougal, a grizzled former BBC presenter, was moved from 5.15 p.m. to 3.45 p.m. when afternoons were opened up in October 1984, and it lasted until 1988.

Popular educational series were promoted to Friday nights at 9.30 p.m., where *Gardeners' Calendar* doubled its audience to 2 million between 1983 and 1986. When the alternate series, *Plants for Free*, was shown, it peaked at 4.3 million, a huge audience for Channel 4. There were also classic documentaries: *Heart of the Dragon*, about the then-closed world of China, was independently produced to a high standard, and another on Vietnam came from Central Television. As Isaacs beadily observed, one was from an independent supplier, one from ITV, and both were of equally good quality. An outstanding natural-history series, *Fragile Earth*, was made by Bristol-based Partridge Films.

By December 1983, the ITV companies were pressuring Channel 4 because it had not bought enough programmes from them. They accused the commissioners of favouring independent suppliers. Isaacs noted that *A Week in Politics* was made by an independent for a lower price than ITV could offer. With 60 per cent of early commissions going to independents, ITV's decision to hang back had cost it the game. Isaacs stood by his rule that Channel 4 commissioned on merit. He was starting to prove that the pioneering publisher-broadcaster model not only worked but was also exposing the inflated cost of ITV production – a revelation that would not go unnoticed in Downing Street.

Meanwhile, programmes with consumer or lifestyle appeal were moved to mid-evening, at 8.30 p.m., including *Take Six Cooks* and *The Wine Programme* with Jancis Robinson. By 1984, Channel 4 had learned the value of timely late-night repeats, and in the run-up to Christmas there was 'another chance' to view *The Wine Programme*. From autumn 1984 onwards it used the afternoons to show classic black-and-white movies, which came bundled with the bought-in packages of American films but were generally left sitting on the shelf. They appealed to older viewers and children.

Isaacs had typically ruled that religious programmes should never be shown on

Sundays. *Priestland, Right and Wrong*, presented by Gerald Priestland, ran for two series, and Karen Armstrong, the former nun turned academic who had been a storming success on *Opinion*, made a six-part series, *The First Christian*, on the life of St Paul. An Easter 1984 series, *Jesus: The Evidence*, from John Birt's department at LWT, looked at the gospel accounts and asked if they were accurate and included a statue of Jesus being blown up in slow motion. This drew around 1,000 complaints from Christian lobbyists before it was screened, but Archbishop Ramsay said afterwards that Christians should not be so defensive and that Jesus could look after himself. Isaacs also panned the programme, not for religious reasons but for its 'vulgar and feeble' dramatic reconstructions.

On Channel 4's opening night, *The Comic Strip Presents* had sent out strong messages to the talent loosely grouped around the Comedy Store that they were wanted. Mike Bolland's accommodating manner towards them had been noted. He chose a promising live sketch show, *Who Dares Wins . . . A Week in Benidorm*, and it started in autumn 1983. Its creators were Jimmy Mulville, Rory McGrath, Andy Hamilton and Guy Jenkin, mustered by Denise O'Donoghue, the business manager and a tough negotiator. This was the group that would eventually form Hat Trick, one of Channel 4's key suppliers until 1998.

An early programme in the first series again offended Christians with a crucifixion sketch, showing Christ on the cross being offered a cigar on a stick, set to the background music of the Hamlet cigar commercials. Isaacs ruled that the item should not have been shown, and many viewers complained to *Right of Reply*, where Bolland and Hamilton defended themselves. But such lapses of taste attracted the elusive young, upmarket viewers, and *Who Dares Wins* was recommissioned that December, but with a safety net attached. It would henceforth be recorded as live on Fridays, with a senior executive present, and any excesses would be cut out on Saturday – a procedure also applied to *The Tube*, after presenter Jools Holland addressed the teatime audience as 'you groovy fuckers.'

But even those safeguards did not prevent an even more serious lapse on 23 June 1984, when the programme grievously offended Leon Brittan, the Home Secretary and the minister responsible for broadcasting. Each week, the programme had a catchline: for example, 'Martina Navratilova's Wristband' was one, at a time before she came out as a lesbian. In the sketch, 'A Camping Holiday with Leon Brittan', Jimmy Mulville interrupted Rory McGrath, who was then led out of the studio to the male lavatory, with a graffiti scrawled on the wall, 'The Cabinet Minister in the sex scandal is Le—' Not many cabinet ministers' names started with 'Le', and Isaacs immediately wrote to Brittan offering an unreserved apology.

A post-mortem was held on how it got on air. It was one thing to upset Christians, quite another to upset the Home Secretary and, potentially, Mrs Thatcher. Isaacs called Bolland in on Monday morning and gave him a dressing-down. Paul Bonner, the Director of Programmes, had not been aware of the newspaper rumours, the Board was later told. The Channel 4 lawyer, Don Christopher, had asked for the offending graffitti to be rubbed out but had left for other duties before the recording. As an extra safeguard, a Channel 4 board member, John Gau, who had run BBC current affairs before setting up as a leading independent producer, was asked to assume the role of editorial supervisor to the series, and a third series of eight programmes was commissioned at a cost of £800,000. Bolland later ordered from the same team a wacky comedy called *Chelmsford 123*, in which characters lapsed into classical Latin. It was not a roaring success, but Hat Trick itself was destined to prosper.

In January 1984, the policy of screening more accessible and popular fare bore fruit with *The Far Pavilions*, a glossy adaptation of M.M. Kaye's novel, for which Channel 4 bought rights, rather than initiating the work itself. It produced three of the channel's highest audiences and, together with *Thunderball* (1965) and a repeat of Granada's *The Jewel in the Crown* on Sunday evenings, Channel 4 won a 7-percent audience share in the first week of January, between 1 and 8 January, compared with BBC2's 11 per cent. When *The Jewel in the Crown* finished, it was replaced by *Upstairs Downstairs*, another ITV repeat, to keep hold of the viewers.

At this point, the budget for 1984/5 was fixed at £112 million, up from £101 million. Isaacs said the increase would allow a shift towards drama and entertainment, with more money for news as well. Discussions began about taking some sport from ITV: horse racing in the afternoons, some of the Olympics and, later, athletics. The expansion of hours would eventually allow live horse racing to add colour and variety to Channel 4, but the vigilant IBA stepped in to stop it running snooker in prime time, because it did not accord with the remit.

There were other bits of fine-tuning as hours expanded. *Face the Press* was moved to 1 p.m. on Sundays to follow ITV's serious current-affairs offering, *Weekend World*. *Voices*, the cultural discussion programme, was deemed too highbrow and was dropped, while plans for a simpler version were discussed. Saturday nights, with its diet of *Union World* and *Twenty Twenty* rather than entertainment, was limping along with a 3-per-cent share. *Treasure Hunt* was recommissioned for a third series.

Black on Black and *Eastern Eye*, the dedicated magazine strands for British Afro-Caribbeans and Asians edited by Trevor Phillips and Samir Shah at LWT, ran on alternate Tuesdays at 10 p.m. for two years until cancelled by the new Multicultural Commissioner Farrukh Dhondy, appointed in March 1984. Dhondy, born in Poona, was a schoolteacher turned writer, with a mischievous touch. He wanted to develop independent alternatives to LWT and to do more drama. He cancelled *No Problem!*, a successful comedy set in Harlesden, and replaced it with *Tandoori Nights*, about adventures in an Indian restaurant, and later the popular *Desmond's*, starring Norman Beaton and set in a Peckham barber's shop. He also initiated *Bandung File*, a controversial current-affairs strand presented by Tariq Ali and Darcus Howe.

Channel 4's first real content debate, which was to set a marker for how far television could go in showing harsh and disturbing X-rated films in a highly regulated environment, was over *Scum* (1979), which it screened in June 1983 at the late hour of 11.30 p.m. It portrayed the brutality of life in a borstal, with the moral, 'Treat people like scum and they will behave like scum'. The BBC originally made it as a television drama but decided not to show it. The rights were sold, and it was remade as a film, receiving an X certificate.

Isaacs bought it but decreed two excisions before broadcast: a homosexual rape and a lingering shot of blood seeping through a sheet after a suicide.

The Director General of the IBA, John Whitney, who happened to be a prison visitor, went against the advice of his officers and decreed that Channel 4 could show it. Two million watched. Mary Whitehouse charged the IBA with dereliction of duty but lost the substance of the case in a famous court decision in May 1984. This emboldened Channel 4 to run two provocative films by Derek Jarman, this time at midnight. They were *Sebastiane* (1976), a modern interpretation of the life of an early Christian martyr who had been a homosexual icon for centuries, and *Jubilee* (1977), depicting the rise of punk rock. This provoked the Conservative MP Winston Churchill to introduce a private member's bill seeking to extend the Obscene Publications Act to broadcasting. The Bill fell, but Channel 4 responded by introducing the 'special discretion required' symbol (a red triangle) on material that might offend viewers. It was withdrawn in 1987 when it was realised it was inciting viewers, including prurient teenagers, to watch sexually explicit material – the opposite of the intended effect.

In the area of sex and extreme language, as in opinionated news and current affairs, Isaacs was struggling to establish a broader right of freedom of expression on television than had hitherto existed. But, in 1984, he was unable to break down the IBA's obduracy over *Life of Brian* (1979), the Monty Python film about Christ which it had bought as part of a package. He was repeatedly prevented from screening it on the grounds of blasphemy, a source of friction until the ruling was relaxed in 1991.

Throughout 1984, the channel's performance and morale were on an upward curve. By June, internal research showed that attitudes towards it were changing and that younger people appreciated it most – as they have continued to do throughout its history. It was also learning to woo audiences with eye-catching titles: a series ordered as *Gay Profiles* became *Eat Your Heart Out*. The advertising dispute finally ended, meaning that proper commercials could flow into the breaks, and then Laurence Olivier won an Emmy for his performance in Channel 4's *King Lear* (1983). In July, Forgan was promoted to Assistant Controller of Programmes, and in September, exactly a year after his fraught confrontation with Dell over opinionated current affairs, Isaacs was offered a further three-year contract until the end of 1988. The following year, when Isaacs was sounded out by the IBA about whether to extend Edmund Dell's chairmanship to June 1987, he was supportive. Peace – or at least a truce – had broken out.

The Board decided that it could only afford one big classical work a year, because they were so expensive. *Nicholas Nickleby* had run during the 1982 opening weeks, followed by Aeschylus' *The Oresteia*, mounted by the National Theatre, which over-ran the budget. It was performed by masked actors – not a method best suited to television – and Cecil Korer criticised it at a programme-review meeting for being elitist and unwatchable: the other commissioners were aghast at his philistine views. It was certainly something no one but Channel 4 would have attempted.

Michael Kustow, the Commissioner for Arts, behaved as an open-handed patron of the arts rather than a conventional television executive. His next ambitious project was *The Greeks*, nine plays and an hour-long documentary for which Channel 4 allocated £1 million towards a £1.5 million budget. Then Peter Brook filmed *The Tragedy of Carmen* in Paris, and in 1987 the channel contributed towards an ambitious version of the *Mahabharata*. Kustow also arranged a collaboration between Peter Greenaway and the artist Tom Phillips on a television Dante: eight episodes of the *Inferno* were completed. Classical ballets were filmed for Dance on Four, and Isaacs took personal charge of his pet area, Opera on Four. Regular opera screenings, latterly from Glyndebourne, were costing £1 million each by the time they were cancelled in 1998.

The channel also felt confident enough to have another go at science programmes after the early disaster of *Crucible*. *Equinox*, which had a wider engineering brief, was launched in 1986 and lasted until 1999, defining new territory from the start with programmes on Formula 1 racing engines, the design of Sir Clive Sinclair's short-lived electric vehicle and deep drilling for oil under the North Sea. There was also a Sunday *The Business Programme*, later expanded from a weekly to daily broadcast, to address the accusation that the channel did not tackle financial matters.

On 2 November 1984, Isaacs wrote, 'We start the third year on the air admired, applauded, and in some danger of being too pleased with ourselves. But it is time to celebrate and congratulate each of you on what you have contributed to this happy result. Stick to it and we'll do better yet.'[9] It had been a hard slog, and at an away weekend in December 1984, Brian Tesler thought he detected signs of burnout in the commissioning team. 'They did not display a crispness of thought or originality of attitude', he observed, and Isaacs replied bluntly, 'They are tired.'[10] The channel was still being deluged with programme proposals, and there was no system to control the amount of work piling up on desks. It was a product of all that pent-up creative energy in the independent sector, but it was becoming apparent that this could not all be focused on one small channel.

The year 1985 began on a notable high. For the first time, Channel 4 achieved its stated aim of a 10-per-cent share of the audience, and within the original target of three years. Congratulations were shared all round. The breakthrough came by virtue of *A Woman of Substance*, an adaptation of a Barbara Taylor Bradford rags-to-riches story about a woman who rose from kitchen maid to global tycoon. Jenny Seagrove played the maid, and Deborah Kerr was also featured. The three episodes ran on successive weekday nights, while ITV held back from competitive scheduling. It was the turning point in the drive to make it a commercially viable channel, as well as meeting the minority remit; but it was a stunt, not typical fare, and, of course, *A Woman of Substance* would have done even better on ITV. It was a 'means to an end' programme for Isaacs, a way to get the figures up and to woo audiences into pressing the 4 button. (He repeated the trick in May 1987 with the sequel, *Hold the Dream*, a two-parter with the same two female stars.)

The IBA exercised a degree of discretion over the annual subscription Channel 4 and S4C were handed by ITV, within the agreed parameters of 14 and 18 per cent of total advertising revenue. It decided to fix the sum at 16 per cent, raising it a year later to 17 per cent. This guaranteed revenue of £129.1 million for 1985/6. For the four weeks in January, the channel went on to deliver a 9.2-per-cent audience share, but the realistic Isaacs knew that this would not be maintained. 'The figures will go down before they go up again. And, in any event, the important thing is to continue to display the diversity of programming that will ensure Channel 4 is not only popular, but distinctively so', he wrote.[11]

All the same, he popped up looking relaxed and happy as a guest on David Frost's TV-am Sunday breakfast programme on 2 February 1985. The two men agreed that while their respective channels had been through stormy seas, they had survived and no longer played the role of Aunt Sallies. Isaacs introduced a show reel illustrating the eclectic mix: *The Comic Strip, Cheers, Fragile Earth, Eleventh Hour, The Oresteia, A Woman of Substance, The Wine Programme, The Far Pavilions, The Snowman, The Beggar's Opera, Treasure Hunt, The Heart of the Dragon, The Tube* and *The Irish RM*. He told Frost that Channel 4 had cheered up in tone a bit since launch and had enabled people to express opinions on television and to have a jolly good argument.

'We had a great walloping when we started', he said, recalling talk of him being sacked as absolute nonsense, like the story of ITV chiefs meeting in secret conclave to oust him. 'We had a clear brief, a free hand on precisely where we spent our money. We had eighteen months' money guaranteed up front, and we never had the added anxiety that the bankers would pull the rug. We have got there . . . I can look ITV in the eye. We can pay our way.'

It was a remark the politicians took note of.

● ● ● ●

In August 1985, the Channel 4 film *My Beautiful Laundrette* went to the Edinburgh Film Festival for the usual screening. It had not been made for cinematic release, but people were captivated by Hanif Kureishi's story of a love affair between a gay Asian and white skinhead boy, who kiss passionately in the back room of the laundrette, and of a Pakistani middle-class family prospering under Thatcher. It was funny, inventive and fresh, and the screening caused a huge stir. Next morning, the *Guardian*'s film critic, Derek Malcolm, wrote a rave review. The film flew from Edinburgh to film festivals around the world and into the cinemas. This had not been planned, and Channel 4, taken by surprise, failed to exploit the success commercially, receiving only 4 per cent of the cinema revenues after an American company bought the rights.

This was the channel's first taste of real popular and international success with its Film on Four venture, and it was totally unexpected. In 1985, the notion of a budget television film making money was inconceivable. *My Beautiful Laundrette* was shot in Battersea in six weeks on 16-millimetre tape rather than 35-millimetre film and had cost just £650,000. It was made by Working Title, a small company founded the year before by Tim Bevan and Sarah Radclyffe. The director, Stephen Frears, had directed the channel's opening film, *Walter*, and was so disenchanted with the pretence of making low-budget films for the cinema that he stipulated it was not to have a cinematic release. *My Beautiful Laundrette*, with its low expectations and flaunting its permissive values, took £5 million in America alone.

The success made a huge impact on Channel 4's image and validated its decision to back low-budget films even though, throughout the 1980s, it kept the red Film on Four logo very small in the end credits for fear of putting off cinemagoers. From the start, Isaacs had decided to break away from the mundane idea of drama – that was why he named the relevant department 'Fiction'. Its output comprised the one soap, *Brookside*, and single films for Film on Four. Some went on theatrical or cinema release first; others straight to television. In the beginning, nobody was much interested in drama series, though one that found success was *Porterhouse Blues*, adapted from Tom Sharpe's satirical novel about life in a Cambridge college.

As the Head of the department, he recruited David Rose, who had run the BBC's English regional drama strand from the Pebble Mill production centre in Birmingham. There, his output had included *Second City Firsts*, half-hour plays by new writers, and regular *Plays for Today*, many of them in the Ken Loach spirit. Directors and writers such as Alan Bleasdale, David Hare, Stephen Frears and Mike Leigh met and mixed in the Pebble Mill bar. They liked working for Rose, who enjoyed a justified reputation as a wizard in the cutting room, where films are put together. Bearded, with watery eyes and usually dressed in a tweed jacket, at first encounter he appeared vague and tongue-tied, with no small talk. Newcomers from outside the charmed circle found him hard to fathom. But his tweediness disguised a fine judgement and the ability to take quick decisions and back them, as happened with *My Beautiful Laundrette*. He was unflappable, as he needed to be when films occasionally collapsed into a chaos of overspending. Even faced with disaster he did not turn on people or panic, because he was near the end of his career and had lived through the anarchic early days of television when drama was performed live.

Sir Richard Attenborough, whose film *Gandhi* had just won an Oscar, played a key role in defining the film policy. 'Dickie attached the same importance to film that David Rose and I did', said Isaacs. 'He was unwavering in his support. We had no studios, we had no brick walls, so we wanted to do as much as possible on location. That meant in those days on film, though a bit later it meant tape.'[12] Channel 4 was fortuitously able to participate in a change in film financing introduced by the Government, securing a place on the newly created British Screen Finance Limited for an input of £300,000 a year. It meant improved access to co-financing, allowing the average total cost of a Film on Four to rise to around £1 million. As a result, the channel could put some money into between fourteen and twenty proposals a year.

At the BBC, the concept of going back to film was watched initially with disdain, but this evaporated as some of its brightest talent migrated to Channel 4. *My Beautiful Laundrette* was to be a prototype for films that portrayed aspects of working-class Britain. Frears went on to make *Sammy and Rosie Get Laid* (1987), and Working Title made *Wish You Were Here* (1987), with Emily Lloyd as a waitress with aspirations. Also making waves alongside *My Beautiful Laundrette* were *Letter to Brezhnev* (1985), about the limitations of women's lives in Liverpool, and *Mona Lisa* (1986), Neil Jordan's film about the sex trade in Soho, starring Bob Hoskins. Another Film on Four, *She'll Be Wearing Pink Pyjamas* (1984), starring Julie Walters, attracted a television audience of over 7 million.

Frears was one of a number of rising British stars eventually lured into making films in Hollywood, and by the end of the 1980s this exodus had weakened Film on Four. But the mix of funding attracted European film producers and directors – including Andrei Tarkovsky and Wim Wenders – to the channel. This gave it international standing and a broader horizon that distinguished it from more parochial British broadcasters. It also had close ties with the BFI[13] and became a co-production partner in a number of successful BFI productions, including *The Draughtsman's Contract* (1982), *The Belly of an Architect* (1987), *Drowning by Numbers* (1988), *Distant Voices, Still Lives* (1988) and (an Isaacs favourite) *Comrades* (1986), about the Tolpuddle martyrs.

The success of Film on Four had its downside, though, as far as the channel's schedule was concerned. For, if the co-producers insisted that the films should first be shown in cinemas, they were prone to holdbacks, the gap between cinema release and eventual screening on mainstream television. There were periods when, even though several films had been completed and had won their cinematic spurs,

Channel 4 had nothing to show. This would make Isaacs' successor, Michael Grade, adopt a far more sceptical approach to film at first and call up the big names of television drama for assistance.

10

Likely lads flourish as Isaacs leaves

• • • •

On Friday mornings during 1985, two likely lads in their twenties would head for Channel 4, regular as clockwork. They were a smartly suited Jonathan Ross and a less flamboyant but equally determined Alan Marke. Ross, soon after graduating from the London School of Economics, had moved into the world of freelance television production, following the example of his older brother Paul. He worked as one of a shifting band of researchers on several early Channel 4 programmes including a music and dance show, *Soul Train*. Ross had to find the dancers; Marke booked the bands.

When Marke was sent to Los Angeles to choose clips for *Soul Train*, he saw David Letterman and brought some tapes back to London to show Ross. *Late Night with David Letterman* had been a minority cult hit in America for some time but was on the way to becoming a mainstream institution. Its format followed that of the classic American talk show perfected by Johnny Carson on NBC's *Tonight*, where the host, supported by a house band, is the real star, and the celebrity guests just the icing on the cake. Letterman, though, was different from Carson: spikier, less cosy, more radical, less deferential to his guests.

Ross and Marke, by now close friends, wanted to make a British version of *Late Night with David Letterman*. Andy Harries, a more experienced older freelance director, was dragged along to discuss the proposal with Channel 4's Entertainment Commissioner, Mike Bolland. Harries admired Ross's quirky sense of humour, but he could see that it was not going to be easy to sell the idea. Ross and Marke were complete unknowns, only distinguished by a burning ambition to launch the best late-night chat and music show the country had ever seen. But you needed contacts to make the bookings that would make it work.

At this point, the most exciting of the new wave of anarchic entertainment shows on the channel was the brilliant but blokeish *Saturday Night Live* (later *Friday Night*

Live), a mix of stand-up comedy and music made by LWT. Introduced by a fast-paced monologue from Ben Elton, it was bringing a stream of new performers to the screen, most notably Harry Enfield, whose character Loadsamoney became a national catchphrase, a symbol of the excesses of the high tide of Thatcherism. Stephen Fry, Hugh Laurie, Rik Mayall and Adrian Edmondson all appeared on the ninety-minute show, but it took three series before Isaacs was satisfied with this potentially volatile mix.

Channel 4 was hungry for fresh entertainment, so Ross and Marke were pushing at a half-open door. But they faced an even bigger problem than simply being unknown: who would be their David Letterman? They certainly did not want someone with the suave confidence of a Terry Wogan or a Michael Aspel. At first they thought of Jeremy Hardy, a stand-up performer they admired, but he rebuffed their approaches. In any case, Bolland, who believed the concept was worth a gamble, had been amused by Ross's unforced wit during their discussions, and, as the debate progressed, a consensus emerged that he should be the one to have a go. Although he had a slight speech impediment, a problem pronouncing his Rs, he had already made one or two brief appearances on screen, and he had charm, even maybe charisma.

Ross and Marke set up a company, Channel X, and made a pilot show, so bad that it was never transmitted. But there was enough potential to work on. 'Part of it was that Jonathan Ross had little experience of television, while Letterman had done stand-up', says Marke. 'But he would work really hard, try and read up before interviews. Jonathan had a lot of guts and the charisma to pull it off.'[1] To kickstart the show, the channel called in Colin Callender, a drama producer who had televised *Nicholas Nickleby* for them and who had made the film, *The Belly of an Architect*, and who would go on to become a senior figure at the US network Home Box Office (HBO) in the USA. His role was to provide interviewees from his film-industry connections.

The first *The Last Resort*, on Friday, 16 January 1987, set a high standard, with a guest appearance by Donald Sutherland. It also featured the actress Amanda Burton and a one-legged acrobat act, The Loonies. Ross was clearly nervous and slightly vulnerable, but the show wears its age well, remaining fresh and energetic. It set the format: a big celebrity, a topical guest, a freak-show element and a band. One of the later freaks was the Regurgitator, a performer who swallowed anything from goldfish to string, which he 'pulled' out of his stomach. Ross closed his eyes in disgust, the audience groaned, but the ratings went up. Bad television made good television; but it was never easy. Ross, as well as conquering his nerves, had to work away between shows cold-calling celebrities, and at first was often turned down.

He was not a scruffy youth presenter. He dressed nattily and kept his language and questioning decent, if sometimes only just. In an interview with Carrie Fisher, who had been filming with Harrison Ford, he asked about Ford's snogging technique – 'Is he rough, does he use his tongue?' – but that was as risqué as it got. And he was game, singing 'It's Not Unusual' alongside Tom Jones with undisguised pleasure. In a circus act, he agreed to become the target and have knives thrown around him. Said Marke, 'It was a lot more loose and silly than *The Letterman Show*.'[2]

There was an immediate buzz about *The Last Resort*, and by March, the Channel 4 Board, recommissioning a further series, patted themselves on the back for finding a very good presenter. It was brought forward to 10.30 p.m., and by the summer of 1987, Ross was on the cover of *Radio Times*. The show in this form ran for two years. It was a classic example of Channel 4's willingness to take risks by backing a novice presenter with hardly any previous experience. It is hard to imagine any other mainstream channel doing that, then or now.

Unlike the brilliant but short-lived appearances by Keith Allen, who proved too anarchic for the channel to handle at launch, Ross was a bona-fide Channel 4 star, springing fully formed from the ranks of runners and researchers. By the second series in 1988, *The Last Resort* was watched by 2.8 million people. He and Marke had devised a classic programme which Ross made his own. (The revived version on BBC1, *Friday Night with Jonathan Ross*, is basically the same show, twenty years later.) Guests soon began to say 'Yes' to his invitations. They included Steve Martin, Dawn French, George Harrison, Sean Connery, Nigel Benn, Jean-Paul Gaultier, Tracey Ullman and Donny Osmond, who was teased with a spoof Donny's pipe-and-slipper set. Ross arm-wrestled with Jerry Hall (he lost) and welcomed David Frost to The Last Resort Village Fête.

● ● ● ●

For now, Ross could do no wrong, but, as he triumphed, *The Tube* ground to a halt without anyone seeming to protest. The *coup de grâce* came after several of the Tyne Tees team who made the programme were involved in a shambolic live New Year show at the end of 1986 in which everything that could go wrong did go wrong. The scripts were late, and during the live broadcast the two-way feedback links from the floor to the control room went down. Ruby Wax, the presenter, became increasingly desperate and loose with her language because she had no direction, and no one could hear what was happening on the set anyway.

The *Who Dares Wins* team were there, except Jimmy Mulville. One of them, singing a song about how to recognise a drunk, picked out from the studio audience the MP Leon Brittan, who had been the satirical butt of a previous ill-judged broadcast. Brittan, who could not hear the words, was smiling away awkwardly, but Sir Geoffrey Howe, the Foreign Secretary, sitting at home, switched on and could not believe what he was watching. He protested to the IBA, while the MP, still unaware that he had been made to look foolish, joined the VIP coach after the show and went on with Mike Bolland to a nightclub.

'I remember us all sitting with double hangovers the next morning at the airport – it was a dismal day', said Bolland.[3] At that stage, all he knew was that it had been a desperately scrappy show, right down to the bagpipe-playing dwarf. He was on his way to Edinburgh to join Isaacs for a meeting with independent producers. When they arrived, Isaacs received a call and asked Bolland to take a walk. 'He told me all the staff involved at Tyne Tees had been summarily dismissed, and they were calling for me to get the sack.'[4] The two Tyne Tees executives involved faced the sack for gross misconduct, though Isaacs told the Board that gross incompetence would have been a better description. From that point, Channel 4 decided it would not commission another series of *The Tube*.

So, the once exuberant Friday-night treat for a generation of students ended its run in April 1987, after five years and 200 hours, with a final programme featuring The Cure and Millie Jackson. It had proved that bands would fly to Newcastle and perform live, forcing British Airways to reschedule the times of its flights so they could get back late on Friday. Malcolm Gerrie, the Executive Producer, was philosophical: after all, the other early Channel 4 pop series had simply disappeared without trace. 'I never thought for one minute *The Tube* would have run this long', he said.[5] It was revived by the channel in 2006, but as a digital radio show.

The end of *The Tube* did not mean that Channel 4 had abandoned youth. It was immediately succeeded, on 3 May, by the snazzy *Network 7*, which gave birth to a new tabloid form of 'yoof' television. It never had a huge audience, settling down at around 1 million, but it spun off ideas, talent and embryonic formats for reality shows in five-minute gobbets, which led to copycat strands on the BBC and eventually helped shape a generation of reality programmes such as *Survivor* and *Wife Swap*.

During 1986, LWT's Janet Street-Porter and Jane Hewland, who ran its factual output, went to pitch an idea to Channel 4's new Commissioning Editor for Youth, the 'hipper than thou' John Cummins. They had prepared a ten-minute sample, but going over in the taxi to Odins, the West End restaurant, Hewland told Street-Porter that was no use: it had to be big. Street-Porter agreed. She said they should aim for a two-hour slot at lunchtime on Sundays, when those who had been out drinking on Saturday night started to wake up.

'We just got out of the taxi, into the restaurant, and winged it. She [Street-Porter] is a damned good saleswoman', Hewland recalled.[6] Street-Porter thought of the title there and then and projected the idea of *Network 7* as a channel within a channel, something young people would identify with. They won an order for twenty-two episodes. What Channel 4 did not know was how young and inexperienced many of the team making it would be, or how sketchy the concept was.

For Hewland, who had risen through the cerebral *Weekend World* as a protégée of John Birt, it was an escape. 'It was my rebellion against God knows how many years of *Weekend World*.'[7] In order to avoid possible obstruction from the broadcasting unions, LWT created a hybrid company, Sunday Productions, with a music producer, Keith MacMillan, who went on to make *The Chart Show*. It was located at the vast underused Limehouse studios, where the Canary Wharf tower blocks now stand. The team – including Simon Shaps, later the Network Director of ITV – worked from offices in painted caravans winched onto the roof. They had single-man camera crews, with the cameras sometimes mounted on shopping trolleys.

The two hours devoured material in a mix of journalism, factual items, gossip, interviews, bands and cartoons. It included a two-minute spoof soap opera, *Flesh and Blood*, themed loosely on *Dallas* and *Dynasty*, starring Diana Quick and a six-foot Australian, Virginia Hey. It borrowed from music videos to make factual items crack along, while nuggets of information of *Reader's Digest* length were moved across the bottom of the screen in captions, so fast that ageing television critics could not keep up. Hewland, Chairman of the new company, was sleepless for four nights before making the pilot, because she did not know how to do it. 'I rang the Royal Free Hospital, and an Irish nurse said, "Do you have any whisky in your house? Pour yourself a large glass and go to sleep."'[8]

Channel 4 thought they were going to get a programme led by presenters, and Street-Porter and Hewland had sat in the front row of *The Last Resort*, hoping to recruit Jonathan Ross. But he was successful enough with *The Last Resort* and had no need to risk taking on this very different programme. Instead, Hewland decided that there would be no script or single presenter and that the researchers would speak to camera when necessary. Sebastian Scott, Charlie Parsons and Magenta Devine, who did a celebrity gossip slot, were all thoroughly briefed, they knew their stories, but they had to wing it to camera, with very few autocues. The pilot took six weeks to prepare, and nobody knew, as they made it, whether it worked or not. It did, but then there was only two weeks before *Network 7* took to the air. Its debut attracted a huge amount of attention from the press, in particular an item on cloned credit cards – or, as the critics saw it, how to rob a bank with a cash card. The second show featured the London Marathon, for the first time on television.

The programme marked a breakthrough for Charlie Parsons, a researcher who had been going nowhere at LWT despite an English degree from Oxford and a training in newspaper journalism that had instilled in him the mindset of a tabloid journalist. He edited the second series of *Network 7*. In one programme, themed on Liverpool, the show hijacked a tourist bus and set up life swaps, including a 19-year-old from Chelsea, with a three-bedroom flat and two cars, who exchanged with a 19-year-old from one of Liverpool's toughest estates. In another first, twenty gay couples were 'married' in a mass ceremony and invited to a wedding breakfast. 'Gay Marriage on Channel 4 Sparks Viewers' Protest', reported the easily shockable *Daily Mail*. Parsons said,

Jane, Janet and Keith all had different skills, but none of them was interested in detail, journalistic detail. I was one of those people who was interested. Janet, when she was editor, wasn't there every single day – often she was off walking in Yorkshire. You'd pick out of her mental address book: she'd say that all her friends were doing Ecstasy, so we did the first story on it. Or she would have met this really interesting bloke at a party – that was Pete Waterman, a record producer, not yet famous. Really, Janet's skill is spotting a story.[9]

Even at twenty-nine, Parsons was much more experienced than most of the people working on the programme. It was his chance to shape a team and run two hours of live television – his big break. In the second series, he put four celebrities on a desert island off Sri Lanka and followed their progress for four weeks. This was the forerunner of *Survivor* on ITV – produced by Planet 24, the company he co-founded to make such ground-breaking programmes as *The Word* and *The Big Breakfast*.

But *Network 7* made Channel 4 executives nervous, and they became positively alarmed when they discovered that its producers had employed a security consultant to bug their own boardroom, where the Programme Review Committee was meeting to discuss the programme's shortcomings. The motive was not to eavesdrop but to illustrate an item in that Sunday's edition on how easy it was to buy surveillance devices. The consultant placed two bugs in the room, one taped under the table and one in a socket. On the following Monday, Hewland sent an apology to Liz Forgan, the Programme Director, attached to a bottle of champagne. 'The idea of bugging the programme review was, I'm afraid, all mine', she wrote. 'No doubt it will call down on my head renewed claims that I am the most irresponsible television executive in Britain – and not fit to have charge of a major current affairs strand.'[10]

John Cummins, the Commissioning Editor, moved on; but after *Network 7*'s first series won a special BAFTA award for originality, Hewland prepared proposals for a third series. Forgan had warned her that the programme had surprisingly few supporters in Charlotte Street, and Stephen Garrett, who had replaced Cummins, was not among them. When interviewed for the job, he had said that he would cancel *Network 7*, which consumed 60 per cent of the annual youth budget of £6 million. Hewland was unaware of this when she and Keith MacMillan, armed with their BAFTA award, went to see Garrett. When he told her his intention, she said nothing but walked straight out of the room. Had she stayed, she would have learned that Garrett had wanted to keep one segment of the programme, 'True or False'.[11]

The abrupt cancellation of *Network 7* was widely seen in the industry as a mistake. Greg Dyke, then Managing Director of LWT (and Hewland's boss) was one of the three ITV directors of the channel at the time. He registered his protest at a July board meeting, but it was brushed aside. Only after the programme was gone was it realised how significant it had been in pioneering a new style of reportage, reflected later in such BBC series as *Reportage* and *Rough Guides*. The fact that Garrett was effectively able to wield the axe single-handed illustrates the autonomy enjoyed by commissioning editors at Channel 4, and in this case the channel's structure worked against its interests. There was a built-in tendency for new commissioners to kill off shows initiated by their predecessors.

To replace *Network 7*, Garrett championed a new talent and arts programme for young people called *Club X*, but it did not work. 'I hated him for a long time', said Hewland, after the team dispersed.[12] Some of them regrouped to make *The Word* and *The Big Breakfast*. Garrett would soon be off to found the independent Kudos and eventually to produce a string of successful BBC1 dramas, from *Spooks* to *Life on Mars*. Ironically, these were developed for Channel 4 but the commissioners turned them down.

A third innovation from the late Isaacs period was *After Dark*, a live Saturday-night-to-Sunday-morning discussion programme that had no fixed ending or resident chairman. As with *The Last Resort*, it was inspired by an existing programme from an overseas broadcaster – *Club 2* from Austria's ORF – where a loquacious therapist and anarchist, asked to fill in with a chat show, became a permanent fixture. The British producer, Sebastian Cody, revamped the format to resemble after-dinner conversation. There were hidden cameras and discreet lighting, but no audience. In some ways it harked back to a more sober precursor, the BBC's *Brains Trust*, and it conformed to Isaacs' belief in unmediated intelligent debate.

But there was one way in which it was different, and it turned out to be the cause of its eventual demise. Because conversation, alcohol and a volatile guest list can be a combustible mix, it is not a formula much seen on television then or since. Although there was no alcohol in the green room, there was plenty on the set. In one programme, Professor A.J. Ayer, the philosopher, drank two bottles of scotch during transmission, with no visible or audible effect. Soon after it began, on 1 May 1987, it became a cult programme watched by insomniac opinion-formers and journalists, even if they fell asleep before the end. It was a brave, risky venture – and expensive for late night, requiring research and an ever-vigilant lawyer. As it happened, though, there was very little legal action, partly because inaccuracies could be corrected while the show went out.

The first programme, *Secrets*, set out the stall. Anthony Wilson was in the chair, and the guests were Clive Ponting, Colin Wallace, Peter Hain and T.E. Utley, the uncompromisingly right-wing *Daily Telegraph* writer. From the start, people watched to see if anyone would behave badly, or even walk out. In Programme 6, on 12 June, they were rewarded when Teresa Gorman, Conservative MP for Billericay, stormed off the set, claiming she had been misled about the nature of the programme. But the most notorious incident came in 1991, not long before *After Dark* went dark for good. The exhibitionist actor Oliver Reed was clearly drunk before the show started. 'How many male chauvinist pigs does it take to change a light bulb?' he asked his fellow guests, then slurred the reply: 'None, let the bitch cook in the dark.' He went on to plant a sloppy kiss on the horrified face of the feminist Kate Millett, then announced 'I'm off to have a slash' – and fell over the sofa. At that point, the show was taken off air and replaced by a film about Welsh coal mining.

When Reed died in 1999, the flamboyant television critic Victor Lewis-Smith revealed that he was the cause of the screen going blank. He wrote that when he saw that Reed was out of control he phoned Channel 4 pretending to be Michael Grade's assistant and ordering that the transmission be halted.[13] Sebastian Cody saw it unfold before his eyes: 'The Commissioner, Michael Attwell rushed into the control room, saying the IBA said we had got to stop the programme. I said it was a hoax. We called Liz Forgan, and service was resumed twenty minutes later.'[14] Channel 4's Deputy Programme Director, John Willis, wrote an internal memo: 'Oliver Reed got drunk and a hoaxer caused the programme briefly to be taken off air. I view the latter with a great deal more seriousness than the former. Steps have been taken to tighten procedures and make sure the integrity of the signal is safeguarded. The shutdown produced the biggest ever response to date, 1,000 calls from an audience estimated at just 300,000. Remarkable.'[15]

● ● ● ●

It was clear by 1987, Channel 4's fifth year on air, that it was becoming a success story by almost all measures. But instead of Jeremy Isaacs and his workforce being able to pause and savour the moment, they were operating in a highly politicised environment that would bring the Isaacs era to what his admirers thought was a premature end. For the first time, the 1987 annual report published the invoices ITV companies had received for the channel's advertising. They were worth £155.2 million, an increase of 38 per cent on the previous year and £19 million more than the subscription it was being handed by ITV. In other words, the channel could probably stand on its own two feet, and in Westminster the feeling was growing that perhaps it should.

This perception was a by-product of an overarching theme of the Thatcher years, her hostility towards the BBC, expressed in a series of ferocious attacks by her and by some of her ministers. Notable flashpoints were the reporting of the Falklands War in 1982, coverage of Northern Ireland, and what the Government alleged was biased reporting by Kate Adie of the American bombing of civilians in Libya. In 1985, the Government had set up a committee under Professor Alan Peacock, a market-oriented economist, to look at the Corporation's future funding and, in particular, to explore the option of replacing the licence fee with revenue from advertising.

The BBC's critics used the example of Channel 4 to advance their argument. Staffed by just 267 people, compared with the BBC's 23,000, it was starting to sparkle as hundreds of small businesses – independent programme producers – demonstrated that they could make public-service programming more cheaply than the BBC and ITV. Despite Mrs Thatcher's dislike of the sexually frank material that often popped up on the channel, and her admiration for the clean-up-television campaigner Mary Whitehouse, she saw Channel 4 as a shining example of private enterprise in action.

To her disappointment, when the Peacock Committee reported in July 1986, it rejected advertising and said that the BBC should have a ten-year index-linked licence fee. But in an unforeseen outcome it made a recommendation that would have a greater impact on the two commercial channels than the BBC. It proposed that ITV franchises should be awarded in future by competitive tender, as a method of controlling their costs. It proposed a socket fitted to television sets to allow for pay-TV and multichannel broadcasting. It suggested a 40 per cent quota for independent production at the BBC and ITV – beaten down to 25 per cent before it was written into law.

Buried at Number 14 in Peacock's list of proposals was the idea that Channel 4 should be given the option of selling its own advertising time rather than being funded by a subscription from ITV. The reason given was that its costs now equalled (at least) its revenue from advertising. A further implication was that this would result in a change in ownership. Channel 4 would no longer be a subsidiary of the IBA, although it would continue offering a complementary programme schedule to ITV rather than competing head-on. Though the committee did not specifically recommend private ownership, the proposal was to start a debate that raged for the next three years.

The Peacock plan ran counter to the evidence put in by the channel that the present system worked and that competition for funds would damage programmes. Sue Stoessl, Head of Marketing, was a dedicated advocate of this point of view and stood resolute in the ensuing debate. 'If you get two people selling advertising in competition, the money will be split, and in the end there will not be enough to make programmes.'[16] She remained convinced that subsequent events bore her out; but there was also a suggestion, twice denied within the Channel 4 Board, that some members had raised separation privately with Peacock.

Whatever the truth of that, the report had certainly put the cat among the pigeons on the Board. ITV, the paymasters, were represented there by three directors – Sir Brian Bailey, James Gatward and Sir Paul Fox – joined by Peter Rogers, Finance Director of the IBA. They all backed the status quo: the IBA could not see why a successful formula should be altered. By contrast, the three most powerful Channel 4 figures – Edmund Dell, Jeremy Isaacs and Justin Dukes – agreed that the option of separation should be explored. According to the minutes, 'Jeremy Isaacs agreed with the Chairman. He noted change might well be thrust upon the channel.'[17] It was a rare instance of the minutes recording agreement between the two men, rather than the usual discord.

The July board meeting duly commissioned independent research from Professor Alan Budd of the London Business School. Dell, who had faced down the IBA previously by submitting independent evidence to Peacock, went so far as to say, 'The structure of funding was crucial to establishing and setting up Channel 4. Now, five years on, the matter has not been, and must be, fully researched.'[18] Isaacs was pragmatic. Although the cable revolution had not materialised as expected, satellite television was being planned. ITV's advertising income had passed £1 billion in 1986 and was growing strongly. The monopoly would be broken in three or four years, so change would come.

The unspoken view at board level was that ITV was badly run, with inflationary production costs impossible to defend. This had a knock-on effect on the BBC's programme costs, and there was every sign that the Government was in a mood to tackle the issue.

Budd's report was ready for the November board meeting. It concluded that a self-financing Channel 4 would be viable if it earned a 14.5-per-cent share of advertising and if its costs were pegged not to rise more than 3 per cent a year. In effect, the channel was being tempted to give up the cosy security of a guaranteed income from ITV, of never having to worry about money, in favour of paying its own way and probably doing better. The Board was split and the atmosphere tense. Sir Richard Attenborough might have provided a calming influence, but he was busy making *Cry Freedom* and could not attend.

Dell, at his most stubborn, said that although the 1981 Broadcasting Act had worked well, the channel should now move towards independence and separation, although 'he did not expect the Board to unanimously agree.'[19] He presented a draft statement – never in fact issued – saying, 'If Parliament were to decide that Channel 4, with its present remit and programme policy should, in the future, independently compete for its own funds, the Board is satisfied that the channel could do so, and remain viable.'[20] He said they should accept the option of self-financing and that competition was desirable, except where detrimental to the programmes. With the remit safeguarded by legislation, the channel should now move towards independence and separation. He proposed to publish the Budd Report immediately after the meeting, so it could be used in parliamentary debate.

Isaacs said that despite difficulties, the channel could carry on, if asked, on a separate basis. But he qualified that opinion with a clear-eyed account of how Channel 4 really worked. The programming was a careful mix of remit programmes and unexceptional ones (such as *Countdown*) for a larger audience. The schedule could easily be manipulated either way, as he illustrated by an actual current example. He had been faced with a decision about Indian films, whether to run straight dramas or

Bollywood musicals. The musicals attracted three times as many viewers as the dramas, but he had just chosen the latter. The moral he drew was that for an independent, competitive channel it would be possible to sustain the remit, but more difficult – and that in those circumstances, Bollywood might well have got the nod.

Dell delayed publishing the Budd Report until 3 December, a fortnight before the next board meeting. This time, Attenborough was in attendance; he was to be named two months later as the successor to Dell, whose dogmatic attitudes had drawn him into conflict with the IBA. A paper from Sue Stoessl, arguing against Budd's conclusions, was provided for directors to study, and they eventually agreed to pull back to an anodyne statement:

> The Channel 4 Board is content with the present funding arrangements based on 17 per cent of net advertising. If, however, Parliament should wish to alter the structure of broadcasting, the Board would not rule out, in advance, alternative structures for Channel 4 and would be prepared to discuss such changes on condition that any new arrangements ensured the maintenance of the existing remit.

That was the point at which the debate on the channel's future funding started in earnest. The options were to leave well alone, to privatise or to seek a halfway house. The channel's executives were faced with the possibility that it might have to stand on its own feet and be run in a more worldly manner. It was only prudent to prepare for what might be inevitable. And just a month later, in January 1987, came a seismic change to the whole broadcasting environment, as the BBC entered meltdown and the tremors spread throughout the industry.

The Corporation had been shaken by a series of libels and rows over alleged breaches of national security when in October 1986 the Government appointed a new chairman, Marmaduke Hussey, a former newspaper manager known as a tough, no-nonsense executive. His brief was to bring the BBC under control, and in January he took the first step by summarily dismissing the Director General Alasdair Milne.

One result of this was to raise ambitions in Isaacs – ambitions which were clearly misplaced in the prevailing political climate. He had already started thinking about the BBC back in 1985, but when Milne was sacked, he had just been sounded out about running the Royal Opera House. He put that on the back burner and applied to be Director General of the BBC. The mere act of putting his name forward showed that he was ludicrously out of touch with the harsh new approach required. Neither temperamentally nor managerially would he have measured up to the top job in British broadcasting. The last thing the BBC governors wanted was a maverick, a champion of troublesome programmes, equipped with sketchy skills of management, running their huge production and editorial machine.[21] Isaacs went for an initial interview with Hussey at his Chelsea home and recounted to his colleague John Ranelagh what had happened. He had gone into the kitchen to make tea with Hussey when Joel Barnett, the Deputy Chairman, arrived. Hussey never came back to the kitchen, and Isaacs was left to bring in the tea tray, like a servant.[22] Only one of the twelve BBC governors is thought to have backed his candidature, and they eventually opted for the in-house Deputy Director General, the accountant Michael Checkland. As his deputy, they appointed John Birt from LWT, who had been runner-up for the job of launching Channel 4.

The BBC's rejection hit Isaacs hard. He was devastated. Ranelagh went to visit him at his Docklands flat in Concordia Wharf with a consolatory bottle of whisky and found him deeply depressed. He had gone through turbulent times: his wife Tamara had died of cancer after a protracted illness in 1986. He was fifty-five, exhausted and downcast.

Isaacs' contract did not expire until the end of 1988, yet by March 1987 the Board recorded that he would be leaving – though it was to be a lengthy departure. Nobody wanted Dell, whose term ended that summer, to be involved in picking the successor. His loyal staff organised a series of dinners begging him to stay, and some on his management team were angry that he was going. But there is no sign that the Board tried to persuade him to stay on, although Dukes did offer to resign instead, so that they would be forced to extend Isaacs' contract. Richard Attenborough said, 'There was a sense his time was up. The IBA were absolutely firm that Edmund had to go and equally firm that the programming, the image of the station needed a new broom. I would have kept him on.'[23]

● ● ● ●

A little later, a weighty five-year independent assessment, funded by the channel, of what people around Britain thought of Channel 4, was delivered by the independent Broadcasting Research Unit, with the title *Keeping Faith*.[24] Here was the voice of the audience at last, saying what it thought of this newish broadcaster with a different agenda. The report found that viewers wanted the channel to continue in its present form and would be unhappy if it became a pale imitation of ITV. They valued its polemical programmes, while respecting the public's right to know the full story. They did not want excessive caution in the areas of sex and morality – an attitude confirmed by the ratings, which showed that audiences for explicit programmes were zooming upwards.

One of the most interesting findings was that a single thread unified views about the channel, which the researchers called 'the adult citizen syndrome'.[25] People recognised that there might be programmes that pleased some and offended others, but adults should be allowed to make their own decisions about whether to watch. But there were blunt voices too: 'Tell Channel 4 not to bother about black-and-white Japanese films – bung 'em back in the archive.'[26] Ethnic groups and gays were unhappy, feeling that the channel had retreated from its initial commitment to serve their interests: they missed the flagship programmes, *Black on Black* and *Eastern Eye*. Many also criticised the serious tone of minority programmes, saying that they wanted entertainment as much as education. On balance, they would prefer it if a realistic version of life as a black Briton, for instance, was represented in mainstream programming, rather than in programmes specifically aimed at minorities.

Respondents found that the channel's attempt to balance its output on political or cultural issues over a series, rather than within an individual programme, was unrealistic, because viewers might easily miss the balancing viewpoint. On the difficult issue of Northern Ireland, the research showed that people wanted television to acknowledge that not all Catholics were nationalists nor all Protestants Orangemen. Overall, Channel 4 was judged to have been successful in opening what the founding father Anthony Smith called 'the sluice gate to change.'

Willie Whitelaw was pleased with the report. As Home Secretary, he had driven through the establishment of the channel and was to act now as its patron saint in troubled times, advising Margaret Thatcher against radical changes. 'I think on the whole it has lived up to what it was asked to do', he wrote.

> It has given new outlets. It has popularised different sports. It has given a new kind of news programme. And on the whole it has given a slightly different slant in the field of music and drama. It hasn't been as adventurous as some people would like, but I think it has been sufficiently adventurous to have an identity of its own.[27]

He was cautious about any change to its status.

With the fifth anniversary in November 1987, and the knowledge that Isaacs would shortly stand down, it was time to assess his contribution. Though it started on time and to budget and had high ambitions, Channel 4 was poorly executed at first: it was a well-intentioned muddle. Jeremy Isaacs provided the essential creative vision to give it a distinctive character, to make the channel different and fresh. Without him, it would have been a somewhat different place. He had the drive, the ambition and the leadership to get it up and running. Part of his enduring legacy was in moulding a cultural organisation that placed great power, for better, for worse, in its future chief executives. But he needed competent people around him of high calibre, prepared to clear up after him. His policy of initial experiment, to let a thousand flowers bloom, had produced some beauties, and a lot of weeds, from a now thriving independent production sector.

As the Broadcasting Research Unit report so correctly observed, he was a broadcaster with a memory, and when starting the channel he had looked back on the previous decades of television not as golden years but as years of missed opportunities that had produced some wonderful programmes but that had also smothered too many voices.

In many ways, his Channel 4 was a reaction against the past. This belief that he was taking broadcasting in a different direction was apparent in almost every early decision: even the choice of launch, 2 November, was the date on which the BBC began its television service in 1936. One frustration was that Channel 4 was never going to be allowed to be too radical because it was owned by the IBA, which policed it carefully, so it was a rebellious child within a traditional broadcasting family from the start.

There had been a lot of important breakthroughs. The hour-long news, eventually, had worked and grew to classic status. His commitment to let all kinds of people put their points of view on television without censorship was sorely tried, but there was debate, opinion and argument outside of the consensus. The channel had broadened horizons, with programmes and seasons for homosexuals and ethnic minorities, though there was constant feuding over their prominence. Although a champion of the liberal depiction of sexual activity on screen, exasperating the Regulator, one of his last decisions was that a series called *Sex with Paula* (featuring Paula Yates) could not be screened in an increasingly AIDS-conscious society.

Isaacs had achieved success for Film on Four, giving single drama and low-budget British film a real boost at home and abroad. One of his proudest moments arrived in January 1987 when *My Beautiful Laundrette* was broadcast on the channel. But this was at the expense of a more regular diet of drama series, which viewers also liked. The modest programme budget was widely spread, with the largest percentages going to drama, film and entertainment; and while film and bought-in (mainly American) programming accounted for 36 per cent of output, they absorbed only 16 per cent of the budget.

Isaacs had driven through a fresh approach to education and leisure with mixed results, and quite a number of the innovations were surprisingly homely: the 1987 schedule included a long series about knitting, *All Stitched Up*, and another, *As Good as New*, about renovating old furniture. Compared with what came later, Isaacs consciously tried to offer something for everyone on his Channel 4, including pensioners, not just youth.

The arts, poetry, opera, music and ideas were taken very seriously and funded generously. There was a strong cultural drive behind the early Channel 4, but the programmes and events were sometimes so highbrow they achieved zero ratings. This was television ordered by intellectuals for the intelligentsia. Isaacs had backed the televising of trials and the provision of funds for community video workshops, to encourage new film-makers, although their programmes were run so late and so long that they did not tend to attract much attention, even from Edmund Dell. And despite brave attempts, it had not really cracked a way of addressing modern working women, who were breaking through the glass ceiling and filling senior executive posts.

More broadly, the authors of *Keeping Faith* accused the channel of working to a narrow agenda, being a showcase for a dated 1960s mindset by which personal and sexual politics took precedence over engaging with hard-edged Thatcherism. Michael Jackson, at this point a successful independent producer making the channel's Sunday night *Media Show*, said his first proposal, *The Sixties*, was instantly taken up because Channel 4 was itself a flowering of the 1960s and its greatest expression.

Ranelagh recalled later that, just after the second Thatcher victory in 1983, Isaacs said in the programme committee that the Labour Party had failed as an opposition, and it was up to them to provide that opposition. 'Jeremy and Co saw their role as crusaders, continuing the 1960s war against the wrong values and wrong politics – which unfortunately for them were the values and politics of most of the voters from the 1980s to the present.'[28]

Finally, Isaacs had not achieved the target he had been set of a 10-per-cent audience share in what was still a four-channel environment. The figure was hovering between 7 and 8 per cent, although Channel 4 was watched by 70–80 per cent of viewers on any given week – almost, but not quite, achieving his goal of something for everyone some of the time. This suggests that, in evaluating Isaacs' overall contribution, a mark of eight out of ten would be appropriate. The authors of *Keeping Faith* concluded: 'Jeremy Isaacs has emerged as the most charismatic and influential figure of his generation; a man of vision and adventure unfortunately ill-suited to the present.'[29] No wonder Channel 4 boycotted the launch: Dukes merely reported to the Board that it had turned up, and was not that good.

11

Dark horse makes the Grade

• • • •

The hunt for Jeremy Isaacs' successor did not start until September 1987, though it had been common knowledge since March that he had decided seven years was enough. So there was a strange summer with Isaacs still *in situ*, licking his wounds after being rejected by the BBC, while many working for him felt betrayed and urged him to reconsider. But the slow-motion departure, all very British, was no accident. It was calculated to ensure that Edmund Dell, who spent much time at Channel 4 burning the tube of his television set, meticulously checking for left-wing bias, was ushered out on 30 June without having a say in choosing the new Chief Executive. Meanwhile, his successor Richard Attenborough had been told by the Regulator not to press Isaacs to stay on, because they wanted a change in the programming.

Dell had one last shot in his locker before he stepped down, a peppery reaction to a series of interviews with the former Labour Prime Minister James Callaghan conducted by Brian Walden, characterised by the retiring Chairman as a 'pompous ass.'[1] The Dell farewell dinner saw Attenborough expressing his 'deep admiration and affection' for the outgoing Chairman, praising his dedication and integrity. Yet, the event did not go as expected. Dell's eyes filled with tears at the eulogies. The brisk Liz Forgan, now Deputy Director of Programmes, looked on amazed, thinking how odd it was: he had, after all, never seemed to have had a moment' pleasure from Channel 4, having spent most of his time there in conflict with his Chief Executive. And now there was this welling up of emotion: he had a funny way of showing he cared.[2]

Once he had left, Dell was free from any restraint about stirring up debate over Channel 4's future and wrote to the *Financial Times* and the *Guardian*, expressing his support for the idea that it should sell its own advertising. In the annual report, released at the same time, he recorded that he favoured independence for the channel.[3] Sandwiched between the all-powerful IBA, which owned the channel, and the full-time executives, intent on doing things their way, Dell had clearly found himself trapped.

George Russell, the canny and personable Geordie businessman now running Marley Building Supplies, was parachuted in as the channel's Deputy Chairman in February to hold the fort while Attenborough finished his great anti-apartheid film, *Cry Freedom*.[4] Margaret Thatcher had taken quite a shine to Russell – he'd broken the ice with her by discussing retiling Number 10's kitchen floor – and he was subsequently made Chairman of the IBA, a key position from which to oversee, *inter alia*, Channel 4's future. The politics of broadcasting were becoming trickier and more dangerous by the month. Mrs Thatcher was now closely involved with what became a crusade to reform ITV, resulting in the ill-conceived 1990 Broadcasting Act. Would Channel 4 be harmed in the fallout? At a seminar she hosted at 10 Downing Street on 21 September, her intentions became clear as she dubbed ITV the last bastion of restrictive trade-union practices.

The future for Channel 4 was unclear in her developing scheme. Raymond Snoddy, Media Editor of the *Financial Times*, reported that a plan by the Home Secretary, Douglas Hurd, for it to become a non-profit-making trust, selling its own advertising, was rejected by the Prime Minister as not radical enough.[5] Options started to be debated within the channel's top management. The business-oriented Justin Dukes, the Managing Director, decided he supported privatisation, with the remit protected by statute.[6] Isaacs, who attended the Downing Street seminar, noted that Mrs Thatcher had seen Channel 4 as a useful low-cost entry point for independent producers. This was true; yet, independents had recently been losing ground to the ITV companies in the contest to supply the channel's programmes. And Channel 4's budgets were generous, a sign of how much production costs were inflated across the board. That month, Isaacs approved two new dramas, *A Very British Coup* (1988) and *The Manageress* (1989), which both cost £600,000 per hour – not so different from prices twenty years later, before factoring in inflation.

With Dell gone, the question of who should succeed Isaacs preoccupied the Board. At their meeting on 22 September, with Attenborough very much back in action, they set the wheels in motion, agreeing to advertise the post but opting not to use headhunters who might arouse expectations. It would be a fair contest. They would not 'nudge' anyone who did not apply. The closing date for applications was 26 October, with a decision promised by 4 December. The Appointment Committee consisted of five board members: Attenborough, Russell, John Gau, Paul Fox and Carmen Callil, the forceful founder of Virago Press. Isaacs was given an assurance that he would be consulted on the shortlist.

There were two internal candidates: Liz Forgan and Justin Dukes, who had done so much of the spadework in setting up the channel. Thirteen people were longlisted, but the figure dropped to twelve as the BBC's arts supremo Alan Yentob pulled out, having decided that his future lay with the BBC. After interviews, the list was reduced to five, still including Dukes and Forgan. One of the three external finalists was Anthony Smith, who was by now running the BFI – also chaired by Attenborough. Smith had great expectations. Attenborough was a good friend, and the previous year, while the two were taking a spin in the film director's green Rolls Royce, he had confided in Smith that he was going to succeed Dell as Chairman. Smith implored him not to, thinking the extra work would kill him. 'I told him it was too much, even for a man of extraordinary energy. He said, "I am going to be Chairman so I can make sure you take over from Jeremy." I believed him, yes.'[7] (Attenborough denies making this offer.)

Even though Callil found Smith unexciting, he did make it to the final three, as did another founding father, Roger Graef, who applied partly to remind the panel of what Channel 4 stood for. The third finalist, the dark horse, was Will Wyatt, a rising BBC executive who would eventually become Managing Director of BBC Television. Wyatt told the panel that Channel 4 was too glum and needed cheering up. It should embrace a wider range of opinions and assumptions. The schedule looked dysfunctional, a compromise between competing interests. He would sort it out and improve Channel 4's audience share.[8]

His interview was held on Monday, 9 November 1987 – the start of a tumultuous seven days for aspiring media mandarins that would end with many hopes dashed and one major surprise. For the BBC was simultaneously selecting new controllers for BBC1 and BBC2, and their headhunting meshed with Channel 4's in a way that was either serendipitous or calamitous, depending on your point of view.

The composition of the BBC interviewing panel had caused great offence to Michael Grade, who was about to assume the pivotal role of Managing Director of BBC Television. The catalyst of the dispute was John Birt, Grade's former friend and colleague at LWT, now flexing his muscles as the BBC's Deputy Director General. Birt insisted that he should be on the interviewing panel for the two BBC controllers, while Grade's friend, patron and ally Bill Cotton, the outgoing Managing Director, was excluded from it.

Michael Checkland said that this was done at the behest of the Chairman, Marmaduke Hussey, but Grade saw it as a power play by Birt and calculated that the new Deputy was bent on maximising his influence in the Corporation's top echelons at the expense of the old guard, which Grade represented. It was, he could see, time to make his exit. 'I couldn't wait to get out of the BBC', he wrote. 'I had no desire to work with a compliant director general down whose neck an ambitious and aggressive John Birt was breathing.' And he told his wife Sarah, 'I'll be gone by Christmas.'[9]

On the Thursday of that week, Wyatt went before the BBC selection panel for controller of BBC2, but he did not gain their favour. They gave the job to Yentob, while Jonathan Powell, a champion of drama, would have BBC1 – ironically, the choices favoured by Grade. Wyatt scarcely had time to rue his misfortune when, on the Friday, he received a message from Channel 4. Would he be ready to see them again next week? He certainly would. It was a weekend full of joyful anticipation in the Wyatt household, but the mood altered at a stroke when he received another call on Monday. 'Terribly sorry, Will, it didn't work out. There'll be an announcement tonight.'[10]

The truth was that the selection panel could not reach a decision. Nobody on the shortlist had convinced them that he had the qualities they sought. Behind the scenes, the crafty Attenborough had started talking to Grade. So, when Grade had telephoned Attenborough around the time of Wyatt's interview, he could not have chosen a better moment. In his autobiography, Grade says he rang on the pretext of disclosing the date of the transmission of a BBC programme about *Cry Freedom*. Having done that, he inquired casually, 'By the way, how's the search for Jeremy's successor going?'

'Well, you know, darling, it's not easy but we're getting there slowly', Attenborough replied. Then Grade made his sally: 'I don't know whether this is of interest to you or not, but I'll say it twice so that there's no misunderstanding. If you were to offer me the job I would take it.' There was quite a long silence at the other end of the phone, then 'Oh, darling!' 'Yes, if you were to offer me the job I'd jump at it.'[11]

Having put down his marker, Grade went through the BBC controllership interviews as if nothing was up. On the Friday – the day Wyatt had been told to prepare for another interview at Channel 4 – Attenborough and Grade talked on the phone again. An interview was fixed for 10 a.m. the following day at Attenborough's grand house on Richmond Green. It was hurried and ultra-discreet, combining elements of a spy thriller with those of high farce. Grade was due to fly to Los Angeles that day, on a trip for the BBC. His wife was already there. But instead of meeting his special adviser at the airport as arranged, he decided to disappear for the weekend, without trace or explanation. He went to stay with his sister, Anita Land, in Hampstead. Then, at the appointed time, he drove straight into Attenborough's garage, who personally closed the gates behind him, and walked into the house through an attached passage, unobserved by any curious Saturday-morning strollers.

The farcical ingredient was supplied by George Russell, who also lived in Hampstead and had agreed to pick up Carmen Callil and drive her to the interview. She had moved into a new home only the previous day, and he had carefully written her new address on a piece of paper and put it into his pocket. But then he had taken his suit to the dry cleaners with the address still in it. When he rang Attenborough's house to see if he knew the address, there was no reply: the movie mogul was in the pergola at the end of his garden, while Lady Attenborough was in the bath. By ringing round, he got an address for Callil, but it was her old one. Flustered and apologetic, he arrived at the house to find that she had made her own way and was sitting with the others waiting for the interview to begin.

When it did finally get under way, it did not take long: the panel were convinced that they had finally found their man. Grade later wrote, 'All my previous experience had been a preparation for Channel 4. I had a CV that was unique in British television. Each aspect of the chief executive's range of duties demanded a particular skill or experience I had acquired at some stage in my career.'[12]

It was true that versatility had been the hallmark of his career to date. While Isaacs had spent his formative years at Oxford University, the younger Grade, with just three O Levels, had run a sports column on the *Daily Mirror*. When Isaacs was making *What the Papers Say* as a Granada junior, Grade was running a family talent agency at a time when stars had shows built around them. He was headhunted by LWT to run entertainment while Isaacs at Thames was backing serious documentaries. When Isaacs was starting up Channel 4, Grade had made an unsuccessful foray to Hollywood, before he was summoned home to resuscitate BBC1.

In fact, he was handling his own career rather like the agent he used to be, getting the best deal for a major if petulant star, switching channels without compunction to win better terms and greater appreciation. Bill Cotton, commenting on Grade's defection, put it this way: 'People have to make the career moves that seem right for them.' (And Grade would repeat the exercise almost twenty years later, when in November 2006 he suddenly jumped from being Chairman of the BBC Trust, at a delicate time for the Corporation, to become Executive Chairman of ITV.)

As Controller of BBC1, he had sat on the top management committees and had been involved in the fraught media politics of the period, while being careful to conceal any party-political allegiance. By boosting BBC1's popularity he had helped the corporation fight off some fierce Thatcherite assaults. The Channel 4 Selection Committee saw him as a big figure, not a grey figure like the three on the shortlist, nor an intellectual looking backwards to Channel 4's roots. He came from the show-business side of the industry, which Attenborough instinctively warmed to.

Indeed, for the panel, he seemed like a fortuitous gift from the gods, an escape route from their seemingly terminal deadlock. They were relaxed about his reputation for favouring populism over minority interests, but there was one problem. He had blotted his copybook over a series of contentious public remarks that summer about Channel 4. At the Royal Television Society's September convention in Cambridge, for instance, he had argued that if he were Home Secretary he would have the channel privatised and allow it to sell its own advertising. Afterwards, an angry Paul Fox – now facing him on the selection panel – had told him to keep his nose out of their business. At the interview, he defended himself before Fox and the others by pointing out that his record showed he had consistently championed public-service broadcasting and would continue to do so. But it was clear that his interest in running the channel had developed late – and opportunistically.

In any case, the Board knew that some fresh thinking about Channel 4's future would shortly be required, for while in public the directors still advocated retaining the status quo, they were themselves starting to prepare for change. In September, as they began their hunt for a chief executive, the Board had received a paper from Justin Dukes and David Scott, the Financial Director, called 'A Changed Status for Channel 4'. Marked 'Private and confidential, not to be left lying around', it was an analysis of possible future options, including setting up an advertising sales force and erecting a series of ring fences to protect the programme remit if the channel were to be privatised. The paper was sent to the IBA, and even Isaacs welcomed it as a useful contribution to the debate. So, Grade's remarks at Cambridge were not complete heresy.

Dukes later said, 'I was pretty clear about privatisation for the channel. I felt it could stand on its own two feet. The team worked well. The taxpayer would realise the value of the investment. I was quite flagrantly pro-privatisation, subject to the Board's approval.'[13]

After Grade's clandestine weekend interview, Attenborough phoned the Chairman and Director General at the IBA, whose approval of the appointment would be required. They seemed positive. It was agreed that Attenborough would inform Isaacs at midday on Monday, that there would be a meeting with IBA members at 4 p.m. at the Hyde Park Hotel, and the appointment would be ratified by the Board at 7 p.m. Paul Fox was deputed to ring the ITV managing directors. On Sunday, Grade wrote out his letter of resignation, to be delivered to the BBC's Director General at 5 p.m. on Monday.

But this finely tuned plan quickly unravelled. Attenborough tried to phone Isaacs but failed, and left messages. Then he went to the National Film Theatre (NFT) on the South Bank where the adjacent Museum of the Moving Image, a brainchild of his and Anthony Smith's, was about to open its doors. Attenborough summoned Smith there and told him gravely about Grade's appointment, picking hairs off Smith's dark businessman's overcoat like a chimpanzee grooming an underling – an encounter observed by this author as she kept an appointment with Attenborough to talk about the new museum.

The Chairman eventually met Isaacs at 3 p.m. and told him the news. There was a huge row. Isaacs was violently opposed, totally amazed and minded to offer his resignation at once. The manner in which the decision was made was completely inappropriate, he raged.[14] 'If Jeremy was capable of murder it would not have been poor old Michael Grade, it would have been me. If I had been facing him he would have hit me', Attenborough later recounted.[15] Isaacs' reaction rocked Attenborough and the IBA, and when Grade arrived at the Hyde Park Hotel as arranged, he realised something was wrong. Attenborough and John Whitney, the IBA Director General, were in agitated conversation.

Attenborough admitted there had been a hitch. 'Jeremy was very upset when I told him about your appointment', he told Grade. 'He thinks it's the end of Channel 4 and he's not going to stand for it.'[16]

Grade found a phone and told his secretary, sitting outside Broadcasting House in his chauffeur-driven car, not to deliver his resignation letter. He offered to withdraw; but the IBA supported the appointment. The Board that evening was not unanimous, but a majority supported the appointment, and Dukes expressed his willingness to work with Grade. The minutes of the meeting recorded Isaacs' opposition in these terms:

> He believed it quite wrong that his view had not been taken. He knew Michael Grade well, he was a most talented television executive, but in attainment and by instinct, he was an expert commercial broadcaster; he would make the channel more popular than it ought to be, and he would work to privatise it. For these reasons he was wholly opposed to his appointment.[17]

This story had leaked, and by the time Michael Checkland received Grade's formal resignation letter on Tuesday morning, the news was already on the front pages. Checkland, who thought Grade should at least have had the courtesy to telephone him before the stories appeared, ordered the errant executive to clear his desk by 2 p.m. At an 11 a.m. press conference at Channel 4, Attenborough, the bespectacled kingmaker, blinked into the cameras and gave his reasons for the choice, rather as if he had been casting the lead in a Hollywood blockbuster:

> We needed somebody like Jeremy Isaacs, who is charismatic. We needed someone who has the same drive, the same energies, the same ability to attract talent. Michael has done this time and time again at the BBC and London Weekend Television – somebody prepared to be courageous, to fight for the channel's remit against all comers. The deal was consummated after great debate, on his assurance that he supported the status quo.[18]

It was unfortunate that Grade, looking wan and sheepish after three nights of little sleep, and having trouble distinguishing the word 'challenge' from 'channel', did not quite fit the script. One-liners eluded him. 'It is a chance to run your own operation', he said, when asked about scaling down from BBC1, with its 40 per cent audience share, to a channel with only 8 per cent. 'There is more to life than mass circulation.' He said that he doubted if he would make many changes and reached for a classic Gradeism to help himself out: 'You don't rewrite a hit.'[19]

This was partly a reference to the flood of complimentary articles marking the fifth anniversary. The industry's magazine, *Broadcast*, had just published a laudatory supplement, praising Channel 4 for writing a new chapter in British television. Grade had contributed as one of ten grandees giving their favourite programmes. The others had tended to include *Channel 4 News*. His selection was *The Emma Thompson Special*, the Jack Rosenthal drama about young love – *P'tang Yang Kipper Bang* – and anything with Ben Elton.

As he left the uncomfortable press conference, Grade ran into an emotional Jeremy Isaacs outside his office. They shook hands warily. Then Isaacs, driven by a sense of ownership and love for the channel he had founded, said, 'I am handing you a sacred trust. If you screw it up, if you betray it, I'll come back and throttle you.' Grade promised he would not.[20] But he was struck by the venom with which Isaacs spat out the words and amplified them to the press: 'I will bloody well hold him to his undertakings.'[21] Anthony Smith, one of the disappointed candidates, said bitterly: 'British television has fallen into the hands of people playing games with instruments of culture.'[22] Much later, his view had softened: 'Yes, I think I have forgiven Dickie for appointing Grade. But was he right to choose him? Well, if he could find no one else [. . .] what came later was worse.'[23]

On 23 December, Isaacs wrote his final 'All at Four' note, before the farewell party. 'To you all my heartfelt thanks for everything. This, the best thing I've done, has been made so by working with you all.'[24] John Ranelagh, his former personal assistant, returned to be with him on 31 December, his last day in the office. He was tearful. It was not a good departure, more an emotional wrench. He walked away from television to run the Royal Opera House, which Dukes saw as a disastrous decision both for Isaacs and the Royal Opera House, because of his doubts about Isaacs' managerial skills.

At 60 Charlotte Street, it would be Michael Grade's name over the door instead of Jeremy Isaacs', but as far as the staff were concerned, it was a lot more than just a change of nameplate. The new Chief Executive was going to take a lot of getting used to. Charlotte Street was a warren inhabited by spiky characters, and their first reaction was absolute shock. The channel was a unique creation, they told themselves; it had a special flavour and a cultural mission, unlike ITV where Grade had seemed most at home. Grade was less starry-eyed: 'As a regular viewer my impression was that the initial impetus of Jeremy's creative flair had spent itself. The channel's entire programme policy was due for an overhaul. So I entered the portals of Channel 4 neither cowed nor complacent. I would do it my way.'[25]

He had been appointed to professionalise Channel 4 and to create a more directed programme schedule. With an audience share of 8 per cent it was not far from the initial 10-per-cent target but depended heavily on imported American programmes to keep up the ratings. As it turned out, though, he did not have quite as much impact on programmes in his first two years as expected, being distracted by the immediate political debate about the channel's future. Ratings were to deteriorate slightly before they improved.

Both Isaacs and Grade attended the annual Nuneham Park meeting in December, where commissioners reviewed the channel's output. Grade said that the content of the programmes was being dictated by independent producers rather than by the requirements of a schedule. Quality control was not always very rigorous. Channel 4 had to lose its innocence and move on to a war footing. At his first board meeting in January, he added that there was an option of the news moving to 7.30 p.m. – which was quietly forgotten – but he was greatly impressed with the financial controls at the channel. By March, he had reversed the expansion into children's television because it would never have the funds to compete, and the channel bought *Sesame Street* instead. But he pushed through a new strand of *Arts Weekly*, later called *Signals*, to challenge the BBC's *Late Show* and continued with Isaacs' expansion into daily business coverage.

Next, he reorganised commissioning, which he said gave too much autonomy to individuals. He confirmed Liz Forgan as Director of Programmes, a sign of continuity, and created two controllerships to marshal the output. Mike Bolland was made Controller of Arts and Entertainment, with a new Controller of Factual Areas – John Willis from Yorkshire Television. He had made his reputation with *First Tuesday*, a strand of courageous and often campaigning documentaries and was highly respected for championing programme-makers in the Isaacs tradition. A Cambridge graduate, Willis was the son of Lord Ted Willis, who had written the BBC's classic early policing series, *Dixon of Dock Green*. Grade has a talent for hiring good people, and Willis's blend of brains, conscience, humour and populism would work well for the channel.

Grade discontinued snooker as out of place on Channel 4, but during 1989 talked of a fourth weekly episode of *Brookside*, later reduced to three. He also identified opportunities to attract larger audiences between 10 p.m. and midnight.

The new commissioning structure resulted in a major turnover of personnel. Naomi Sargant, who ran education and stayed on for a year, said,

> Michael didn't honour the educational commitment in the way Jeremy did. He left in the iconic good works, like disability and multiculturalism, and the big audience things like gardening, but he cut back by 20 per cent on the rest. Classic example: I was commissioning an afternoon live programme from Thames with Mavis Nicholson three days a week. It was replaced with Oprah Winfrey: she was black and cheap. I was there for a year and I never once had a serious conversation with Michael about educational programming. Education never had the pride of place that it had before.[26]

At a conference at Selsdon Park in Surrey on 30 June, Grade told the commissioners what he thought of the schedule. It was vital for them to respond to proposals within two weeks, he said, and they had to take responsibility for programmes up to transmission, including the crucial task of viewing them in advance. He said the target audience share should not be 10 per cent but 15 – a proposal that was forgotten quite quickly.

But it was politics, not programmes, that dominated his initial agenda. As soon as he joined, he was drawn into the big debate on the future of Channel 4, taking place against the backdrop of Mrs Thatcher's full-throttle attack on ITV for tolerating restrictive labour practices. He had pledged to keep the channel as a public-service broadcaster and to oppose its privatisation, and he felt obliged to stick with that commitment. There were a number of challenging developments to factor in. The threat of competition was springing up everywhere. The IBA had awarded a direct-to-home satellite broadcasting licence to the ultimately unsuccessful British Satellite Broadcasting (BSB), and this prompted Rupert Murdoch to bring forward plans for his own satellite service, Sky. Then, in the aftermath of the Peacock Report, the Department of Trade and Industry had confirmed that there was potential for a fifth terrestrial channel, and maybe even a sixth, although Channel Five was eventually delayed until 1997.

Grade said in January that there was only a short window of time for Channel 4 to influence the future of television, and it must grasp the opportunity.[27] Attenborough saw clearly that it needed to start selling its own advertising, but without exposing itself totally to the marketplace. Yet, the channel was playing a cautious game. Its first response, to a Home Affairs Select Committee, was to back the existing hand-me-down subscription. It was then faced with the prospect of a White Paper on broadcasting to be published in November 1988, with the principal object of bringing in a licensing system and competitive tendering for ITV.

A few weeks before the White Paper was published in November, Channel 4 was given a glimpse of the section pertaining to its own future and was galvanised into action.[28] While praising the programme remit as a 'sterling success, which must be fully sustained', the White Paper continued, 'It does not follow that the structural arrangements for Channel 4 should remain unchanged [. . .] Greater competition between those selling television airtime [. . .] is essential.' In other words, the Government's wider proposals for a more competitive commercial television sector made structural change unavoidable.

Channel 4 realised it had to be more proactive, more daring even, and put forward viable compromises to save itself and tip the debate. The Finance Director and Company Secretary David Scott drew up a sixteen-page paper, with input from Grade's consultant, Peter Ibbotson. Called 'Six Options for the Future', it was never published nor widely circulated outside government circles but went for ratification to a specially assembled board meeting on 29 September 1988. It was an intelligent and forthright contribution from a channel that knew the chips were down and that it must speak for itself.

The paper assumed that a separation of Channel 4's advertising from ITV's was bound to come, that there would be a new Channel Five and new satellite services, and that BBC1 and BBC2 would work together more closely. The first option, for no change, was now formally ruled out. The next two options, it said, were consistent with the survival of Channel 4's innovatory programme remit. They were:

- The channel would continue to receive a subscription linking it with ITV, but separate selling was possible.
- Separate selling of ITV and Channel 4 advertising, but with an incentive for ITV to continue to cooperate with the smaller channel.

The next option, involving greater risk to the remit, was for Channels 4 and Five to be in joint public ownership, with complementary scheduling. And finally, there were two courses that would put the remit even more at risk – a stand-alone privatised Channel 4, or a Channel 4 Trust. The option of separate selling, but with an incentive for ITV to cooperate, was thus floated as a possibility for the first time. It involved defining a base level of funding that would allow the channel to continue unharmed. The aim would be to persuade ITV not to attack Channel 4, because it would have to meet the resultant deficit if it did. An arrangement could be devised by which if the channel was in loss one year, the gap could be funded by ITV, then recouped from Channel 4 in subsequent better years. This was the basis of the compromise that would secure the channel's immediate future, lasting from 1993 until 1999 when ITV still promoted Channel 4's up-and-coming programmes at no charge. The paper concluded,

> Some months ago under our previous chairman the option of stand-alone privatisation held some attraction. However, at that time we took no account of the effects of channels five or six, the introduction of Astra [satellite] channels, the possible lifting of public service obligations on ITV, a more complex set of equations.

When the White Paper was published, it set out three options:

1. Channel 4 as a private company.
2. The middle way: a non-profit-making body, selling its own advertising, with a minimum level of guaranteed income.
3. Some form of link between Channels 4 and Five.

It showed that the Government was in three minds and signalled that privatisation was not necessarily going to be the chosen course. Channel 4's own suggestions had made a crucial difference. The second option, the middle way, was backed by the Parliamentary Home Affairs Committee in a second report in March 1989, but there was no consensus amongst the massed ranks of lobbyists. Advertisers were pushing hard for privatisation, as were some newspapers, while the powerful IPPA, which would gain a statutory right to supply all broadcasters with a 25-per-cent share of their programmes, wanted a not-for-profit Channel 4 Trust. The only thing agreed by all was that the channel would no longer be funded by a handout from ITV.

Over the following months, a guarantee was devised at a base level of 14 per cent of net terrestrial advertising accrued by ITV. This harked back to the funding formula on which Channel 4 was founded and was close to the level which the Budd Report had identified as workable. By spring 1989, it was the turn of the Treasury to pick over the baseline guarantee, concerned to ensure that any risk was offloaded on to the ITV companies, not the public purse.

On 13 June, the Home Secretary announced that Channel 4 would indeed be a public trust, licensed by the IBA, but the refined funding formula came as a shock. If the channel's income fell below the 14 per cent mark, the difference would be met by ITV, but never to more than a 2 per cent shortfall. The sting was that any surplus revenue over 14 per cent would have to be split equally between ITV and Channel 4. Further, Channel 4 must hold half of the excess it banked in a surplus fund, to be used as a first call. In other words, if Channel 4 did well, or very well, it would transfer large sums across to ITV, while keeping only 25 pence of every pound over the 14-per-cent limit for programmes.

This formula was enshrined in the Broadcasting Bill published on 7 December 1989, and the reaction within Channel 4 was that they had been shafted. In retrospect, it was clear that Attenborough and the channel's lobbyists had not given a sufficiently high profile to the safety-net deal. Clearly, it had been rushed through, and it had a glaring flaw that could have been identified earlier. For if the commitment from ITV to meet the channel's losses was to be capped at 2 per cent, fair play surely demanded that the surplus payment should have been capped as well. Surprisingly, though, the Board, which never encouraged a wider debate on the details, was relieved to get the deal it had. The downside would not be revealed until later.

Grade, addressing the Royal Television Society in Cambridge from the safety of 1991, in the forum where he had once advocated privatisation, explained what had happened. The high-powered Cabinet Committee on Broadcasting that decided the terms of the Act had been chaired by Mrs Thatcher herself.

> Outright privatisation was what they wanted. If that powerful body had had its way, Channel 4 would have been auctioned to the highest bidder.

It was a real threat. It took a very long time to wear down the ideological self-certainty of the privatisers; and the argument was only won at the eleventh hour.

If that battle had been lost, then Channel 4 – in any recognisable form – would have been lost, and we would not be enjoying the luxury of debating the finer points of the meaning of the remit. The fight for the soul of Channel 4 did not take place in the letters column of the *Independent*. It took place in late-night drafting sessions, in endless meetings with civil servants, ministers and MPs, not to mention a number of trips through the dustbins in Downing Street. But it was won, and the channel survived a lethal threat to its very existence. The price of victory was the acceptance of separate selling. To those who ask why we didn't go to the last ditch for the existing funding arrangements, I must bluntly restate that the status quo wasn't on. This was 1989. It was a considerable achievement to rescue what we did.[29]

For the next Chairman of Channel 4, Sir Michael Bishop, it all looked pretty simple: the company was a victim of rogue legislation. But there is another ancillary explanation. Until February 1991, ITV supplied three directors to Channel 4: Greg Dyke from LWT, Richard Dunn from Thames and James Gatward from TVS; and for ITV, the funding formula was a good thing. It contained within it a rough-and-ready element of repayment to ITV for supporting the channel through the early years until 1986, when advertising was thin. The Broadcasting Minister, David Mellor, who handled the details of the amendments, said that since ITV would have to pay for the downside, it was only right they should share in the surplus.

The general belief was that there was plenty of scope for Channel 4 to fall into loss, though this did not in fact happen. Perhaps, too, the will to fight the formula was stifled by a last-minute flurry in the House of Lords over a tough new impartiality clause concerning the reporting of politics and public affairs, which was successfully watered down. There were three plus points for the channel in the Bill:

1. It was not required to bid competitively for its licence.
2. The programme remit was technically unchanged.
3. The legislation allowed for a change in the funding formula after 1997.

The arguments made at this pivotal moment remain highly pertinent for what happened over the next two decades. The 'Six Options' paper maintained that, left on its own without ITV's protection, Channel 4's programme remit could not, over time, survive the pressures. Yet, in 1999, after the final links between the two networks ended and unrestrained competition began, Channel 4 became a small but prosperous channel, standing on its own two feet and coping well, for a time. Second, 'Six Options' regarded a link between Channel 4 and the as-yet-unlaunched Five as entailing some risk, but less risk than privatisation. Fast forward to 2003–4, when an increasingly vulnerable Channel 4 looked at the possibility of such a merger, to create a relationship like that between BBC1 and BBC2. Finally, the funding formula was resented from the moment it was mooted and irrevocably soured relations between Channel 4 and ITV. It would cost the channel £412.5 million between 1993 and 1999, paid in annual cheques, representing half the surplus the channel made over the 14 per cent share. However, in its infant years, between 1982 and 1986, it had received in total a subscription income of £744.5 million distributed through its parent and owner, the IBA. This had cost ITV a net £234 million when adjusted for the early start-up burden and then the income ITV subsequently reaped from selling the channel's advertising. So, there was a sort of rough justice involved.[30]

The Bill was passed on 1 November 1990, and the channel would be weaned from its parent, the IBA, on 1 January 1993. It had been saved from the ultimate fate of privatisation. But here's a well-kept secret. The founding share capital of £100 in the original Channel 4 Television Company, dating back to 1980, was passed during autumn 1992 from the IBA not to private-equity owners demanding dividends but to the newly separated Channel 4 Television Corporation, established by the 1990 Broadcasting Act. So, from that date, Channel 4 had no external shareholders.

The channel still owns these 100 shares in the original company, now a dormant subsidiary, though the archivist was unable to locate the certificate. More to the point, no new shares in the new statutory Channel 4 Television Corporation were issued. In future, it would be regulated by the replacement and lighter-touch Independent Television Commission (ITC), which had the right to hire and fire its non-executive directors. But, contrary to the widely held belief – which Channel 4 never discouraged – no arm of Government, neither the Treasury, nor the Department of Trade and Industry's shareholder executive own any shares in Channel 4 (though, as a statutory corporation it is a publicly owned asset). This fostered its sense of independence, though it would be vulnerable to any change of government policy as to its programme remit and structure. Now it was standing on its own two feet there would have to be major changes, and Grade had two years to prepare for them. The doubters were essentially correct about the impact of the new arrangements on the channel's programming. The Rubicon would be crossed in 1993 as the programmes and the audiences they attracted were linked directly to income for the first time. In preparing for that moment, Grade had to make sure the channel could attract a healthy 10-per-cent audience share and package enough advertising around its programmes to earn its way.

12

Breakfast with handcuffs

• • • •

Fifteen months after joining, Michael Grade decided that he had been distracted by all the politicking and had to focus on programmes. By March 1989, the channel was treading water, audiences were flat, and its appeal to youth, the most valued asset, was declining. It needed more viewers, to gain the elusive 10-per-cent share of audiences by the end of 1992. That meant adding a minimum of 1 per cent a year over the next two years.[1]

It was not a propitious time for such a venture. Britain was entering a short, sharp recession, and after a decade of exuberant growth, television advertising was about to stagnate, then decline by 2 per cent in 1991 – the year of the first Gulf War. This nasty blip, though brief, would constrain the programme budget for the first time and make Grade's job harder. Hired to professionalise the channel in a transitional period, he was having to accelerate changes in relatively tough conditions.

Lacking any emotional ties to the early experimental period, he deployed a number of devices that would provoke his critics to sharpen their spears, detecting threats to the sacred remit. He bought more American imports and made more use of them, so that they provided better value for money. He introduced longer runs of successful programmes, a new emphasis on entertainment and high-impact drama (see Chapter 15). He tried to give the audience more regular, themed strands: Sunday nights became film nights, and from Monday to Thursday there was always a strong factual hour from 9 p.m. Friday, as before, was entertainment night.

Grade never showed any overt pride in *Countdown* nor schmoozed its presenters Richard Whiteley and Carol Vorderman, but the brain-teasing quiz, with a strong following among older viewers, was now extended throughout the year, soon making a positive impact on audience figures. In September, *Brookside*'s production was cranked up from two to three episodes a week, though when this first became part of the schedules in July 1990 the stretched storylines pleased no one. Grade even considered working up another soap, until the sensational 'body under the patio' story emerged to revive the flagging interest of *Brookside* fans.

There was also a need to harvest new revenue from outside the traditional evening peak time: *The Big Breakfast* eventually helped to do that.

The swiftest change, though, was in factual programmes. These had been vital to the channel from its birth – and remain so – because it could never afford large quantities of home-grown drama: Channel 4 is, at heart, a factual channel. A new series, *Cutting Edge*, set up during 1989 by John Willis, went out on Monday evenings at 9 p.m.

Grade told Willis that his job was to make the channel grow up, but Willis was relatively protective of its early history and character, so different from the more narrowly focused ITV with which he was familiar. His arrival in autumn 1988 marked a diminution of what Paul Bonner recalls affectionately as the 'truly surprising, off-the-wall, anarchic, left field' programmes.[2] Grade was not a great fan of these, and, as a result, some of the pioneers began to leave, disgruntled and ostracised, soon after the new controller arrived.[3] As a newcomer, Willis detected the whiff of a disappearing world which seemed rooted, two decades on, in the culture of the late 1960s.

> It was a very distinctive culture, very different from others in television. It could have been a magazine, a university department, maybe an independent production company. It was a channel made up of outsiders: it was outside the system, and everyone felt there was a licence to be cheeky and frank. You did feel you were in an amazingly privileged place. Film-makers from all over the world got in contact with you because there were so many slots. An amazingly wide selection of ideas was available.[4]

But procedures could be slack: sometimes documentaries were broadcast without being viewed and formally checked. This was a remnant of the notion Channel 4 was there to publish the ideas and work of others, but Willis saw it as sloppiness and insisted that it was tightened up: 'The danger was that people were making films for themselves and their friends.'[5] The new Scheduler, Ashley Hill, who joined from the BBC, recalls that programmes occasionally appeared out of the blue, as a documentary-maker ambled in to the Charlotte Street foyer, bearing the fruit of a long-forgotten commission. There was a lengthy list of unplaced programmes waiting for slots – cupboards stuffed to overflowing with the untransmitted and the untransmittable.

Cutting Edge was an hour-long report on contemporary life, a conscious attempt to tell the story of modern Britain as the Thatcherite era drew to a close. It was clearly inspired both by *First Tuesday* and BBC1's *40 Minutes*, an eclectic and uplifting popular strand curated by Eddie Mirzoeff during the 1980s. Peter Moore, a London School of Economics politics graduate, was brought down from Yorkshire to deliver the new programme. This was an era of series and magazine shows. For nine years, until 1997, he had a major impact on the channel, inventing or overseeing thirteen regular strands and series, from *Undercover Britain* to *True Stories*. Like Willis, Moore felt wonderfully liberated in Charlotte Street. Programme reviews took his breath away with their frank appraisals. One of his first memories is of two commissioning editors fighting in a corridor at an away weekend in Brighton. Soon afterwards, Richard Attenborough stood up and said how very proud he was of the channel and burst into tears.

Grade neither set nor discussed audience targets for *Cutting Edge*, which had a generous budget of £120,000 for each hour. For the first two years, the controllers and Michael Grade went to a new overflow building along the street on Friday mornings to review the week's ratings. 'We didn't look at them every day, just once a week', says Willis. 'Scheduling was about choice, choosing the most exciting programmes for the amount of money available.'[6]

Adds Moore: 'Michael Grade never interfered, though I would upset the *Daily Mail* regularly. He would poke his head around the door from time to time, cigar in mouth. Farrukh Dhondy called him "Puff-puff".'[7] But the bid to impose a consistent house style on *Cutting Edge* produced a barrage of criticism, particularly from independents who hated being required to conform and saw this as part of Grade's process to make the channel more like ITV. Moore even had a favoured narrator, Mark Halliley, a BBC professional. 'Yes, I probably did seem like one of the first barbarians [to the old guard]. It got a lot worse when the BBC arrived, with Michael Jackson.'[8]

The first *Cutting Edge*, on 19 February 1990, was *Just Some Stories for Eleanor*, about living with motor-neurone disease. It set the style for a run of twenty, covering subjects that ranged from Eton schoolboys to London binmen, then back to *Anyone for Polo?* Claudia Milne's *Island of Outcasts*, a heart-rending programme about mentally ill patients in a primitive institution on a Greek island, kept naked and hosed down like animals, won a Royal Television Society award. By April, a year after Grade had said that programmes needed his attention, he proudly reported to the Board that the impact of reshaping the channel's documentary output had been an uplift in ratings and press coverage.

Cutting Edge gathered steam and gained its highest audience on 14 February 1994 with *Shops and Robbers*, about a Marks & Spencer serial shoplifter, watched by 9.4 million people. Such was the strength of the brand that, though it lost favour when Channel 4 fell out of love with programme strands in 1999, *Cutting Edge* never disappeared – though its revived form in 2007, which opened with a programme about urban foxes, was weak, a far cry from its original specification.

The other key factual innovations were *Female Parts* – which opened with *Rude Women*, watched by 7 million – *Dispatches*, the still vibrant current-affairs programme, and *Rear Window*, featuring documentaries with an international and multicultural focus. The channel's enthusiasm for interesting documentaries from around the world directly inspired the BBC's *Fine Cut*, later renamed *Storyville*. New educative strands, pioneered by Naomi Sargant's successor, Karen Brown, would include, in 1994, *Time Team* with Tony Robinson – the start of popular archaeology – alongside *Equinox* and *Witness*, dealing with science and religious faith.

Despite Willis's insistence on imposing a house style, there was still some room for self-expression. One talented film-maker who came up with a long documentary about Rupert Murdoch was given the choice of making cuts so that it could go out at 9 p.m., running for an hour and a half to a large audience, or keeping it at two hours, to be screened between 11 p.m. and 1 a.m. He chose the latter and a tiny audience. Willis tried to create a set of tiers, so that documentary-makers could work up the ladder from half-hour *Short Stories*, for new directors, to *Cutting Edge* and *True Stories* at ninety minutes or longer.

Nick Broomfield's film, *The Leader, His Wife and the Driver* – about the South African right-wing populist Eugène Terre'Blanche – was an early highlight.[9] A singular young producer, Phil Grabsky, was making his first series, for £480,000, on how Spain had changed since Franco. He was commissioned before Willis took over and, after spending two years in Spain filming, he returned to London to find that far more exacting standards now applied. He had designed the series around the stories of four Spaniards, with a minimum of narration.

> I went to a screening with Peter Moore. I was a twenty-six-year-old. It was a beautiful film, but Moore went very quiet then he said to me: 'I fucking hate it, I want wall-to-wall narration, facts, statistics, what is changing [within Spain].' I had to reshoot. Film-makers were coming out of viewing rooms fuming. I think documentaries lost their way then. The UK became insular, narrative driven.[10]

But Moore and Willis did ask him what he wanted to do next.

In 1991, Channel 4 broadcast *The Committee*, one of its most difficult and controversial programmes, which would have a legal fallout lasting a decade. It was commissioned and managed by David Lloyd, who ran the news and the hard-edged current-affairs strand *Dispatches*. It was a political tinderbox because it made allegations of collusion between Protestant paramilitaries and security forces in Northern Ireland to commit murders. The film, made by a small independent company, featured an anonymous witness, Source A, who was disguised and whose name was never disclosed by the channel. He was the only source for the allegations; but the channel decided that was sufficient.

The refusal to name the informant led to contempt-of-court proceedings, and the channel was fined £75,000 by Lord Justice Woolf; in a worst-case scenario, it could have been shut down. Grade, Attenborough and the rest of the Board adhered throughout to the fundamental tenet that you should not reveal your source; otherwise the whole process of investigative journalism becomes undermined – and in this case someone's life was at risk as well. Grade weathered the attacks from a section of the press, and Roger Graef, who was to become one of his fiercest critics, always praised his stand.

The programme naturally infuriated the Royal Ulster Constabulary (RUC), and the channel became embroiled in bitter libel actions fought across the next decade. The issue remains so sensitive – it is generally accepted that the programme itself was flawed – that even today requests to see the full files are routinely refused. It was not until January 2007 that the Northern Ireland Police Ombudsman confirmed that collusion had actually taken place, and the Attorney General, Lord Goldsmith, was passed a file containing the names of seven RUC officers. Understandably, *Channel 4 News* reported this more extensively than any of the other channels.

● ● ● ●

Entertainment was Grade's forte. He appreciated talent and was naturally a fan of Jonathan Ross; but for a variety of reasons Ross's career did not thrive. The second successful run of *The Last Resort* ended in the autumn of 1988, but Ross was easily bored. A more ambitious venture, *An Hour with Jonathan Ross* – a Sunday night mix of celebrities, chat, quizzes and music – flopped, despite the involvement of Vic Reeves, Bob Mortimer, Paul Whitehouse and Charlie Higson with sketches and scripts. Undeterred, Grade thought Ross could solve another problem. He had stood in successfully for Terry Wogan on his BBC1 chat show, so Grade decided to screen *Tonight with Jonathan Ross* three times a week at 6.30, to boost audiences for the news at 7 p.m.

Ross and Marke, his off-screen producer, were given the star treatment. 'We had a meeting with Grade and Andrea Wonfor [by now running entertainment at Channel 4] on 7 March 1990, a slap-up dinner in Mayfair', recalls Marke.[11] By June, he had booked the Greenwood Theatre, near London Bridge, as a venue for the programme. *Tonight with Jonathan Ross* was launched on 5 November 1990 and ran for two years and 149 episodes, but despite a huge effort, it never really took off. Terry Wogan continued to dominate the format with 7.5 million viewers at 7 p.m., and the best celebrities in town went to him. Ross, at best, hovered around 1.6 million viewers, declining below 500,000 during the Gulf War.

'It was a big miscalculation, a grave error', said Marke. 'It killed off the whole feeling he'd created through *The Last Resort*. Grade is a charismatic guy, I must admit, but it did seem like we were staring at a cash register.'[12] The principal flaw in the concept was that the chat show was on too early for Ross's fans still returning from work. With Grade's backing, they tried taking it to America, but that flopped too. In 1993, Ross returned with one last throw: *Saturday Zoo*, a mix of comedians and chat involving the newcomers Steve Coogan and Mark Thomas, with Rowland Rivron (Dr Martin Scrote from *The Last Resort*) and Joanna Lumley as an occasional co-host. Savagely reviewed, it fizzled out – and that was the end of Ross on Channel 4. 'It ended in a non-confrontational way', reflected Marke, who went on to found his own production company. 'Once a broadcaster perceives that's happening, they can decide it's over for you.'[13]

Chris Evans, the zany host of *The Big Breakfast*, became the channel's flavour of the time, even though, according to Forgan, Grade never really understood Evans or the new wave of entertainers and satirists – including Chris Morris, the sublime exponent of black humour. The roster of new shows included *Drop the Dead Donkey*, the topical send-up of a television newsroom, and *Rory Bremner, Who Else?* Bremner had been brought over from the BBC, and his first series in 1992 brought biting political satire to the channel for the first time. Clive Anderson was another Channel 4 discovery, while the stand-ups Jack Dee and Sean Hughes were given their television breaks.

When *Network 7*'s replacement, *Club X*, failed at 6 p.m. on Fridays and was replaced by *The Word*, Grade quickly moved it to late night, 11.15 p.m. to 12.15 a.m., where it gained cult status. Gaby Roslin, also a graduate of *The Big Breakfast*, was later given *The Real Holiday Show* to present. This was an early popular reality show about people misbehaving on holiday: they took a video camera and an assistant producer with them. It went out led by *Friends* and *ER* after *Brookside*, and Roslin was credited with adding 1 million viewers to the show's 5 million. Grade had some personal input into this show, suggesting to its commissioner, Peter Grimsdale, that the holidaymakers should be brought into the studio at the end to comment.

When Grade arrived, there was already a flashing light warning that the new satellite services, BSB and Sky, merged into BSkyB in 1990, were pushing up the prices of the American programmes that made such a significant contribution to Channel 4's ratings and economics. American programmes cost the channel £6.9 million in 1991; when Grade left in 1997, this had more than trebled to £23.6 million. The amount of American material broadcast, including repeats, rose by 40 per cent in that period. It was hugely cost-effective, as Channel 4 had discovered with its first sneaky deal for *Cheers* back in 1982, then *Roseanne* four years later.

An hour of British-made original drama would cost between £300,000 and £600,000, while two half-hours of US sitcoms were £10,000 to £20,000. That meant that in effect they subsidised the prestige programmes – and they were usually more popular. In 1991, two-fifths of the channel's weekly top tens were American imports, mainly sitcoms, led by *The Golden Girls* and *Cheers*. Six US series averaged more than 3 million viewers against three British ones.

Among the four terrestrial channels, Channel 4 was at this stage unique in count-ing so heavily on programmes made for another market. Here, though, were the seeds of danger. Because they were cheap, and the best were popular, American pro-grammes, led by *ER* and *Friends*, would attract rival bidders – first satellite television, then Channel Five – while the rights to back catalogues of British programmes were not easily available, and probably not all that suitable even if they were. Under Isaacs, American programmes were 'tellyfilla', presented as exhuming old hits in a discrimi-nating fashion for the amusement of viewers – although this justification clearly did not apply to freshly made first runs of transatlantic comedy.

'Both in daytime and evenings, it [Channel 4] would be very vulnerable to a bidding war with another broadcaster such as a satellite, which aimed to secure a basic minimum audience by purchasing rights to multiple runs of recent US sitcoms', noted *Broadcast* magazine's ratings guru William Phillips in 1991. But, like a choco-holic, Channel 4 could never wean itself from its addiction. The European Commis-sion, which tried to regulate satellite television through the first Television Without Frontiers directive in 1989, was fostering European television and film production to fight off American influence. Channel 4 was supposed to become more oriented towards the Continent, but attempts at productions funded by a number of national television channels led to series mocked as Europuddings. There was *Black Forest Clinic* from Germany and *Châteauvallon*, 'Dallas sur Loire', played out in dubbed and subtitled formats. Channel 4 also invested in *Mission Eureka*, a sex and space drama so bad it had to be played at midnight. None of the shows caught the audi-ence's imagination.

Under a forceful new commissioner, the *Guardian* critic Waldemar Januszczak, there was a fresh approach to the arts, a shift away from high culture and filmed per-formance; though live opera continued, including a wonderful production of *Tosca*, in 1992, performed on location in Rome and shared with the BBC. Januszczak, a televi-sion novice, invented an iconoclastic new strand, *Without Walls*, a weekly hour-long tilt at a topic or artist, often barbed and sometimes wayward. It was introduced by a mascot, Douglas the Armadillo. The programme staked out its territory with Tony Parsons' bitter denunciation of the English working class; Michael Nyman's musical tribute to his football club, Queen's Park Rangers; an exploration of homosexuality in Shakespeare, D.H. Lawrence and Michelangelo; an examination of Alf Garnett and *Expletives Deleted*, examining British attitudes to bad language. The show also includ-ed a denunciatory *J'Accuse* strand, as in 'J'Accuse Santa Claus of stringing along small children'. It was altogether less cosy than ITV's arts flagship, *The South Bank Show*.

In 1991, the channel ran its landmark late-night Banned season, packed into twenty-one days for impact and to foster debate. It followed the vigorous but unsuc-cessful attempt to impose a form of censorship on television in the 1990 Broadcast-ing Act. Willis, in a Channel 4 press release that now seems quaint, said, 'We are delighted to offer viewers an opportunity to make up their own minds about *Life of Brian* and other programmes.' *Life of Brian*, the most successful of three Monty Python films – and now a regular Christmas standby on Channel 4 – had been the subject of a long dispute between the channel and the Regulator since 1984, when it was refused permission to screen it on grounds of blasphemy. Several of the other films in the season, including one on sex education, still required cuts or pixillation to comply with the regulations. Channel 4 ran into serious trouble with the Regulator with *Sex and the Censors*, clips of banned bits from films, which was carelessly scheduled earlier, at 9 p.m. at night.

This season included one of the most extraordinary minority-interest programmes, shown to a tiny audience at 11 p.m. on 11 April, a textbook example of something only the early Channel 4 would have backed. It was called *Mother Ireland*, and it had already provoked a major row between Forgan and George Russell, by now the Chairman of the ITC that had replaced the IBA. *Mother Ireland* was made by the Derry Film & Video Workshop in 1987 and bought in April 1988. It was backed by the channel, perhaps naively, after assurances that the workshop was not run by IRA terrorists.

The programme told the bloody and emotional story of Ireland through the perspective of republican feminists – no unionists were included. Much of it was in black and white, and it included songs and poems of martyrdom and suffering. One of the contributors was Mairéad Farrell who, shortly after it was completed, was shot dead by undercover SAS officers in Gibraltar in 1988 in an incident that caused yet another explosive media row between the Government and the Regulator, when Thames Television's *This Week* investigated it in a programme called *Death on the Rock*.

The inquest into Farrell's death held up transmission of *Mother Ireland*. Once it was over, Grade told the Board in October 1988 that the channel needed to make a decision about whether to show it. There were extensive consultations with lawyers. Forgan and Willis were in favour of transmitting it unedited, but Grade, supported by Attenborough, disagreed. He said it should not be shown as it stood because Farrell had deceived the programme-makers, and he wanted it adapted to exclude her. Greg Dyke, another director, thought it was wrong in principle to exclude Farrell, but he understood the pragmatic reasons. Carmen Callil thought it should be screened intact.

George Russell, then still the channel's Deputy Chairman, inquired about another contributor, Rita O'Hare, who had been Editor of a republican newspaper in Dublin. Russell felt very strongly about it because his secretary had been injured by an IRA parcel bomb delivered to his office, and a similar parcel – though not containing a bomb – had been delivered to his Northumbrian home. The bitterly split Board was rescued the next day when the Home Secretary, Douglas Hurd, announced new emergency regulations banning interviews with extremist Republican organisations, including Sinn Féin. The Channel backed down. So the programme was finally included, three years later, in the Banned season. By that time the Derry workshop was a thing of the past.[14]

● ● ● ●

By September 1991, everyone was jumpy: the new ITV franchises would be awarded the following month, and Channel 4 was nervously preparing for a new era. Over the summer it had inadvertently lost £5 million, placed on deposit just as the Bank of Credit and Commerce International (BCCI) collapsed. The Board rejected a resignation offer by the Finance Director, David Scott. This was a rare lapse: Channel 4 from time to time initiated audits of independent producers it felt were not delivering value on screen, but its business systems usually ran well. It was also planning to quit Charlotte Street – another cause of concern to the original founders – and to build new headquarters to accommodate an expanding staff that would rise to 554 by 1993.[15]

The year 1991 was the worst time for British advertising in twenty years, and the subscription from ITV fell by £4 million. In the wake of the 1990 Broadcasting Act settlement, the channel had to shoulder a new responsibility, hived off by ITV, for commissioning schools programmes, which would cost around £10 million to make. The independents, important stakeholders in the channel, watched the programme budget suddenly shrink by between £25 million and £30 million, a cut of a sixth. At the same time, the channel was imposing more rigorous standards of programme-making. The IPPA's Director Margaret Windham Heffernan called it a managerial mess, and her members attacked Grade for abandoning the Isaacs mission.

The row went public at the Edinburgh Television Festival that August at a packed Saturday session: Channel 4: Remit or Ratings. The debate was led by Roger Graef, a disappointed contender for Chief Executive in 1987. He said the quizzes, sitcoms and repeats were 'irrelevant to the channel's original task.' The freedom of the Chief Executive to interpret the remit in whatever way he or she chose should be challenged, if necessary under the new Broadcasting Act. 'I fear we will have to fight to save Channel 4 once again.'[16] Beforehand, he had rehearsed the arguments to sympathetic groups in a quiet voice, cloaking his passion. But at the debate in the Assembly Rooms, he received little overt support from other producers, fearful of inciting their paymaster's wrath, and he was left exposed to Grade's furious counter-attack. Yet, John McGrath, the independent producers' representative on the Board, later told Grade that while he may have defeated Graef, he had not won the argument nor won hearts.[17]

Just as that debate seemed to be fizzling out, a bombshell landed on Grade's desk on 12 September. The front page of the *Independent* reported that Channel 4 had paid him £500,000 in a 'golden handcuffs' deal, in return for staying put for at least five years and not joining bids for the upcoming ITV franchises. A further £300,000 had been paid by extending gold-plated deals to six other executives, who got a year's extra salary for three-year contracts; Scott, for instance, received £80,000. Even John Willis and Andrea Wonfor, the newish Controller of Entertainment, were included: they were not board members, but they were the most marketable executives because they were ITV-trained.

The reason why the news of these deals caused such a shock was that Channel 4 had not been perceived as a place to get rich quick, though talk of privatisation had whetted some appetites. Even Grade's habitual supporters did not think the channel had behaved well: they pointed out that Isaacs had been paid only a modest £65,000 salary when he left. Grade's take-home pay in 1991 was lifted by the deal from £235,000 to £485,000.

The executive bonus scheme was leaked to the *Independent* by a rival broadcaster incensed by the news and was reported by this author, then the paper's Media Editor. It was confirmed, after a delay, by the channel's assiduous Press Officer, Chris Griffin-Beale, who seemed shocked: he was, after all, a long way below the rank required to be in on the deal.

The scheme had been devised off-stage by the Chairman, Attenborough. It was minuted as a decision of the Remuneration Sub-Committee on 26 March of that year, before a full board meeting. It was obliquely mentioned in the 1990 annual report, published in June 1991, where he wrote, 'We are giving consideration to taking steps [...] to secure the services of our key people in the longer term.' Though agreed by the Remuneration Sub-Committee, the full Board had not had the chance to discuss or reflect on it when the story broke. There was no board meeting in August, and in June and July they had been too tied up with other matters. The first that most of the channel's staff heard of it was from the *Independent*. The unions protested, as did aggrieved independent producers, who called an emergency meeting.

Heffernan wrote to Attenborough on behalf of the IPPA:

> When five million disappeared into the maw of BCCI we attempted to be sympathetic [...] after all, nobody's perfect. But I have tried and failed to identify the moral and managerial high ground the channel occupies while doling out a million pounds to its executives. If the channel depends so exclusively on a few individuals, then its managerial problems are severe. If it can keep them only through cash then probably those problems are insurmountable. If it expects any sympathy from its suppliers, it is desperately out of touch.[18]

The effect of the row was to reignite the debate over whether Grade was really the right custodian for Channel 4. Anthony Smith was pained. He wrote to the *Independent* on 15 September 1991, saying the news was 'shocking to many of those who worked hard to establish the channel.' The Board, after all, had taken the view that senior staff should stay in post for only about four years, so that the programmes could constantly be revitalised with fresh ideas. 'That the Board should scatter gold along its top corridor suggests it has misunderstood its future as well as its past', his letter concluded.

Attenborough replied to the IPPA:

> The channel was and is facing a critical period. Channel 4, as a publisher broadcaster, is the model for all the new applicants for Channel Three (ITV) licences and therefore could expect to be the first port of call for headhunters. Our fears proved only too real, since all the senior staff did in fact receive offers.[19]

But the view persisted that the deal was really structured around Michael Grade. Did everyone else really get offers?

A week later, at the Royal Television Society's Cambridge Convention, Grade accepted some blame for not preparing people for the change and agreed to a special session on the Friday evening. This author, according to the *Royal Television Society Journal*, asked the most dramatic question, wondering whether Grade had persuaded other board members to take payment in order to implicate them all. Grade said the suggestion was defamatory, but one board member, Liz Forgan, did respond: 'I think it would have been better if the well thought out, properly discussed reasons for all this had been made apparent at the time [. . .] then it wouldn't have looked quite so furtive as it appears to look now', she said.[20] She subsequently argued in favour of publishing the figures at once, to clear the air, but was overruled on the grounds that disclosure would fuel further press comment.

Peter Fiddick, chairing the session, asked Grade why it took so much money to persuade him to stay. Grade replied that the decision was a commercial rather than a moral judgement. He had never seriously considered leaving but had been approached. He had told Attenborough that he might expect to get other job offers and that 'if I am going to take myself off the market, we should have a negotiation [. . .] I don't want the market rate but I would like you to make me some offer.'[21] Later, he told staff that he needed the money because he was between a divorce and the break-up of another relationship and in need of a new house.

Michael Darlow, a former Chairman of IPPA, was critical:

> If that is the ethos that now governs Channel 4 then we have an uneasy feeling that this is an ethos which is inappropriate for a channel which has a special remit. It is not so much that Channel 4 has lost its way – but if it has lost its soul it will lose the map altogether.[22]

The charge of losing its soul would ring down the years, resurfacing with the *Celebrity Big Brother* row in January 2007, when it was accused of fostering racist behaviour.

Attenborough, who was by now in Hollywood making a film about Charlie Chaplin, was absent from the September board meeting four days later – the first time the matter was properly discussed at board level. By then, the deal he had agreed could only be endorsed. As Carmen Callil said, it was a fait accompli. Under the new contracts, any board member who attached their name to any ITV franchise bid would have to leave.

David Lloyd, Senior Commissioning Editor for News and Current Affairs, now became the de-facto shop steward of the commissioners. He remembers:

> It was one of those revolutionary moments where you honestly wondered whether the commissioning body wasn't going to walk out. It was very febrile. For all that Michael had modernised the place and was making it more professional, the culture was not one of get rich quick. That was the last thing it was [. . .] It still had a cottage-industry quality, and that was seen as its fundamental difference and strength. So it really was a seismic shock to the system.[23]

The Rubicon had been crossed, and it provoked the most serious crisis of staff relations in the channel's first nine years. In his report to the Board, Grade wrote: 'It has been very damaging. It has been a difficult three weeks.' Shaken by the reaction, he vowed to introduce informal gatherings with commissioning editors to improve communication and to deal with the criticism that he was distancing himself from them. Eventually the fuss died down, as his critics reflected on the damage Channel 4 would have suffered if Grade – an obvious candidate to run the ITV network schedule – were to have left at such a critical time. Directors who benefited from the scheme described their inducements later as tin handcuffs, compared with the huge amounts given to successful independents and ITV directors on future such occasions.

Were the payments justified? There was legitimate concern that directors could be poached for ITV franchise bids, their names kept secret until the new franchises had been awarded. This would create instability leading up to Channel 4's own crucial change of status in 1993: the channel had already paid some generous overall salary rises in an attempt to head off poaching. Grade was clearly very marketable, because at heart he was a mainstream broadcaster. He had been approached by Richard Branson, whose ITV franchise bid was destined to fail.[24] They had three conversations, but Grade's price, £250,000 up front plus £250,000 a year, was too steep. Michael Green of Carlton, who was to win the London weekday franchise as a publisher-broadcaster on the Channel 4 model, was another rebuffed suitor. John Willis had six approaches but turned them all down. It is not clear whether anyone else would have been poached.

In the event, Liz Forgan was the only executive to breach her three-year loyalty agreement. At the Edinburgh Television Festival the following year, she gave a ringing speech about her belief in public-service broadcasting in the presence of John Birt, about to become Director General of the BBC. He hired her to run BBC Radio in January 1993 and, as part of the deal, the BBC had to repay the amount of her handcuff to Channel 4. As Director of Programmes, and high priestess of the channel's founding values, she had chipped in to defend Grade at Cambridge, but in autumn 1991 her relationship with him started to deteriorate fast, and she was stung by his description of her departure in his memoir, *It Seemed Like a Good Idea at the Time*.

> I was so amazed by what he said in his book. He accused me of disloyalty, leaving the place in the lurch. All totally untrue. Complete nonsense. At Cambridge I did stand up and defend him. I said it could have been better handled . . . In fact, I was bitterly against golden handcuffs and had argued till I was blue in the face against them. I hated the whole idea. If people stay in a place they should stay because they want to, because that's where their heart is.[25]

She had predicted accurately that there would be a tremendous row about them but forfeited the moral high ground by going along with a modified scheme for herself.

> I didn't want to refuse to have it, because it would make it look as if all my colleagues were wrong. I didn't want to look snooty. The impetus for this came from Michael. He got the lion's share, then it was extended to the rest of the Board. I think you are quite right, it was cover for Michael. It was exactly what happened.[26]

Despite the reservations of the Isaacs old guard about Grade's commercialism, as the channel's tenth anniversary arrived in November 1992 it remained identifiably different from ITV, not only in programming but also in its audiences. Under Grade, the distinction was becoming blurred around the edges, but the essence of the original ethos had not been betrayed. The changes he had made would strengthen its chances of survival when it had to sell its own advertising next year. Its audiences in daytime had risen sharply, and in peak time they were also on the rise. In 1992, it finally broke through the 10 per cent barrier. After 6 p.m., it was reaching 9 per cent of the audience, while in daytime the figure spurted to over 13 per cent, in spite of the new obligation to provide schools programmes.

Under Grade, Channel 4 had found its second wind. One of his key insights was that there were discontented viewers who wanted an alternative in the afternoons, a lesson that the channel has never forgotten. Towards lunchtime and on the fringe of weekday peak time, where he was already doing well with *Countdown*, Grade extended the cheap but watchable programming: old black-and-white movies, Oprah Winfrey chat shows, a few American sitcoms and a sprinkling of teen series after 6 p.m. What the channel now needed, to become a commercial success, was to be more distinct from ITV and to woo the youth and upmarket audiences even more determinedly.

Liz Forgan's departure did not leave a hiatus. John Willis was instantly promoted to fill her post, which pleased the commissioners and the new advertising sales side. The channel was just starting selling its own advertising and, coming from ITV, Willis understood the score. He says, 'We felt the worry acutely but the previous system was so strange, a strange British compromise, that we were pleased to stand on our own two feet. But we had absolutely no idea how it would work out, and ITV was extremely aggressive. We needed really strong programmes.'[27]

Back on 3 April 1989, the channel's original breakfast programme, the long-forgotten and unmourned *Channel 4 Daily*, was launched to run from 6 a.m. to 9.25 a.m. It increased the channel's broadcasting time by 20 per cent for a disproportionately modest outlay of around £15 million a year, but it never worked, completely lacking a 'switch me on' factor. Designed as an upmarket grapefruit, with segments supplied by ITN, 'Business Daily', 'Countdown Masters' and arts and entertainment from Mentorn, it was Channel 4 being nice, committing the classic mistake of doling out bits of a single programme to different independent producers to make. Its aim was to attract an upmarket audience, weaning them from their loyalty to Radio 4's *Today* programme – a hopeless task. But then, because of the channel's links with ITV, it was constrained from going head to head with TV-am by challenging its appeal to housewives.

With ITV about to cease its support, the task of figuring out a solution to the breakfast dilemma, one that made money, was handed to the seasoned entertainment controller, Andrea Wonfor, who had brought in *The Tube*. The tender was won in May 1992 by the talented makers of *The Word*, Waheed Alli and Charlie Parsons – who had also been a key force in *Network 7* – together with Bob Geldof. *The Big Breakfast* was launched on 28 September 1992 before GMTV took over from TV-am, and, to everyone's surprise, proved both a commercial success and highly innovative, almost instantly quadrupling audiences for the slot. Parsons organised the team to work on it, with Bob Geldof presenting – though this petered out quickly – and his wife Paula Yates conducting interviews in bed, including one with Michael Hutchence: this was a reference back to *The Tube*. Sir David Nicholas, the former Editor of *News at Ten*, who was by now a director of Channel 4, quipped, 'The new

show made Roland Rat look like Lord Reith but that is clearly not preventing it finding an audience.'

One of the formative off-screen talents was Duncan Gray, who had filmed Chris
Evans' first-ever audition piece when he worked as a student on Greater London Radio.[28] Gray worked for Parsons as a development researcher in the year before launch
and helped devise what would basically be a live, freewheeling radio programme
adapted for television, based loosely on the Radio 1 breakfast show. Evans and Gaby
Roslin were the uninhibited disc jockeys, and when they stopped talking, there was,
instead of a music track, a silly and deliberately embarrassing three-minute feature,
such as 'Whose Washing Line Is It?' The many gaffes were part of the flow. Emma
Forbes was offered the job of female host – in effect, Evans's sidekick – but she got
cold feet. Roslin, then a children's television presenter, was chosen for her sunny
personality and because she would never try to upstage Evans on whom the show
depended. In effect, it was a channel within a channel, bringing 'duvet television' into
being for kids and teenagers, who increasingly had sets in their bedrooms. Grade's
regime had produced a breakthrough, a long-running hit, just when it was needed
commercially. And that shut the critics up – for a bit.

13

The golden formula

● ● ● ●

Channel 4's emergence as a small and surprisingly wealthy independent television station began in 1993, when it took control of selling its own advertising. This was a key turning point, not only in financial terms but also because of the effect it had on the programming ethos. Exposed for the first time to raw commercial pressures, its executives had to face the reality that without solid ratings it faced trouble. Stewart Butterfield, Director of Sales and Marketing, would become a key figure in this, the channel's more worldly second decade. In the two years before that turning point, from his arrival in 1991, commissioning editors had taken hardly any notice of him as he sat in his tiny, cramped office on Charlotte Street's first floor, quietly preparing for this challenging new era.

Butterfield, who had been with the McCann-Erickson advertising agency for sixteen years, handling their big European accounts, was approached by head-hunters in the late autumn of 1990. He had relevant experience and a certain reassuring gravitas. He was good at presenting strategy to the Company Board and to outsiders, and he did not panic under fire. Since some involvement in Channel 4's launch back in 1982, he had not had any contact with the channel but said he was willing for his name to go forward.[1] He went before what he thought of as an 'oddly democratic group' of the Executive Board: Michael Grade, Liz Forgan and Colin Leventhal, Director of Acquisitions. Grade offered him the job but said this must be approved by the Chairman, Richard Attenborough, who gave his assent at a long lunch at the Savoy Grill, dominated by Attenborough's theatrical reminiscences. (Although change was in the air, some things remained the same.) Butterfield was chosen on the hard-nosed assessment that he would bring in most revenue. Liz Forgan favoured another candidate, Tess Alps, but she was outvoted.

As the channel moved towards selling its own advertising, conditions were in some ways propitious. BSB had been captured and then ruthlessly dismembered by a triumphant Sky. The ITV franchises were changing hands, so a lot of experienced people were on the job market as the losers disgorged staff. A debate on whether to contract out sales to an agency was swiftly settled. 'With Michael, we decided early on we'd have our own sales force', Butterfield recalled. 'An independent sales force was never going to understand the nature of Channel 4.'[2] The success of the 1990s was to be built on the 1980s. Unlike most new ventures, Channel 4 had a ten-year track record, so the problems inherent in a start-up were largely avoided. Advertisers knew the channel. Media buyers, usually young men, watched its racier programmes. ITV was losing its monopoly of advertising, exercised since 1955, but still operated in a strange, federal world, with the companies' sales forces competing ferociously against each other rather than uniting. 'That was the basis on which I joined', says Butterfield. 'I was pretty sure, given the nature of ITV and given my belief that Channel 4 could evolve, that there was a very good chance of commercial success.'[3]

When he arrived, he found a channel essentially dominated by programme commissioners. He was not impressed with the way the schedule zigzagged around, or the tendency for programmes to turn up seemingly out of the blue. No one had the faintest idea how this new melding of commerce and artistic idealism was going to work. With Michael Grade and David Scott, the Finance Director, Butterfield went to sound out the ITV companies to see how they saw the change. At LWT, they met Ron Miller, the legendary Sales Director, in relaxed mood, just off to play golf in Barbados. Clearly he did not see the pesky little channel as any threat to his lucrative empire. 'I watched David Scott's face drop', recalls Butterfield. 'I don't think anyone in Channel 4 realised how ITV sales worked.'[4]

Andy Barnes, who was to be the key force in founding the sales team, joined as Head of Sales in November 1991, followed by Hugh Johnson as Head of Research. They had to decide on an approach. Until this point, Channel 4 was a television publishing house in the happy position of spending a guaranteed pot of money without worrying too much where it came from or how the programmes fared in terms of ratings. Under the funding formula agreed back in 1980, the ITV companies handed over a subscription every year, to convert into programmes made by independent suppliers. Advertising was handled off site by ITV sales teams they never met.

Channel 4 was fortunate to be launched in the Thatcher era when television advertising was booming, regularly exceeding projections, as it would do for a further twenty years, until 2000. Launching early into this growth period was rather like surfing a wave. As the advertising cake expanded, Channel 4's 14-per-cent slice of ITV's overall annual sales income steadily grew. In the first five years, until 1987, as the channel experimented with programmes of variable quality, it was protected from its mistakes. The dispute with the actors' union, Equity, which often meant commercial breaks were just empty space, lasted until 1984 and would have destroyed the channel had it operated as a normal business.

The initial aim was for a 10-per-cent audience share, but by 1987 only 8 per cent had been achieved. In the next five years, a clearer, more orderly schedule started to emerge, and ratings improved. Channel 4, instead of being a drain on ITV, was starting to be of increasing benefit. As 1993 loomed, maximising audience share and advertising revenue became a priority, which is why the programming under Grade began to move away from Isaacs' schedule. But in 1991, as Butterfield set to work, the extent of the changes that would flow from an independent advertising sales force were still not fully understood, either by the channel itself or by advertising agencies and the ITV sales teams that would now be competing with it.

Since 1982, ITV had, in effect, bundled Channel 4 sales with its own advertising. Advertisers would be urged to spend a bit of their total budgets on Channel 4, which was customarily priced at about half as much per viewer as the ITV rate. The conviction grew within Channel 4 – certainly within the boardroom – that it was being undersold. Subsequent events proved this, but no one was going to shout about it in the tense period of 1988/9, when the threat of privatisation loomed. Increasing its advertising rate would make the channel more valuable and, therefore, more vulnerable to a predator.

The deal struck in 1989 between Channel 4 and the Government, enshrined in the 1990 Broadcasting Act, was that instead of being privatised, it would be allowed to sell its own advertising. The link with ITV would be weakened, although the network would provide a safety net if Channel 4 ran into financial difficulties; so there could be no question of a call on public funds. Channel 4 would have guaranteed slots on ITV to promote its programmes in return and would pay back to ITV half of any advertising revenue that exceeded a 14-per-cent share. So, from 1991, the channel began to build a sales force of around sixty people, who would expect cars and bonuses, like sales forces everywhere.

One unforeseen consequence was that programme commissioners began to wonder why they should not have cars as well. Some time later, it was decided to offer company cars to commissioning editors to play fair. There was an outcry along the lines of 'How dare you give me a car', recalls David Scott. Michael Grade countered by saying that they didn't have to take one if they didn't want to. In the end, most did.

In the run-up to 1993, Grade began to tinker with the schedule to maximise potential revenue throughout the day. The popular *Countdown* would be screened all year, and *Brookside* moved from two episodes a week to three. *The Big Breakfast* was launched in September 1992, deliberately timed to take advantage of ITV's vulnerability when GMTV was taking over its breakfast service from TV-am. Schools programmes were taken off ITV as part of the changeover, and Channel 4 had to do them instead, but, as a reward, it was allowed extra advertising minutes, adding 5 per cent to its inventory, which it smartly moved to more lucrative commercial breaks. The ITV companies complained at what they saw as sharp practice, and the dispute continued into 1993, the beginning of worsening relations.

Then there was the channel's own brand positioning. From the start, its experimental approach had attracted younger people to programmes such as *The Tube* and *The Last Resort*, while the tastes of people who watched less television, the 'light viewers', were catered for by news, documentaries, the arts and films. By 1993, this was an established pattern, and it proved to be a lucrative formula if deployed carefully. These were the niche audiences who advertisers wanted to reach.

Grade explained that the remit was elastic. 'Our task is now to adapt to the changes imposed on us and to develop and propel them along the route that means Channel 4 remains a real alternative for viewers', he said. He referred specifically to Jeremy Isaacs' formula of means-and-ends programmes.

> Our responsibility is to take that formula, adapt it, stretch it, pull it and push it into a programming policy which will continue to offer into 2003 [i.e., ten years on] an alternative. Commercial survival doesn't mean a ratings war with ITV. I cannot predict just what specific programmes that philosophy will deliver in 1993, or 1998. But we must offer something different for cultural and commercial reasons.

The roots of Channel 4's decision to market its advertising in a different way from ITV can be traced back to a defunct ITV company. TVS, based in Southampton, had been the franchise-holder for southern England since 1980 but lost out to Meridian in the 1991 franchising round and was formally replaced on 1 January 1993. It covered an area stretching from Kent to Dorset – the prosperous deep south of England, whose well-heeled and well-educated residents generally preferred the BBC to ITV. TVS sales teams could not, therefore, sell advertising slots in the conventional way, on the basis of high ratings. Instead, they talked up the audience demographics: this programme was reaching primarily ABC1 professional and managerial males, and that one appealed to young people between sixteen and thirty-four – both categories highly valued by advertisers.

It was not easy, though, because computers, vital for swift analysis of audience trends, were in their infancy when TVS took to the air, and the audience-measurement system was not as sophisticated as it would be by the 1990s – when, as computers improved, the Channel 4 team was better able to show potential advertisers that they were delivering exceptional value.

Andy Barnes had pioneered the TVS approach and was now recruited to Channel 4. At thirty-seven, he had a sharp brain, the gift of the gab and was cheery, brave and shrewd. Salesmanship was in his blood: his father was a new-business director at an advertising agency and his brother Simon was Advertising Sales Controller at the *Mail on Sunday*. In December 1991, he walked into the new department in Whitfield Street, close to the Charlotte Street building, where it had been decided to house the sales team to keep them separate from the creatives. 'There were no desks, no sales policy, nothing', he recalls.[5]

Channel 4 Sales was seen as a poisoned chalice by the rest of the advertising industry. After the calamities at TV-am and BSB, the received opinion was that, in television start-ups, the pioneer habitually failed, leaving the successor company to sort it out. Barnes knew how ITV treated Channel 4. 'ITV had sold Channel 4 the way any good monopolist would do it. We lumped it up, sold it as one. If you control the sales on both channels you can allocate funds and advertising campaigns as it suits you.'[6] He knew, through a careful reading of the research, that Channel 4 had under-exploited potential. Radical, challenging programmes were likely to appeal to young, upmarket people with disposable income. It would be fatal for Channel 4 to plunge downmarket and turn itself into ITV2.

The first change Barnes engineered was pragmatic. 'ITV, in all honesty, wasn't worried where Channel 4 put the advertising breaks, so the channel's schedulers had a massive amount of control over the breaks, which was barmy. They put them in the wrong places and didn't allow any breaks in certain programmes'.[7] This analysis that is still disputed, though, by Sue Stoessl, Channel 4's first Head of Marketing.[8] The new Sales Department took over the scheduling of commercial breaks, placing as many as they were allowed into the top-rated, prime-time programmes.

But it was not plain sailing. Back in Charlotte Street, the programme commissioners became edgy. 'We told them what they were doing didn't make any sense', says Barnes.

> *We* had to decide where breaks go. *Cutting Edge*, for instance, was a fantastic programme for upmarket viewers, but at the time the programme department was only allowing one break an hour, and sometimes no breaks at all: it was absolutely insane. Stewart and I had a meeting with Liz Forgan. I said, 'Liz, we've got this fantastic property, we want two breaks in it.
>
> She said, 'Well Andy, you don't understand. We have to get the viewer in, create tension, build them up to a state of frenzy. If we go to a break we have to build them up again. Sometimes it is just not possible.'
>
> I said, 'Liz, we are going to lose millions of pounds.' We agreed to put in two breaks.
>
> But we'd listen. We'd have a discussion. I never personally got any animosity. In the first three or four months of us selling our airtime, in 1993, the programme schedules came out. When we saw them in sales we'd

think, 'Hell, we've got a homeless fortnight season – not a homeless day but two weeks. They must be joking!' But then it was a huge success. After that, we all said, 'We're not programme-makers: we'll just sell the stuff.'[9]

One barometer of change, though, was the ritual of the overnight ratings from BARB, the audience-measurement service. This gave crude audience figures each morning at around 11 a.m., showing how well the programmes of the day before had performed. Jeremy Isaacs had never released them. Michael Grade had held them close. From 1992, Hugh Johnson released them to the Programme Department as part of the educative process.

One far-reaching decision was to sell Channel 4 advertising at fixed prices and to refuse to negotiate downwards. This set a base price on which future increases could be calculated. It was an important difference from ITV, whose advertising was linked to a system of average station price, calculated each month by adding together the advertising revenue and dividing it by the commercial impacts (how many people viewed an advertisement) in that month. It could go up and down and create all sorts of bargaining opportunities. When 1993 came around, Channel 4, as a smaller channel, remained much cheaper to buy into than ITV, but because of the increase in slots, the team had more to sell than in 1992. And with fixed prices, it could more accurately calculate its potential revenue.

Channel 4 also organised its sales team differently from ITV. It divided the UK into just six regions – Ireland, Scotland, London, North, Midlands and South. The ITV map, by contrast, was split into thirty-nine sub-divisions. Barnes's sales team laid down the rule that within any advertising break, one or two spots – or about 20 per cent of the break – would be for local or regional advertisers. They could not all go to Procter & Gamble or Unilever. This created a kind of rationing, which in turn encouraged demand. 'We had to sell some airtime regionally', Barnes explains.

> In 1992, there were fifty-two airlines flying out of airports in the south-east, compared with a handful in the north-east, all wanting to advertise. That's the cream on the cake, the 20 per cent of regional advertising. In effect, it gives us two channels to sell, 80 per cent nationally and the rest locally.[10]

It also gave Channel 4 a clear advantage over the emerging satellite channels, with their purely national coverage.

Next came the decision to sell only the three most expensive groups of viewers to advertisers: sixteen-to-thirty-fours, light viewers and ABC1s. Channel 4 was the first to introduce a computerised system called optimisation. This looks at the type of programme and matches the advertisements to the audiences. It remains the key to Channel 4's operation. Only certain advertisers could gain access to programmes attracting the sixteen- to thirty-four-year-olds, which is why there were no Persil ads in breaks during *The Word*. ITV reached the mass audience with programmes such as *Coronation Street*, and its advertising remained very expensive. Channel 4 was able to exploit the peaks and troughs.

Television advertising sales houses divide the population into fourteen categories. The price of slots depends on how much television that audience watches. Men aged sixteen to thirty-four, who watch 41 per cent less television than housewives, are currently the most valued and, therefore, the most expensive group to advertise to. Big advertisers trying to introduce a new product to 70–80 per cent of the audience do not only want ITV's couch potatoes, they want the people who are harder to reach. For example, an ad in *Coronation Street* might deliver 30 per cent of the total impact needed. If the advertiser also took a spot in *Emmerdale*, the impact might rise to only 36 per cent, because the same people watch both soaps. Channel 4 had light viewers and also upmarket ones, so the sales team could make a strong case for not being left off an advertiser's schedules. The channel was also efficient and cost-effective for some youth brands, such as music. The approach would adapt well to the future, with the introduction of digital channels E4 and More4, which specifically target sixteen- to thirty-four-year-olds and light upmarket viewers. But it was clear that this approach would find it hard to coexist with the scatter-gun 'let a thousand flowers bloom' programming of the Isaacs era. This, then, was the grand strategy. But putting it into practice needed nerves of steel.

In 1991, as the ITV companies realised Channel 4 was going to run as an independent company in competition with them, they reduced even further the money they allocated to the channel. In 1992, Stewart Butterfield went to an infamous meeting with ITV advertising directors, who declared they would drive Channel 4 into the sea. When Butterfield told Barnes, he laughed.

> I said that we would fight them on the beaches. I thought we could do far better than anyone thought we could, although I knew the advertising agencies were very conservative. ITV was a very, very big monster in the marketplace and would endeavour to use its muscle to hurt us.[11]

ITV, after all, controlled three-quarters of the television advertising market.

> Like nobody ever got fired for buying IBM, no media buyer gets fired for buying ITV. We couldn't compete on its level. I always told people, 'ITV is great. If I were you I'd buy it; but you will get a better, more rounded schedule if you include Channel 4. We have lots of light viewers, young viewers, upmarket viewers.' We were very self-effacing, not arrogant. We

said, 'You don't have to buy us but if you do, this is what we will deliver.' The fear we had was that ITV would exert its muscle but in fact we benefited from their system of divide and rule. Their system was set up so that they competed against each other as much as against us.[12]

By this time, as consolidation in the ITV network began to start, its advertising was sold by three sales houses, each trying to cut the others' throats. Their bonuses depended on how well they fared compared with their rivals, with the result that they saw themselves competing primarily with each other rather than with Channel 4. The exception was in Scotland, where ITV did see itself competing with Channel 4 over what was, in effect, a discrete national market and tried to warn off advertisers tempted by the upstart channel. At the beginning of 1993, Channel 4 had only one advertiser in Scotland, a double-glazing firm. Naturally, it gave this sole customer the best possible slots and used the consequent uplift in sales as an example to other potential advertisers.

The channel's sales force came under immense pressure to bargain on lower rates during 1992, but they stood their ground. The first advertiser to agree a deal on the terms was Renault, which gave the channel 40 per cent of its television budget. In November, Barnes went for a meeting with the leading media buyer Zenith, to discuss £10 million of business with a big confectionery client.

He came away with nothing. 'What pissed me off', he recalls, 'was that the company and the two agencies it used, Zenith and Mediavest, had been spouting off for years about the system. I said, "You pontificate in public about the ITV monopoly, but in private you are just as bad. We want to be a catalyst." They said they wanted to buy at average station price – the conventional ITV formula – and if I refused they wouldn't buy anything. I was walking out down the stairs and the director I'd been dealing with rushed out and said, "I do hope you don't think we were overly aggressive." I said, "I have come away with nothing. If I ring you up in the next year the only reason will be that I am desperate, and then you can screw me into the ground. But for now we won't deal".'[13]

During the course of 1993 agreement was reached, on Channel 4's terms.

The tension was reflected at board meetings. Advertising revenue during the last quarter of 1992 was down by 1.6 per cent on 1991, Butterfield told them in December.[14] But he saw flickers of hope and stood by his projection that the channel would earn £305 million in 1993, even though bookings for January were running very late. 'That's the nature of deals', he told the Board. 'People hold back.'[15] But he knew that, if his projection was to be met, his clients would have to stop holding back very soon. Channel 4 was spending heavily on marketing in the run-up to January, with posters promoting its daring new British programming. The aim was to reach out to groups who had never watched the channel, assuring them that, in contrast to its image in some hostile sections of the media, it was not all about permissiveness or deviant sex, but neither was it a clone of ITV.

January was tough, but the target of £20.4 million was slightly exceeded. Then, month by month during the year, Butterfield was able to report to the Board that Channel 4 was exceeding its sales targets, as the programmes performed strongly. By the end of the first quarter, the company had earned £8 million more than expected, and advertising was growing strongly, 10 per cent up on the previous year. In the event, it took 18.2 per cent of net television advertising revenue, just above the target of 18 per cent it had hoped for, compared with the 14 per cent ITV had formerly been paying over to it. Income was £343.9 million, up 29 per cent on the previous year's £252.2 million, and audience share was 11 per cent, compared with 10.1 per cent in 1992. As Michael Grade wrote, 'Channel 4's sales team [. . .] won the confidence of advertisers and agencies – and provided ITV with more competition than it had expected.'[16] Its top ten advertisers by importance included most of the big guns: Unilever, Proctor & Gamble, Nestle, Cadbury Schweppes, Kellogg, Renault, Ford, British Telecom, Central Office of Information, Whitbread.

The task of the sales team as it limbered up to 1993 had not been helped by the marked scepticism of the programming side – led by Liz Forgan, torch-carrier for the Isaacs old guard, who would in fact leave the channel at the beginning of that year. 'She thought this was bound to be a compromise and would undermine Channel 4', says Butterfield. 'I liked Liz a lot, I admired her probity, but there was always a degree of tension between her and Michael. She saw him selling out to some extent. He saw her as not commercial enough to make the transition.'[17]

There was a debate about whether Channel 4 could be 'semi-competitive', settling for a 12-per-cent share of advertising revenue and taking advantage of a top-up from the ITV safety net. 'It is almost impossible to aim for a target like that', Butterfield insisted. 'It is also impossible to set out to be half successful. I thought that debate was completely barren, because the decision had been taken. The skill was to implement it. That's why 1993 was a very dangerous moment for Channel 4.'[18]

There was also a tortured discussion about introducing sponsorship as part of the more relaxed regime now allowed by the Regulator. Forgan, who predictably, as the conscience of the channel, opposed such a measure, conceded that instead of individual programme sponsorship there could be a single 'bucket' for companies who wished to identify themselves with the channel.[19] She lost out, and the 1993 sponsors were Budweiser in American football, Carlsberg in Italian football, Kronenberg in the Tour de France, McDonald's in Gamesmaster, and Thomson Directors for the weather forecasts. 'Liz never really believed in her heart in this. She believed strongly in the concept of public-service broadcasting and thought it could not be harnessed to commercial competition. She was terrified of losing control of the schedule.'[20]

Butterfield would avoid formal meetings and confrontation with her, instead dealing directly with Ashley Hill, the Scheduler.

Butterfield thought that under Forgan the programming side was 'an awful shambles',[21] though it began to change as Grade disciplined people to commission programmes to a schedule and demonstrated the link between ratings and revenue. He found John Willis, who succeeded Forgan as Director of Programmes, a lot more sensitive to his strategy. 'He had come from ITV and he was a very useful bridge. He understood the advertising dynamic: he had worked at Yorkshire Television, which was driven by it. But he had a huge reputation as a programme-maker.'[22] Butterfield also held a high opinion of Andrea Wonfor, who, as Controller of Entertainment, had championed *The Big Breakfast*. He saw her as combining cutting-edge thinking with commercial reality – just the mix that the channel had to perfect in its bid to maximise audiences while not sacrificing its unique character. Executives had begun to understand that when something did not work, it was no use persevering: it had to be moved.

Michael Grade's skill was to hold the ring between the commercial and the commissioning sides in a fundamentally changed company. To some extent, this change was disguised, because the Sales Department was still barred from direct intervention in programming. Not until 1994 was Andy Barnes allowed to present his sales perspective directly to the Programme Department as a whole. 'I told them not to change much, that our job was to sell their programmes. I realised they just assumed we would do it. The Programme Department has always just assumed the Sales Department will deliver. In some ways that's the biggest compliment my team can ever be paid.'[23] After the meeting, he asked Grade if he should talk to the programme-makers on a regular basis. Grade smiled, took a huge drag on his cigar and said: 'No, I don't think they're quite ready for it yet.'

14

Britain's Pornographer-in-Chief?

• • • •

Channel 4 might have expected to coast happily through 1995 as awards rained down upon it for programmes as diverse as *Don't Forget Your Toothbrush*, in which its new star Chris Evans refreshed the game show, and *Beyond the Clouds*, a beautiful series documenting life in a remote rural village of China. Film on Four was flourishing, and *The Madness of King George* (1994) had landed an Oscar.

Yet, the year was overshadowed by allegations that it was sleaze, tackiness and a desire to shock that were setting the tone at Channel 4, rather than its range of distinctive programmes. When the Regulator, the ITC, published a ruling on 7 June that it had breached the programme code – an item about a Mr Powertool pulling a woman across a stage by a rope attached to his penis was the most eye-catching offence – this precipitated a vitriolic attack on Michael Grade, led by the *Daily Mail*. Columnist Paul Johnson, in one of the most memorable rants ever mounted against a broadcaster, pronounced the following day that it was 'time to sack Britain's pornographer-in-chief'. 'Michael Grade has made Channel 4 a haven for filth', he wrote,

> He says he caters for minorities but that is, at best, a half truth. Lesbians, homosexuals, sex perverts, necrophiliacs, fanatical anti-papists, students of scatology and animal cruelty, extreme feminists, people who like watching other people being grossly humiliated and abused or want to see a man whose penis was cut off by his wife – these minorities, if that is the correct word for them, are well catered for by Channel 4.[1]

In fact, the Channel 4 Board ignored Johnson's advice, and that very month offered their Chief Executive 'pornographer' a new five-year contract.[2] But there was no denying the channel's image was being damaged. This was not to be one of those mutually beneficial 'storm over' rows in which Channel 4 enjoyed the publicity generated by provoking the *Daily Mail*, which in turn could then promote itself as the mouthpiece of middle England. 'The unpleasant and inappropriately personal press coverage had resulted in a smear on the channel's reputation which could have repercussions for some time', the Board reflected.[3] Grade, the master publicist, was wounded and tried to say as little as possible in response, hoping the fire would die down.

There were a number of provocative programmes and strands that fed the *Daily Mail's* indignation, but the specific cause of the Johnson outburst was the excesses of *The Word*, an anarchic, laddish Friday-night programme, easily avoided by those Johnson claimed to champion: 'groups who go to church regularly, love their country, who are faithful to their spouses, who bring up their children to be truthful, law abiding and honest.'

When *The Word* started in 1990, it was seen as a brilliant, if unstable mix of cutting-edge live music, from (Kurt Cobain's) Nirvana, Pulp and Oasis, disrespectful interviews with celebrities – which might start with the remark, 'Your film is crap, how much do you earn?' – and surprise stunts and pranks pulled on people in the studio. The producers tried to ratchet up the ratings with a series of ever more shocking weekly antics. In series four, for example, they invented a thing called 'Win or Weep'. It was filmed in a scrapyard, with people competing to win a dream prize. The weeping came in because if you lost, you'd see your prize possession smashed up – one couple got their car crushed; another had a sofa sawn in half.

The researcher on the programme, Andrew Newman, later made a BBC2 programme on youth television called *Watch This or the Dog Dies*. The title was a reference to a bizarre episode in the fourth series of *The Word* when he was asked to find an old lady who would bet her dog for a hip operation. If she lost, her dog would be put down live on the show. It was to-be-talked-about telly, even making a good point about NHS waiting lists, reasoned the producer. This item proved impossible to set up, but he did find a family who would bet their dog for a trip to Disneyland. Channel 4 quite rightly said at an editorial meeting they couldn't do it.

By 1994, the show, said Duncan Gray, its editor, had become very dark indeed.[4] In its urge to shock it had crossed a line. He knew it was probably doomed and likely to be cancelled by a newly promoted Channel 4 Commissioner for Youth and Entertainment, David Stevenson, a Edinburgh University sociology graduate. The two sides did not get on, which did not assist trust.[5]

Yet, while Channel 4 was increasingly attempting to exert control over the production, another team at Planet 24, in the same office, was responsible for *The Big Breakfast*, a big hit which had made stars of Chris Evans and Gaby Roslin. They were in a powerful position, and Channel 4 had to tread carefully.

On 14 February 1994, Grade had written to David Glencross, the seasoned but stern Chief Executive of the ITC, seeking to reassure him, setting out editorial procedures, which required that all pre-recorded items (i.e., the stunts) were sent to Channel 4 for preview and approval. Dawn Airey, Controller of Entertainment, wrote that Planet 24 are 'still trying to push back the acceptable bounds of taste and decency.'

By the fifth run, which started in the autumn of 1994, the press coverage generated from what was, after all, just one hour a week of late-night television was starting to overshadow the rest of the channel's output, rather in the way that the 'racist' *Celebrity Big Brother* would overpower Channel 4 for a time in early 2007. Yet, broadcast at 11 p.m., it was well away from the mainstream and designed for and appreciated by a youth audience of around 2 million, composed of those just home from an evening in the pub, and younger teenagers up late at the end of the school week, vicariously letting their hair down. They had no complaints.

By now, *The Word* was under review by the channel as the 100th show loomed, so the makers were seeking even more 'shock horror' coverage and tabloid front pages, aided by a sharp young publicist Mark Borkowski. It was still hosted by Mancunian ex-radio presenter, Terry Christian and Dani Behr, but Mark Lamarr had left after being secretly filmed in his dressing room with actress Margi Clarke, who had been instructed to 'make up to him.' The resulting footage was screened round the studio loop for the production team to have an eyeful, and Lamarr protested furiously.

Everyone involved with *The Word* was engaged in a balancing act. It was meant to be edgy. Anything could happen since it went out live, in front of a noisy audience. The presenter Terry Christian once walked off the stage in the middle of the programme. Viewers watched, fascinated to see what would go wrong and what bad-taste item would make them groan.

A lot was illusion and fakery, for this was a programme dominated by smart producers with reputations to make. The Editor of the series, Gray, was a Scots-born Oxford classics graduate and former President of the Union, who would by 2006 be running the ITV network's entertainment programmes, where *The X Factor* and *Dancing on Ice* drew large family audiences. He was overseen by Charlie Parsons, another Oxford graduate, who had created 'this circus of madness'.[6]

The director was Philip Edgar-Jones, who later was the Endemol executive in charge of producing the notorious *Celebrity Big Brother* in which Jade Goody was accused of leading racist behaviour towards Bollywood actress Shilpa Shetty. The researcher, Newman, would become Channel 4's Entertainment and Comedy Commissioner in 2004.

The lightning conductor that focused questions about the moral compass of *The Word* and Channel 4 presented itself in the form of Peter Kerry, a fourteen-year-old grammar-school boy, who had attracted media coverage as the 'home-alone' boy. Kerry ran away from his suburban semi-detached home in South Harrow, Middlesex, after taking his father's credit cards and pasting his own photograph into his father's passport. He flew to Malaysia and wandered around. The press competed with stories of where he'd last been sighted. On his return to England on Monday, 27 February 1995, he was met at Heathrow by hordes of reporters. They included the resourceful Newman, who managed to woo the family sufficiently to be invited into their home, as the tabloids posted notes through the letterbox and knocked on the door. Kerry was signed up exclusively to *The Word*, and his mother's consent was gained to take him to New York.

Channel 4, it now appeared, planned to reward the runaway by sending him on an all-expenses-paid, but nicer, jaunt to America, where he would be interviewed at the Empire State Building for a live item on *The Word*'s programme on Friday, 3 March. No one asked the question of whether this was irresponsible behaviour towards a confused teenager. But then, Channel 4 knew nothing about it.

What the press and producers also did not know at this point was that the Regulator was preparing to pounce on Channel 4. Middle-aged and elderly members of the ITC had been watching *The Word*'s latest string of bad-taste items with mounting concern. Series five had introduced a new short-lived strand, 'The Revengers', in which a member of the public would ask for a spiteful stunt to be pulled on someone who had annoyed them. This had backfired, so a more popular insert, 'TV Hopefuls' was brought back halfway through. 'TV Hopefuls' was founded on the cynical if true premise that people will do anything to get on television for a moment of fame (in this case it was a minute and a bit of fame). It remains a basic impulse that drives programmes from classic talent shows to *Big Brother*. The entry bar, in the case of *The Word*, was a willingness to take part in nasty challenges, such as munching a worm sandwich, and would later inspire (in watered-down form) some mainstream television dares, such as the bush-tucker trials of ITV's *I'm a Celebrity . . . Get Me Out of Here!*

The 'TV Hopefuls' strand had been invented after producers auditioned new presenters, in their annual 'Word Search' for a fresh face. (In the previous 1993/4 series, they had found Hufty, a bald-headed lesbian this way.) The hopeful new presenters were gathered at Channel 4, put in the studio and deliberately confused by turning off the ear pieces connecting them with the control room so that, without instructions, they floundered.

Duncan Gray heard Paul Ross, the then Editor, say to Charlie Parsons, 'these people will do anything to be on TV.'[7] So they were ordered to crawl around the studio, on all fours, like dogs – Davina McCall, who served her time as a failed 'Word Search' candidate, assisted her later career by refusing.[8] 'Something went ping in Charlie's brain' said Gray.[9]

The 'TV Hopefuls' inserts were filmed, and carefully edited. At first, the volunteers did pranks which fell just on the right side of the line. For example, a young man had to snog a toothless old woman. The show's publicist Deborah Goodman was so disgusted by it she refused to go to the recording. However, it transpired that the old woman was an actress briefed on the joke. In another 'TV Hopefuls', a woman bathed in a bath of horse manure and cow's urine, all done after consulting public-health guidelines that had ruled out pigs muck as insalubrious.

Up to now there had been two interventions in *The Word* by the Regulator, over the treatment of a woman seeking a boyfriend on Valentine's Day and American actor Alexis Arquette for unscripted swearing. The rival standards body, the Broadcasting Standards Council, had largely kept quiet, seeing the dares as belonging to the spirit of student rag-week pranks.

But, by spring 1995, Sir George Russell, Chairman of the ITC, had drawn up a list of the ten Worst of *The Word*.[10] *The Word* offended them every single week.

The list was as follows:

- 25 November: The Revengers carry out a fake leg amputation.
- 9 December: The Revengers: an elderly man's colostomy bag is emptied over a viewer's flatmate.
- 16 December: The Revengers push a stake through someone's stomach.
- 23 December: The Revengers: a Santa Claus filled his mouth with vomit and spat over a victim.
- 6 January: The Hopeful, a student, drinks a glass of his own vomit.
- 13 January: The Hopeful, clad in Jesus sandals, paddles in dog excrement.
- 20 January: A very fat man sponges himself all over and the Hopeful drinks from it.
- 3 February: The Hopeful licks an old man's dirty foot.
- 10 February: The Hopeful drinks a milkshake of raw worms and liver.
- 17 February: The Hopeful puts his face in a cow's intestines.

The ITC also compiled a videotape of the excerpts, which members had solemnly viewed. 'I will gladly send a copy of the ITC tape to your board', Russell wrote. The ITC's list didn't seem to distinguish between fake stunts and real ones. Channel 4's Director of Programmes John Willis later told the Board in the privacy of a (minuted) meeting that in the most offensive one, a colostomy bag emptied (by an actor) over a studio guest, the bag had been filled with tea, and the old man with the dirty foot was also played by an actor.

However, the 'drink your own vomit' was real – the sound man on the filming had rushed off the set to be sick when the Hopeful drank salty water, vomited, then drank the result. There was a shadow over the Hopeful's face to prove it.[11]

The dog excrement was also freshly collected from a local London park by Newman. He had been sent back to get some more soft, squelchy stuff by Edgar-Jones and asked to try it out in rehearsal, confirmed Duncan Gray and Andrew Newman. The vomiting Santa had also been played by an actor. This was the decade before *Little Britain*, with its regular joke featuring projectile vomiting, moved to BBC1.

In defence, Dawn Airey listed items that had been rejected – nose-picking with an amputated finger; a Revenger item running over a pet rabbit, faked with a dead lookalike bunny; and, most disturbingly, an interview with mass murderer, Dennis Nilsen. In this one, the production team had managed to get a tape of Nilsen making synthesised music in his prison cell. They planned to play it accompanying a clip of the murdered young men's bodies being exhumed. Channel 4 spiked that story.

That was the context for what happened next. Michael Grade initially described the clash as the ITC going on the rampage, though it was not clear if he had watched *The Word* regularly.

On 22 February 1995, David Glencross, Chief Executive of the ITC, wrote to Grade, firing a warning shot. The two sides were about to meet to discuss the Regulator's annual review of the channel's performance. 'The Commission spent some time discussing certain elements of *The Word* following the 25 November edition', his letter said. As well as the offending Revengers and Hopefuls – the Worst of *The Word* list – he now highlighted another questionable item, with an American called John Bobbitt whose penis had been severed by his wife but later sewn back on. Viewers had been treated to a prosthetic penis being waved around. It was 'tacky and sleazy' said Glencross. They had decided to take a more detailed look at whether 'certain items in the Revengers and Hopefuls slots were consistent with the ITC programme code strictures that content must not be an offence to good taste and decency.'[12]

Channel 4 had just published its annual statement of programme policy, its promises for the current year. 'I can find nothing in that statement which foreshadows some of the items we have had', observed Glencross. He was warning Grade that the channel may have breached the statutory code.

The Channel 4 Board was shocked by this intervention, and when the performance review between the Board and ITV took place, the minutes record 'a robust exchange', a euphemism for a row. The initial response was to stand and defend the show. It was decided that Channel 4's Deputy Chairman David Plowright should send back a letter – basically drafted by Grade, backing *The Word*. They did not consider more straightforwardly tackling the question of whether the content needed to change. But at this time, not all of them were aware of what *The Word* was up to. The belief was that the ITC was meddling and acting beyond its powers.

On 27 February, the Channel 4 Board met, and Michael Grade told them he believed the letter contravened the 1990 Broadcasting Act because the ITC strayed into subjective issues. They agreed that 'the strongest representations' should be made by letter to the ITC. A defiant reply was drafted during the exact three days when the Peter Kerry trip to New York was being set up.

The Word team began working on the Friday, 3 March show on the preceding Monday, oblivious to the board meeting, with a pretty empty slate. As ever, they were looking for something provocative. Kerry's return was a gift. Mrs Pat Kerry's (the mother's) permission was obtained. Mrs Kerry later said she thought her son would be hosting some kind of travel item. She had never seen *The Word* and was horrified when she did.[13] *The Word* saw it as a 'happy-ending' story.

The helter-skelter chain of events would become so controversial they were chronicled in a detailed investigation carried out for the Channel 4 Board, on Grade's orders. The Board felt they'd been made to look foolish. Each participant gave a blow-by-blow account, including David Stevenson, Commissioning Editor; Dawn Airey, Entertainment Controller; John Willis, Director of Programmes; and the production company, Planet 24.

According to Stevenson's testimony, he had contacted Charlie Parsons on 23 February, the day after Glencross's warning letter, to tell him about it and to ask for every item on *The Word* to be thought through very carefully. On Monday, 27 February at an editorial meeting with Parsons and Gray, he expressed concern he was being relayed too little information.

The first anyone at Channel 4 knew about the 'home alone' item was on Wednesday, 1 March, and this was from the Press Association, which was running the story. Duncan Gray told him the decision to do the item had only just been taken and yes, Kerry did have a full passport and full parental approval. Gray said Kerry would testify on air that he had had a harrowing experience in Malaysia.

Stevenson's account says he then checked with Dawn Airey, who said the item was all right as long as it was done responsibly and was not condoning his behaviour. But that was before extensive coverage in Thursday's papers – the first that John Willis knew of the item. He too agreed it could go ahead if pre-recorded and responsible. It still did not cross anyone's mind that the boy appeared to be being rewarded for running away from home, causing great distress, racking up bills on his father's account, and was only fourteen.

By Friday, the *Daily Telegraph* waded in with an editorial headed: 'Words Fail Us'. The show, it said, 'is trivial, ugly and obscene but without a redeeming shred of artistry.' Channel 4 specialised, it said, 'in mindless stunts, the only point of which is to cause embarrassment, distress and humiliation to victims of varying degrees of innocence, gullibility and exhibitionism. Its stable stage props seem human vomit or worse.' In all, it was an item of 'gross irresponsibility.'

Stevenson that morning also learnt that the piece from New York was going out live. Peter Kerry, with a chaperone, producer Anne Lavelle, presenter Dani Behr and Andrew Newman were already in New York by the time the channel reacted. They had flown out that morning.

Versions of the script were shuttled between Planet 24 and Channel 4. The central point did not change: Kerry was supposed to be taken, blindfolded, to the Empire State Building, where a five-piece brass band would be playing. By 12.30 p.m., John Willis decided the piece must be pulled. And Michael Grade swung into action. He rang the school and spoke at length to the boy's headmaster, Dr Alan Robinson, of Langley Grammar School, near Slough, who had been wrongly reported as having given permission on behalf of the school. 'I do not condone this trip at all', he said to Grade.[14] At that point Grade took complete charge. Stevenson called to Grade's office, was told David Plowright and Michael Bishop, the Chairman, were now involved and angry at the apparent lapse of editorial judgement. Stevenson said Grade behaved well towards him. Grade, astute at managing upwards, announced a full inquiry to be conducted by David Scott. Grade was going on holiday the next day.

At 6.40 p.m., Dawn Airey joined John Willis and Stevenson at the programme recording at Teddington Studios. It had been decided *The Word* in its entirety could not now go out live. Sarah Andrew, the lawyer involved, rose from her sick bed to attend. There was then a final last-minute panic at 7.30 p.m. when Grade and Willis were told that the first item, a song from a rap band, Gravediggaz, contained seven 'muthafuckers'. Grade asked Stevenson to inform *The Word* series editor, Gray, that this was 'totally unacceptable. There are to be no swear words on the show.'[15] If there are any swear words, Stevenson emphasised, Grade would pull the programme off air, and it would not return. Charlie Parsons confirmed the show was to be pre-recorded, and the song would be the band's 'day version.'[16]

As Airey wrote in the internal inquiry, 'the show goes out for live with the viewers thankfully not knowing the behind the scenes angst this show had caused.'[17] In fact, the channel could rightly say that its editorial controls had worked. This is what David Scott's inquiry concluded. The Kerry item was pulled, no rules had been breached. In New York, Newman scuttled around for an alternative *Word* item to fill the gap and found a cat show.

This did not stop another broadside from the *Telegraph*. '*The Word* makes the legendary behaviour of anarchic youth in the sixties look like teatime in a Carmelite convent', it opined. The channel's teeming duty log included a sour comment: 'I hope Michael Grade's children turn out like that boy. Maybe then he'll understand.'[18]

In the mainstream media, only Anne Robinson, then a columnist for the mid-market tabloid *Today* newspaper (now defunct) stuck up for the show. 'Do not knock *The Word* for its misjudgement. TV is full of fearful executives who would rather make dull programmes than risky, original ones.'

But behind the scenes, concern was still building. The Board's leading figures felt they had been made to look out of touch by their executives. David Glencross had also warned that *The Word*'s antics risked 'damaging the channel's reputation with the public, if it has not already done so. To put it squarely, Channel 4's commitment to innovation, to quality [. . .] is not a matter of raising the shock threshold. [. . .] I have written frankly [. . .] I do not want there to be any misunderstanding about our concerns.'

On Thursday, 2 March, the day of the *Telegraph*'s 'Words Fail Us' editorial, and the day before *The Word* went out, David Plowright had replied to the ITC robustly. 'It was [. . .] a shock to see a letter from the ITC asserting that the channel's reputation with the public had been risked and/or damaged by some items in *The Word*', he wrote. 'For our part, we do not believe there has ever been a time when the channel's reputation has been higher. The Board believes *The Word* is justified by the Channel 4 remit. We recall a similar unease about *The Tube*.' He added that it was 'far from being a juvenile self-indulgence.'[19]

Clearly, the Kerry incident, though not broadcast, challenged that rosy assumption. Sir Michael Bishop had decided to issue an unusual public statement and rebuke late on Friday 3 March. 'Channel 4 has made an error of judgement in enabling Peter Kerry to travel to New York, notwithstanding his parents' permission.'[20]

Mrs Kerry wrote to the producer during the post-mortem to say, 'Within hours of his return you had spoken to him and offered him a trip abroad to do a travel report [. . .] there was no opportunity to reflect [. . .] We are also very unhappy you never discussed with us your decision to interview Peter in New York.'[21]

Bishop also drafted a letter to the *Daily Telegraph* on 3 March but did not send it, pointing out that *Channel 4 News*, *The Rector's Wife* (a Joanna Trollope drama adaptation) and operas from Glyndebourne, solid middle-class programming, were also part of Channel 4.

Grade could have sounded the alarm on Thursday, after reading the press coverage and before the letter from Plowright was sent.

'I certainly missed the moral significance of the New York trip', he conceded in a memorandum of 21 March, a month later. He added, 'I have to say that in my experience of the entertainment areas I have never come across an issue quite like this one.' Of the lessons to be learnt, there was a failure to see the moral dimension. 'We have certainly had more than our fair share of shock headlines of late.'[22] Commissioning editors would address this, he promised the Board. Grade also wrote that if Planet 24 wished to propose another series, it would have to be on the basis they were convinced the show has not run out of steam. He would tell the Chairman of any decision before the producers.

In other words, *The Word* could not recover. Duncan Gray knew he was running a doomed show. He threw himself into going out with his head held high. When it ended, at the 'wrap' party, he, at least, was in tears at the passing of a television legend.

On 22 March 1995, the ITC acted. It threw the book at Channel 4. Sir George Russell wrote to Sir Michael Bishop citing the 1990 Broadcasting Act, Section 6(1) requiring a channel to transmit nothing that offends against good taste and decency. Channel 4 had debased individuals in three items: the colostomy bag, the vomiting Santa and a third item not on the original worst list, Mr Powertool – a man pulling a girl on a chair across a studio by means of a rope tied to his penis. At their next meeting, the ITC would decide on sanctions. He asked for their views before 4 April.

Channel 4, faced with a possible fine, played for time.

John Willis, Director of Programmes, let the cat out of the bag. It was then that he told the Board the colostomy bag was full of tea, not urine; that an actor had played the part of the man wearing the colostomy bag. It was also significant that the audience watching at home had not objected. Mary McAleese, a key board member (later President of Ireland), responded that it was difficult to 'have a sensible public debate given the items complained about – they did not push any creative boundaries.'[23]

On 31 May, the decision arrived. The three items were breaches. Channel 4 had 'overstepped acceptable limits', though there was no fine. Grade's confidential assessment was 'this was probably the least we could have expected.'[24] For Grade, who surely realised the individual items could not be defended with a straight face, the issue that still rankled was the detailed involvement of the ITC in the channel's output.

As a back-up, Channel 4 had hurriedly commissioned research into sixteen- to twenty-four-year-olds' views of *The Word* in April 1995. This found that virtually all respondents who watched enjoyed being shocked by it. The Hopefuls was very popular and enjoyed as a voyeuristic endurance test. 'It makes you laugh and heave at the same time', said one.

Not natural readers of the *Telegraph*, most were unaware of the media criticism. But tellingly, those canvassed who were aware of the Peter Kerry incident generally agreed it had set a bad example.

John Willis reflected with hindsight:

> We were in a moment of cultural change. The audience was dividing into two: on the one side there was this younger more independently minded relaxed audience, for whom *The Word* was biblical, it was for them. And on the other their parents and grandparents, who were outraged. They had seen what might happen at a teenage party. The audience was culturally divided, in an interesting way, and we, Channel 4, were at the sharp end of it.
>
> I am sure we got some decisions wrong, but there were no riots in the streets – it probably kept people at home watching TV rather than in the centres of town binge-drinking. *The Word* was a fantastic series; there are so many people working in television who started on it. I was a fan, but it started to take an abnormal position in the channel's life, it was causing a lot of pain, getting in the way of other things the channel wanted to do, and it was probably running out of steam creatively.[25]

The publication of the ITC's decision was on 7 June 1995. It unleashed the vehement response from Paul Johnson. The *Guardian* played it differently: 'Mr Powertool Drags C4 into Big Trouble', observed its headline. The ITC and Channel 4 closed ranks in the face of the *Mail*'s onslaught. They had a constructive and unemotional discussion about the adjudication.

Glencross went onto the *Today* programme to try to defuse the row, saying that *The Word* represented a 'tiny fraction of Channel 4's otherwise outstanding programme performance.' But the reaction continued.

There were other factors that spurred Johnson to write more broadly about the 'tide of filth and pornography' on Channel 4. The channel chose that week to screen, as part of a Martin Scorsese season, *The Last Temptation of Christ* (1988), a film that provoked controversy in its depiction of Jesus as subject to the same temptations as ordinary mortals, who, while on the cross, has an erotic fantasy about Mary Magdalene. There were 1,500 letters of protests from Catholics and fundamentalist Christians who believed the film to be blasphemy. They started writing to the advertisers. So, every advert that ran around the film was very carefully selected.

It was also running *The Red Light Zone*, a late-night Saturday series of documentaries and short films about the sex industry, or, as ITC delicately put it: 'the seamy side of life outside the mainstream.' A video diary of the life of a prostitute in multiracial Bradford was typical fare. The series drew on the independent film and video workshops Channel 4 had helped fund since its inception. Also weighed in the scales was *Dyke TV*, a short series about lesbianism, which led the *Daily Mail* to investigate the background of its commissioner, Carolyn Spry, whose worst failing, apart from being a lesbian, was choosing to live in the left-wing borough of Haringey.

Belatedly, the Broadcasting Standards Commission (BSC) charged in, deciding that the John Bobbitt incident was lewd, but not the others.

Grade, who felt it best to sit it out without responding publicly, in a defiant private response pointed to the opposing views of the ITC and BSC and said the ITC were out of touch.

> These rulings will not influence our decision either way about the future of *The Word*. [. . .] While the storm seems to have blown itself out for the time being, the smear will undoubtedly stick. There is no quick antidote to the *Daily Mail*'s poison. Looking back on the last few months, since the ITC decided to go on the rampage, you cannot blame the newspapers for getting our misdemeanours on *The Word* out of proportion. That is how the ITC have handled it.

In July, the Channel confirmed the cancellation of *The Word*. David Stevenson was glad to see the back of it; he'd finally pulled the rug on lads' TV. 'It was Oxbridge prankery, the worst aspect of it was a cynicism about working-class people. It was a bit too clever and a bit too cruel in places. It had the same prurience about other people's lives which *Big Brother* has.'[26]

This left an important Friday-night gap to fill, and Stevenson had an answer. He wanted a different studio-based show but one based on a similar 'broken' entertainment format of stunts, discussions, guests and audience participation, hosted by women. Fed up with the *Loaded, Men Behaving Badly* culture, it was 'Time for the Girls to Be on Top'.[27] He put out a closed tender to four companies, and Planet 24 was not among them. 'I had to get something fast, that hit the ground, made as big a splash as *The Word* for the autumn of 1995.'[28] This led to the creation of *The Girlie Show*, billed as 'a celebration of women in the 1990s', with a title inspired by a tour Madonna was making in Britain at the time. Rapido, the company behind *Eurotrash*, the cheeky youth magazine show, was in charge.

The first series was presented by American lesbian supermodel Rachel Williams, with co-presenters Sara Cox, later a Radio 1 breakfast DJ, and Claire Gorham. Gorham, previously a journalist on the black magazine *Pride*. Gorham knew the programme was designed to entertain but was unprepared for the stunts: waxing a man's bottom, judging a sexy fireman's competition and an item called 'Naked Apes', which took four Geordies on outings, for example, to a gay club, where Gorham instructed them to keep their backs to the wall.

The first series attracted the attention of the Regulator for an interview with a convicted shoplifter, full of helpful hints on how to be one. Then a discussion about men's underpants, or rather, what was in them, got out of control when Williams slid a plate of eels down one model's pair. As the eels slipped down his legs, he muttered 'bitch' to her, while the audience groaned in unison, 'Oh my God.' *The Girlie Show* was relaunched for a second, more restrained series in 1997, but by now its depiction of 'ladette' culture seemed as dated as the male version.

For anyone angling for the top job at Channel 4 after Grade, having a pop at *The Girlie Show* was a no-brainer. Michael Jackson, running BBC2, and a driving force in its creation, pointed to it as an example of the danger of cynically commissioning for the sixteen- to thirty-four-year-old audience in a speech to the Royal Television Society in 1996. Stevenson was ousted on 21 April 1997.

The debate about Channel 4's tackiness had a serious political context. As ever in broadcasting, the channel needed influential friends. Lobbying remained high on the agenda.

Since 1993, it had clearly been making a highly successful job of selling its own advertising and standing on its own two feet, and it began complaining bitterly about being the victim of a costly piece of 'rogue' legislation.

Grade, while dubbed 'Pornographer-in-Chief' by one section of the press, was running a high-profile campaign to end the 'funding formula' by which Channel 4 was obliged to pay the ITV companies half of any advertising it earned above a share of 14 per cent of the total market, in return for a limited degree of financial protection. The annual cheque had risen from £57.3 million in 1994 to £74 million in 1995, and handing over these huge cheques really hurt. 'No public purpose is served by the continuation of these rogue arrangements', said Bishop,[29] and the channel listed the extra programmes it could order instead. A new Broadcasting Bill was published in the autumn of 1995 and presented a golden opportunity for a change. But the Government was so far unconvinced by the channel's lobbying and was inclined to let the funding formula run.

The realisation that Channel 4 was throwing off huge amounts of spare cash was quickly grasped. No wonder that in the autumn Channel 4 prepared a twelve-minute video for MPs, with a range of programmes, including its brand new drama, *The Politician's Wife*. Channel 4 was about to face a rude shock – it had commercialised itself to the point that it could become an asset for privatisation.

There are two postscripts to the events of 1995. Paul Johnson was unmasked as a long-standing adulterer two years later by the *Daily Express*, and, when Michael Grade left the channel in 1997, he was presented with 'The Worst of *The Word*' tape as a farewell present – by Sir George Russell.

15

Drama! GBH, Potter, Film on Four

● ● ● ●

One characteristic of the Grade era was his decision to lavish significant sums of money on two established television writers; but with mixed results. Between 1988 and 1996, Dennis Potter and Alan Bleasdale were backed in five drama series, costing around £26 million in total – an eye-watering sum at the time. This spending produced one outstanding hit in 1991, Bleasdale's *GBH*, a significant commentary on the Britain of the 1980s. Its success allowed the process to roll forward pretty much unchecked, because of Grade's close interest. But Potter was well past his peak, and the spending came to an abrupt halt with his posthumous flop, *Karaoke and Cold Lazarus*, in 1996. Bleasdale's third work, *Melissa* (1997), an unremarkable glossy remake of a Francis Durbridge thriller, was the last thing he would contribute to the channel.

In supporting these two artists, Grade diverted money that could have been directed more fruitfully towards new writers and fresh fiction, in keeping with the channel's remit to experiment and provide a platform for unexposed talent. The débâcle culminated in a frank boardroom debate led by the Chairman, Sir Michael Bishop – otherwise a firm Grade supporter – who regarded it all as an example of how creative types could collectively lose their heads. This was why, in selecting Grade's successor in 1997, one stipulation was that there had to be a fresh approach to drama.

By instinct, Michael Grade was an old-style broadcaster and patron. At the BBC he had supported the two playwrights, regarding them as among the greatest television writers of their generation – which they were, when on song. He was proud to offer them a congenial environment at Channel 4, where they could be free to innovate at a time when the BBC, under his great rival John Birt, seemed less fertile ground for creativity.

Grade had been in America when Bleasdale, a garrulous hypochondriac Liverpudlian, wrote the outstanding *Boys from the Blackstuff*, screened by BBC1 in 1982.

One character in particular, Yosser 'Gissa Job' Hughes, played by Bernard Hill, seemed to encapsulate the tragedy of unskilled workers dumped on the scrapheap by uncaring Thatcherism. After Grade moved to the BBC as Director of Television, he became involved in Bleasdale's next project, *The Monocled Mutineer* (1986), a powerful serial about Percy Toplis, who led a munity at Etaples in the First World War. Although it was based on a true incident, Bleasdale had heavily embellished the facts; but Grade foolishly authorised a press release claiming that it was historically accurate. This caused an outcry, with the BBC being accused of denigrating the officer class – depicted by Bleasdale as cynical and vicious – for political reasons. Yet, the serial proved a ratings hit.

Not long after Grade arrived at Channel 4, he was approached by the independent producer, Verity Lambert – a guiding force behind *Dr Who* – bearing a vast unfinished script-cum-novel from Bleasdale which, after substantial rewriting, would become *GBH*. It was centred on Michael Murray, a manic leader of a Labour council in a northern city, played by Robert Lindsay and clearly inspired by Derek Hatton, the most prominent member of the extreme left-wing militant faction that ran the council in Liverpool – Bleasdale's home city – in the 1980s.[1] The drama's pointed message was summed up in the memorable line, spoken to Murray by a former colleague he had victimised: 'The further left you go, the more right-wing you become.'

Grade called in Peter Ansorge, the Deputy Director of Drama, who had overseen two successful series: the satire *Porterhouse Blues* and *The Manageress*, starring Cherie Lunghi as a female football manager. He was in the final stage of bringing to the screen *A Very British Coup* by Alan Plater – based on a book by the Labour MP Chris Mullin – and *Traffik* (1989), a taut thriller about the international drugs trade, later remade into a Hollywood movie. Channel 4's drama policy, in other words, was already shifting. Because it would never have the money to make long-running drama series, the defining strength of its output, Isaacs, with Attenborough's blessing, had concentrated his resources on the gritty soap *Brookside* and low-budget British films that might have a cinematic release. But Grade and Ansorge were convinced that strong, home-grown dramas were what audiences really enjoyed.

Ansorge had known Bleasdale when he worked at BBC Birmingham, whose tradition of fostering single plays and writers had helped shape Film on Four. When Grade moved to Channel 4, Bleasdale had reassured Ansorge that he was a good person to work for. Ansorge recalled,

> Michael one day called me in and asked me to read this enormous script, or it might have been a novel. There were about 800 pages typed up. He asked me to read it and said he had promised an answer in the morning. I went home. I got to a scene which happened in episode five, where Murray goes loopy [in a hotel corridor outside the bedroom

where a blonde was lying in bed waiting for him]. The dialogue was all there. I went in with absolute confidence the next day and said we could do it. Michael never read it. Then Liz Forgan got hold of it. She got half way through and phoned me to say it was crazy and wouldn't work. But although she was Director of Programmes, she had no say. Michael Grade just said: 'We're doing it.' I can't remember a single controversy about the budget. It was £6 million.[2]

Bleasdale was even given the creative freedom to make episodes of unequal length. Grade took infinite pains over it and exchanged letters with the author about the scheduling. The original idea had been to show it at 10 p.m. on Sundays, but Bleasdale pleaded against this as being too late. Grade eventually hit on Thursday nights, with a Sunday repeat. Bleasdale, in turn, wrote and thanked him: 'You've given us an extraordinary amount of money at a difficult time for any major broadcaster. You've given us unrivalled and complete freedom of opportunity and expression. You've given us total straight line support and you've given us a narrative repeat and a Sunday night.'[3]

An important key to success had been a tough producer, Verity Lambert. 'She summoned Alan down to London to script edit it', says Ansorge. 'I visited. These were seriously long scripts. She knew it scene by scene, better than Alan. She was incredibly frank and straight.'[4] Lambert worked with her dog, a Great Dane called Arthur Daley, sitting next to her. 'At 4 p.m., Alan would say that he would take Arthur for a walk. We walked straight to the Bush Tavern, where the barman pulled the dog a pint [. . .] Alan will listen. That was the key.'[5]

Nine years after *Boys from the Blackstuff*, Bleasdale had again created a drama that caught the contemporary national mood. *GBH* was broadcast in May and June 1991 to critical acclaim and large audiences – 5.7 million for the opening, 5.3 million for the second. Young and upmarket viewers flocked to it while the BBC looked on enviously. It is still repeated and packaged on DVD, and in some ways it is Channel 4's equivalent of ITV's totemic serials, *The Jewel in the Crown* and *Brideshead Revisited*. While they were based on novels, *GBH* was an original work. Channel 4's board basked in the critical reaction, made sweeter when Will Wyatt, then running BBC Television, wrote a congratulatory note to Grade.

The serial could not stay out of the news. There was a row when it lost out to *Prime Suspect* in the 1992 British Academy Awards, despite the fact that four of the seven judges protested that they had voted for it. As a result, the judging procedure was tightened.

Naturally enough, Grade was keen for Bleasdale to produce another blockbuster, but when the writer confessed he had nothing up his sleeve, he was allowed to present a season of four films by newish writers under the title *Alan Bleasdale Presents*. This was a quasi-flop: the screenplays were criticised as not living up to the glossy production budgets. His next original serial came in 1996 and was *Jake's Progress*, starring Julie Walters and – again – Robert Lindsay. It was about a dysfunctional family and a disturbed little boy who tries to murder his baby brother. It cost £6.1 million and was unenthusiastically received, but it remains one of Robert Lindsay's proudest achievements.[6] Bleasdale's period at Channel 4 petered out later that year with *Melissa*, stripped over two weeks. Grade, his principal patron, was to leave in January 1997. But although his work at the channel had enjoyed mixed fortunes, it had made Bleasdale a wealthy man, able to afford the luxury of a central London pied-à-terre.

● ● ● ●

It was Dennis Potter, writer of *Pennies from Heaven* (1978) and *The Singing Detective* (1986) – two of the greatest television serials – who illustrated the weakness of Grade's strategy of indulging an established talent from the past, no longer able to deliver outstanding creative work that could justify the high price tag. Grade had been Director of Programmes at the BBC when Potter wrote *The Singing Detective*, a complex tale of memory featuring Michael Gambon as Philip Marlow, an ailing detective in a hospital ward reliving his life through flashbacks.

Grade had personally given the go-ahead to the most controversial scene, when the detective as a boy scaled a tree in the Forest of Dean and looked down to see his mother having sex in the grass with a stranger. The bobbing male bottom was more explicit than anything then seen on television and sent Mary Whitehouse, the morality campaigner, into overdrive. Seven million people watched, but Potter's reputation as 'Dirty Den' was reinforced by his next work, *Blackeyes*, in 1989, which was supposed to be about the exploitation of women by men. It was panned by the critics, and Potter, who insisted on directing the play, admitted he had gone too far. After this, he received no more commissions from the BBC, but by then Grade had moved to Channel 4 and said he was proud to have Potter writing for him. He believed in creative talent and was confident that, even if one project flopped, the next could be another work of genius. So Potter took Grade his next script, *Lipstick on Your Collar*, made for around £4 million and screened in 1993. It was a semi-autobiographical serial set in 1956 at the time of the Suez Crisis, about two young men in the War Office pitched into the intelligence service. The charting of a social order changing around them, and the experience of falling in love, were played out with popular songs of the period – by now a Potter trademark.

Potter wanted to direct this too, but Ansorge resisted, questioning whether he was the best director for the job. Deeply wounded, the manipulative Potter then behaved disgracefully. He approached Alan Yentob, the Controller of BBC2, and phoned Ansorge as the Drama Department was having its Christmas lunch. 'I've sold it to the BBC, he told him. 'You're fucked. Have a really miserable Christmas.'[7] However, when Yentob studied the small print of the proposal – a budget of £4 million or £5 million, with Potter directing – he declined to go through with the deal.

A chastened Potter then went back to Channel 4 and had to accept that another director, Renny Rye, would take charge. During filming, when Ansorge visited the set, Potter beckoned him to his office, took out a bottle of champagne and said, 'I'm not saying you are right; but you might have been.'[8] Ansorge believed the work brought back humanity to Potter's writing.[9] It was a modest success but not a resounding one. The critics called it derivative, especially in the use of period songs.

Potter was never physically robust, and in 1994, on St Valentine's Day, he was diagnosed with incurable cancer of the pancreas and given three months to live. He went to see Grade and poured his heart out over the customary bottle of red wine. As he left, Grade asked him if he wanted to put any of his life on record.

The outcome was one of the most memorable programmes in Channel 4's history, Melvyn Bragg's extended interview with Potter, during which the playwright, in almost constant pain, comforted himself three times with swigs of morphine from a special hip flask, which Bragg had to unscrew for him. The interview had to start at 9.30 a.m., because Potter was at his most lucid in the morning. The two men sat in a bare studio, with technicians and the floor director in view. As Potter reviewed his life, describing his childhood in the Forest of Dean and the rural mining community he had been born into, he displayed a sweetness of character that had not always been apparent in his work or his professional life, as well as an absence of fear in the face of imminent death.

Writing, he stressed, had been his life, his vocation, and he spoke fluently of his deep fears about the future of television as commercialism came to the fore. He called his cancer 'Rupert', after Rupert Murdoch, the media mogul who had been one of the targets of his James MacTaggart lecture in Edinburgh the previous year, in which he described television as 'ripped apart by and reassembled by accountants and politicians.' He reserved special venom for the two men who then ran the BBC, the 'croak-voiced Daleks' John Birt and Marmaduke Hussey.[10]

Yet, despite his scorn for the BBC, he used the Bragg interview to make a heartfelt dying request which was also an audacious programme pitch. He asked the BBC and Channel 4 to collaborate to produce his final works, two interlinked drama series: *Karaoke*, already scripted, and *Cold Lazarus*. *Karaoke* was built around a writer, Daniel Feeld, played by Albert Finney. Diagnosed with cancer, he finds his fictional plots becoming inextricably tangled with real life. *Cold Lazarus* is set 400 years in the future and features the same character, or rather his frozen head, whose memories are being accessed by scientists.

Potter wanted the BBC to start with *Karaoke*, with narrative repeats on Channel 4, then Channel 4 to kick off with *Cold Lazarus*. He said his doctor had calibrated the right amount of morphine so that he could work: he was writing ten pages a day, and it was flying. Ansorge was shocked when he watched a pre-transmission tape of the interview and heard what Potter was suggesting. He rushed in to see Grade, knowing that he would approve the project because, in his book, loyalty superseded everything.

However, these plays were the work of a dying man on strong drugs, in immense pain, unable to eat solid food. He was asking for a collaboration that had never happened before and has not since. The two series would cost £10.1 million, with Channel 4 essentially running the production through Potter's independent company, Whistling Gypsy. Renny Rye was director, and the producer was Kenith Trodd, a former collaborator with Potter before they fell out. The channel paid 60 per cent of the costs because *Cold Lazarus* required special effects.

The agreement was driven by Channel 4. When negotiations looked like grinding to a halt, Grade wrote a stern letter to Alan Yentob, urging him to stop messing around. 'Let's appoint a producer and tell that producer what we expect of him. Let's get back to basics and get the show on the road.'[11]

The plays were transmitted in May 1996. Of the two, *Karaoke* was the more successful. *Cold Lazarus* needed a strong script editor and several rewrites, which it never got. Ansorge insists that the morphine was not to blame. 'I know because I used to talk to him. He had four hours every morning when it didn't affect him. He wasn't out of his brain.' All the same, some of the script – delivered six weeks before he died in June 1994 – suggested that he was. Many speeches were far too long. And by the time production began, there was no writer around to adjust them.

Because of the cost of the project and the unusual nature of the deal, expectations were high. But when *Cold Lazarus* was previewed before the press at the ICA cinema in the Mall, the reaction was ominous. It had not helped that the screening equipment had broken down, and the mood of the assembled critics was thunderous when Ansorge and Michael Wearing, the Head of BBC Drama Series and Serials, went on stage to handle questions. 'I have never experienced such a completely hostile crowd', said Ansorge.[12] *Cold Lazarus* got audiences of 1.5 million and was critically panned.

John Willis, Director of Programmes, said, 'We were in a difficult situation [. . .] Dennis Potter was probably the best television writer we had. Channel 4 unfortunately didn't have so much money it could do other things as well. All Picasso paintings are not perfect. It just might have been the best thing he ever wrote.'[13]

Liz Forgan was not so forgiving. She had never possessed Grade's legendary patience with talent.

> Michael was obsessed with Dennis Potter's genius. He could do no wrong, and nobody could say, 'Dennis this is crap, please do something else with it.' Absolutely nobody – because Michael would pre-empt it.

He would agree things with Dennis, sign off scripts, and nobody – not me, not the commissioning editor – could come near it. That was utterly Michael's fault. It was completely shocking. Dennis had done some absolutely good work, but he was not in good shape in the 1990s. Then millions of pounds went on this completely unwatchable stuff.[14]

She had left by the time *Cold Lazarus* was conceived but she could have stopped *Lipstick on Your Collar*.

I should perhaps have done something but I left that area to Michael because he was good at it. But he had a blank spot when it came to Dennis. When television thinks it has a real genius, you think you must stand by this genius through thick and thin. There is nothing wrong with that but we went on too long with Dennis Potter. Nobody ever sat down and said: 'Now look Dennis, look at this appalling mess.'[15]

Grade's selective relationship with talent was part and parcel of the very personal power exercised by strong chief executives in a small organisation. Jeremy Isaacs also had his passions: in 1986 he famously ordered a series on *The Great Moghuls*, costing £500,000, from a former Thames Television colleague, Douglas Rae, when they stood side by side at the urinals in Charlotte Street.[16] But this kind of unquestioning patronage has not been repeated since. Paul Abbott, the writer of *Shameless*, is pegged to tight budgets, while Peter Morgan wrote *The Deal* (2003) and *Longford* (2006) as one-off dramas.

If Bleasdale and Potter represented expensive investments with mixed results, there were genuine drama triumphs in the Grade era, notably Jimmy McGovern's *Hearts and Minds* (1995), about an idealistic schoolteacher, played by Christopher Eccleston, in a tough comprehensive. But, as critics pointed out, some serials had a safer middle-class appeal and could have equally well been shown on BBC2: *The Politician's Wife* (1995), *The Camomile Lawn* – an adaptation of a Mary Wesley novel (1992), *The Rector's Wife* by Joanna Trollope (1994) and *The Fragile Heart* (1996). There was a feeling that, under Grade, the channel was retreating from the cutting edge.

This appeared to be confirmed with the commissioning of an ambitious adaptation of *A Dance to the Music of Time*, Anthony Powell's wistful cycle of novels chronicling the decline of upper-class England in the middle years of the twentieth century. Screened in 1997, with Simon Russell Beale playing the insufferable Widmerpool, it was popular with viewers but not primarily with the kind of viewers the channel had originally set out to attract. Yet, there were still some adventurous commissions: an adaptation of Caryl Phillips' novel, *The Final Passage* (1996), about the lives of Afro-Caribbean immigrants to Britain in the 1950s; and *Tales of the City*, Armistead

Maupin's Balzac-style account of the lives and loves of a group of San Franciscans in the 1970s and 1980s (1993). There was also a big comedy breakthrough with *Father Ted* in 1996, though Grade had to be persuaded it was funny.

● ● ● ●

Compared with all the expensive drama, *Brookside*, costing around £20,000 per half hour, had a more down-to-earth purpose. It was there to anchor audiences and, from 1993, to help earn the channel's keep. Grade increased its frequency to three times a week, with an omnibus edition on Saturdays; and if it wasn't in the top five programmes, everyone was worried. But much depended on the unbiddable personality of its creator, Phil Redmond. The problem in 1990/1 was that Redmond, secure in his Merseyside mini-empire, decided to bid for Granada's ITV franchise. This led to a lack of focus on *Brookside* and a serious slide in the ratings, to 1.5 million. The original cast had mostly moved on, and Jimmy McGovern, who had written it for eight years, was making his way as the author of ITV's *Cracker*.

Redmond remained Executive Producer but was never in the office when a worried Ansorge tried to get in touch. Ansorge told Grade that the soap was a rudderless ship and that the storylines that had once sustained two episodes a week were being stretched out across three, with predictable results. Grade's response was, 'Right. I'll give you some money and you can start developing three ideas for a soap to replace *Brookside* – and don't keep it a secret.'[17] What he meant was that Redmond should be made aware of the threat to his project.

When Redmond called, Ansorge gave him an ultimatum: find a competent producer or get back to doing it yourself. Redmond chose to promote the personable, hard-working Mal Young, raised in a working-class Liverpudlian family, who had been working on the soap for some time. Young knew *Brookside* inside out, and he revitalised it by introducing sensational storylines, attracting audiences that would peak at 9 million, keeping it at the very top of the channel's home-grown hits. Grade was delighted: 'I knew it was out of the doldrums when I started getting complaints from the ITC about it.'[18]

The story that turned around *Brookside* was the body-under-the-patio saga. It was brewed over two years and reached a climax in the spring of 1993, the year Channel 4 was selling its advertising for the first time. It centred on the occupants of Number 10 Brookside Close which, unknown to the rest of the close, was a safe home for abused families. Into it moved the Jordache family: mother Mandy, her eighteen-year-old daughter Beth – played by Anna Friel – and youngster Rachel. Later, their estranged father, Trevor Jordache, played menacingly by Bryan Murray, who had featured in one of the channel's very first dramas, *The Irish RM*, bullied his way back into the family, started sexually abusing Rachel and beating them all up.

They first tried to poison him with weedkiller. When that didn't work, they gave him ground-up painkillers, and in case that was not enough, Mandy stabbed him in the back with a kitchen knife.

The audience-appreciation index for the episode, a device used by broadcasters to judge success, stood at 85, seven points higher than usual. The *Guardian's* columnist Suzanne Moore watched it with her eight-year-old daughter and supported the storyline. By contrast, the *Star's* Stafford Hildred called it 'Brookside Bilge.' More significantly, the family murder sparked a debate about domestic violence. The three episodes that portrayed the beating and abuse provoked 400 calls to the special helplines that had been set up, with one in two callers saying they were currently being victimised.

But it was screened at a point when sensitivities about screen violence were running high. The stabbing of Trevor Jordache led to direct confrontation with the Regulator, the ITC, some of whose members were becoming more and more concerned about the storylines and were horrified that the murder was shown in the omnibus edition, at 5.05 p.m. on a Saturday, when many children would be watching. The ITC first published an intervention in its complaints bulletin, then went on to issue a formal warning on 20 October 1993, stating that the channel had been in flagrant breach of the guidelines, covering 'portrayal of dangerous behaviour easily imitated by children.'

After the killing, the family buried Jordache's body under the patio, with the assistance of a neighbour. It was dug up the following January during a week of stripped programmes that drew the record 9 million viewers. The murder trial, in May 1994, provoked more intense debate when Mandy and Beth were found guilty. And Young, unintimidated by the Regulator, followed up with the first-ever lesbian kiss exchanged on television before the watershed – between Beth and a nanny, Margaret Clemence, also living in the Close.

By January 1994, the ITC was demanding tapes of the soap dating back to 1982, to test if it had become more extreme and violent. Questions were raised about another storyline in which a long-standing character, Jimmy Corkhill, was taking cocaine. All this led to intense debate about what was allowable according to the conventions of the day. Channel 4 and its defenders argued that the knife in the stabbing was static in the character's hand, the blade had no blood on it and the actual stabbing was not shown.

Grade, concerned that the ITC wanted the series watered down, turning it into just another cosy soap, continued to argue – implausibly – that it was a matter of fine judgement. 'Members of the ITC do not appear to be regulating on behalf of anyone', he wrote. There had been no 'groundswell of public disquiet' about the issues they had raised.[19] The channel compiled a list of incidents in previous omnibuses that had gone unchallenged: date rape, murders and a siege with guns and killings.

But in January 1994, the Board conceded that great care would have to be taken with the teatime omnibus, and some ground would have to be given. Peter Salmon (standing in for John Willis) and Peter Ansorge decided to cut the lesbian lovers' kiss from the omnibus edition. John Willis then had to go on *Right to Reply* to apologise to those viewers who complained about the cut being made. In the longer term, this sensationalism carried the seeds of disaster, initiating a trend that in less careful hands would lead to *Brookside* losing touch with its audience.

Redmond continued to have a difficult relationship with the channel right until *Brookside* was cancelled in 2002. Ansorge said,

> There is no question part of him is very gifted. When he focused on Brookside he was extremely clever, intelligent and creative – rather exciting. He was very, very suspicious of commissioning editors and didn't want it to be seen that there was any interference from Channel 4. He was one of the few independents with a consistently successful programme, responsible for commercial success.
>
> The big problem was that he felt he was the most important person. Quite often he'd sack an actor, and, in too arbitrary a fashion, he would write them out of the storyline. In the early days, he had in his writing team the young Jimmy McGovern and the young Frank Cottrell Boyce. I would sit in the writers' meetings. They locked the producers and writers together over a few days. Phil would axe a storyline, but they would fight their corners. They gave him a hell of a time. It could be very creative.[20]

Redmond's contract was watertight and very generous. The channel was afraid of losing him and of losing *Brookside*. While Mal Young ran the show, all went well: he listened to suggestions from Channel 4 and kept the plots bouncing along. But he was so good at it that in 1996 he was poached to start a new soap, *Family Affairs*, for Channel Five.

Brookside went downhill from there with far-fetched storylines, too much noisy argument, unlikeable characters, another strong incest line, the overuse of favourites such as Lindsay (Claire Sweeney) and Jimmy Corkhill, and a lesbian love triangle. A soap audience can be patient, telling themselves it will get better, but when it doesn't, they start to disappear. There was a brief revival in 2000 under a new Executive Producer, Paul Marquess, who brought in a new family and discussed screening the soap five nights a week.[21] When Marquess left to run *The Bill*, Channel 4 hoped that Young could be tempted back, perhaps as part-owner of the production company. But it did not happen, and *Brookside* passed on in 2002, after a fairly protracted illness.

Redmond, though, had hedged his bets by launching in 1995 what eventually became a new soap, *Hollyoaks*, aimed at teenagers. It was filmed at the former further-education college where Redmond's production company was based. Its unique quality was that all the stories were led by the young characters, with their parents in less prominent roles. Envisaged as the junior partner to *Brookside*, *Hollyoaks* was the youthful sibling that would eventually become the survivor, screened every weeknight.

● ● ● ●

On arrival at the channel, Grade, still haunted by his earlier bruising failure in Hollywood, was suspicious of Film on Four, asking what it did for his television channel as opposed to nurturing the ailing film industry. He saw film as vanity publishing, there to make the channel look good rather than to boost ratings. He observed, for instance, that *My Beautiful Laundrette*, though a tremendous hit in the cinemas, did not get a television screening until January 1987 and had produced a poor £4,000 return from a US distribution deal. He instinctively preferred television drama, especially when it involved the big-name writers.

His case was strengthened by figures showing that audiences for films on the channel had halved between 1987 and 1991: not everything could be a runaway hit. The new head of Film on Four was David Aukin, a shrewd and warm man who attracted talent but had no television experience, having been recruited from the National Theatre by Liz Forgan. For that reason, Grade had his doubts about him and kept his distance at first. Forgan suspected that he really wanted someone who had been brushed by the magic gold dust of Hollywood.

Aukin said, 'I was on a four-year contract and was pretty sure they would not renew it. It took a long time to forge any kind of working relationship with Michael.'[22] When the two men had discussions about the future of the unit, Grade would hint that his favoured option was to close it down.[23] In 1993, Peter Moore, the forceful Commissioner of Documentaries, proposed that very course at a programme strategy meeting, adding that money earmarked for films would be better spent on first-run drama. Aukin fought his corner, pointing out that you could get six to eight runs out of a film, while drama is difficult to repeat more than twice.

It was certainly true that Channel 4 was at that point playing an important role in a British film industry going through one of its periodic bouts of decline. Film on Four, despite Grade's scepticism, was one of the industry's few reasonably active production units – and under Aukin, it began to recover some of its former prestige. The 1990s would turn out to be a stunning decade. Aukin inherited a sparsely filled cupboard, because the early successes had not been followed through, artistically or financially. His starting annual budget of £8 million was cut by the Board in 1993 but quickly restored as success followed success, and the channel's balance sheet ben-efited accordingly. By 1997 he had £30 million a year to invest.

'I remember arriving in 1990. It was a channel on the cusp of change. Grade saw the future – but at the point of joining they would still play films without commer-cials. I asked about ratings, and everyone was aghast at the question. Who is this philistine among us?'[24] One of his tasks was to devise two Film on Four seasons a year, starting in January. Finding little worthwhile material in the cupboard, he im-ported some theatre disciplines, notably a quest for good-quality scripts: the play's the thing. On David Puttnam's suggestion, he hired a Hollywood script editor, Jack Lechner. 'He was terrific – I didn't think the scripts were quite good enough and I really needed a hot-shot editor. He's a very eccentric man but he would get on with the writers. He's not just a critic – he offered solutions.'[25]

The turnaround came with *Shallow Grave* (1994), a violent black comedy, bris-tling with greed, murder and mayhem, about a group of flatmates whose mysterious lodger dies leaving a suitcase of money.

> When I first read *Shallow Grave* I recognised the intelligence and den-sity of a Pinter play. This was written by someone [John Hodge] who understood the rhythm of modern speech. It is thrilling and it is rare. It was given to me in Scotland by Andrew Macdonald [the film's pro-ducer]. I read it and the following morning phoned him to say it was wonderful.
>
> Grade had told me when I joined that the only mistake you could make was commissioning something you didn't believe in passionately. That meant when something didn't work – and most things don't – that was all right. If you keep backing your judgement, enough will.[26]

Aukin was pragmatic. He saw he needed to back at least fifteen films at any one time because you never knew where the successes would be. He was flexible: some projects were fully funded, others he bought a licence for, or took a bit of the equity. Because of the broader crisis in the British film industry, Channel 4 was a first port of call for writers and producers. By spreading the risks, if three or four films were really successful, five broke even and five were failures, that would be all right.

When *Shallow Grave* came along, Michael Grade hated it. 'It was the first Thatch-erite film', Aukin maintains, 'depicting her view that there is no society. It was about the children of that age. In terms of all arts, the breakthrough is the play that divides the generations. This was it.'[27]

The film gave star roles to the then-unknown Ewan McGregor and Christopher Eccleston. Usually, Grade's judgement and handling of talent were impeccable, but not this time. After the screening, in a room off Leicester Square, he rounded on

Aukin in front of the two stars. He had laughed at the beginning, then became more and more appalled at the gratuitous violence, murders and dismembering of bodies, with the knife going in and in again. He was thinking in terms of television and decided it was untransmittable. After speaking his mind, he stormed out.

Yet, in cinemas the film was a big commercial success, the first one to recoup its costs – £1.3 million – in the British box office alone. That year, Michael Grade and Jeremy Isaacs were together presented with an international Emmy recognising the channel's contribution to film. And Grade had the pleasure of handing out an award to Aukin at the Dinard Film Festival in France. *Shallow Grave* paved the way for a follow-up from the same team in 1996 – *Trainspotting*, adapted from Irvine Welsh's novel about Edinburgh heroin addicts, again starring Ewan McGregor. It was nominated for an Oscar.

Not all of the Films on Four were about low life and violence. In 1994 came the huge success of *Four Weddings and a Funeral*, a mainstream social comedy, on which Aukin took a lucky punt. Sceptics thought that Hugh Grant would not appeal to American audiences, so the main producers, Polygram, did not want to fund it fully. They let Channel 4 shoulder some of the risk and the eventual profit. Grade had by now discarded his reservations about Film on Four and was in his element as a successful movie mogul, especially as host of the VIP reception after the London premiere, where guests wore wedding-style buttonholes.

Another hit in the same year was *The Madness of King George*, a film version of Alan Bennett's play for the National Theatre, starring Nigel Hawthorne and Helen Mirren. For a while, Aukin could do no wrong, with blockbuster after blockbuster flowing off the production line: *Howard's End* (1992), *Peter's Friends* (1992), *The Piano* (1993), *Ladybird Ladybird* (1994), *East Is East* (1999), *Brassed Off* (1996) and more. Wisely, the Board left him to get on with it.

> No one was looking at my results. Every year I'd get another £30 million, come what may. I wasn't trying to make a business out of it – that wasn't the name of the game. The sort of British films we're good at making are not Hollywood action movies. If you aim at commercial success you almost certainly miss. The astonishing thing is that if you don't aim at commercial success but aim at trying to make a really good movie, then the miracle happens, and every now and then you do have a huge commercial success.
>
> What I understood was that if you are not able to get a film transmission quickly on the channel you get something else, people going to see a Channel 4 film in the cinema. It's a wonderful way of marketing your product.[28]

The larger the audience that saw a Channel 4 film in the cinema, the larger the television audience for it. 'It was my aim that if you wanted to know what Britain was like in the 1990s, you'd have as good an idea as any from watching Channel 4.'[29]

But towards the end of the decade, the mood changed. Like an addict seeking rehabilitation, the film industry wanted to reduce its reliance on television. The film-makers thought they were getting a raw deal from the broadcasters, and the arrival of National Lottery money gave them an alternative source of income. By the time Aukin left in 1998, to be succeeded by Paul Webster, Channel 4 had ceased to be as important to the industry as hitherto, though this was the point the channel changed its priorities and invested in more ambitious films. The great days of Film on Four would probably never return. The irony was that Grade had been coolly dismissive of the channel's film arm when he took control but that it turned out to be one of the great successes of his regime.

16

Whitehall warriors fight privatisation

• • • •

Champions come in many guises. During 1996, Channel 4 was defended most passionately from being put up for sale by a grey-haired Conservative businessman who exploited to the limit his personal ties to the Prime Minister, John Major. Sir Michael Bishop, born of an Australian father, had founded British Midland Airways and had made a fortune. He owned a magnificent country house (Donington Hall, near Derby), kept a suite at the Savoy Hotel and developed into as effective, if less charismatic a lobbyist as the redoubtable Sir Richard Branson. His contribution to preserving Channel 4 as a hybrid publicly owned company has remained largely unrecognised, because he was pushed out in 1997 by the new Labour Government, even though they were aware of the service he had performed for the station.

Bishop was drawn into Conservative Party politics when he was forty, as Margaret Thatcher arrived at 10 Downing Street. His airline, which specialised in short-haul flights, was being held back by British Airways' effective monopoly of landing slots at Heathrow Airport. In 1981, Bishop met Ian Gow, Margaret Thatcher's Parliamentary Private Secretary – later murdered at his home in Sussex by the IRA – and told him about this barrier to competition. Gow advised him to write a very concise letter to Mrs Thatcher and promised that he would put a star on it, to make sure she read it.

'I finished my letter on Wednesday', says Bishop, 'hand-delivered it on Maundy Thursday – and then the Falklands were invaded.'[1] Nevertheless, a week later, he received a personally signed letter from Mrs Thatcher, which led ultimately to the loosening of British Airways' grip on Heathrow. Bishop was highly impressed by the Prime Minister's commitment. Moreover, his success in doing down a much bigger operator conditioned his thinking, so that later he would understand Channel 4's role as the minnow – but a feisty minnow – in the shark-infested pond of commercial television.

He had been recruited to the channel's board in 1990 by the canny Sir George Russell, Chairman of the IBA, as Deputy to the busy Richard Attenborough, forced to retire as Chairman at the age of seventy. By then, he was close to John Major and the Chancellor, Kenneth Clarke, as well as the moderate wing of the Conservative Party. He was also a member of Brooks, the most gracious of the St James's gentlemen's clubs, where Tory grandees wine and dine – a far cry from Charlotte Street. In 1992, he had spoken at a Wembley Arena rally in support of John Major and his commitment to privatisation.

Bishop been on a board of Central Television, the ITV company that served the Midlands, between 1981 and 1990. 'I am under no illusions of why I was appointed to Channel 4, and of the thought processes that went on', he admits.

> I had access politically. I didn't know the metropolitan broadcasting circle, neither did I know Michael Grade [though the two would form a close working relationship]. I found everything the total opposite of public perceptions, in particular as far as Dickie Attenborough was concerned. He was slightly ridiculed for his style, yet he is one of the most efficient people I have ever met, He is a very shrewd judge of character. Dickie has an amazingly disciplined mind and an ability to respond in a light-hearted way.[2]

Bishop was delighted when he was made Chairman in 1992. He thought that probably 90 per cent of the workforce at Channel 4 voted Labour, and he knew that this, along with partisan coverage in other parts of the media, had understandably angered the Conservative governments of the 1980s and 1990s. 'To be quite honest, I thought they were justified in feeling stung. But Michael Grade was always popular with politicians. He gave no hint of his allegiances – he was completely neutral.'[3] As Chairman, Bishop kept his distance from the programme-makers but made sure he maintained a tight grip on staff numbers and other costs. Thus, he was able to convert some of the channel's surplus cash into a freehold asset: a purpose-built headquarters in Horseferry Road, Westminster.

During the summer of 1996, the Board was shocked to hear about a new threat to privatise Channel 4. Triggered by the 1990 Broadcasting Act, the channel became a statutory corporation, in effect owned by the Treasury, though the £100 founding share certificate was lodged in Channel 4's archive, where it remains to this day. The debate sprang from an idea within the Number 10 policy unit, and the Prime Minister asked the Treasury to look at it. There had been rumblings about privatisation from several quarters from the moment the channel began to find its feet. Justin Dukes, the founding Deputy Chief Executive, had been enthusiastically in favour and had provoked debates among executives in the late 1980s, mirroring the political debate about the channel's future. In the run-up to the 1990 Broadcasting Act, Attenborough went to Number 10 to charm Margaret Thatcher into limiting any change to the provision that Channel 4 could start selling it own advertising.

Now, nearly a decade later, the channel dangled like a low-hanging ripe plum. Years of rolling back the state, following the first successful privatisation of British Telecom, meant that potential candidates for selling off were drying up. Meanwhile, the channel had been stunningly successful at selling its advertising breaks. But the major changes to the programming, initiated by Michael Grade, had set hares racing. During 1995, the channel was rocked by ferocious criticism of some of its output, culminating in the row over *The Word*. In the *Daily Mail* the spiky columnist Paul Johnson sustained a persistent campaign against Grade and all his works (see Chapter 14).

Yet, the timing was bizarre. During 1995 and the first half of 1996 there had been a thorough debate in Parliament to set the legislative framework for digital television. This new Broadcasting Act would receive royal assent on 24 July. Channel 4's status had not been discussed in the process, except for a refusal to remove the hated 'funding formula' – a hangover from its dependency on ITV, which forced it to hand over ever larger cheques to its rival every year. The Government had swept aside Channel 4's objections, because the payments ensured that ITV would provide a limited guarantee in the event that the channel's advertising dried up. The fact that privatisation did not rear its head until after the Act was passed led Channel 4's executives and supporters to suspect dirty tricks. Had they been lulled into thinking that digital television was really the big policy issue, when all the time privatisation plans were going ahead in secret?

An indicative vote in Cabinet, to explore a privatisation option, was passed thirteen to one in June, with only Virginia Bottomley, Secretary for State for National Heritage, favouring the status quo. It transpired that the Budget forecasts (in the annual 'red book' government update) revealed a £500 million shortfall in privatisation receipts for 1996/7. The political imperative was to project a lower public-sector borrowing requirement for the following year, when the election loomed. Channel 4 appeared to be one of four candidates that could plug the gap. It would have to be a post-election privatisation, but it could be used as a factor in election campaigning on lower taxes for 1998/9. There was talk of a valuation of £1 billion.

A febrile atmosphere grew at Channel 4, though nothing was said in public. Approached for advice, Samuel Montagu (a subsidiary of HSBC) wrote to Finance Director David Scott: 'A realistic valuation might well be in a range very substantially below what the public expect.'[4] There were no costs to take out because it was very efficiently run.[5] The problem was that the fierce public campaign to end the funding formula, spearheaded by Michael Grade, had highlighted Channel 4's success and potential wealth. It seemed that it could end up with the worst of all worlds: the formula stood and privatisation was being debated behind closed doors.

Sir Michael Bishop was alarmed. He believed that privatisation was only a whisker away because the Government was desperate for cash. He had to fly to a conference in Boston, and during the seven-hour flight he drafted and redrafted a letter to his friend John Major, setting out the reasons why Channel 4 should not be privatised.

> I faxed it back to Michael Grade from my hotel. It was only three pages. There was a deep silence from his end of the phone. He asked for no changes [. . .] Michael, the Board and I, as a Conservative supporter, thought this was the best shot, to go to the politicians rather than civil servants.[6]

This is what Bishop wrote:

> Dear John,
>
> As you will know, I am a wholehearted and totally committed supporter of the consumer advantages and financial benefits which the privatisation programme implemented by successive Conservative Governments have brought to key areas of British commerce and industry. Indeed, we together shared a public platform extolling the virtues of this policy [. . .] However I am equally convinced that Channel 4 is not a suitable case for this treatment. To propose the channel for the momentous change of privatisation fails to meet the criteria for such a change in two ways.
>
> Firstly, the unassailable track record of privatisation to date is that the standards or quality of products or services dramatically improved. That is a key test. Sadly, as evidenced by the downmarket and generally poor content of the vast majority of satellite television output and the increasingly similar trend within the ITV network, it is only too clear what happens when conventional shareholder pressures are applied to the TV industry. Quality and choice are diminished. For Channel 4, with new shareholders seeking to maximise profits, money for dividends would have to be taken directly from the screen, at viewers' expense, by diverting programme expenditure.
>
> Second, an important qualification for privatisation has been that the targeted corporation has required access to Government funding. Channel 4 has never required nor sought financial support from the Government. It would be particularly unpalatable if the excellence of British public service broadcasting, exemplified by the channel and recognised worldwide, has to be held to ransom for the short-term expedient of fund-raising for other purposes.

I believe such a Philistine approach towards an organisation that has contributed so much to bringing the arts, music, education, film and current affairs to a vast new wider audience at no cost to the public purse would elicit widespread condemnation from many of those who are strong supporters of the Government. It would, undoubtedly, encourage a broad coalition of opposition inside the Conservative party, and right across the political spectrum.

Finally, privatisation would not make Channel 4 more accessible. The contrary is the case. Channel 4 is fully accountable to Parliament through the ITC, Additionally, the ITC has power to appoint and dismiss the non-executive directors, a majority on the Board. It has no such powers over ITV plc licensees. Knowing my credentials in supporting privatisation where a valid case can be made, I hope you will understand my candid and forthright representation in seeking an assurance from you that the perverse suggestion that privatisation would be pursued by the Government is unfounded.[7]

So why would such a keen proponent of privatisation be so adamantly opposed to it in this instance? Bishop knew from first-hand experience the rapacious demands of the City for high returns. Investors would have expected the same from Channel 4 as they expected from ITV, and Bishop understood that such a marketplace could not support the mix of public-service programmes that viewers were accustomed to. Nor would privatisation have benefited Channel 4 financially. Later, he could say, 'I feel proven correct by events at Channel Five [launched a year later] and by what has happened to ITV.'[8]

It proved, though, to be a long, sweaty summer. The letter was acknowledged, but after that came silence from Downing Street. An edgy Grade composed a memo to his directors:

I believe the Board must have a searching debate to examine if there is a point at which a willing privatisation might be something we would have to consider. I am certainly not advocating it, but we must think this through most carefully. We will fight the principle with all the cunning and vigour we can muster.[9]

On 23 July, nearly a month after Bishop's letter, Grade and David Scott met with the Financial Secretary to the Treasury, Michael Jack, who confirmed that the matter was under review. The pair made their case, pointing out that with their programmes still costing just £30,000 an hour, the same as at launch, compared with ITV's £86,000, they were a highly efficient outfit. Moreover, they had funded their new office themselves. Grade said he could boost profits by £12 million a year by removing *Channel 4 News* and replacing it with American movies. That was what any profit-seeking executive would do in the private sector, but was that really what the Government wanted to see happen to Channel 4? Jack, clearly on the defensive, repeated that the proposal was at a fluid stage and, indeed, implied that he knew precious little about it. Grade told him that Kenneth Clarke, the Chancellor, had been to lunch at Channel 4 in mid-July and had raised the matter privately. When told that the Board were not in favour, he had replied that he was not himself advocating it.

After the meeting with Jack, Dermot Finch, the Minister's Private Secretary, showed Grade and Scott out of the Treasury Building in Horse Guards Parade. Grade asked him what he thought. 'If you ask me, it's bonkers', Finch replied, 'but they are desperate for cash. They don't watch TV and wouldn't even know who Dennis Potter is.'[10] Bishop then wrote to enlist the support of his old mentor Sir George Russell. 'There is a strong resolve within the Treasury to secure the privatisation of Channel 4, with perhaps an announcement at the Conservative Party conference', he warned.[11]

Senior civil servants were suddenly not returning Grade's calls, so he went public at the Edinburgh Television Festival on 26 August, playing for sympathy and support: 'Sorry folks, no jokes', he told delegates. 'I'm too angry and too sad.' Channel 4, he explained, was caught somewhere between the Treasury and Downing Street. Anthony Fry, the merchant banker (and brother of the comedian Stephen Fry) pitched into the debate. Channel 4 wasn't a gold mine, he said, because it was a mature company, and certainly worth less than the £1 billion and more being talked about: perhaps £700 million would be nearer the mark. But in the discussion, Grade had to defend the channel against the charge that it had abandoned its remit anyway – the fallout from the 'dumbing down' debate that had raged damagingly during 1995 and had left a sense that everything was not rosy.

In response, Grade weighed into what he called the 'rose-tinted glasses brigade'. He was especially riled by the Granada Director Steve Morrison who labelled it Channel Three and a Half – illustrating his belief it was moving into ITV's populist territory. Peter Rogers, the incoming ITC Chief Executive, spoke up in Grade's defence: 'We do not believe the remit is being broken. We have our quarrels with Channel 4, some of them pretty serious, but nobody has ever suggested the problems are systemic', he said. Grade afterwards wrote to Morrison's boss, Charles Allen:

> Not for the first time Steve Morrison declared himself to be a dangerous enemy of the channel. In no other industry would one business trade with a competitor in the light of such potentially damaging and false allegations. It is my strong belief that we should cease trading at any level with LWT/Granada.[12]

As a follow-up, he asked his staff for an analysis of all the business done with the ITV programme supplier as he prepared for war. It took until 12 September for Grade to simmer down and accept Allen's apology.

His mood was lightened by the arrival, finally, of Major's reply to Bishop's letter. It was, on the face of it, a non-committal thank-you note. 'I am sorry to have taken so long to reply to you. I warmly congratulate the Board of Channel 4 on their achievements. The Government has <u>not</u> taken any decisions, but we are keeping all options open.'[13] The Board noted with satisfaction that Major had underlined the word 'not.'

Bishop replied on 16 September, the day before a government strategy meeting at Chequers called by Major. He added a fresh argument: Channel 4 currently dealt with over 500 independent production companies, and privatisation would be certain to affect their businesses. It would be like unleashing a swarm of angry bees.

Bishop opened a second front in September, when he had a private meeting with Michael Heseltine, the Deputy Prime Minister, founder of the Haymarket Publishing Group and a contemporary of Jeremy Isaacs at Oxford.

> He was filtering views for the budget. We had a good hour – it was just him and me, with no civil servant present, no note. It was very trenchant. I said privatisation would severely prejudice the quality of the channel's content. I had to make my case and he was playing Devil's advocate – every point I made, he took up. It was a very interesting interview. At the end I had no idea if I had succeeded or failed.[14]

At the same time, the Regulator waded in, making some highly relevant points that remain at the heart of the debate about Channel 4's unusual status. Sir George Russell warned Virginia Bottomley that the ITC thought the channel's programme remit 'cannot be guaranteed under a shareholder regime.'[15] Its licence to broadcast included a programme policy statement that demanded a minimum number of broadcasting hours in only a few areas – education, news and current affairs. The remit did not specifically require *every* programme to be experimental, innovative, distinctive and appealing to viewers not generally catered for by ITV, it ruled only that a sufficient or suitable proportion be justifiable in these terms. It could be rewritten, but a rigid formula covering a wide range of programmes would restrict its freedom and the ability to respond fast. He pointed to the lesson of ITV, where commercial pressures forced commissioning editors to play safe, resulting in too many predictable crime and police dramas.

He also reminded her that there had been no consensus on what the licences for ITV had been worth, so 'the risk of an excessive bid for Channel 4 on privatisation is a very real one,'[16] with the result that programme costs would have to be squeezed to fund the acquisition. Without its statutory remit, Russell warned, it would be a much more attractive proposition than ITV, because it is a national service, free of obligations to make regional programmes. 'If privatised, Channel 4 could break away from, or gradually but significantly erode, the statutory programme remit. It could go populist.'[17]

ITV would not give ground to Channel 4 without a fight, and it would seek to move further downmarket by eroding its own public-service obligations, including regional programming. 'Over many years it has been my experience that when broadcasting and commercial considerations come into conflict it is the broadcasting side that loses out. Serious damage can be caused very quickly. Recovery takes years.'[18] This was a serious statement from a man overseeing a flawed system created by the Thatcher Government. It was also prescient about what was to happen to ITV.

Meanwhile, the party-conference season came and went. At the Channel 4 board meeting on 23 October, it was noted that there was no mention of Channel 4 in the Queen's speech or at the Conservative conference. 'The position is changing almost hourly', wrote Michael Grade dramatically.[19] He fixed up a meeting with Sir Terry Burns, Chief Secretary at the Treasury, telling him, 'When this came up before I saw it off with Mrs Thatcher. At least she engaged with us over the arguments and in the end she agreed with us.'[20] Burns, wisely, repeated that only general discussions were taking place at a political level and no decisions had been taken but added that 'decisions can be taken very fast in the rough and tumble of the public sector.'[21] He asked what level of support Grade had among Conservative MPs. He was told that the old Tory guard, men such as Douglas Hurd and Timothy Renton, wanted to maintain the status quo. The ideological right, though, smelt blood.[22]

But the moment passed. Channel 4 was erased from the list of privatisation candidates in the red book. Grade was able to report, 'Fear is receding. People are surprised we have not run a megaphone campaign, but the key factor here was the Chairman's personal intervention.'[23] At its meeting on 25 November, the Board recorded its thanks to Bishop. By December, when Major finally responded to his September communication, promising opaquely that if the Government were to reach a point where decisions were imminent, he would offer the prospect of a meeting, it was all was starting to sound academic.

'As far as privatisation was concerned, we canned it,' said Bishop in 2006.[24]

> From 1997 to the present there has been no serious attempt to privatise Channel 4. Even Jeremy Isaacs, who would pick a fight with anyone, eventually became cordial towards me. He didn't like the idea of committed capitalists being involved in the organisation – it was total anathema to him – but he gradually realised that Michael Grade and I knew what we were talking about. I showed people that my politics

were irrelevant and I fought the Conservative Government very, very hard. There are always those who think they can have a halfway house, that they can use private money and keep the formula untouched [. . .] There was no way Channel 4 could be held in aspic: it would have had to be either a full-blooded privatisation or not. If it had been privatised, it would have been sold on at least twice by now – you only have to see the state ITV is in.[25]

With the benefit of hindsight, it seems reasonable to question how realistic the threat of privatisation ever was. Did Bishop's and Grade's determined lobbying amount in effect to tilting at imaginary windmills? Were they casting themselves as heroes in a mini-drama of their own concoction? The Conservative Government, after all, was dying on its feet, as the opinion polls showed quite clearly. Selling off Channel 4 would require legislation and a full debate, and there were many other interested parties, aside from the channel's own executives, who would vigorously oppose any sell-off. It patently could not be done within the remaining short life of Major's Government.

Despite those polls, Labour's landslide victory on 2 May 1997 was not a foregone conclusion: certainly there is nothing in the board minutes that presage it. Those involved remain convinced the threat was real. The passion with which they fought, the solid support they received from the Regulator and the advice from senior Treasury figures suggest that it was a real threat. They believed that once Channel 4 was in the 'red book', it would be very difficult to remove it. And the most significant gain from the campaign of resistance came, not from fighting off a desperate Conservative government looking for cash in the short term but by recruiting the government-in-waiting to the cause.

On 3 July 1996, Michael Grade had written to Tony Blair, as Leader of the Opposition, picking up on a statement by the then Heritage Opposition Spokesman Dr Lewis Moonie, who had said, 'I place on record our implacable opposition to the privatisation of Channel 4.' Included with the letter to Blair was an elegant seven-point summary of the anti-privatisation argument on a single sheet of paper. Point six noted that a privatised Channel 4 'would be open to subsequent take-over by European broadcasters' and, with the introduction of digital services, by American or Australian operators – in other words Rupert Murdoch.[26]

On 16 July, in a response that Grade carefully filed away for future reference, Blair replied, 'I believe Channel 4 [. . .] has strengthened and diversified Britain's public-service broadcasting. It has proved itself enormously popular, financially successful. [. . .] It has fostered a thriving independent production sector. Channel 4 is a success and I believe it would be wrong to place in jeopardy its achievements by privatising it.'[27]

Since then, three Labour manifestos have included a commitment not to privatise Channel 4 during the life of that Parliament, and the Conservatives have dodged the issue.

But once the channel was 'saved', Bishop knew there had to be a quid pro quo and that it would have to involve improvements in programming.

> We had to doff our caps to the original issues if we were keeping the channel as it was. I wanted to see a period of creative programmes, a real statement of programming values, which would justify all the political capital put into it. I felt that saving the channel from privatisation had to be followed with a real knockout blow.[28]

What he also knew was that Grade intended to leave. In September 1996, Grade asked to see him, and the two men dined at Brooks. Grade's five-year contract was at an end, and he was tired of being a lobbyist. A lucrative appointment beckoned with First Leisure, the entertainment and bingo-hall conglomerate founded by his family, allowing him the opportunity to acquire substantial capital through share options – something he could not do at Channel 4. He had served nine years and had faced down privatisation attempts at the beginning and at the end of his term. And he was out of sympathy with some of the more outrageous elements of the schedule, such as the *Brass Eye* series, from the satirist Chris Morris, which had had to be cut and delayed from autumn 1996 to spring 1997.

As for Bishop himself, he planned to stay on for a while, if for no other reason than to ensure a smooth transfer from the tempestuous Grade to what he believed should be a more self-effacing successor.

However, he had not counted on the mood of political vindictiveness that would accompany the triumphalism of a New Labour government finally returned to power in 1997 after seventeen years in the cold. Even though defeat for the Conservatives was widely expected, Bishop had not shrunk from identifying himself publicly with the lost cause. He leased an aircraft to the party for the election campaign, and when Labour activists (including Waheed Alli) sat in their Millbank headquarters and saw the Chairman of Channel 4 on camera, next to Major on the campaign trail, his fate was sealed.

They did not know the full story of just how far Bishop felt indebted to Major in particular, who had listened to his heartfelt pleas to keep Channel 4 as a public corporation. So, although the ITC recommended that he should be kept on for at least another year, Chris Smith, Secretary of State in the renamed Department of Culture, Media and Sport, declared that Bishop – whom he had never met – would keep the chairmanship 'over my dead body.' Asked for his reaction to that remark by the *Sunday Telegraph*, Bishop commented tersely: 'Rather shallow.' Chris Smith, with the benefit of hindsight, thinks that Bishop should have been kept on.[29]

As he bowed out, Bishop observed that Channel 4 had to reinvent itself, not just by finding dramatists to succeed Dennis Potter or comedies to succeed *Father Ted*. 'Channel 4 has got to go to great lengths to be contrary. If it is not contrary in every sense it will lose its bite and impact.'[30] He noted that for the first seventeen years of its existence it had known only Conservative governments and had seen itself, in effect, as being in opposition. 'I'm not foolish enough to ignore the great sentiment of support the new government has throughout broadcasting', he reflected. 'That is the reality. But it was very effective when it was in opposition. Now it has to show exactly the same bite under a Labour government – even if the commissioning editors have to grit their teeth and force themselves to go over the edge.' And, with that, he went back to running an airline.

17

Lexus man arrives

• • • •

During 1996, a persistent young producer called Andrew Newman rang the prison where Reggie Kray, the East End gangster, was held and asked him to get in touch, to support a charity campaigning for elephants in distress. When Kray phoned back, he was put on to Chris Morris, the satirist, and they spoke for twenty-five minutes about the fate of Clara, an elephant in a German zoo who was slowly inflating because her trunk was stuck up her anus. Kray was one of a handful of celebrities who sent messages of support when they learnt of Clara's unfortunate plight; others included the actress Britt Ekland and the comedian Paul Daniels. The next day came a knock on the door of Talkback, the television production company, in Percy Street, off Tottenham Court Road. Newman opened it to a Kray henchman. 'Someone has been taking the piss out of Reggie', he observed menacingly. 'Remember, there are three Krays – and only one is dead.'[1]

The company's part-owner, Peter Fincham, worried about the safety of his staff, was naturally keen that this item did not go forward into the first turbulent series of *Brass Eye* for Channel 4. He was the Executive Producer of the six programmes, which had taken a year and £1 million to film and were themed around stitch-ups, the notion that some people will believe anything. The series, scheduled to start on 19 November, had originally been planned for the BBC, but they had backed out – and when Grade previewed it, he too was horrified at the number of important people who had been duped by Morris and decided it could not be broadcast as it was.

Apart from the inflating elephant, another main worry was over a cod news report of a statue of the Virgin Mary in Ireland apparently weeping. Morris played the role of the reporter: 'It's probably just rain dripping down the front of the statue, but try telling this to these bog-brained Murphys and it would be as likely to be believed as getting a blow-job from the Pope.' Fincham, who became Controller of BBC1 in 2004, said in

2006 that he thought that line was broadcastable by modern standards: 'I didn't think personally that line would have led to a complaint being upheld – but they wouldn't broadcast it. These storms at the time now look like storms in a teacup.'[2]

Grade had resolved to leave Channel 4 and television once his second campaign against privatisation was concluded, but the crisis that blew up over *Brass Eye* would sour his final months, showing how remote he had become. Grade told the Board later that he had experienced the feeling that the same old problems had been resurfacing again.[3] What nobody realised outside the channel – including the Chairman, Sir Michael Bishop – was that John Willis, the Director of Programmes, had essentially been running the place for the past eighteen months, while Grade mainly confined himself to high-profile lobbying. In January 1997, he announced that he would be quitting the following May. His departure would accord with what has become a tradition of Channel 4's chief executives stepping down gracelessly.

The *Brass Eye* row was the point where the commissioning team turned against him. They saw him as out of touch, and they resented his retaining the power to block programmes they passionately believed in. Grade's confidence had been shaken by his being dubbed Britain's 'Pornographer-in-Chief', by rows over *The Word*, the critical disdain for *The Girlie Show*'s vulgarity, frequent interventions from the Regulator, notably over *Brookside* and, most recently, Sean Ryder swearing on three editions of Chris Evans's *TFI Friday*. As the big name over the shopfront, he, as Isaacs had done, took all the glory and all the criticism. Yet, at programme launches, he had for some time seemed at sea, self-consciously sipping lager out of a bottle.

Grade had withdrawn the series initially because the producers had not received meaningful written consents from the people duped. As he prepared to kill it off completely, he called an editorial meeting, where it was made clear to him that he had overreacted and that everyone else was determined to put the programme on air. A junior commissioner, Dan Chambers, thought he detected the whiff of a palace revolution, with most of his colleagues convinced that Grade had lost the courage of his convictions.[4] Willis, by contrast, supported *Brass Eye* with the fervour of a man who had just had his contract renewed until the end of 2000. He was determined that it should be broadcast. Grade gave way, the cuts and compliance issues were sorted out, and the series was given a new start date, 29 January.

One of the most extraordinary episodes to reach the screen was a bizarre hoax on the Conservative MP for Basildon, David Amess. He was briefed by Morris about a new drug called 'cake' being imported from the Czech Republic. First, he recorded a campaign message – there were special T-shirts printed with the acronyms 'F.U.K.D. and B.O.M.B.D.' – then he raised a question in Parliament, eliciting a reply from the Home Office that they would ban this (imaginary) drug. It was a send-up of the way prominent people in public life are prepared to take up campaigns without delving deeply or stopping to think. In another segment, the serial killer Peter Sutcliffe was reported to be the starring in *The Ripper, The Musical*, and in a ludicrous twist Sutcliffe's 'agent' was shown describing how his client was allowed out of prison each night to take the lead role as part of his therapy. This infuriated John McCririck, the channel's racing and betting commentator, who thumped the table, incensed in particular by the notion that a mass murderer should have an agent.

Part of the channel's public-interest defence was that a number of celebrities had seen through the hoaxes and had refused to play. But a foolish gesture by Chris Morris rather spiked the notion of lofty intentions. During the delay caused by the extra editing, he had doctored the tape of the final programme, on 5 March, inserting a flash frame that read, 'Michael Grade is a cunt'. Neither Channel 4 nor the production company, Talkback, knew anything about this, but Morris told Newman and some other friends what he had done when they gathered together to watch the programme go out. Next morning, Fincham, on holiday in Barbados, received a fax message saying that Channel 4 was thinking of suing Talkback, and in a subsequent telephone conversation with Grade he was at pains to assure him that Morris had acted alone. David Scott, promoted to Managing Director before Grade left, has an explanation why Grade was so offended by the prank: 'You have to remember that Michael had always been incredibly supportive of programme-makers. I think he was depressed by it.'[5]

The race to replace Grade began as soon as he announced his forthcoming resignation. He had run Channel 4 for nine years, the longest-serving chief executive. The channel was in rude financial health,[6] but there was an urgent need for fresh, strong, creative leadership. From the moment he was appointed, the suspicion never quite went away that Grade was somehow not quite right for Channel 4. At first he was thought to be Mr ITV, too mainstream, and now the criticism was that he had been shaped by the BBC of the 1980s and was out of date. In 2006, Isaacs pounced on the fact that when Grade took on the Executive Chairmanship of ITV, he said he was 'coming home' – something he had also said when he became Chairman of the BBC Board of Governors. Home is where the heart is, but where exactly was Grade's heart?[7]

His achievements in the transitional years between 1988 and 1993 had been immense. With Attenborough, he succeeded in establishing a viable future for Channel 4 as a hybrid operator, a publicly owned corporation undergoing relatively light scrutiny. He achieved this despite a prevailing atmosphere of hostility towards broadcasters in Westminster, which would cause irrevocable damage to ITV. He had been an effective, if sometimes histrionic, Whitehall warrior – and he had done it all over again in 1996. Though the old guard might deplore the compromise of selling advertising in competition with everyone else, he had pragmatically embraced it once he saw there was no choice, and he found the right people to carry it out successfully.

He had overseen the transition from a totally subsidised channel, kept by ITV, to one that paid its own way by pushing up the price of its advertising, and he had ensured that there remained a degree of separation between advertising and programming. Then he had led a crusade against the unfair funding formula, an insurance policy that worked against Channel 4's interests to such an extent that in February 1997 it had to make out a cheque to ITV for £89.9 million: the argument was won later that summer, after Labour swept to power.

In this battle, he formed a close – perhaps too close – bond with his Chairman, Sir Michael Bishop, who had made an extremely successful business out of running British Midland as a feisty regional airline challenging the giant British Airways. On the face of it, the situation with Channel 4 was similar, as it battled doughtily against the mighty ITV. But that David-and-Goliath approach ultimately worked against Channel 4, provoking mutual hostility between the two channels and scotching any idea of working together after 1993 with complementary programmes and scheduling. The only link remaining was ITV's obligation to give promotional spots for Channel 4 each day on ITV, and vice versa for Channel 4, yet during the first year of the new deal, even that had almost broken down, and the Regulator had to step in.

A more moderate course, of making the funding formula fairer but keeping its skeleton, in recognition that a safety net of some sort might one day be needed, was considered, but rejected. Ending the funding formula and keeping the channel in public ownership were the guiding principles of Grade's final years. (At one point, the Board had considered whether Channel 4 could be made into a trust but had baulked at the complications.)

The Board's preoccupation with the channel's essential structure had one especially damaging effect: it had made no significant preparation for the digital age. The Channel 4 website started on 1 July 1996, but no broader plans for new media were discussed. The conservative Grade found it hard to get his head round such far-reaching developments for which nothing in his background had prepared him. New media was not his style. Yet, the 1996 Broadcasting Act was about setting up digital terrestrial television – eventually to come good as Freeview. The channel responded sluggishly with a sketchy proposal for a pay film channel, code-named 'C4B' during late autumn 1996 and spring 1997.

Meanwhile, competition was hotting up. Channel Five, the last old-style terrestrial channel funded by advertising, was starting on 30 March under David Elstein, one of the early campaigners for Channel 4, and Dawn Airey. An effective marketing campaign projected the new channel as modern and mainstream, and it made its first impact when Kirsty Young read the news while perched on rather than sitting behind a desk – an affectation that later spread to rival channels. Multichannel viewing had trebled from an untroubling 4 per cent of total hours in 1991 to 12 per cent in late 1996, and over 20 per cent of homes now received signals via satellite or cable.

Channel 4 had rejected a number of proposals from would-be partners, and in 1995 turned down the offer of a chunk of Channel Five from the winning consortium, chaired by Greg Dyke. Channel 4 assessed its profit potential to be low and did not wish to fund 25 per cent of its £500 million start-up. The Board had been advised that an investment could be justified under the terms of its operating rules, but they were financially conservative, and Grade ruled that any new activity must complement and support the role of Channel 4 as a public-service broadcaster. This complacency was fuelled by the Board's belief that at the point of Grade's departure they had created a virtuous circle of sharply rising advertising income, providing more each year to invest in programmes. In 1988, the programme budget was £135 million, and by 1997 it had risen to £310 million.

'Money was slopping around', recalls Graham Smith, Commissioner of Entertainment and Comedy from 1996 to 1997, responsible, *inter alia*, for Chris Evans's *TFI Friday*. He estimated that the *TFI Friday* production budget, for an hour-long tea-time mix of guests, comedy and two or three bands, should have been £160,000 an hour, whereas it came in at £275,000 an hour. 'There was a lot of that. The channel was immensely cash rich. There was no great necessity to be economical.'[8] Evans was paid £50,000 a show for this third series.

Grade had achieved the elusive 10-per-cent audience share, then consistently exceeded it, and he had attracted talented people on and off screen. But those indisputably impressive ratings had come at a price. Reliance on American imports, comedies such as *Friends* and *Frasier*, was growing. Part of Grade's legacy to his successor was that 23 per cent of the audience ratings came from American sitcoms and drama and 19 per cent from films – these, too, mainly American. With *Brookside* accounting for another 9.2 per cent, that meant that half the total viewing was for just three kinds of content, which was unhealthy. After all, the channel had more than £300 million a year to spend on programmes and was meant to be innovative, catering for tastes beyond the mainstream.[9] Channel 4's primacy in the field of American sitcoms was about to be challenged. At the end of 1996, as Grade was preparing to bow out, there was an ominous scuffle when Sky and Channel Five bid together for the rights for the fourth and fifth series of *Friends* and *ER*, in a deal orchestrated by Elstein. Channel 4 offered $37 million, but negotiations with Warner Brothers faltered when Sky and Channel Five jointly offered a munificent $170 million. Warner wanted a slot on a satellite pay service, which Channel 4 could not offer but Sky could.

Grade moved fast to head off the threat, in the knowledge that *Friends* and *ER* had provided the channel with its fifth and sixth top-ranked show during the year. In the resulting deal, Channel 4 kept the terrestrial rights but Sky gained the pay-TV rights to series two to six. But as part of the deal, they had to buy a number of other drama series they did not want. During Grade's era, he was able to insist that Sky was not granted a broadcast window ahead of the channel, but that could not now be sustained indefinitely, and Channel 4's pitch of offering the best of the imports would start to sound increasingly hollow over the coming decade.

The changes in the Grade era were best symbolised by the steel and glass head-quarters in Horseferry Road, Westminster, that the channel moved into during 1994 – a freehold asset valued at £55 million. The muddled inadequacies of Charlotte Street were replaced by an achingly cool sculptural building in steel and glass de-signed by Richard Rogers, with lifts on the outside. It was designed for the exact number of staff employed, 550. Willis liked the building but found the surrounding area 'dead' compared with Fitzrovia, a widely held view.[10] Michael Darlow, the inde-pendent producer and one of the original campaigners for Channel 4, thought that the inside was like an American penitentiary: all that was missing were the grilles and caged prisoners. It would now go through a changing of the guards.

● ● ● ●

The trio in charge of selecting Grade's successor were Sir Michael Bishop, Deputy Chairman David Plowright – the ousted Managing Director of Granada – and Mary McAleese. They turned to the established media headhunter Gill Carrick, of White-head Mann, for help. There was not a large field. Greg Dyke, by now long dispos-sessed of LWT, was an obvious choice, but he was running Pearson Television as well as chairing Channel Five and would not apply; he would have to be approached. Three internal candidates came forward: Stewart Butterfield, Colin Leventhal and John Willis. Only Willis stood a chance, but Carrick warned him that an insider would find it hard. Alan Yentob, who had set BBC2 onto a creative course that com-peted with Channel 4 and was now running BBC1, was an obvious candidate, but he did not go through to the final round. His one-time protégé, Michael Jackson, did.

Staffers, led by David Scott, threw themselves behind Willis and encouraged him to make a serious pitch for the job. At his interview, he produced a paper explaining how he understood the heartbeat of the channel. 'We would not have stood still', he said later. 'We would have introduced new commissioning editors and changed the drama. My paper was about continuity and change at the same time – keeping the channel stable while introducing a lot of change.'[11] Bishop told him it was brilliant, but Willis suspected he thought Grade had written it. Bishop also asked him why he had not spoken up more at board meetings.

> I explained that I was content to be Director of Programmes and enjoy-ing it. I was making my way and was keen to continue in my role. But [. . .] I also realised that with a new chief executive my job would be vulnerable anyway, so I might as well have a go.[12]

For the first and only time in its brief history, Channel 4 had a credible internal candidate for Chief Executive. But Willis's weakness was that he had focused mostly on factual programmes and was not a great self-promoter in a sector where people rush to take credit for successes that are often not theirs. On the selection panel, David Plowright was his principal advocate. He said:

> I felt a lot of what he had championed at Channel 4 showed he understood what it stood for [. . .] Sir David Nicholas also supported him on the Board. Of the candidates we interviewed, John had the track record and understanding of the channel. I felt Michael Jackson would do it well but on a temporary basis. We were in despair over the drama: it was a dead cat.[13]

Michael Jackson, thirty-nine, was seen by Grade, now fifty-four, as the broadcaster of his generation, and he emerged as the obvious successor. As a young man, he had campaigned energetically for the channel's foundation and produced programmes for it early on. He had pleased those of the founders with traditional tastes in television by winning a commission for a series on the 1960s, and then for *Open the Box*, about the way people view television, which led to the more innovative and influential *Media Show*. Michael Grade got to know him when he produced a session, 'The Scheduling Game' at the Edinburgh Festival in 1996, which saw Grade pitted successfully against Birt. Impressed, he encouraged Alan Yentob to lure him to the BBC, where in 1989 he had started *The Late Show*, a cool nightly review of arts and culture that ran after *Newsnight*. Two years later, he moved to the executive ranks as Head of Music and Arts – elbowing aside Janet Street-Porter – then after another two years, he was made Controller of BBC2.

John Birt, by now the BBC's Director General, took a close interest in Jackson's career: he was one of a select group of high fliers groomed for greater things by being sent to Wharton, an American business school. Under him, BBC2 had given Channel 4 a run for its money, buying up *The Simpsons* and *Video Diaries*, encouraging an appetite for leisure programmes and backing *This Life*, a drama series about twenty-somethings made by Tony Garnett. In 1996, Jackson became the BBC's youngest-ever Director of Programmes, briefly running BBC1. That was the year when he made a speech at the Royal Television Society warning that Channel 4 was losing its credibility – a swipe at programmes such as *The Word* and *The Girlie Show*:

> Am I alone in thinking that the pursuit of demographics – in particular young, lager-drinking, upwardly mobile men – has led to a sapping of Channel 4's originality? [. . .] Treating the audience simply as categories of consumers is the worm in the bud of any channel that wants to be taken seriously.

For all his accomplishments, and his instincts for what made a new television programme, Jackson was socially shy and reserved. When he spoke, or had made up his mind, it was always to the point and worth hearing. But he liked to work through a small, trusted group. He was not a natural leader in the Isaacs or Grade mould: he did not communicate by megaphone. Born in Wilmslow, the son of a baker, he was the first senior figure to come not from the debating grounds of Oxbridge or from the gilded aristocracy of light entertainment but from a media-studies course at the Polytechnic of Central London, now the University of Westminster.

He was never a great public speaker, but he is self-disciplined and steeped in the visual media, spending hours watching television and films, reading, thinking, identifying trends, hoovering up ideas and jotting them down. People who worked with him waited for him to come in after a weekend, with files of cuttings to pass on. He liked the fruits of success: good restaurants, fine wine and luxury hotels. He had moved house from Clapham, south London, to Notting Hill, buzzing as it was with media types. His one eccentricity was to walk over his office furniture without his shoes on.[14]

In the job interview, Jackson promised he would mastermind a creative revival in line with the channel's original values and purpose. He would be innovative, saying things in a direct and provocative way that the BBC could not easily manage. This would be accompanied by a rigorous overhaul of commissioning and a complete review of any new digital-channel plans. Entertainment needed fixing, as well as drama. He pointed out that the rising new comedians, from Vic Reeves to Jack Dee, were going to ITV and the BBC, which were, in effect, stealing Channel 4's clothes. The channel's scheduling reflected the BBC Grade had left in the 1980s: Jackson would epitomise the fresh thinking of the ensuing decade.

Mary McAleese favoured him: she had always wanted an outsider. But Bishop, who now, in effect, had the casting vote, wavered. If psychometric testing had been in vogue, he might well have asked Jackson to undergo it, because the nagging question, despite his stint at the business school, was whether he had all-round executive skills. Was he a leader? Will Wyatt, Managing Director of BBC Television observed, 'He had a natural aptitude for television programme-making and commissioning, but at the BBC he avoided managerial chores whenever he could. He was quickly bored with money issues.'[15]

As the panel wavered, Richard Eyre, the very successful Chief Executive of Capital Radio, was asked to go to meet the selection committee at the Savoy Hotel, where Bishop kept a suite. Capital had an historic link with Channel 4 because Richard Attenborough had chaired both and was involved in their launches. Eyre, a born-again Christian, recalls:

> Very late in the day Sir Michael Bishop rang and asked if I could I meet with him. There was a clandestine meeting at the Savoy. They were go-

ing to the Board imminently and had to decide. He asked me to see Mary McAleese and David Plowright, but it went disastrously badly. Mary McAleese asked me if it was possible to do the job of running Channel 4 and be a Christian. I said I couldn't understand why not – after all, I was running Capital Radio, another media company. We then moved on to talk about morality. Plowright suggested to me that viewers could always push the on and off button. I responded by asking whether he thought a broadcaster had no responsibility for what is being broadcast.

Afterwards, Eyre realised that Plowright was deliberately provoking him.[16] But it was an adversarial meeting, neither friendly nor positive. Eyre knew he was out of the race almost before he realised he had entered it.

Bishop had to struggle with the notion that very successful people are not the easiest of personalities to deal with and that he was not best equipped to judge creative men and women. Even taking that into account, though, Jackson was not his idea of a perfect candidate, largely because of his perceived lack of interest in the nitty-gritty of day-to-day management. However, he eventually overcame these doubts, recognising that they had appointed a managing director, David Scott, to strengthen the business side, and that could leave room for a different kind of person at the top. Jackson's role would be more that of a Chief Creative Officer than a Chief Executive, although he would retain that title, and the salary that went with it.

On 2 May 1997, that sunny day after the General Election that swept New Labour to power ('A new dawn has broken, has it not?') Jackson announced he was leaving the BBC. He was recruited to Channel 4 on a three-year contract, renewable a year at a time after that, at a salary of £350,000, shortly to rise to £478,000. He quickly moved to shore up the non-creative side of the business by making Andy Barnes Sales and Marketing Director, reporting to Scott, not to him. Unlike Grade, he showed very little interest in the advertising sales side. 'We hardly saw him, after a first visit', says Barnes.[17] But Jackson also brought in his own marketing man, David Brook, from Channel Five and the *Guardian*, to handle the broader issues of marketing, branding and strategy that needed attention: the famous logo had been abandoned in 1996 and replaced with four empty circles.

Any change at the helm of a large organisation inevitably brings casualties, and the most significant was John Willis. His new four-year contract, at a salary of £250,000 a year, had a protective clause covering a change of chief executive. This had been agreed by the Remuneration Committee, consisting of Bishop – who knew of Grade's intentions – David Plowright and Bert Hardy. Plowright thought he had negotiated an agreement with Bishop that if Jackson were appointed Willis would stay on, and soon after his appointment Willis said he hoped to work with him. But that was not how Jackson saw it. Itching to get his hands on the channel's programming, he intended to double up as Director of Programmes.

On 4 June, he sent out a memorandum:

> I'd like to meet each commissioning editor individually before I start in July, to get a sense of your area. To make our time as productive as possible I would be grateful if you would prepare a short paper detailing:
> - How you feel your area contributes to the overall vision of the channel.
> - Who are your key audiences (include appreciation indices, reach and share figures).
> - Who your key suppliers are.
> - How do your plans relate to the competition?
> - Programmes commissioned over the last two years.
> - What you see as key opportunities in your genre over the next two years.
> - How your area could contribute to marking the channel's 15th anniversary in November.
> - Any other thoughts about the channel's strategy, programmes or structure.

If this was calculated to send the commissioners into a panic, diving for their ratings experts, it certainly succeeded. They did not tend to have this kind of information to hand: Grade dealt with that sort of thing. Peter Moore, as he surveyed his broad factual empire, realised with a sinking heart that *Undercover Britain*, with its appeal to audiences in the lower social groups C2DE, was doomed, despite a 10-percent share on Wednesdays at 9 p.m. *True Stories* would suffer the same fate. Jackson was to institute a new disciplined approach imported directly from John Birt's BBC, which Grade loathed. It marked a switch of priorities: the start of the rise of schedulers who expected programmes to be commissioned for slots, rather than slots found for programmes. The meetings with the commissioners took place at smart hotels: among the favourites were the Goring near Victoria Station and the Ritz in Piccadilly, where a waiter pursued Jackson a tie so that he would conform to the dress code.

On 1 July, he formally started work. At his first board meeting, he announced that he was going to be Director of Programmes for the next six to twelve months, as he reviewed the schedule. He abolished the two big posts that Grade had created – Controller of Factual and Controller of Entertainment and Arts – and said he intended to create five new editorial posts, most of which would be filled by recruits from the BBC. Willis was absent, consulting his lawyer (he eventually went to Cherie Booth, the new Prime Minister's wife) before he beat a retreat to his house in France.

The changing of the guard was dramatically underscored by a set-piece dinner two weeks later at the Dorchester Hotel on Park Lane. Some 500 people had gathered to pay tribute to Michael Grade, who, at the age of fifty-four, was to quit television for a more lucrative position heading the family business. Alongside the broadcasters, as they sat through a surprisingly tedious string of speeches, were a few of the rich and famous: Elisabeth Murdoch, Bruce Forsyth, Melvyn Bragg and Lord (Lew) Grade, Michael's uncle. A pair of bright red socks – Grade's flamboyant trademark – tied with golden string nestled by each place setting.

The conversation in the mirrored ballroom – and some of Grade's most cutting remarks – concerned Jackson, notable by his absence. There was some macabre humour about people leaving the channel in body bags, for already the new man was making sweeping changes, in addition to sidelining Willis. There were plenty of stiff upper lips in evidence, as the speeches wound to a weary midnight punctuation point. Grade paid a pointed tribute to Willis: 'It is important Channel 4 reinvents itself from time to time if it is to stay ahead [. . .] But no matter how many changes he must make, show respect for the past. The achievement of John Willis and all his teams has been absolutely unmistakable.' And he counselled Jackson to 'forget much of the tosh he was exposed to at the BBC'.

This speech bore some resemblance to an ancient curse, for everyone Grade singled out for special praise was destined to be dispensed with, including the Editor of *Channel 4 News*, Sara Nathan. The entire commissioning process was being revolutionised, and no part of it would escape Jackson's direct scrutiny. At that point, five commissioning editors had gone or would soon be going. Lucinda Whiteley, who had reintroduced home-grown children's programmes and pioneered what was designed as an exclusively teen soap opera, *Hollyoaks*, was leaving voluntarily for a better job at Polygram. Peter Ansorge, running drama, would leave within months after tidying up projects under way; but he was expensive to lose, for he too had been given a new four-year contract, at £90,000 a year, just before Grade left.

Farrukh Dhondy, Head of Multicultural Programmes and one of the channel's longest-serving executives, left of his own accord and was replaced with Jasmin Anwar from the BBC. David Stevenson, Commissioner of Youth Programmes – including *The Girlie Show*, which Jackson had roundly attacked – had already left that spring. Seamus Cassidy, the Senior Commissioning Editor running *Father Ted* and *Brass Eye*, went to Planet 24, where *The Big Breakfast* was in decline. Stewart Butterfield and Colin Leventhal, who had put themselves forward for Grade's job, both left: Butterfield for Granada and Leventhal to set up a film company with David Aukin from Film on Four.

The most notable new recruit was thirty-eight-year-old Gub Neal, Granada's Head of Drama and the original producer of ITV's hit series *Cracker*. It was a major coup for Jackson to entice this rising star of television drama. Apart from *Cracker*, he had produced *Band of Gold*, *Hillsborough* (1996) and *Moll Flanders*

(1996) and was skilled at selling drama formats as co-productions to America. His dynamic blend of creative and commercial nous was now to be given its freedom at Channel 4, even if the channel's annual drama budget of £40 million was much less than he had enjoyed at ITV.

Jackson wanted drama to strike out in a cheaper and more modern direction. He wanted a home-grown version of *Friends*, and Tony Garnett's World Productions had already been asked to devise pilots. Jackson was signalling from the very first day that he intended to take the channel on a new path. Yet, in effect, he was behaving like Jeremy Isaacs, the founding father, who always acted as Director of Programmes and thus was able to create and nurture the brand. Jackson was reasserting that role, and in doing so rediscovering Channel 4's essential simplicity of purpose as a broadcaster buying in all its programmes. It was his chance now to stamp his own personality on it. He was taking back the territory.

There were still loose ends to tie, though. At the autumn programme launch in late August, a lavish event with pink champagne at Shakespeare's Globe Theatre on the banks of the Thames, Jackson was shadowed by a spectre at the feast, a nervous-looking Willis, who had been advised by his lawyer to keep turning up for work until his status was clarified. A week later, David Scott went to the Edinburgh Television Festival and detected a feeling in the industry that Willis was being treated shabbily. He stepped in to broker a deal. Jackson hated sacking people in direct encounters, while Bishop deplored the idea of paying out, convinced that media executives operated in their own rarefied world, very different from the rough and tumble of mainstream business. But the contract had to be honoured, and Willis was offered £710,000 to compensate for loss of office. On 29 August, the announcement finally came: John Willis quits. He later reflected, 'I just wanted to be treated with a bit of graciousness. Instead of that I had to dangle on for a very long time and I found it hard to get my legal rights [. . .] I was left in an outrageous position.'[18]

Bishop himself, having fought off any sale of Channel 4 so successfully that the issue of privatisation would be nothing more than a background noise for the next decade, was now facing the axe as well, as the new government made its own appointments. The cultivated Chris Smith, Labour MP for Islington, was the unexpected choice as Secretary of State for the Department of Culture, Media and Sport. He came into office committed to seeing Channel 4 remain a public-service broadcaster, perhaps truer to its original remit than before. He saw it as an inspired creation and was amazed that Willie Whitelaw had persuaded Margaret Thatcher to let it happen:

> There were question marks against its programming – some were valid, some were not. There were ways in which it was perhaps not fulfilling its original purpose: you had to question whether there was too much im-

ported programming and not enough UK-based production. This out-cry over *The Word* and so on – that was all part of what Channel 4 was about: it was supposed to take risks. If it didn't annoy some of the people some of the time it wasn't doing its job. I certainly hoped it would get back to encouraging innovative production. It had two big advantages: it had seen off privatisation and it sold its own advertising.[19]

He found Michael Jackson distant.

He was certainly shy – difficult to have anything but an awkward con-versation with, apart from very early on. I remember one quite wet af-ternoon, we had both been staying for the weekend at Waheed [Alli] and Charlie's [Parsons] house in Kent, and we went to Sissinghurst on the Saturday afternoon. I remember wandering around the White Gar-den with Michael: me the very new Secretary of State, him the new Chief Executive. We had a very pleasant conversation but subsequent to that it was difficult to get Michael to unwind and unbend, to have a free-flowing discussion.'[20]

Over the first big decision, dismantling the safety net, most of Smith's negotiations were with David Scott. 'The formula to secure Channel 4's existence had become a money-spinner for ITV. I had a very careful look at the way it was operating. I was lobbied strongly by all parties and after careful analysis I decided that it was time to end the formula.'[21] It was cut by a third in 1998 and set at zero for 1999. This was now vital for Channel 4 because the explosive advertising growth it had been able to har-vest was now subsiding; it had reached a plateau, and from 1996 it was reaping just modest increases. The channel was now being given a substantial boost to its funds – a golden hello for Jackson – but, in return, Smith asked the ITC to ensure that it stayed truer to its founding purpose. 'A quid pro quo was that it invest the money saved in things Channel 4 was set up to do.'[22] In return, the channel committed to a new licence from 23 February 1998. The key points were:

- 60 per cent of programmes were to be specially commissioned for the chan-nel by 1999. (The ITC had complained that the percentages for 1995 and 1996 had been too low at 53 per cent and 50 per cent respectively.)
- A commitment to originate 30 per cent of programmes outside London by 2002.
- A new maximum for repeats – 20 per cent in peak time and less than 40 per cent overall. (The ITC had complained that repeats had risen to 43 per cent in 1996, and to 20 per cent in peak time.)

- A major commitment to the British film industry, giving preference to inno-vative and risky subjects and treatments.
- A commitment to provide at least three hours of multicultural programmes a week, and a new requirement to introduce diversity in peak time in news, current affairs, educational, religious and multicultural programmes.
- A new commitment to programmes about people with disabilities and a strengthened statement on education and training.
- By 2004, 80 per cent of programmes were to be subtitled.

All the programme targets were perfectly achievable under the new settlement, barring unforeseen disaster. Channel 4 created a new senior post in Glasgow to drive its push to commission more programmes from out of London. In 1998, the channel handed over its last cheque to ITV, of £66 million. Between 1994 and 1998, the ITV companies had received £412.5 million, while the value of the promotional slots they gave to the channel was just £20 million in 1998.

● ● ● ●

New Labour was in a rush to appoint its own people. Though it would have been wise to allow Sir Michael Bishop a year to ease Jackson into his new role, that was not a consideration. Labour peer David Puttnam was interested in becoming Chairman, but Chris Smith asked him not to apply because the vice-chairmanship of the BBC would be coming up.[23] So, shortly after the May General Election, a City lawyer called Vanni Treves was phoned by Gill Carrick about the chairman-ship of Channel 4. Treves lived in Islington, and Smith was his MP, but this was not a piece of New Labour patronage. They had had no previous connection and only met a long way into the process – and Treves has never been a member of the Labour Party.

'If my name was not a pretty unusual name, I would have thought she had got the wrong guy', said Treves, the Florentine-born son of an Italian Second World War resistance leader, a Jew shot dead by the Nazis. Treves had been bundled out of an apartment overlooking the Boboli Gardens as a toddler when the Germans came searching. His mother remarried an English officer, and after this dramatic start to life, he was brought up in a classic upper-middle-class manner, rising to head an es-teemed City law firm, Macfarlanes; but with his extravagant sweep of hair, he always seemed a shade exotic.

Carrick told him she had been given a mandate to open up the field to people with-out substantial experience in the media. Treves replied, 'Look, I know nothing about Channel 4. I watch it a bit but I am not a great television watcher [. . .] but send me the stuff.'[24] His wife tried to dissuade him from pursuing it, saying the job ought to be given to someone who did know about television. But Treves was intrigued and let his name go forward. The selection process narrowed the field to two: him and the Chairman of EMI, Colin Southgate, subsequently Chairman of the Royal Opera House. Treves was interviewed eight times before the job was finally offered to him at the end of 1997. 'It was very rigorous and rightly so, given my ignorance of the subject.'[25]

First was an extensive grilling by Carrick, then by several members of the ITC, from the Chairman down. Next came a curious joint interview with the outgoing Chairman Sir Michael Bishop and Michael Jackson. Finally, he was called in to see Chris Smith. 'He asked me perfectly fair and conventional questions. Next thing was I heard from [Sir Robin] Biggam [Chairman of the ITC] that I was appointed. The reason clearly was I had a lot of experience in corporate governance, running difficult large organisations, be they law firms or industrial companies.'[26]

On joining Channel 4 in 1998, he found it was run more efficiently than he had expected.

> One of my preconceptions was: this place is full of luvvies, none of them wears ties, I'm the biggest stuffed shirt around – it will be hell. But it was throughout a rigorous regime, partly due to David Scott, and the people I dealt with were very professional, so that was a big, big plus.[27]

Despite the bonus of the abolished funding formula, there were still doubts whether the channel could earn its keep.

> I came in and saw all these worrying projections about the audience share. We were between 10 and 11 per cent, but we were most likely to decline to 7 per cent. To me it is pretty marvellous that it is still about 10 per cent year by year. We hung in there [. . .] A phrase David Scott, a realist, used a lot, was, 'we feel fragile'. The word 'fragile' is the one I remember from that period. The sense of fragility was never far away.[28]

The first thing Treves had to do on appointment was to try to establish a good relationship with Jackson. He never succeeded. The shy and reserved Jackson mystified many of those around him. 'There was mutual incomprehension', said Scott, who found it took eighteen months to gain Jackson's trust, but once he had done so he played a role not unlike Justin Dukes to Jeremy Isaacs.[29] Treves found his Chief Executive difficult to get to know or to hold a straightforward, businesslike conversation with. He spoke elliptically, almost in riddles. He was opaque. Treves, a lawyer, liked clear language to express clear lines of thought. He respected the fact Jackson was self-made and had worked his way up from a poor background, but that did not aid communication between them.

'Michael Jackson, both as a tool of management and as a function of his personality, almost encouraged uncertainty', Treves said.[30]

> He never made people comfortable and was reluctant to give out praise. He was very bad with figures. Although he was personally very money-conscious, he didn't really care about finances. The controls were rigorous: at all times we knew exactly where we were, but we were often uncomfortable with the things he did. He didn't try to learn what it takes to be a chief executive.[31]

One sore point was that Jackson had a company Lexus, with a driver he had brought over from the BBC. Treves thought he had bad manners: he, the Chairman, was left standing in the rain after the Cambridge Royal Television Convention while Jackson swept back to his hotel in the car. The fact that he seldom offered lifts to his colleagues in it was not the main issue: people wondered whether it was really a Channel 4 sort of car. Treves thought it should be changed for something more humble, but it was leased, so it stayed. When the lease came up for renewal, there was talk of a bigger, better Lexus, but Treves squashed the idea. He also resented Jackson's spending on a coterie of consultants, who wrote strategy papers and speeches for him. And the Chairman took a hard line on expenses, insisting on mandatory disclosure of gifts and free facilities accepted by staff members.

Treves got on much better with David Scott, Jackson's deputy.

> I had a lot of time for him. He was the man who held the channel together, the glue, a man of great probity, a gentleman of the first order. But the downside was that he had been there before the channel began, so questions like 'Why are we doing that?' were questions he probably hadn't asked himself for a while [. . .] None of these people had worked outside the industry.[32]

It was, thus, an inward-looking organisation at a time of great change.

It was not at all clear, though, what Vanni Treves, with no knowledge of the media or media politics, and with a chief executive who did not trust him, would bring to the party.

18

New things in the air

• • • •

Jon Snow, the veteran anchor of *Channel 4 News*, suddenly switched to wearing trendy ties, in graphic blocks and brightly coloured stripes, in late 1998. He recognised that he and the programme had to smarten up to gain the approval of the channel's new boss. The news, a protected area under Michael Grade, was one of the first to fall under Michael Jackson's critical eye: he thought it wooden and dull. Moreover, he had come from the BBC, where news and current affairs were a law unto themselves, out of bounds even for senior executives. Here he was in charge and, at last, could flex his muscles.

This area of television was in turmoil anyway, because Sky News and Channel Five were setting the pace; the BBC's News 24 was gearing up, while audiences for regular news programmes were starting to fall as choice and competition grew and younger people turned off. Within two years, ITV would axe *News at Ten*. Yet, this meant that *Channel 4 News* had the chance to stand out, as nightly brain food, if it sharpened up. Eye-boggling ties would be only part of its salvation.

To understand why this prestige programme was suddenly judged to be stale, we need to go back to its roots. *Channel 4 News* had a disastrous launch in 1982 but then was rescued and shaped into the format that survives to this day. In the process, it became the industry's darling, and for fifteen years ITN was largely left alone to run it, without facing competition from rival providers – though back in 1988 Grade had briefly toyed with the idea of cutting it back to half an hour. It became the symbol of the channel's serious side, a vital defence whenever critics attacked its reliance on American programmes or on sex and general tackiness.

The last upheaval had been back in 1989 when the presenter Peter Sissons, a master of the telling interview, was poached by the BBC to replace Sir Robin Day in the chair of *Question Time*. The BBC doubled his money to £500,000 over three years, and he spurned Grade's efforts to woo him back. Jon Snow, reporting on the fall of the Berlin Wall at the time, was unexpectedly called in as the standby presenter and was soon offered the job permanently. Once Grade realised that Sissons was going despite his best efforts, he decreed that Snow represented the future of newscasting. A lanky bishop's son, who cycled everywhere in grey suits that could have come from a school outfitter, Snow was a surprise choice. He had been Washington Correspondent, then Diplomatic Editor and principally enjoyed being on the road rather than in a studio, but since foreign news was a key part of the programme's agenda, his extensive experience was an asset.

One problem, though, was that he could not read an autocue. The then Programme Editor, Richard Tait, later a BBC governor, had to coach him in this and other aspects of the newsreader's art:

> I was not a natural presenter. The early days were pretty bumpy. I waggled my head around, I was too exuberant – it was like letting a wild animal loose in the studio. Richard Tait sorted me out. He was an intellectual and he intellectualised me. It was the construction of interviews that concerned them most, not the autocue, and he was very good at helping with that [. . .] It was only a question of what sort of personality you stamped on the show.[1]

Snow's principal extra contribution was his restless energy. He wanted to present the programme from where the news was – an instinct that worked well in turbulent times. By the time of his abrupt change of ties, Snow had been filling the presenter's seat for nine years, and the programme had developed a comfortable rhythm, though broadcasting from a rather nasty orange set. It was unusual for its time in having both a woman editor, Sara Nathan, and a woman deputy, Sue Inglish. The audience was fairly modest – just over three quarters of a million – but 52 per cent were upmarket, though most of them were middle-aged to elderly. Grade decreed that it must not be changed, because the chattering classes liked it just as it was. Even if they did not watch it much, they were reassured to know that it was there.

Then along had come the new Channel Five, stealing headlines with its cool young blonde presenter, Kirsty Young, perched on a desk rather than sat to deliver a refreshingly snappy brand of news in a sultry Scottish brogue. Channel 4 had never managed to find an authoritative female presenter to stand in for Snow: Sheena MacDonald was tried, but the Board was not keen. One of its most tenacious and brave foreign correspondents was Lindsay Hilsum, but there were complaints, at first, about her voice.

Jackson's criticisms rankled, especially with Stewart Purvis, who had rescued the programme in 1983 as its second editor and was by now Chief Executive of ITN. 'We regarded ourselves as right royally stitched up because the next person in decided that he didn't like it, without understanding the context', Purvis lamented. 'Under Grade we were under instructions to preserve it almost in aspic, so it could be seen as a treasure.'[2] Michael Jackson wanted to discard the aspic – difficult to do without also discarding what is being preserved.

There was no question of ducking out of the commitment to serious news. The updated programme agreement with the Regulator, which Jackson had to honour, said the channel must transmit substantial programmes of national and international news. But Jackson decided to approach rival suppliers, with the aim of putting pressure on ITN to make the changes he wanted. He extended the Channel 4 news contract only to mid-1999, to give him time to seek an alternative solution, and he invited proposals by January 1998.

Possible bidders were presented with a document called 'Open to Ideas', drawn up by David Lloyd, Head of News and Current Affairs. It asked questions such as how many items there should be in a news programme and how long they should be? What is the role of the interview? Where did investigations and foreign bureaux fit in? Is there a case for a news bulletin at the start?[3] 'Only if we receive constructive ideas will we proceed to a full tender', Michael Jackson said.[4] And, after commissioning research into Snow's appeal, he told would-be bidders: 'Please do not assume anyone other than Jon Snow will be presenting the programme.'[5]

In November, on the day the move became public, the ITC agreed that *Five News* could move to 7 p.m., so it would run head to head with *Channel 4 News*. The *Guardian* responded with a cover story in G2, its tabloid features section, by Kamal Ahmed, pitting Jon Snow against Kirsty Young in 'News from the Battle Front.' This irritated Jackson enormously. 'The *Guardian* jumped to the conclusion that we were in some way responding to that move, seeking to compete with Five's populist, youthful agenda, and hared off with an appallingly glib feature.'[6]

But this trawl for new ideas set alarm bells ringing at ITN, as it had been meant to do. ITV had just cut the price it paid ITN for its news by 28 per cent, and the stability, even the survival, of the grand old news operator was suddenly at stake. ITN had to woo Jackson, and Purvis went to enormous lengths to ensure that he won his man. 'I used to know an ex-girlfriend of Jackson. We quizzed her: What were his favourite colours? What magazines does he read? We enlisted the style guru Peter York. I chucked the kitchen sink at it – I studied my target.'[7]

Sara Nathan, the Editor since 1995, was a sacrificial victim. She had been appointed after winning accolades for relaunching Radio 5 Live as a rolling news and sports channel, but Jackson regarded her as an odd choice for a television news hour and told Purvis he would not win with her. Tait, by then Editor-in-Chief of ITN, described their plight to Purvis as 'One more step and the kid gets it.'[8] They knew that Nathan had, in effect, been a victim of the earlier decisions not to modernise the programme.

Snow said:

> We had a divine situation: a woman editor and a woman deputy editor.
> I was absolutely committed to making it work. I thought we would get
> a whole different perspective. But I think it proved too much for Sara.
> She was very nice, but you began to realise that however we may laugh
> about intellectualism, *Channel 4 News* really has to be led by quite a
> cerebral individual: they have to bring things that no one else in the
> team can provide [. . .] I felt in the end there was nothing coming down
> to me, no tablets of stone, no input.[9]

During this autumn of turmoil, ITN recruited Jim Gray, the thin, nervy Deputy
Editor of *Newsnight*, to be Editor-in-Waiting of *Channel 4 News*. With him came his
close colleague Peter Barron (who later returned to *Newsnight* as Editor). In effect,
Purvis had poached the cream of *Newsnight*'s editorial team. The joke at ITN was
that Gray had been chosen because, in build and intelligence, he was the nearest
they could find to Jackson himself. Jackson explained why he thought a change was
needed: 'I thought the look, the production, wasn't as crisp as it should have been.
I had never met Sara Nathan and I didn't say I wanted Jim Gray – that was done by
Stewart Purvis.'[10]

Gray and Barron made an immediate impact. There was a less predictable running order, more news updates, sharper graphics. 'They want us to make trouble', said
Snow. 'I want to make trouble.' Jackson, already placated, observed in January 1998:

> The current ITN team and Channel 4 news seem to be trying harder.
> The programme is attracting news coverage not just after transmission
> for its live interviews but before, for a number of exclusive investigations,
> including Swiss mistreatment of wartime refugees and a re-examination
> of Bloody Sunday [. . .] Our ratings are quite unaffected by Five's deci-
> sion to move its news head to head with us. Indeed, it is *Five News* whose
> ratings have slumped.[11]

Apart from ITN, only one group responded to Channel 4's invitation to apply for
its news franchise. George Carey, whose production company made *Question Time*
for the BBC, linked with Sky News to put in an impressive bid. Both contenders went
for interviews with Jackson on 3 February 1998. ITN's proposal, designed like a style
magazine, was slapped on Jackson's immaculate glass office table, and it easily carried
the day. In April, Jackson confirmed that he would continue to commission *Channel 4
News* from ITN. The new agreement ran for five years, but with a break clause halfway
through, in June 2001, and at the end of the five years it would roll on year on year.

The debate had never been about price: ITN was given a bigger budget, subsequently linked to the retail-price index during Jackson's era, whereas ITV, after foolishly killing off *News at Ten* in 1999, continually tried to cut its news budget until 2005.

'I have respect for the way Channel 4 has done it, compared with ITV', Purvis reflected. 'They were always very professional.'[12] Jackson now had so much confidence in Snow that he invited him to accompany him to the Super Bowl, the climax of the American football season, in San Diego in 1998. The two sat together on the plane and talked at length. 'We stayed in the Hotel where *Some Like It Hot* was filmed', Snow remembers. 'It was a real schoolboys' outing. Initially I thought we were chalk and cheese and he was shy. But as soon as he got the measure of you, it was different. He decided to get pally, and we developed a very good relationship.'[13] It proved to be a busmen's holiday. The Monica Lewinsky affair blew up while they were there, and Jackson bought the world rights for the first interview with her – later conducted by Snow – for $400,000.

The relaunch of *Channel 4 News* in January 1999, together with a Saturday edition, was more about style than substance. The quality of the journalism was already good, but the approach had been freshened up. They added new specialists, a website and a UK editor, and the programme's studio set was redone as a glass cube within the newsroom, set with a low table and glowing lights – a look that still survives. Audiences moved up towards 1 million. 'That was when I started wearing bright ties. I was suddenly aware I was very dull – we just needed to get our act together. The graphics improved, everything changed. News wasn't Michael's bag, but he had a very imaginative and creative approach to it.'[14] With Jackson's backing, Snow was able to be more exuberant, presenting the programme from hotspots around the world, sometimes tied in with Channel 4's broader interests. So, in the summer of 2001, when the England cricket team was playing India in a Test series televised by the channel, Snow roamed around India for the news.

However, some inside the channel still harboured reservations. A strategic programme rethink in 2000 was frank.[15] The hour of news was uncompetitive commercially. It had never paid its way, covering only about half its costs with advertising. The 7 p.m. start, always too early for the south-east, was now far too early and did not fit in with modern working lives. The news was well regarded but little noticed – a fact confirmed by the political journalist Michael Crick, who observed that when he moved on to *Newsnight* his reports got much more attention. It would have made commercial sense to extend the 'happy hour', beginning at 6 p.m. and aimed at young viewers, for an extra half-hour, with the news starting at 7.30 p.m. However, 'the attack on our reputation that would follow an ill-thought-out move would be extremely damaging [. . .] Jon Snow is the face of the channel. There is no clear successor.'[16] Between 2001 and 2007, it remained remarkably stable, buttressed by a revamp in 2006 and a new bureau in China, with audiences varying between

900,000 to 1.1 million, a 5 per cent share. The composition is unique: half of its viewers are upmarket, from social groups ABC1, over fifty-five and male. But 20 per cent are also young, between sixteen and thirty-four, staying on after *Hollyoaks*, and it is the news programme most trusted by ethnic-minority groups.

So, *Channel 4 News* sailed on into the twenty-first century; and Jon Snow's collection of dazzling ties swelled inexorably.

● ● ● ●

When Michael Jackson was at the BBC, the joke was that he ran BBC2 by stealing Channel 4's clothes; John Willis had even called him a copycat criminal. But now that he was Chief Executive, he said many of Channel 4's programmes, not just the news, were out of fashion or not up to scratch for a channel that was no longer the new kid on the block. 'We couldn't be a child of the 1960s, we had to be an adult of the 1990s', was one of his mantras. He wanted more quality control, echoing Grade's criticism back in 1988 that stemmed from the continuing difficulties of marshalling feisty commissioners and independently sourced programmes. In short, he embarked on what his allies saw as dragging Channel 4 kicking and screaming into the modern age.

This was the period of changeover when the last dregs of the Isaacs hippy era seeped away. Peter Moore, the Factual Commissioner, would shortly leave, having blotted his copybook by offering a new BBC recruit a spliff, with the words, 'Welcome to the hippy channel.'[17] Jackson wanted landmark programmes for sure, but of his own sort. So he made no apologies for leaving concerns about the advertising sales and business side to his deputy. 'There was a big job on the creative and strategic front. If I hadn't done that there wouldn't have been any programmes to sell.'[18] His initial assessment was that 'for a service committed to the contemporary, it could be surprisingly insular.'[19] The daily press clippings, he noted, referred only to Channel 4's output, not to the competition.

One of his first acts was to switch his offices from the back to the front of the Horseferry Road headquarters, so that he overlooked the grand, fan-shaped entrance to the Richard Rogers building. 'I didn't want to look out over suburban flats', he explained. His new glass office was furnished with two milky-white sofas, rock-hard benches – no slothful lounging – and the glass table for meetings. He was as impatient with sloppy minds as with sagging sofas; and he was wound up to deliver. 'Every chief executive of Channel 4 says it's amazing how small it feels. The point is that at the BBC no one fundamentally matters, it goes on. But at Channel 4 it feels much more vulnerable.'[20] A reminder of that vulnerability came when Channel Five took advantage of the handover period by trying unsuccessfully to poach *Brookside*, which provided Channel 4 with 9.2 per cent of its ratings.

Over eighteen months, as he carefully went through the programming with his hand-picked team – mostly imported from the BBC – Jackson injected a shot of creative and analytical energy. The channel and his era would be remembered for and should be judged by its British-produced shows. But change takes time, and in the short term the channel seemed to go backwards, with more repeats of things like *Whose Line Is it Anyway?* – discontinued because Clive Anderson, the host, had been recruited by the BBC.

The ITC, in the annual review for 1997, tartly remarked that the station had lost its drive for innovation. Jackson disliked so many of the ongoing programmes that he commissioned fewer of them, which meant a hiatus before his new style of programmes came on stream, many of them dealing with the concerns of consumers and homeowners. There were misfortunes, too. *Father Ted*, which Michael Grade had originally thought not funny at all, had assumed the status of a classic sitcom, but the third series in 1998 was to be the last because the actor who played the title role, Dermot Morgan, had suddenly died.

Jackson did organise an early repeat of *Brass Eye*, which he admired. He had not arrived with a master plan on paper; it was a case of renovating drama, comedy, entertainment and factual by sifting ideas, developing new pilots with trusted suppliers and choosing new talent to work with. This is how a creative manager works. He had pledged to cut American programmes, but he was a great fan of the best of them, and 1998 saw *King of the Hill* launched to critical appreciation. To handle buy-ins, he hired June Dromgoole from the BBC, a former army officer who had been competing against Channel 4 for the previous decade.

There were key building blocks. *Friends* and *Frasier* ensured that Friday nights were entertainment nights, and *ER*, on Wednesdays, trundled on. *The Big Breakfast* was briefly stabilised in September with new presenters, Johnny Vaughan and Denise Van Outen – promoted from being the airborne weather girl. They replaced the failed pairing of Sharron Davies, the Olympic silver medallist, and Rick Adams, an ITV children's presenter. Vanessa Feltz briefly did the celebrity interviews in the boudoir. It remained a money-spinner but never regained the popularity of its halcyon days between 1993 and 1995. A few things moved. Mel and Sue's *Light Lunch*, a rare entertainment chat-show success, became the *Late Lunch* at 6 p.m. A successful new teen zone, T4, started on Sundays, then spread to Saturdays. Melvyn Bragg anchored a short-lived live review of the Sunday papers on Saturday nights.

'Obviously it would be easy to get on, commission some new shows and hope for the best', said Jackson. 'I thought it needed more than that. The first year I spent thinking about the programmes, the commissioning structure, the schedule [. . .] Sometimes it felt like the channel was still fighting the battles of the 1960s, thirty years on. The mindset was still left versus right.'[21] One of the programmes the new regime inherited was an observational documentary by the high-profile director Paul

Watson, *The Dinner Party*, which held right-wing Tories up for ridicule. Jackson thought that this was the wrong target. In the new Blair era, it would have been better to expose the Cool Britannia mindset.

He noted that programmes were still put in boxes marked popular, obscure, challenging or unchallenging, and he ordered a retreat from the approach that people called minorities somehow lived in a parallel universe. 'We're all minorities now and sharing more than we know.' The channel's remit should be eventually built into all programmes, even if that sometimes meant failure. 'If I look back on my time at Channel 4, it was time for the next turn of the wheel, one era coming to an end, time to move on to the next infinitely more competitive multichannel age.'[22]

He hired Rosemary Newell, a cool analyser of audiences who had scheduled BBC1. She arrived in October and quickly established herself as a power behind Jackson's throne and those of his successors.

Another crucial change symbolised Channel 4's commercial approach: Jackson switched the energetic Jules Oldroyd from the Advertising Sales Department to the inner Programme Scheduling Team. She had joined in 1992 to sell advertising and was by now a senior business manager handling a group of media agencies, who placed £100 million of advertisers' money with the channel each year. She would now work with Newell and Michael Jackson at the heart of the channel, eventually becoming the programme scheduler, making sure they picked programmes that would deliver the right kind of audiences: upmarket viewers, the ABC1s, young adults aged sixteen to thirty-four and light viewers of television. She was also involved with the budget round, looking at the offers and pointing out gaps in, say, the provision for contemporary young males.[23]

The immediate issues included how to fill the happy hour between 6 p.m. and 7 p.m. to attract young viewers avoiding the BBC and ITV news; how to develop new leisure programmes to chime with the rise in general living standards, and a new focus on contemporary drama, which would result in *Queer as Folk*. Twenty independent production companies were set to work on drama pilots, in the hunt for new series. Jackson had arrived well briefed on the staid drama and excessive dependency on American imports: the BBC had been monitoring it for several years.

This was the point when the two wings of Channel 4, programmes and advertising, formerly often at loggerheads, began to communicate in a pragmatic fashion. Jackson said it was not because Oldroyd would lead the hunt for sixteen- to thirty-four-year-olds that he moved her into the control room, but because he liked her: she was bright and hard-working.

> I was very aware of the sixteen-to-thirty-fours, but I tried very hard to break with the view that we do things we don't really like to pay for the others. The great thing with British public-service television is that

it never wanted to be an arty ghetto, but to engage. I always wanted to achieve that.[24]

Said Oldroyd, 'Michael was a massive sponge. He was firing questions all the time. He would continually ask where we could make a difference.'[25]

Jackson had a strong competitive instinct, and no part of the schedule was overlooked in his forensic study. The people he brought in enforced the discipline that the programmes must be commissioned to the schedule, not the other way round. The argument was that if you commission into a void you have no idea whether the programme tapes you end up with will deliver the audiences you want. He introduced a clear process for commissioning, through regular budget rounds in spring and autumn – the BBC system writ small. All the programmes were minuted and given a grade. Before, the commissioners had autonomy within a looser system: they were given a budget, a sum of money and a number of hours each year, which they then spent. The new schedule set goals for programmes and prices for the slots.

Apart from Jackson himself, his team of modernisers had little or no connection with the channel's original ethos. An exception was another hiring from the BBC: Steve Hewlett, the Editor of *Panorama* when it had landed the astonishing Princess Diana interview, but also a veteran of Channel 4's early current-affairs battles. He was now handed responsibility for the entire factual area. However, after a year, he was appointed Director of Programmes at Carlton.

Programmes reflect the interests of people who commission them. Channel 4 had been a hotbed of ideology, with some diehard left-wingers and others with more or less radical opinions. Most of them now quit, and a new wave of commissioners arrived. Reflecting the style-conscious era of New Labour, they were in favour of consumerism and unapologetic about acquisitive lifestyle television. Jackson had widened BBC2's leisure strands with *Home Front*, *One Foot in the Past* and *Changing Rooms* and had boosted its daytime performance with *Ready Steady Cook!* The question was whether his rigorous BBC approach would quash the natural spirit and energy of Channel 4.

When Jackson arrived, the programme schedule was still put together manually. 'It used to circulate like a kidnap demand, in hand-written block capitals', he observed acidly.[26] It was a throwback to Liz Forgan's methods, to the so-called 'Primrose lists' – the schedules she used to devise in her garden at Primrose Hill in North London. Kevin Lygo's early impression was of the outgoing scheduler sticking his head around the door and asking: 'Anything for Thursdays?' From now on, the schedulers would use computers to crunch viewing data. The search was on for insights, to exploit weak spots in rival channels. Jackson's deputy Scott said,

It didn't stop them fiddling all the time with the schedule – it used to drive me mad. Even though we had a beautiful plan to the year end, with programmes commissioned slot by slot, every single week they'd be poring over the BARB audience figures, trying to optimise their ratings, reacting to other channels.[27]

It was competitive, reactive and nervy. The last-minute changes made promotion difficult and costly. Said Jackson, 'I brought in a lot of new people. I changed programming. It was a huge process of change, and we also had a brand new board within two years. I have never worked harder before or since.'[28] In the early months, he looked drawn. He hated sacking people: one commissioning editor came out from his glass office not realising he had been given his notice. Jackson leapt like a gazelle out of the way of unknown staff. It was not defensiveness, he insisted,

It was just taking on a ship where you were the captain, with not a lot of crew, reconstructing it. I had to do a lot myself. At the beginning I was very reluctant to say things to people who might be leaving, or to promise things. As time went on I became more communicative. As things become successful you are able to communicate more effectively.[29]

● ● ● ●

Kevin Lygo was commissioning comedy and entertainment from independent producers for the BBC when Jackson moved – perfect training for Channel 4. He had started all sorts of new strands for BBC2, including *They Think It's All Over*, from the expanding Talkback production company, which Peter Fincham co-founded with Mel Smith and Griff Rhys Jones. On joining Channel 4, Lygo threw himself at his new task with such zeal that he sacked almost the entire entertainment department and hired new people to work for him.[30] 'The main thing was there wasn't enough entertainment and comedy at all, so I doubled the spend and the hours and almost completely dispensed with the team', he said.[31]

He dropped most of the old programmes, including the long-running *Drop the Dead Donkey*, while *Eurotrash*, the camp late-night review, faded as Antoine de Caunes went on to produce films. Rory Bremner and Mark Thomas with their political satire were safe, though. Their producer, Geoff Atkinson of Vera Productions, said, 'We had minimal contact with Michael Jackson, though we were told Mark was part of the Channel 4 gene pool.'[32]

Hat Trick, the company that had produced *Drop the Dead Donkey*, as well as such early fare as *Who Dares Wins*, saw its business from Channel 4 go into a sharp decline. But Fincham's Talkback, under a cloud since *Brass Eye*, enjoyed a revival in its fortunes, winning five new commissions.

Jackson, Lygo and, to some extent, Fincham went on to plot a new wave of entertainment programmes: *Smack the Pony*, *The Sketch Show*, *Dom Joly's Trigger Happy TV*, The 'Ten Best' and '100 Greatest' list shows and the Graham Norton chat show. *Comedy Labs*, half-hour showcases for up-and-coming talent, gave early opportunities to Peter Kay and Dylan Moran, who had emerged from the stand-up comedy circuit. Money was never an issue with Jackson, bolstered by the extra millions no longer diverted to ITV pockets.

Fincham recalled a key turning point. 'Michael, Kevin and I had dinner one night early on at a very smart restaurant in Park Lane. We talked about various ideas, and over coffee I suggested doing a sketch show that featured mainly women – this was at the peak of the Bridget Jones craze.'[33] Jackson liked the idea, and the three men agreed what was originally called *The Girlie Sketch Show* but which became *Smack the Pony*.

> It was an example of a simple idea, well executed. It doesn't have to be a very sophisticated or a clever idea. Oddly it hadn't been done: all sketch shows had been three blokes and a girl, or just four blokes, and nobody had ever flipped that round the other way. In itself it's not a Nobel prize-winning idea, but it was timely.[34]

Fincham was then offered the opportunity to make a nightly topical sketch show, *The 11 O'Clock Show*, which would refresh television entertainment, send several stars to Hollywood and create Ali G. Jackson had decided to force something to happen by applying the pressure of time and money to find new talent. Here he was most clearly fulfilling his role as a creative leader.

The 11 O'Clock Show was the biggest single comedy commission around and, even better from Fincham's point of view, it was not put out to competitive tender.

> I remember Kevin stating he didn't want to do that. It was legitimate: this [Talkback] was the company for the moment, comedy-wise. They knew I came from a slightly different generation of independent producers. I worked in a partnership way with the channel, not in an adversarial way. Michael, Kevin and I all got on very well. To be absolutely honest, this is the story of Channel 4 and independents – they go through phases. It's a lot to do with individuals.
>
> I remember an occasion when we were planning the *11 O'Clock Show* in 1998, and I drove to Channel 4 in the family car, a muddy jeep full of nappies, put 50 pence in the meter, and as I did so a limousine

pulled up, and out got Waheed Alli and walked up the steps. His chauf-
feur got out and started polishing the car.

I thought, there's something in this contrast in style. They had *The
Big Breakfast*. Talkback had a future.[35]

The 11 O'Clock Show was pulled together fast. It was on air by 30 September 1998,
a year after Lygo and Jackson started. A key to it was the input from the gifted producer Harry Thompson. But for everyone concerned, it was a painful experience.

> You've got to fill the bloody airtime. We put out calls to all the agents. The
> scripts that might have gone unread were studied. Tapes were watched:
> it's like prospecting for gold. Suddenly, the rush was on. Michael and
> Kevin had a very clear view that if you commission like that you may
> not create a perfect show – something that comes from the top down
> rarely is – but you are hanging a net over the side of your boat and you'll
> catch a lot in it.[36]

The show eventually ran three nights a week as a satire on the day's news, recorded
that same evening, using spoof newsreaders and spoof interviews. It was especially
harsh on vox pops, where reporters mug people for their opinions on the street. The
first series ran for two weeks, then for six weeks, then three months, even though it
was of uneven quality and nobody at first could decide whether it was working or
not. Jackson never really liked it and often quizzed people about their views. A few
weeks in, though, it became apparent that they had struck gold with Sacha Baron
Cohen, alias Ali G. Said Fincham:

> Sacha was a guy with a tape. He had sent this tape of himself as a comic
> rabbi in to Channel 4 and it had been rejected. The rumour was that
> his mother, being an archetypal Jewish mother, had called the channel
> to berate them. He went within a few months from being a bloke who
> turned up on the bus and asking who wanted a cup of tea – then mak-
> ing it – to being the most famous comedian in Britain. I have never
> known anything like it before or since.[37]

One inspiration for Ali G was a black dancer called Normski (briefly the partner
of Janet Street-Porter), who wore a yellow tracksuit and spoke street gobbledegook.
Another was Radio 1 DJ Tim Westwood. Baron Cohen created him as a spoof youth
reporter, drawing on the techniques of *Brass Eye* in that interviewees were duped
by being asked to sign a consent form saying that the producers were making a new
late-night topical show for young people that dealt with serious issues in a way that

made them entertaining. It was all true, but what it did not say was that a very clever Cambridge graduate in a funny hat, dressed as a rapper, with his catchphrase 'Is it cos I is black?', would make the victims look stupid. Fortunately for the producers, most of them took the joke in the spirit intended. Andrew Newman, who helped write and make the early Ali G video sketches, said:

> We shot about six before the three-minute strand was finally called Ali G. The first one was with the economist Madsen Pirie of the Institute of Economic Affairs, but he refused to sign the release form. Sacha is easy to work with and had a brilliant mixture of the acting and clowning skills of Peter Sellers and the barefaced cheek of Rod Hull.[38]

Other stars of *The 11 O'Clock Show* included Iain Lee, Ricky Gervais and Mackenzie Crook, a regular presenter (later to feature in Gervais' BBC sitcom, *The Office* and then *Pirates of the Caribbean*). Harry Thompson noted that the show's receptionist, Daisy Donovan, had a terrific personality, and she went on air as a newsreader. 'It was a scary ride at the time', Fincham recollects.

> Comedy is the hardest thing. I'm not sure the talent was there to sustain it either in the writing or performance. It never felt quite good enough, it aways felt patchy. What it says about Channel 4 generally is that shows with relatively modest audiences can have enormous impact. Whereas you could be on an ITV sitcom, get 8 million viewers and walk down a street and nobody would know you, Ali G seemed famous at once.[39]

Audiences for the programme were never more than 1 million, but they were young and trendsetters. By the time of its second big run, in March 1999, Channel 4 had embraced it warmly, and Jackson had achieved his first breakthrough – although he never personally found the show very funny. Baron Cohen moved quickly on to *Da Ali G Show*, a satirical interview series that differed from his slots on *The 11 O'Clock Show* because by now everyone was in on the joke. Then, with a film and America beckoning, he invented a new character, Borat from Kazakhstan, who featured in two specials made in partnership with America's HBO. At the time, this failed to light up the audience: only later did Borat turn Baron Cohen into a Hollywood star, marking, in retrospect, British comedy's growth in international reach and status.

Graham Norton had already been spotted by Channel 4 in 1997 when he stood in for Jack Docherty on Channel Five. Graham Smith, Commissioner of Entertainment (before being briskly ousted by Lygo) realised that Norton was a potential star and opened negotiations. That summer, Lygo and Fincham flew up to the Edinburgh

Festival to ask Norton to host *The 11 O'Clock Show*. Norton refused, saying he did not like news. When he won an award for the best comedy newcomer, Lygo gained the confidence to give him a pilot chat show. Norton wanted to call it *The Frolic Room*, after a bar in Los Angeles, but he was overruled and it became *So Graham Norton*. 'I thought it was a bad omen to have my name in the title', he says. 'It gave me so much power – one person will be the arbiter. I did have a lot of control going into the show.'[40]

Initially, the channel ordered six shows, which were really one-man comedy gigs disguised as a chat show, but suddenly Norton found himself placed on Friday nights, taking over the 10.30 p.m. *Eurotrash* slot. He therefore inherited an audience who expected a bit of Friday night rudeness, in the tradition of *The Word* and *The Girlie Show*. His audience figures quickly doubled from 2 million to 4 million. 'We were there at a very interesting time. Kevin was very dynamic – he turned the department around, and entertainment became a very big area.'[41] Originally, Norton resisted signing exclusively for the channel, and after the first series, he was asked to do *Room 101* for BBC2. Lygo got wind of that and, having just recommissioned the series, was reluctant to give up a star that Channel 4 had created. He therefore persuaded Norton to sign exclusively for the channel. After two series, he and the producer, Graham Stuart, set up their own production company, So Television.

In 2001, Norton was again thinking of going to the BBC, but Jackson and Lygo convinced him to stay and do a five-nights-a-week show for three years. 'Channel 4 were great to work with', he says. 'We were a success. There was a sense of freedom.'[42] But while he thought it important to hang on to Norton, Lygo was prepared to let Johnny Vaughan go to the BBC in 1999. On the other hand, he was the first senior executive to go out of his way to cultivate Carol Vorderman, and Richard Whiteley, recognising *Countdown*'s solid performance year after year. Vorderman was given a five-year contract in 1998 worth £5 million – nearly £4,000 a programme.

The defining programme of the Jackson era was *Queer as Folk*, which made its debut at 10.30 p.m. on 23 February 1999. 'It was the apogee for me', says Jackson. 'Before, gay programmes were all about problems. This was about gay life.'[43] The writer and creator was Russell T. Davies, who had been working at Granada on *The Grand*, a drama series about the workings of a great hotel. Gub Neal's deputy at Channel 4, Catriona MacKenzie, had been impressed by an episode that Davies had written, centred on a gay barman. At the same time, an ambitious young producer, Nicola Shindler, was setting up Red Productions in Manchester and commissioned Davies to write the series, based on the gay scene around Canal Street in Manchester. It was to be a positive portrayal of gay life from the inside, with no preaching about issues such as safe sex. Other series had featured peripheral gay characters – for instance Ferdy, the motorcycle delivery man in *This Life* – and there had been gay subplots in *Brookside* and *EastEnders*: here they would be at the centre of the drama.

'You'll be seeing a lot more than men holding hands', Davies promised.[44] The provocative opening episode depicted casual initiatory sex between Stuart – a successful, promiscuous public-relations man, played by Aidan Gillen – and a fifteen-year-old virgin schoolboy he had picked up. Next morning, with the faithful Vince (Craig Kelly), the three drove to school. There were 321 calls to the channel that night, of which 136 complained about filth being poured into their homes. It was the first programme for two years that Mary Whitehouse felt the need to complain about. Between December 1997 and June 1998, Davies wrote the entire series, and it was produced just as rapidly. Gillen proved to be an inspired piece of casting, and, on the strength of it, he was taken up by Hollywood.

Queer as Folk was the first major series marketed by the new Strategy and Development Director, David Brook – who was having a whirlwind effect on the channel, initiating at this time the bid for test match cricket. Middle-aged women were shown the tapes, their shocked reactions recorded and used in radio commercials. It was pushed hard on the poster sites now booked permanently at major junctions and stations. When Becks lager withdrew its sponsorship, the marketing department was jubilant: still more press coverage. The series never did well in terms of pure numbers, averaging 2.1 million viewers over the eight episodes, but 49 per cent were upmarket ABC1 consumers, and 45 per cent were aged between sixteen and thirty-four, which was commercial heaven for the channel.

Davies started writing a second series, and Jackson saw its potential as a twenty-two-episode soap, but then he decided against it, and Davies and Gub Neal came round to his view, agreeing that, having breached the barrier, it was time to move on. They just did a one-off Christmas special, a wedding between Stuart and Vince. An American version ran for five years, with spin-off merchandising for which Channel 4, not Davies, pocketed most of the royalties.

Davies found Jackson chilly.

> There wasn't much contact with him. I did go to a meeting in which he made the Channel 4 lawyer sit in the room and write down everything I said – we were discussing possible spin-offs from the show – in case I ever claimed copyright over what he considered to be a Channel 4 idea. So, no, not exactly best friends, no.[45]

ITV's Drama Controller, Nick Elliott, asked Davies to lunch, and, as a result, he went on to write a more popular variation, *Bob and Rose*, for ITV, about a gay man (Alan Davies) falling in love with a woman (Lesley Sharp). It attracted 6.6 million viewers. 'It was the best thing I have written, and I could not have done it without *Queer as Folk*', said Davies.[46] He finally fell out with Channel 4 in 2000 when Tessa Ross, who had replaced Gub Neal, turned down his drama *The Second Coming*, based on the idea of Jesus coming back to earth in present-day Manchester. He took it to ITV, which made an award-winning version, and Davies, one of the freshest television writers of his generation, never worked for Channel 4 again. Later, he masterminded the immensely successful BBC revival of *Doctor Who*.

Drama, overall, remained a disappointment. What Jackson chiefly wanted from his drama commissioners was long-running 'returnable' series on the American model. There were several failures and false starts – *Psychos*, *North Square*, *Buried* – until they hit on *Teachers*, *No Angels* and, in 2004, Paul Abbott's *Shameless*. Jackson points out: 'It takes a long time to make these shows. Getting out of the disaffected BBC writer phase, as represented by Dennis Potter and Alan Bleasdale, to the newer generation was hard. So was getting some returnable series. It has taken a long time to get there.'[47] The snag was that drama concentrating on people in their twenties and thirties, drinking and having sex, while attracting more male viewers than usual, was serving too narrow an audience.

19

Spending spree

• • • •

Jackson had spent eighteen months gingering up the channel, finding new entertainment stars such as Ali G, pioneering living history strands such as *The 1900 House* and splashing out on cricket. He had reached a point where he felt happy handing some decisions over to his new Director of Programmes Tim Gardam and freeing himself for more strategic thinking. David Brook was already trying to steer the Board in new directions. He told them that Channel 4 was more than just television, it was a brand 'ahead of the mainstream – in a word, upstream – engaged in the pursuit of emerging values, a discoverer of ideas and talent, pioneering, pleasurable, stimulating while risk-taking.'[1] He had Jackson's ear, but the Chairman, Vanni Treves, would listen with increasing suspicion and his Deputy, Barry Cox, would soon explicitly warn that some of their activities were increasingly out of step with what viewers expected. Jackson had independently come to the radical conclusion that the days of being a single channel were over, but he had a lot of ground to make up.

Channel 4 had, in any case, been given explicit directions to expand. The Government had made a drive towards digital television a key point of its media policy and expected the channel to pull its weight, after giving it and ITV new digital frequencies.[2] But BSkyB retaliated by trumping the digital terrestrial offer, with ten to twenty times more digital satellite channels. The question for Channel 4 was what to put on the spare channels. Research had long identified Film on Four as one of its strongest cards, so Jackson had reviewed the scheme for a pay FilmFour channel as soon as he took over, but he decided it was too modest. He believed it must go on all networks and try to reach as big a set of subscribers as possible. That was why he rebuffed financial inducements to resist the satellite platform from Michael Green, Chairman of Carlton Communications, who slapped a cheque on the table worth, by some accounts, £10 million. Green wanted the film channel to be exclusive to the new British digital broadcasting pay-TV service, OnDigital, which he co-founded with Granada. This pale rival to BSkyB would collapse in 2002.

The Board decided that FilmFour would be solely under the channel's control: in other words, that it would shoulder all the risk. BSkyB were keen to share owner-ship and, as an inducement, had offered Channel 4 thirty titles a year from the Sky library. But Channel 4 turned down the offer. 'We felt uncomfortable with some of the controls', said David Scott.[3] The film channel launched on Sunday, 1 November 1998, after a massive party in King's Cross the night before, where cool film-industry people packed marquees under the arches to drink champagne and cocktails and watch 'extreme cinema' – reels of violent and sexually explicit cinema clips projected on white walls and huge screens. The message was that this was a channel for people who wanted edgy, uncut, uninterrupted independent films.

The marketing and positioning, overseen by Brook, was judged a triumph inter-nally. Johnny Vaughan, host of *The Big Breakfast* and, for a time, much in favour, was the face of the new channel, introducing the launch night that ran as a simul-cast on Channel 4 to encourage subscribers. Jude Law's untested but glamorous new production company, Natural Nylon, delivered the launch programme, a series of comedy sketches played to canned laughter, but this was a mistake: a launch night is really about marketing, not striking a pose.[4]

In a linked move, FilmFour Production, the film-making side of the channel, was made into a separate company, FilmFour Ltd, in May 1998. It settled into renovated freehold offices at 76 Charlotte Street, near to the original Channel 4 headquarters, and had a separate staff that rose to sixty-two. The subscription rate for FilmFour was set at £5.99 a month. By Christmas, 25,000 had signed up, and 50,000 by Janu-ary. A year later, it had around 250,000 subscribers and seemed to be doing all right, though Jackson conceded it would never return a fortune: it had cost £20.4 million to start up in 1999 and lost £14.8 million in 2000. The principal flaw in its business model was that it stood alone and was not part of anyone else's bundle of movies. That made it uniquely isolated, in its own little groove.

The aim for FilmFour Ltd, set out in April 1998, was to make fewer but bigger films, doubling investment and attracting international co-production partners, and to be successful in America. This was broadly what the Culture Secretary, Chris Smith, wanted within the new licence terms for the channel. Jackson readily agreed, although he kept a small, experimental FilmFour Lab going.

'The traditional small UK film had to be perfect to succeed', he would point out, in his defence,[5] but then the same applied to the bigger budget films. The Film Council, under the producer Alan Parker, was also raising its sights and allocating lottery funds. The channel's board was told in 1999 that theirs was a high-risk strategy, with the potential to lose £15 million a year. Everyone was aware of the risk, but they ploughed ahead, seemingly star-struck.

FilmFour was, after all, part of the channel's tradition. Since 1982, it had invested £220 million in British films. Richard Attenborough had become Channel 4's founding Deputy Chairman on the condition that it supported film-making. David Puttnam, another patron saint, went out of his way to offer advice and to introduce Jackson to Warner Brothers in Cannes in 1998 in the hope they would strike a distribution deal.

It had enjoyed a wonderful run in the first half of the 1980s and in the 1990s, culminating in 1999 with *East Is East*, a story of a mixed-race Asian family in 1970s Salford, which took £10 million in British cinemas. But then success dried up. There was no *The Madness of King George*, *Trainspotting* or *Shallow Grave* in the pipeline. The most promising British film, *Ali G in da House* (2002), starring the Channel 4 star, was made not by FilmFour but by a rising British film company, Working Title, and that really rankled. The intention was to spread costs and risks by striking deals with German and Spanish co-financiers, but despite its best efforts, the channel never nailed the deal they really needed – with a Hollywood studio for a three-year stretch. In 1999, Scott and Jackson went to see all the Hollywood studios. Scott said,

> We wanted them to put in a percentage of the budget, and we would get
> distribution around the world. The studios were nervous about having
> to take films of the channel's choice – nervous of their lack of creative
> choice. While FilmFour had been through a purple patch, it was going
> off the boil.[6]

Channel 4 did not get that vital financing. It did not enjoy creative success, and the sixty-strong film team, working in that separate building back in Charlotte Street, were distanced from the main television operation. David Aukin, who had run it so successfully in the 1990s, had simply been a commissioning editor, part of the channel team. But Paul Webster, an experienced film producer hired from Miramax, was the Chief Executive, reporting directly to Michael Jackson. His priority was not to supply the needs of the channel but to compete in the broader movie market and to create a business.

The Channel 4 television executives, particularly Dromgoole, did not think they were getting the films they wanted at economic prices, and as the films declined in quality, they resented the cost.[7] Suddenly, from being the centrepiece of Channel 4's output and public-service mission, Film on Four was nobody's darling. Flop followed flop. In 2001, there was *Charlotte Gray*, a film based on Sebastian Faulks's novel, about a woman agent in France during the Second World War. Despite starring Cate Blanchett, it failed in America because Faulks was not known there. *Lucky Break* and *Crush*, released in the same year, similarly failed to make an impression on the box office. In 2002, the channel made an initial £5-million investment in *Death to Smoochy*, a $50-million Hollywood film starring Robin Williams that brought in revenue of just $8.3 million. Scott recalls, 'When I saw this proposed deal, I said to Michael Jackson, this is not *Death to Smoochy*, this is death to FilmFour [...] Michael got Paul Webster to get the deal toned down, but still did a deal.'[8]

The over-expansion of FilmFour Ltd continued to drain resources through 2001, at the same time as advertising income, the channel's lifeblood, started to collapse. Jackson's successor, Mark Thompson, slammed on the brakes in the summer of 2002, and in the autumn the separate company was ruthlessly wound up. Jackson later said, 'Channel 4's film production was something that we got wrong – not strategically but creatively. The films weren't good enough. Mark was quite right to make changes.'[9] He explained that he had fundamentally misunderstood the film market. 'The Government was pumping huge amounts of money into the marketplace and it was getting hugely over-heated. We followed the market rather than leading it.'[10] The near-destruction of a great tradition would rankle. Jackson was tarnished. But so too, in time, was Thompson, as the dust settled and the closure of FilmFour Ltd began to seem too ruthless, disrespectful of a great tradition.

● ● ● ●

California, here we come! Michael Jackson and his team from Channel 4 were in a buoyant mood when they checked into the swish Hotel Bel-Air in Los Angeles in December 1999 for what they thought would be a leisurely stay. They were there to renew the rights to *Friends* and *ER*, their top imported shows, and to combine that with film-studio meetings. But it would be far from leisurely: they were to endure an intense, nerve-racking twenty-four-hour negotiation, during which none of them slept a wink. At the end, they signed an unexpectedly large bill. To stop BSkyB, in the person of Elisabeth Murdoch, walking off with the trophy shows, they were obliged to commit Channel 4 to accelerating the start of a new entertainment channel, E4, to showcase the pricey pay-TV rights they had bought for £10 million a year.

It was policy-making on the hoof, for the Board back in London had not yet given approval to E4, though it had been under discussion. (David Scott disputes this interpretation.) Jackson had inherited from Michael Grade only the sketchiest plans for the multichannel future in the shape of a single digital film channel, FilmFour. New media and the Internet hardly registered on Grade's radar. He was once said to have quipped, 'When I hear the word digital I reach for my pension.' This lack of long-term strategic thinking about how to adapt would cost the channel dear in the period between 1997 and 2007. By 1999, it was apparent that subscription channels, with themed programmes ranging from sport to history, were the future, or at least a means of squeezing funds from viewers. Subscriptions to Sky were growing fast, and the key was to buy up exclusive content to drive sales. How to develop Channel

4 as a multimedia brand was by now such a priority for Jackson and David Brook, his Director of Strategy and Development, that they risked taking their eye off the main network and straying into schemes of dubious merit.

June Dromgoole, the well-connected expert in acquisitions who had followed Jackson from the BBC, had more immediate concerns on arrival in Los Angeles. She had arranged the face-to-face negotiations with Jeffrey Schlesinger, who ran the distribution arm of Warner Brothers, the owners of the *Friends* and *ER* rights. She was determined to avoid a repeat of 1996, when Grade was forced into fighting off BSkyB and Channel Five by renewing the series on such bad terms that it created internal friction. This salutary experience ought to have triggered heart-searching about whether the channel could possibly hold on to its supremacy in screening the pick of American imports, but by now they had become an addiction.

Jackson, who resented being saddled with Grade's bill, regarded it as a parable of how badly Channel 4 was equipped for multichannel. This was because there might have been better terms on offer if the channel had understood earlier what Warner wanted: a pay-TV service with a local British partner, which could well have been Channel 4. Warner had shrugged its shoulders at the lack of response and went to BSkyB, selling them the pay rights to *Friends* and *ER* for Sky One. Only with difficulty did Channel 4 salvage secondary, free-to-air rights. It was forced to run, as new, series of *Friends* and *ER* that had been seen on Sky One six months earlier and also had to sign up for makeweight programmes and films that it mostly did not want. The deal was described by insiders as a huge albatross.[11]

Jackson determined that this time it was going to be different. He opened the meeting with Warner by saying, 'We've come to buy the rights.' The American team replied that this time they were going to sell pay and free rights together to one company. When asked why, the Channel 4 team was told that this was what the market demanded. They guessed correctly that this meant it was what BSkyB wanted, so that they could control *Friends* completely. It would tear a hole in Channel 4's Friday nights.

'We began to explore, from 10.30 a.m., how much it would it cost to buy both free and pay rights', said David Scott. 'We had known it was in the air.'[12] As the morning wore on, Schlesinger and his team began to get edgy: they clearly wanted Channel 4 out and began to murmur about having other meetings and having to go to New York the next day. Both sides knew that you cannot do a complicated deal in two to three hours. Jackson and his team smelt a rat, but Dromgoole insisted that they were not going to be fobbed off. A determined Scot, she impressed Americans because she lived in a stately home (Penkill Castle in Ayrshire), from which she commuted to London weekly.

Ranged against her, though, was Schlesinger, whom she found a 'serially aggressive negotiator, but perfectly pleasant and rather fun in a social situation – one of the most astute heads of distribution of any US studio.'[13] She recalls, 'I told them we had not finished our conversation, and I arranged to return later that day.'[14] By now, they suspected that Elisabeth Murdoch, in charge of the Sky entertainment channels as Managing Director of Programming, had been tipped off and was in town, so they went down slowly to the Warner carpark below and hung around to see what would happen next. 'Surprise, surprise, Murdoch turns up, and we have a chat with her in the car park lift', said Scott. 'We told her we had come for the free rights but they were trying to sell pay and free together and it was all very expensive.'[15]

The team went back to the luxury of the Hotel Bel-Air and waited tensely until a call came through at 4 p.m. from Warner asking them to return. Jackson and Scott had arranged a movie-industry dinner, so Dromgoole and the lawyer went and struck a deal that evening, then had to work clause by clause through the contract overnight. After dinner, Jackson and Scott joined her, and they negotiated until 5 a.m. They did not get out of it cheaply. Warner demanded a £75 million three-year contract for *Friends* and *ER*, with Channel 4 paying £15 million a year and E4 £10 million. They had also been obliged to buy six other comedies and five other drama series – some makeweight but one at least that would prove an unexpected hit: *The West Wing*.[16]

It was this deal, rather than months of strategic planning, that drove the timetable for launching E4 in January 2001. The Board's first formal debate about the new channel took place at their meeting on 13 December, the week after the team returned from Hollywood. It was to be aimed at young adults between sixteen and thirty-four, promising 'Friday night every night' or 'Channel 4 with the boring bits taken out.' One director, the economist Andrew Graham, Acting Master of Balliol College, Oxford, was not impressed. He cautioned that his experience of that age group was that they did not want Friday night every night. 'They want to learn, too.' Jackson asked for E4 to be given fast-track approval, and this was reluctantly agreed subject to the business-plan figures working. Jackson put his successful Controller of Entertainment and Comedy, Kevin Lygo, in charge, with his trusted Commissioner Andrew Newman running it day to day.

With the Warner rights, E4 became a strong proposition. It was a home for *Ally McBeal*, *Dawson's Creek*, *ER* and *Friends*. But Channel 4, having poured its energy into FilmFour, had not properly digested its first digital lesson. Now it was venturing off into a somewhat different operation, a basic subscription service where the income was counted in pence per month per subscriber, not pounds, and where income from advertising was needed too. On the plus side, it was using broadcasting spectrum freely gifted and would reinforce the channel's role as a place for entertainment appealing to young adults. The target was a 0.8-per-cent share of digital audiences, and the first year's programme budget was £42 million. It would ultimately provide profits after it reached break-even in 2005.[17]

What Jackson did not know at the time was that *Big Brother*, which was a surprise late addition to the schedule in the summer of 2000, would be a huge draw for the very same young adult viewers, who were about to become even more valued by advertisers. The second series in 2001 would come to E4's rescue, with spin-offs from the broadcasts on the main channel essentially keeping it going during the summer months, proving at least as important to it as *Friends*. The pay channel's ratings shot up from 0.5 per cent to 0.91 per cent when *Big Brother* began.

There were several consequences to live with, though. By taking *Friends* and *ER* away from Sky, it had rattled their bars, while it had also kept at arm's length from OnDigital. The channel was like a small barque in danger of being crushed between the looming icebergs of BSkyB and ITV. At the next board meeting, in February, Jackson said, 'Channel 4 is either a profound ally or constant competitor to Sky.'[18] He raised the possibilities that they could liaise over acquiring programmes and that Sky could take a stake in E4. Barry Cox, though, was worried about both the principle and the politics, questioning how it would play with the Government. A new Communications Bill was being shaped, involving a new regulatory regime.

As it had been with FilmFour, it proved hard to strike a carriage deal for E4 with BSkyB, which had the largest network of 6 million homes, compared with 1.6 million cable homes and 1.1 million digital terrestrial homes. BSkyB simply hoped that E4 would not launch, because it would threaten Sky One, and while negotiations dragged on, the new channel's debut was put back. In the event, the carriage deal with Sky was struck just three days before the launch on 18 January 2001. The lever that worked was that BSkyB is essentially divided into two, a programming company and a platform company. It was the platform company that ruled that it did not want to be left without E4 to sell. But they played tough over the subscription terms, originally offering nothing but finally agreeing £15 million over five years.

The first programme on E4, the opening of a new series of *Friends*, attracted 628,000 viewers, or 6 per cent of those with multichannel television. E4, as it emerged, was three-quarters repeats, a quarter new content. The nineteen new programmes for the first year included *As If*, a trendily shot teen drama, and an early cult hit, *Banzai*, a spoof of a Japanese game show that quickly graduated to Channel 4. One third of digital homes sampled E4 within a month. A related E4.com website was rolled out in March, but it did not work properly, because entertainment clips needed powerful broadband services which were then in their infancy. Advertising on E4 was sold at a third of the Channel 4 rate and did not meet its first-year target of £10 million from this source. Editorially, the positioning was correct.

Jackson reasoned that to move into a multichannel world, he needed new people. There was a knowledge gap. ITV built OnDigital, later rebranded as ITV Digital, with their existing people, and it cost them £1 billion before it collapsed and closed ignominiously in 2002. His strategy, largely developed by David Brook and executed by David Scott, was to try to get a pay-television team in place. The key managers were Gerry Bastable from Nickelodeon, Dan Brooke from Paramount and John Keeling, who had a Sky and Disney background. He then added interactive media and new-media departments, and almost every board meeting brought requests for new posts to be approved. In the beginning, these were largely waved through, and the staff soared to 1,158 by 2001 – almost double what it had been in 1997. The custom-built headquarters in Horseferry Road were too small within four years, and extra new offices had to be located.

Brook was in a hurry. The new digital departments were at arm's length from the main channel and had their own life. Shortly after Jackson arrived, he commissioned business consultants McKinsey to advise on internet strategy, as they had done at the BBC. Their report suggested an annual expenditure of nearly £100 million which the channel ignored because it could not possibly afford it. Exposure to new media was limited to less than £20 million a year. In the heady days of the dotcom boom, almost every day brought another new proposal to Jackson's desk, requiring development money. New dotcoms approached the channel to see if it was prepared to barter share stakes for free advertising. Brook paid £1.5 million for a stake in a software company, Finger Tips, which later collapsed.

Jackson also began to look hard at buying independent production companies, although this went against the principle upon which Channel 4 was founded – as a publisher buying in the best ideas. He was concerned about securing rights to key programming. The favoured first acquisition was Wall to Wall, which supplied *The 1900 House* series. There were also talks between Andrew Brann, the Board Secretary and Head of Business Affairs, and Tiger Aspect. In July 2001, the Board agreed to consider taking a 20–25 per cent stake in Wall to Wall. The proposed policy switch was put to the ITC, but it petered out and by then the channel was in financial difficulties.

Jackson was keen to recruit staff who shared his modernising approach. He thought the Head of Personnel, Gill Monk, was old-fashioned and had to go. By the end of 1999, one of the channel's last stalwarts, Director Frank McGettigan, who had helped set up the administrative company, had had enough and, disgusted with the profligate ways of the new team, took retirement. The old guard was being swept away and replaced by people they regarded as the new-media barbarians.

It was hard keeping pace. Brook, still in his thirties, was difficult to pin down. He was great fun to be with, possessed of real marketing flair, but not a systematically organised person best suited to long-term strategic thinking. He had a shock on joining Channel 4, where his unbounded enthusiasm for the new and unexpected met suspicion, especially when he strayed into editorial matters. For a time, he acted effectively as Jackson's deputy. FilmFour, with which he was closely identified, was a project that needed his marketing skills. The channel never had access to the new films and Hollywood blockbuster premieres acquired by its rival,

Sky Movies, but it was still asking for a substantial monthly fee. So it relied heavily on brand expectations, the established Channel 4 film image. Jackson virtually scheduled the first month of FilmFour himself, pronouncing: '*Bicycle Thieves* is an important film.'

The film-channel expert, Tom Sykes, arrived from BSkyB to manage the new channel in September 1998, two months before it launched. As an experienced outsider, he spotted an immediate paradox. The mandate was to be edgy, high-quality, challenging, always entertaining, appealing, especially to male movie fans. But everyone running a film and entertainment channel has a set of rights to exploit, and subscription-film channels have to resign themselves to screening a significant proportion of much dross alongside a few big hits.

After the launch, it was decided that the FilmFour channel was to be about quality and range. The important thing was to sell the package to sceptical viewers, to emphasise choice and films in wide screen. It was 'films you know and films you don't know', chosen by the experts. At the start, it was showing 130 films each month, with a different theme almost every day, and it packaged up movies into seasons. It was trying too hard. 'It was a thinking person's film channel', says Sykes,[19] though it was never marketed as such. They set in train a big research project, nicknamed the Bufometer research because it centred on how 'buffy' the channel should be, in other words, how cool and art-house. But the reality gradually percolated through that the channel was a retail business, not an art-house venture, and it was operating in Sky's shadow. The deal with BSkyB saw subscription income split fifty-fifty between Channel 4 and Sky, which meant that far too little came to the channel.

The second fatal flaw was that although FilmFour was run by Channel 4, whose experts bought and scheduled the films, Sky ruthlessly kept information about customers to itself. 'We would have preferred to know the names of our subscribers', says Scott, in an understatement.[20] The procedure effectively ruled out deals with other broadcasters because when they made proposals for collaboration they had to be told that there was no such thing as a FilmFour subscriber, only Sky subscribers who took FilmFour as part of their package. Such valuable data was never shared. 'Conspiracy theorists would say it was a complementary service to Sky', says Sykes. 'We periodically looked at retailing ourselves, but in the early years it was decided it was better to collaborate, to stick with Sky.'[21]

Then a third flaw became apparent. The extra cost to the consumer was very visible because it was a single channel. While Sky, with its bundles of channels, could disguise costs, FilmFour was a clear price per month. That meant that the churn rate – the number of cancelled subscriptions – rose persistently to peak at 50 per cent. Channel 4's perception was that BSkyB always wanted to keep FilmFour small. They never killed off the patient, just throttled it sufficiently so that it never could cannibalise Sky Movies.

The problems mounted during 2001, Channel 4's dark year. The break-even point kept receding until the Board was told it needed 1 million subscribers to make a profit – three times the current level. Worse was to come. FilmFour lost 90,000 subscribers overnight when ITV Digital collapsed in March 2002. The BBC led the relaunch with Freeview, but it was free to air. Furthermore, ITV Digital had done well at marketing compared with the cable operators, who were abject failures at selling FilmFour. At one point, Telewest recruited 60,000 subscribers, through telemarketing paid for by Channel 4, but three-quarters of them were never connected, probably because they were not logged on to its computer base. So it limped on: just to stand still required a continuous and expensive level of telephone marketing to bring in new subscribers.

The most clear-cut digital-channel failure was attheraces, an attempt, tortuously negotiated over three years, to create a racing channel financed by a cut of the bets on the races placed internationally via the Internet. The logic was that Channel 4 was building on its long association with live racing, renewing programme rights in a sport for a lengthy ten-year period for a reduced cost, buying international and new-media rights, with the potential to make tens of millions of pounds. When finally agreed in the autumn of 2001, it was, at least, a controlled deal. Channel 4 and BSkyB each had a third share and capped their investments at £23.5 million. The third partner was Arena Leisure, which owned many leading racecourses. It went wrong from the start in 2002, though Channel 4's exit took until 2004 and absorbed a huge amount of management time. The net loss to Channel 4, after tax, was around £5 million. It remains a sorry tale, a footnote to an era that saw euphoric multimedia madness quickly transformed to hangover. It contributed to a growing sense of pessimism about how to expand.

All this wheeling and dealing aroused the critics, who accused the channel of extravagance and misallocating the new influx of money that should have been spent on home-grown programming. Too much of the channel's newly retained income was going on dubious digital escapades that did not work. The critics were on to something. After 1993, Channel 4 had emerged, to most observers' surprise, as a surprisingly wealthy channel, small but tough. Now it was intent on using the digital expansion policy encouraged by the Government to become bigger than a just a single television channel. Some £138.2 million was spent on new ventures during Jackson's four years between 1998 and 2001, the outlay rising sharply from £9.8 million to £71.4 million over the period, with FilmFour absorbing the most, £55 million.

The well-targeted attack was led by David Elstein, the former campaigner for Channel 4 and Chief Executive of Channel Five. First, in 2000, in front of government ministers, he pointed to the missing £250 million in Channel 4's accounts, the difference between its 1999 income of £642 million and the programme budget of £390 million. The Board was also startled by interventions first by City lawyer Bruce

Fireman and then by Elstein, who argued that the multichannel expansion was, in effect, being pursued in a manner that made them *ultra vires*. Elstein had re-read the 1990 Broadcasting Act and the 1998 order that had finally set the funding formula payment to ITV at zero. It said that the core function of the Channel 4 Corporation was to support 'the continued provision [. . .] of the television broadcasting service known as Channel 4.' David Scott described this as 'emotive rubbish': the missing money was going on these other activities.

At issue was whether the channel should be funding its new services through its annual surpluses of cash. Elstein got an opinion supporting his interpretation from David Pannick QC. 'It was [also] entitled to do such things and enter into such transactions as are incidental and conducive' to securing Channel 4, he said.[22] But surplus funds should be going to a reserve fund to support the channel, not to new services such as FilmFour and E4. In short, there was a difference of opinion between the lawyers about Channel 4's powers. Fortunately for the channel, this was never taken up by the Government or the Regulator, but the upshot was that Channel 4, after its own legal advice, had to make changes in the way it organised itself and presented its accounts. It was advised it was clearly acting within the law by setting up websites, such as E4.com, or sharing content with EMAP, with which it had a joint venture, but it was not with FilmFour or E4. The Board, accordingly, had to set up a qualifying company and put FilmFour and E4 into it.

All this raised another issue: whether the Board's scrutiny, its track record of governance, was adequate. Elstein asked basic questions about the business plan. What was its purpose? In a paper to the Board, David Scott said, 'We will need also to fully explain our strategy and vision to the ITC, the DCMS and Downing Street, in anticipation that there will be external pressure to limit and restrict the scope of Channel 4's developments.'[23] In the event, this did not blow up into a big political issue, but the next annual report was changed to split off the new channels and to record their losses more clearly.

These well-targeted darts began to raise doubts among board members about Jackson's grip on the business. They were becoming ever more wary of the proposals he brought to them. It was a sign of their weakness, and the ITC's distraction, that the real checks on Channel 4 came at first from outside, including the press. This was when the breakdown in trust and relations between Treves and Jackson began to accelerate, though at first it was well concealed. The Board started to question the numbers needed to run the digital channels and the costs of new-media ventures. At the end of 2000, Barry Cox queried the salaries and increased staff numbers. Directors scolded Jackson for writing too gentle a letter to department heads, without setting firm targets for reductions.

Because of the fuss, the new channels and commercial activities were in 2001 placed into a new company, 4Ventures. They were E4, the FilmFour channels, Interactive,

FilmFour Ltd, Sport on Four and Go Racing (later renamed attheraces). A new Chief Executive – the merchant banker Rob Woodward – was headhunted from the City to run 4Ventures and to carry out a complete review of the business plan. He divided up the operations in terms of assets and loss centres and set out a range of options, including closure.

The separation of new activities into 4Ventures would become divisive over the next few years, when the team that ran 4Ventures implied they were the future and Channel 4 itself was the past. It became much harder to manage the two entities, with their separate ambitions and cultures.

Fatally for the channel's commitment to schools programming, he also decided that his empire should include 4Learning and that it should move from being a core area of public-service content to a commercial one, expected to make money – prompting the resignation of Karen Brown, the Deputy Director of Programming, who ran schools programming. Specific educational content targeted at teenagers went into sharp decline, the low point marked by a *Teen Big Brother* in which a couple had unprotected sex. This was not addressed until 2006, when plans began to migrate the service to the Internet.

John Newbigin, the channel's Head of Public Affairs, said in retrospect that it was like a dysfunctional family at the top of Channel 4.

> There were these three weird teenage boys – Michael Jackson, David Brook and Tim Gardam. Michael Jackson wasn't Chief Executive, he was the Chief Creative Officer. They were all cracking on with interesting ideas. It was as if David Scott and Janet Walker [Managing Director and Finance Director respectively] were Dad and Mum. They ran the business side. The problem was that the budgets they agreed were often ignored.[24]

One outcome of the new financially focused regime was a protracted renegotiation of contracts with BSkyB for the FilmFour Channel and E4. Sykes said, 'The pitch was that FilmFour doesn't work and it won't work. You've taken all the value out of the business, so we want a greater share of the revenues we generate.'[25] The split finally moved, in the case of FilmFour, from the original fifty-fifty to eighty-twenty in Channel 4's favour, but not until 2004, when the price went up to £7 a month. But in the longer term, access to Sky's subscribers was not enough. The churn rate, which at best fell from 50 per cent to 35 per cent, was three times that of BSkyB's. FilmFour, as a pay channel, was on a slow path to oblivion.

Jackson insists that it is easy to forget the context in which the new channels were devised.

I would say about my time at Channel 4 that we future-proofed it – we were able to make a channel which had been very much a single terrestrial television channel into a cross-platform organisation that was able, culturally, to occupy the future [. . .] Look now at the move into online, into radio: you can't do that overnight. The foundation stones were laid at this point, and not just by me [. . .] Of course, not everything worked, but the actual sums of money were comparatively small, compared with the money spent on the schedule.[26]

He might also have added that every other broadcaster was making costly mistakes too.

David Scott reflected later,

Whilst not everything was perfect, I would say this was a fine achievement, which has transformed Channel 4 and provided the digital channel strategy, which in 2007 sustains group audience share and advertising revenues. Think how much smaller Channel 4 would be if it had remained as a single channel![27]

The spending spree, in most areas, came to an abrupt end during 2001, because the tap of advertising money suddenly stopped gushing freely. Channel 4, which had known only good times for eight years, suddenly became a much grimmer place. In some ways, it never again recovered its optimistic bounce.

20

The wall of leisure

● ● ● ●

In the first twenty-five years of Channel 4's existence, it operated a fairly stable programme schedule, and any significant changes, such as the arrival of *The Big Breakfast* in 1992, made news. This is why the period from 1999 to 2001, the late Jackson
era, is so important, for during these three years the channel's direction up to 2007
was largely determined. The most dramatic change came in 2000, with the runaway success of the first *Big Brother*, discussed in Chapter 24. But the rise of leisure
programmes and undemanding factual strands, built around the dilemmas of real
people, was another critical change. They were about to spread, albeit erratically,
across weekday evenings, eventually eroding the original concept of a channel that
was constantly innovating and experimenting – making it look stale.

Changes to weekday evenings between 8 p.m. and 9 p.m. would be described ret-
rospectively as building a wall of leisure, based initially on property shows. This wall
did not derive from any architect's overarching vision: it was more a result of trial
and error. Frequently, the enthusiastic reaction of viewers to new programmes, such
as the gentle *A Place in the Sun*, came as a surprise to everyone. This broader reliance
on leisure and features was accelerated by the need to invent reliable alternatives to
soap opera at 8 p.m., to entice viewers in after the *Channel 4 News* ended. They had
to compete with the aggressive expansion of *Coronation Street*, *EastEnders*, *The Bill*,
Holby City, and ITV's first use of stripped entertainment nightly, with *Who Wants to
Be a Millionaire?* Then, on a different front, Jackson suddenly found that *The Weakest
Link* on BBC2 was stealing his thunder at 5 p.m. With a third of homes now connected to multichannel television, the youth-oriented happy hour from 6 p.m. was
no longer very happy either.

So, the wall of leisure was only the most eye-catching and controversial part of a
range of responses and reactions to fierce competition. This was a period that saw

Right: 'Lexus man': Michael Jackson, Chief Executive, 1997–2001.

Below: Jon Snow, Presenter of *Channel 4 News*, with Editor Jim Gray.

Above: Kevin Lygo,
Director of Television, 2003–.

Left: 'Is it cos I is black?'
Sacha Baron Cohen as Ali G.

Above: Graham Norton welcomes Elton John to *So Graham Norton* (1998–2002).

Right: Nathan Maloney (played by Charlie Hunnam), Stuart Jones (Aiden Gillen) and Vince Tyler (Craig Kelly) in *Queer as Folk* (1999).

Above: Kevin McCloud with home builders on *Grand Designs* (1999–).

Left: Kirstie Allsopp and Phil Spencer prove it's all about *Location, Location, Location* (2000–).

Above: Tim Gardam, Director of Programmes, 2002–4.

Below: Richard and Judy welcome Prime Minister Tony Blair to their Channel 4 sofa.

Left: Mark Thompson, Chief Executive, 2002–4.

Below: Noel Edmonds and his red boxes: *Deal or No Deal* (2005–).

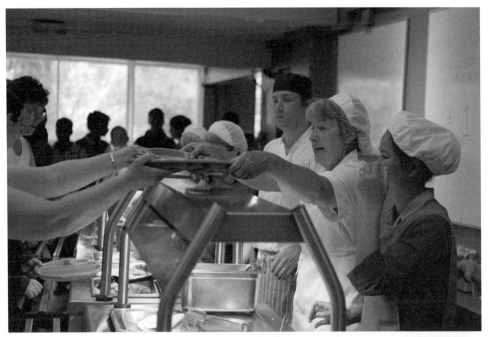

Above: Jamie Oliver and dinner ladies in *Jamie's School Dinners* (2005).

Right: Luke Johnson, Chairman, 2004–.

Below: Alastair Campbell makes an unscheduled appearance on *Channel 4 News*.

Andy Duncan,
Chief Executive, 2004–.

Carl Gallagher (played by Elliott
Tittensor) examines his plate in
Shameless (2004–).

A penitent Jade Goody watches
footage of her confrontations with
Bollywood actress Shilpa Shetty
on *Celebrity Big Brother* (2007).

the collapse of *The Big Breakfast* and the slow wilting of *Brookside*, which ran on Tuesdays, Wednesdays and Fridays at 8 p.m. and which at its peak had delivered almost a tenth of the channel's total ratings. There was, too, about to be a retreat from long-running strands of serious programmes at 9 p.m., such as *Equinox, Cutting Edge, Witness* and *Dispatches*.

Though *Cutting Edge* and *Dispatches* never died, they were chopped up into short runs, then partly replaced by shorter series and eye-catching single documentaries. *Dispatches* was eventually sent marching to Sunday nights and obscurity. In summary, this was the period when most vestiges of the old Channel 4, left over from Isaacs and the early Grade era, started to fade away – and when its older, faithful viewers, who had been watching since 1982, started to feel alienated.

The best place to start this story is with the glamorous Daisy Goodwin, a former BBC producer, known to viewers for pioneering events such as *The Nation's Favourite Poem*. Goodwin, who has the knack of effortlessly thinking up new programmes as others bake cakes, had made a series called *Home Front* for BBC2. Within it there was a segment about a man building a timber-framed barn house, which provoked such a positive reaction from viewers that she knew self-builds would make a separate series before long. On *Home Front* she met a Cambridge architecture graduate, Kevin McCloud, who was married to a friend of hers and who proved a natural in front of the camera. He then presented a series for BBC2, *Don't Look Down*, about spires and towers, but the controller, Jane Root, did not take to him, and BBC2 was anyway under pressure to move back to more serious fare, such as history.

After 1999, BBC2 was the channel for middle England, as Jackson put it – and that left the yuppie lifestyle field open for others to exploit, at a time when incomes were rising and advertisers and sponsors were detecting a mood of change. Channel Five, snapping at Channel 4's heels by now, was already busy with Ann Maurice's *House Doctor* – she was a sassy American who advised British homeowners how to sell for more by repainting their walls magnolia and eradicating pet smells. This was the start of the property explosion that provoked an upsurge of interest, some vicarious, in buying a second home or moving to the country or abroad, while buy-to-let mortgages encouraged a generation of amateur developers and speculators. Aspirational self-improvement chimed in with the arrival of Cool Britannia, the unashamed enjoyment of the good things in life, with programmes to match that expanding from home design into food, grooming, diet, health, cleanliness, raising children and training dogs. Jackson was well attuned to this: when running BBC2 he had asked Peter Bazalgette to make *Ready Steady Cook!* and *Changing Rooms*.

By 1998, Daisy Goodwin was working for Talkback, Peter Fincham's independent production company, and she put McCloud and the self-builders back together in *Grand Designs*. Jackson bought the series from her but did not like the title: he wanted to call it *Build Your Own House*. Goodwin insisted that was not aspirational enough and stood her ground, so *Grand Designs* duly appeared in May 1999. 'The thing is, everybody who builds their own home is a nutter', she reflected. 'That makes good TV. Second, there is a start and a finish – it's an inbuilt format.'[1]

But it was a nightmare to do for 1999. Building takes time. The series included a couple developing a water tower on the Chilterns into a house: when they had finished, it still looked like a building site. 'We had to cheat, dress the houses to look more finished than they were', Goodwin admits. Critics found the projects – and thus the programmes – too grand in scale and chilly in tone, more about the architecture and the thermal qualities of insulation than about people and their dreams. The first series was only a modest success when screened at 8 p.m. on a Thursday, attracting 1.6 million viewers – 400,000 short of the target; but research showed it had the potential to be a core Channel 4 programme.

The second series, in August 2001, started later, on Tuesdays at 9 p.m., and attracted 2.8 million viewers. *Grand Designs* would soon become one of the channel's biggest homegrown hits, built on the twin British passions for property and eccentric characters, and McCloud developed into a leading presenter.[2] The success gave the channel confidence to develop more easily formatted and lighter property programmes. May 2000 saw the debut of the first eight-part series of *Location, Location, Location*, fronted by Kirstie Allsop and Phil Spencer, finding new homes for picky movers. It was followed by two spin-offs, *Relocation, Relocation* and *Selling Houses*.[3]

Property Ladder with Sarah Beeny, about making money from doing up property, started a six-week run on September 2001 with a pleasing 2.3 million audience and 10.5-per-cent share. In 2002 came *Other People's Houses* and *A Place in France*. By 2002, after Jackson had left, the lifestyle and property shows were burgeoning, with fourteen episodes of *Location, Location, Location* ordered at a time. You can track them spreading like a dye, at first tentatively from Tuesday to Wednesday, then onwards through the week, embracing Thursdays and finally into Friday at 8 p.m., as a process of experiment turned into approval and almost uncritical embrace. *A Place in the Sun* moved from daytime to 8 p.m. in October 2000 and into a *Brookside* slot as the channel started to shift the soap around. In 2003, it was joined by a new slant on domesticity, *How Clean Is Your House?*

Every one of the property shows had a clear, distinguishing premise. It was house-buying, house-selling, how to have two houses for the price of one, moving from country to country, city to country, how to make money on property. The great danger was not that the property market might go down but, with other channels piling in, the market for the shows might reach saturation point. And the critics began to ask how innovative Channel 4 could claim to be when it was running its sixth property spin-off. When other channels follow suit, should that not be the signal to move on? That is certainly what the founders of the channel would have done. But the schedulers just saw reliable performers.

A broader wall of leisure was built up from 2001 as Jackson targeted young male viewers with shorter-lived car shows, *Driven* and *Deals on Wheels*, backed up by a successful website, 4Cars.com. Then there was *She's Gotta Have It*, a fashion and shopping show, and *Nigella Bites* and *Forever Summer with Nigella*, so-called family cooking in a real home. *Dinner Party Inspectors* suddenly marched in to assess how well their victims entertained their friends in their well-appointed homes. The channel already had run two series of *River Cottage* with Hugh Fearnley-Whittingstall, the old Etonian who championed self-sufficiency and real food from his smallholding, but it was only after 2001 that it was embraced as part of the lifestyle boom and really promoted.

This wave of lifestyle programming brought a new set of independent producers and no-nonsense presenters into favour, recruited by the style-conscious commissioner, Liz Warner, and guided by the bustling Ben Frow, with a driven personality and popular touch. Frow had trained for a year at the London College of Fashion as a tailor and had gone into television as dresser to Richard and Judy in 1990, ironing his shirts, buying her tights and rinsing them out. He loved peering into other people's homes from the bus going to and from work. Frow never showed much grasp of the wider Channel 4 mission but he had a nose for a hit and was promoted to run features in the 8–9 p.m. slot. 'I promised Tim Gardam I would deliver him returnable formats, predictable shows that came back year after year', he said.[4] And that is exactly what he did.

> Other people [at the channel] didn't really like doing them. Also, I just
> wanted success. *Selling Houses*, showing you how to sell your house for
> as much as possible, was cynical – but we had a hole in the schedule and
> I wrote the format out on the back of an envelope.[5]

How Clean Is Your House? came about in a serendipitous fashion. Goodwin, as she was leaving Frow's office, asked conversationally: 'How clean is your house?' Frow's eyes widened. 'That's a title for a show. I know there's a great show there', he said, and he commissioned it on the title alone.[6] The key was finding presenters, Kim Woodburn and Aggie MacKenzie, and marrying their cleaning tips to the human-interest side, dealing often with people with problems or dysfunctional families. There were some flops, though, such as *From House to Home*, for which the channel bought a gutted house which interior designers did up, a room at a time, over six weeks. At the end, a viewer would win the house; but the designs were terrible, and it broke the unwritten rule by choosing an outré design rather than having real people at its heart.

In the main, though, the lifestyle programmes were successful and commercial, with costs pegged at around £150,000–£160,000 per hour. Women made up 60 per cent of the audience, which made it the most female terrestrial channel at this time, alongside BBC1. Tim Gardam, the Director of Programmes, developed a theory about them:

> The future lies in popular, information-packed, easy but sharp factual features. But our programmes here need a very clear discipline. They must be easy to join, clear of purpose, direct in appeal, utterly focused on what they offer a target audience to take away. We aim for a minimum 2 million audience in every slot from 8 to 9 pm.[7]

That strategy, devised after the event, was a key to Channel 4's ability to hold its audience at a steady 10 per cent overall – double the 1 million who had been watching the 7 p.m. news – despite the growth of digital television, while extending its share of advertising. It also gave Gardam the confidence to contemplate the once unthinkable, abandoning *Brookside*, and to shrug off failures at breakfast time.

Gardam had been recruited as Director of Programmes in July 1998 at £200,000 a year and formally took over that December, eighteen months after Jackson arrived.[8] Entertainment, comedy and drama were basically controlled from separate mini-empires at first, and he never had much enthusiasm for drama and was attacked for ending the promising *North Square*, about young lawyers, after one series. He was there mainly to handle factual programming, the bedrock of the channel. Dan Chambers, then a programme commissioner, said that what no one anticipated was the thoroughness and brusqueness with which he altered the essence of Channel 4. 'He introduced rigour and order to the schedule.'[9] He was also the person who commissioned the first *Big Brother*.

Gardam had a double first from Cambridge, where he was a contemporary of Peter Bazalgette. At the BBC, he edited the 1987 General Election coverage, then *Newsnight* and *Panorama*, before becoming Chief Executive of News. But he was too individualistic to swallow John Birt's rigidly dogmatic and structured approach to covering public affairs, arguing instead for rational scepticism, for weighing up ideas on their merit. His impatience with Birtism led him to quit the BBC in April 1996 to join Channel Five's launch team as Controller of News, Current Affairs and Documentaries. There he was responsible for the ground-breaking format of Kirsty Young's news and also commissioned some of its most successful factual programmes.

He had been at Channel Five for two years when Jackson offered him the Channel 4 job. Before it was finalised, he had to be interviewed by Vanni Treves, the Chairman, who resented not having been consulted about Jackson's approach to him. Treves asked him where he wanted to be in five years' time. 'I said this was a job for three years', says Gardam. 'My last job in television.'[10] That appealed to Treves, who had by now a deep distrust of Jackson and many of his inner circle.[11]

Jackson, for his part, was aware of how editorial crises erupt most often from hard-hitting factual programmes. Gardam was extremely articulate, used to making the case in defence of his programmes and a good public debater. The most publicised problem as he arrived was a programme called *Chickens, Too Much Too Young*, about the plight of young people blighted by years of Thatcherism. Overseen by David Stevenson, the now departed commissioner of *The Girlie Show*, it was about the lives of young male prostitutes in Glasgow. To illustrate how they dealt with clients, someone from the production company got a car and picked the boys up. But they failed to label the sequence a reconstruction and did not tell the channel what they had done. When the cover was blown by the *Times* columnist Matthew Parris, blame fell on Maire Devine of Wall to Wall Scotland, who had made the film.

Gardam held an inquiry and made his view clear: 'The fabrication of this film is an extremely serious matter for Channel 4. It has badly damaged the credibility of serious television documentary. We found no evidence that anyone involved from Channel 4 knew, or was in a position to know, what Maire Devine had done.'[12]

The channel was fined £150,000 by the ITC, and the incident sparked a debate about standards and truthfulness in television. Carlton had already been fined for *The Connection*, faking an investigation about the way drug mules from Latin America brought in drugs, and the use of actors instead of real people on Vanessa Feltz's BBC chat show was also exposed.

Gardam was well equipped to defend a controversial *Brass Eye* special from Chris Morris about the hysteria surrounding paedophilia in May 2001, which created the kind of storm of moral outrage from politicians, including Tessa Jowell and David Blunkett that Morris was expert at sending up. Jackson gleefully called it 'a nice little stink bomb', and Gardam saw Morris as being in the tradition of the satirist Jonathan Swift.

Gardam personified the tensions within the channel as advocates of the serious, the old, the new and the formulaic jostled for position while he mentally beat himself up striving to hold the 10-per-cent audience share. Even before he formally started work at the channel, and without telling anyone else there, he bought two series featuring the historian Dr David Starkey: *Elizabeth* and *The Six Wives of Henry the Eighth*. History was one of his signature themes: he backed the female historian, Bettany Hughes, who made *The Spartans*, and ordered an adaptation of Evelyn Waugh's *Sword of Honour* trilogy, starring Jeremy Irons, although he found the result disappointing. Around the time of the millennium, it seemed that people wanted a fix on the past. Wall to Wall's 1999 hit *The 1900 House* freshened up social history by putting a family in south-east London back into the lifestyle of the period, and it was followed by *The 1940 House*, *The Edwardian Country House*, *The Frontier House* – exporting the concept to America – and, in 2003, *The Regency Country House*, which flopped because it bent the rules by being a dating show as well. Dan

Chambers invented *Secrets of the Dead*, a new history strand that exhumed histori-cal figures and applied forensic science to them, producing programmes such as *Murder at Stonehenge* and *What Sank the Mary Rose?*

Coming from penny-pinching Channel Five, Gardam was shocked at the money gushing around – epitomised by the free bottled water, sparkling or still, given to staff. He saw the same independent producers he had been dealing with at Chan-nel Five pitching the same ideas to Channel 4, but at a higher price. Wider changes, beyond the wall of leisure, were plotted in his core channel strategy paper of 26 April 2000 when he was looking forward to a relatively stable programme budget. The paper pointed out that a typical factual entertainment programme cost only 2 pence per viewer, a soft feature was 3 pence, Graham Norton's chat show 2 pence and a documentary series 5 pence. This compared with 18 pence for *Queer as Folk* and 10 pence for new comedy, such as the 'slack com', *Spaced*.

> Our reputation cannot be achieved on the back of entertainment and
> drama. We have to build a greater reputation for all our programmes,
> notably our factual brand [. . .] Our ratings and programme economics
> are dependent on the success of our factual programmes [. . .] We have
> not achieved a clear focus in our factual entertainment, the one genre
> where we can afford to expand our entertainment appeal.[13]

He moved on to discuss the long-running strands that John Willis had intro-duced as his big idea ten years before and which were the mainstays at 9 p.m. 'Our strands do not always [. . .] live up to their name. We still need strand programmes to give weight to single documentaries by grouping them. But we will develop subject-specific short series out of the strands.'[14] Sometimes it would be better to do ninety-minute single-event programmes dropped into the schedule.

He addressed the generation gap, the fact that the over-thirty-five viewers were beginning to feel restless.

> In some areas we have been too slow to change, to invent programmes
> that explore popular culture in peak time, programmes for the video-
> game, celebrity-fixated generation. Yet, we are also accused by the gen-
> eration of our original supporters of abandoning experimentation and
> a campaigning internationalism [. . .] No need to be nervous about al-
> ienating the audience that has most passionately identified with it in the
> past. The single most important challenge for Channel 4 is to break out
> of the cast of mind that opposes the older and serious versus younger
> and tabloid.[15]

This amounted to a blueprint for the rise of features, light documentaries and factual entertainment, while a black mark was placed against strands such as *Real History*, *Equinox*, *Witness*, *Cutting Edge* and *Dispatches*. This was the point when serious factual programmes started to go out of favour, a trend later highlighted by Ofcom in its 2007 financial review. There was an irony here, for Jackson had himself invented *Modern Times*, a documentary strand lovingly curated by an outstanding producer, Stephen Lambert, when at BBC2. The switch in emphasis was heavily influenced by marketing, for strands often fared badly in pre-publicity, seldom nominated as the pick of the day by newspaper previewers.[16] Dorothy Byrne, the commissioner responsible for *Dispatches*, was opposed to the new thinking. 'It was a fashion. I completely disagreed with it. Strands mean the audience know what they are going to get. It felt as if the channel was ashamed of having current affairs.'[17] The changes did not all come at the same time. The first stage was to chop strands into shorter runs, while *Dispatches* was moved around the schedules, finally settling at weekends, until in 2005 it was revived as a hard-hitting peak-time series.

Meanwhile, Gardam hit upon a new brand of formatted reality documentaries at 9 p.m. with *Faking It*, whose premise was to tutor a novice until he or she could compete with experienced professionals – transforming, for instance, a pole dancer into a show jumper. It began with a pilot in September 2000, with a shop assistant breaking into high society, and attracted 2.41 million viewers, for an 11-per-cent audience share. The idea had come from the now independent producer Stephen Lambert, creative director of RDF – or rather from his wife, Jenni Russell, who suggested it as a modern reworking of George Bernard Shaw's *Pygmalion*.[18] January 2002 saw the launch of *No Going Back*, about people who sell up in Britain and venture on a new life. The first episode achieved a 15-per-cent share, but there was a shock when a couple who went to a Nicaraguan island were attacked by pirates, with tragic consequences.

Faking It, *No Going Back* and, in January 2003, another durable and more commercial RDF strand, *Wife Swap*, started to elbow out the old style of fly-on-the-wall documentaries which, while they chronicled life in all its awkwardness, did not necessarily produce a neat resolution or large audiences. *Wife Swap* was actually inspired by a *Daily Mail* article, looking at the contrasting lives of people, and was commissioned as a personal-finance programme. The first series attracted 5.3 million people, gained a 21 per cent share and was exported to America. But by the eighth series, in 2007, it was another of the programmes which the channel's critics saw as proof it had lost its way.

There was also an end to regular seasons of Film on Four – as a strand it disappeared. *Right to Reply*, in which viewers expressed their views about programmes, was banished after a run of four in December 2001, on the specious grounds that with so many programmes being aired it was difficult to choose those seen by enough people to have a meaningful debate. This had been a key weekly programme for Jeremy Isaacs. The real reason, though, was that being held to account was always a pain for programme-makers. This decision distanced the channel from its viewers and critics, removed the opportunity for debate and was yet another live and unpredictable element banished from its schedule.

In his job application, Gardam had written a manifesto for Jackson in which he said that independent authorial voices would make the channel stand out: it had to get back to people who had something to say. Starkey and McCloud fitted that, but, as Gardam was soon to discover, Channel 4 was increasingly about marketing, and the wall of leisure was easier for the marketing department to promote. He would later reflect about his tenure: 'I think I left Channel 4 with its heart and soul intact; but it was a very tricky balancing act.'[19]

Just how far the channel felt forced to go to shore up its ratings was demonstrated in the spring of 2001. While it pursued a policy of catering for young adults and upmarket viewers after 6 p.m., it had always relied on bulky audiences in the afternoons and early evenings to hold up its overall share. So now, its head of daytime, Jo McGrath, told Amanda Ross, who ran the independent production company Cactus with her husband Simon, that she had a specific problem between 5 p.m. and 6 p.m., up against *The Weakest Link* on BBC2. She needed something that stood out and could be run across the week. One of the shows devised in 1996 was *Pet Rescue*, a clone of the BBC's *Animal Hospital*, from Peter Bazalgette, but that was now over.

The Rosses were mistress and master of *The British Soap Awards*, shown by ITV, hosted by Richard Madeley and Judy Finnigan. The high-profile couple had confided to Amanda Ross that they were really unhappy at ITV, where they had presented a morning programme for thirteen years, but they did not have that many options for change. 'I told them I could help reinvent them', she said. 'ITV didn't value them.'[20] She had discovered this for herself when Andrea Wonfor, Managing Director of Granada, invited her to her table at the Broadcast Awards in January 2001. Wonfor made a loud joke about Richard and Judy having nowhere to go from ITV, and the whole table dutifully laughed – except for Ross, who thought it was unnecessarily rude. 'They were arrogant and didn't seem to value people.'[21] Richard and Judy's contract with ITV ended in June 2001, and the network eventually offered them a one-year extension.

Ross told McGrath that Cactus were developing a new magazine show suitable for the 5–6 p.m. slot – harder-edged, with topical interviews and no cookery. McGrath asked who would present it. 'You will either think I am mental or not', Ross replied. 'But what about Richard and Judy?'[22] McGrath said she would love it, and Ross phoned Richard Madeley. By the time she had driven home to Clapham, it was agreed in outline. The Board said the deal could go ahead, but it had to be presented as a trophy signing, and a period of negotiations began that remained secret until there was a leak at the Montreux Television Festival in late April.

The press started asking questions, but Matt Baker, Chief Press Officer and Jo McGrath's partner, managed to ward them off until the deal was signed. After Richard and Judy finished their show on Thursday, 3 May, they went to their lawyer's office near London Bridge, where they had agreed to stay around the table until the deal was done. Judy climbed in through a back window, assisted by an upturned milk crate. The channel's commissioners were on an away day in Cannizaro House, Wimbledon, so draft agreements were faxed backwards and forwards. The deal that emerged was for two years, five nights a week, forty-two weeks a year, with a production contract worth around £16 million a year, £6 million more than *The Big Breakfast*. The Rosses would build a studio in Kennington specifically for the programme.

By switching from ITV, the presenters doubled their money. They would earn an additional fee as executive producers, not just performers. The final agreement was signed at midnight by Judy Finnigan at their home in Hampstead, and Channel 4 set up a mystery news conference for Friday afternoon. Clutching a big 4 logo for the photographers, Richard and Judy posed on the steps of the Horseferry Road headquarters, as staff trooped onto the glass balconies to cheer the new arrivals.

The euphoria soon evaporated, though. The programme had originally been due for launch in January 2002 but was rushed forward to November 2001, as the channel battled with its financial problems, and it showed signs of hasty preparation. On ITV in the mornings, the couple had averaged 1.3 million viewers. On Channel 4 they drew 2.4 million on the first evening but then the figure collapsed to a disappointing 1.6 million. The first show – introduced with a nice role reversal touch by Finnigan who said: 'Hello, I'm Judy Finnigan; this is my husband Richard' – was curiously hyperactive, cramming in seventeen items including a bizarre slimming experiment where one person sat still, thinking himself slim, while the other exercised on a bike for an hour. 'Nobody knew what the mood of a 5 p.m. show should be', said Ross.[23] (By 2007, they had worked it out, with only seven items per show.) It all confirmed many people's doubts about whether Richard and Judy were really Channel 4 material.

Peter Bazalgette, by now a director of the channel,[24] had thought the signing odd when Gardam told him about it. It was hard to see how recycling ITV faces fitted in with Gardam's grand strategy of a year before, when he said the channel was to be 'the place for the curious viewer to locate television's new talent and creative imagination.' But he believed that having a live magazine programme that reflected the day's events was important. The couple attracted enough upmarket viewers – and hence advertising – to pay their way, and their reputation was such that prestige interviewees such as Hillary Clinton agreed to appear. They added a wine club and an influential book club to the mix, allowing them to qualify as an addition to the channel's educational output.

Although it was not altogether a cosy transplant, and the programme was almost continually under review, the contract was renewed for three years in September 2003. 'We were really happy. We were locked in to the end of 2007', said Ross.[25] But, as she would find out in January 2006, when the channel suddenly signed up Paul O'Grady to alternate in the slot, in television, contracts can be torn up; security is never guaranteed.

• • • •

The Big Breakfast was really a radio programme on television, custom-designed for the zany Chris Evans. The programme floundered after Evans's departure, although the pairing of Denise Van Outen with Johnny Vaughan sparked a brief revival. But at the end of 1998, Van Outen announced she was leaving, and, to Gardam's frustration, Planet 24's boss Waheed Alli would not tell him who the next presenter would be. Eventually, Alli lighted on Kelly Brook, a nineteen-year-old former stage-school actress, in a bid to go back to the show's tabloid roots. It did not work. *The Big Breakfast* had to hold a minimum audience of 500,000 to make money, but it was falling short. A leaked internal memo asserted that Brook had trouble pronouncing long words such as 'satirical' and 'intrepid' on the autocue, and the *Daily Mirror* columnist Sue Carroll called it a 'sloppy hasbeen show'.[26] Brook was fired in July 2000 and went on to star in advertisements for the Triumph Flaunt It range of brassieres, commenting: 'I was fired for being too working-class and not luvvie enough for Channel 4 chiefs.' *The Big Breakfast* ended that Christmas.

Gardam trawled for new ideas, shortlisted five and picked a show called *RI:SE* from Princess Production, run by Sebastian Scott, who had worked on the first *The Big Breakfast* and Sky News. It started in March 2002 but came off in a year. 'The truth is there wasn't a new show to put at breakfast time', said Gardam. 'It was exhausted. You can't always innovate.'[27] There was no gap to be filled: GMTV served mainstream ITV viewers, especially housewives, while the BBC's breakfast news show catered for adults of a more serious turn of mind. There were a dozen or more children's channels and music channels galore for teenagers. Everyone else was listening to the radio. Instead, the channel ran cheap repeats of American sitcoms, from *Friends* to *Everybody Loves Raymond*.

Chris Evans, meanwhile, briefly beguiled commissioners when he made a reappearance at the Edinburgh Television Festival in 2002 after a sojourn in Hollywood with his young wife Billie Piper. He made a passionate case for the return of live-entertainment television programmes, but his attempt at a comeback on Channel 4 with *Boys and Girls*, a big Saturday-night studio show, was a dismal and expensive flop.

The happy hour between 6 p.m. and 7 p.m. was a recurring problem, a crucial time for a channel needing to harvest ratings before the news came along. Gardam saw it as a teenage and young adult zone, but the bulk of those viewers were tuning into *The Simpsons* on BBC2. Channel 4 had tried all sorts of programmes – *Crossfire*, *Crystal Maze*, *Shipwrecked*, *Gamesmaster*, *Late Lunch* with Mel and Sue, *TFI*, *Fit Farm* and *The Salon* (dispensing haircuts and beauty treatments) – as well as American programmes from *Dawson's Creek* to *Stargate SGI*. *Hollyoaks*, on the up as *Brookside* declined, became a lynchpin, at first three times a week and then, from November 2003, increased to five. The schedulers were, again, looking for consistency, stripped shows from reliable producers delivering 2 million plus young viewers.

In June 2001, June Dromgoole heard through her Hollywood contacts that *The Simpsons* was again up for grabs and that Channel Five was preparing such a huge bid that the BBC would be forced to withdraw. This was a matter of urgency, for Five was now hovering just below a 6 per cent share and had already captured *Home and Away* from ITV. During the autumn, the able Dromgoole approached the owners, Fox, with a lower bid than Channel Five but with the promise that she would market it with vigour in what she insisted was a better environment for the show. On that basis, she bought the free-to-air rights to new series and the back catalogue: Sky One kept the first-run pay rights. When the new series was launched on Channel 4 in November 2004, it attracted 2.2 million viewers. The happy hour was sorted.

The outstanding problem became *Brookside*, one of Channel 4's original programmes. Back in 2000, when the last successful producer Paul Marquess left, there had been discussions about turning it into a daily soap. 'Our current strategy is to persevere with *Brookside* and restore credibility and depth to its characters', Gardam had told the Board at that time. 'However, its future and positioning will depend in part on the movement of other channels' soaps.'[28] One of the ongoing issues was the difficulty of working with Phil Redmond, and Gardam was not the man to solve that. By December 2000, it remained vulnerable, ratings were down by 25 per cent – and ITV was stripping *Who Wants to Be a Millionaire?* against it. Gardam reported, 'The company [i.e., Redmond] is complacent and resistant to Channel 4 editorial involvement. We are negotiating a more robust editorial structure.'[29] A plan to give the serial a one-hour slot on Wednesdays was shelved until this was agreed.

There were attempts late in 2001 to persuade the former producer, Mal Young, to return, or even to buy into the Mersey television company. These failed, and scrapping the programme now became a serious option, although there remained considerable dissent within the channel about its fate. It was seen as an illustration of the drawback of working through independent producers. If the channel had made the soap, they would have simply sent in their own team to turn it around, as ITV and the BBC did periodically with *Coronation Street* and *EastEnders*. In the event, it was left to Mark Thompson, Jackson's successor, to deliver the *coup de grâce* after he formally joined as Chief Executive in March 2002. *Brookside* had outstayed its welcome. It had begun as a fresh, innovative soap but by now the territory it covered had become commonplace, and the number of rival soaps between 7 p.m. and 9 p.m. squeezed it to death.

The schedulers did not help by moving it around a lot, infuriating Redmond. Rosemary Newell, the scheduler responsible, insists that she was trying to protect it from the competition,[30] yet, on 27 March 2002, she left it against a double epi- sode of *Coronation Street*, where it drew just 500,000 viewers against the Street's 11.4 million. In September, a programme review happily reported that 'the combination of two personable and atmospheric documentaries, *River Cottage* and *A Place in France*, gained an audience of 2.8 million, indicating the potential once *Brookside* is removed.'[31] It was duly deprived of its evening slot in November – coinciding with the channel's twentieth anniversary – and switched to the afternoons, while notice was served that the contract would end in December 2003. The very last episode went out past midnight.

There was bitterness on both sides. Redmond felt slighted – even though his *Holly- oaks*, now in its fifth year, had become a mainstay of the channel – and he put most of the blame on Jackson. Mersey Television's contract fell in value from £35.5 million to £23.9 million, and the slow run-down ensured that *Brookside* was in too feeble a state to sell to a rival channel. The Board, too, was aggrieved: they were having to spend £17 million during 2003 on a weekend afternoon soap they did not want. Without a widely appealing prime-time soap for adults, the channel was vulnerable, and without the gritty flavour of Liverpool, it seemed southern and aloof.

● ● ● ●

Channel 4's budget approach to sport had been limited to minority enthusiasms until 1999.[32] Then Channel Five started to buy football rights opportunistically, so Channel 4, in a tactic devised by David Brook, decided to go after cricket, seeking the rights to test matches played in England, until then always screened by the BBC. It was a last-minute decision, and it took less than three weeks in October 1998 to tie up the deal. It came at a turning point for the sport, which had a new struc- ture devised by the England and Wales Cricket Board, chaired by the former Tesco boss, Lord MacLaurin. Jackson relished springing the coup on a complacent BBC, although he had little personal interest in sport. 'The BBC had no conception that they could ever lose it', he said.[33]

Channel 4 bought four years' rights to the home test matches for £56 million and pledged £13 million in marketing. There were two strands to the channel's ap- proach. First, it took a sport with a wide following but a moribund structure and applied the Channel 4 touch to it in terms of enterprising production. Second, it involved a multicultural approach – part of the channel's remit – with big screens in parks and an urban cricket programme. When the West Indies came in 2000, it brought in reggae groups to play at the Oval and Lords. The coverage itself was well received by viewers, involving more cameras, more close-ups, better graphics and greater crowd participation. It was all made more exciting by the use of modern technology: devices such as the snickometer and Hawkeye plus a comprehensive website with regular updates and a live scorecard.

In its first season, 1999, the production company Sunset and Vine won a BAFTA award and the Royal Television Society's TV Sports Award of the Year. The *Daily Telegraph* commented, 'If anyone 18 months ago had said that Channel 4 and cricket would be natural partners, it may have been difficult to believe.' Audiences gradually improved. In the first summer, the average was 1.2 million viewers for each session, with the highest 2.1 million – mostly young, upmarket viewers with a fair proportion of women. The audience for the climax to England's victory over the West Indies at Lords in July 2000 peaked at 5.3 million, with an average 4.2 million. Terry Blake, the England and Wales Cricket Board's Marketing Director, said, 'It's been a wonderful partnership which has exceeded our expectations.'

It was not all plain sailing, though. One early problem was that when it rained, the channel had no archive footage to fill the gaps in play. There was, too, a clash with summer flat racing. There were ten occasions in 2000 when the channel's commitment to racing and cricket coincided, sending cricket off to FilmFour – tough on cricket fans who did not subscribe to cable or satellite. The starting time of 10.30 a.m. also proved an embarrassment, because that was when the channel was supposed to run its educational programmes. And if play continued after the advertised stopping time, it wreaked havoc on the commercially geared early evening schedule, which could affect revenue.

Despite such irritations, halfway through the contract, in April 2001, the Board renewed it for three years until 2005, when England won the Ashes from Australia. The new rate, though, was £20 million a year, which some board members thought too steep because cricket was a loss leader that never made money or appealed to its target sixteen- to thirty-four-year-olds; and this was at a point when Channel 4's finances began to deteriorate. Losing the cricket after 2005 came as a relief to some board members, and the channel has not reinvested on that scale in any other mainstream sport since, though it did bid for a package of Premiership football rights in 2006. Cricket would be seen, in retrospect, as a Jackson-era bubble, the product of the period between 1998 and 2000 when the programme budget rose by a third and it could afford to do a fast deal without the strategic planning to back it up. It was wonderful while it lasted, but not sustainable for a small channel about to face an uncertain future.

21

Caught out by 9/11

• • • •

There is a moment when the party has to end, when the lights are switched on and the hangover starts for those who have overindulged. That is what happened at Channel 4, and we can pinpoint the precise moment: 11 December 2000. The Directors were at the Marriott Hotel on the banks of the Thames, looking at five-year plans[1] when a question was posed by Robin Miller, the toughest and most commercially minded of them, who had risen from founding *Motorcycle News* to be Chairman of EMAP, the publishing and media company.[2]

'What happens if there is a downturn?' he asked. The question hung in the air like a bad smell on the day, but it would be remembered long after he retired. He warned his colleagues that it would not be easy to turn the tap off once funding new ventures had begun in earnest during 2001. The budget plans being discussed that afternoon included nearly £50 million for the cost of the launch year of E4. As a consequence, the company was planning for a minimal profit. Surveying the past year, he noted a decline in efficiency and worrying signs of overspending on overheads. Looking ahead, the returns from new investments were too marginal. He saw a lot of cash going out and too little coming in – the classic recipe for going broke. 'The main channel will not always be a cash cow, and the rationale must be that the new businesses will, in time, fund Channel 4.'[3] Yet, for the time being, the company was wholly reliant on Channel 4 income, mostly from advertising, and it was not giving itself nearly enough room to manoeuvre. Already the global economy was slowing, and the dotcom bubble was about to burst, bringing down the overpriced, over-hyped technology stocks.

As it turned out, Miller was spot-on in his timing; but the collective response from the executives was to shrug off his warning. 'They could not believe it until it happened', said Barry Cox, the Deputy Chairman.[4] They had become complacent, accustomed to growth and prosperity. Just before the warnings began, Tim Gardam had committed £2 million to a project, *Finding the Bismarck*, a great Nazi battleship which had sunk the British ship, *The Hood* in the middle of the Atlantic in 1941. 'Crazy. But it changed that fast. When I took delivery of the programme a year later, in 2001, I thought, how did we get the money for that?'[5]

Although advertising growth in general had been quite modest after 1997,[6] the benefit of the abandoned funding formula in 1999 had produced a sudden injection of cash, and those on the receiving end thought there was no reason why the good times would not continue to roll. After all, in 2000, television advertising had risen by a healthy 11 per cent. But then it suddenly ground to a standstill and, after April 2001, went into reverse, with frightening monthly falls of between 15 and 20 per cent on the previous year.

An air of suspended disbelief was maintained until that May. Andy Barnes, the Commercial Director, was still saying that the outcome would be flat, that they would hold their income steady at £638 million and that it was ITV who would suffer most. While Channel 4 had the second outing of *Big Brother* to look forward to, ITV had invested much money and energy in a pre-recorded reality format called *Survivor*, which flopped. Savings were identified rather than implemented, and department heads were politely asked to shave 5 per cent off their budgets for 2002.[7]

After E4 was launched in January, the channel continued to splash out, signing Richard and Judy to solve the 5–6 p.m. slot in one of its most expensive contracts, justified by the argument that it helped the channel hold on to its target of an overall 10-per-cent share of audiences, even though advertising in the evening peak period was four or five times more valuable than in daytime. By July, the profit forecast was slashed to £4.3 million, and Tim Gardam had to take £40 million out of the programme budget. Films were deferred, and two factual series postponed. Then an already frail global confidence was shattered by the terrible events of 11 September, as the Twin Towers of the World Trade Center were destroyed by suicide hijackers. The impact on advertising was immediate, with two airlines cancelling their spots overnight. Over the next few weeks, the decline accelerated.

This was another point in the channel's history when questions were raised about the efficacy of its system of corporate governance. Only two years earlier it had been freed from the hated funding formula, and in the mood of euphoria, nobody thought to ask whether it would be sensible to look for some sort of replacement insurance policy, just in case times became tough. The Board had deliberately opted to walk the tightrope without a safety net and had spent their cash cushion. Perhaps they felt that if they did not look down they would never fall off.

As the financial position worsened, Jackson was negotiating his exit, using his own undeniable part in the channel's creative revival as a calling card to land the job he had always hankered after. Ali G, taken up by HBO, was launching into America.

Channel 4 had been one of the first broadcasters, after Holland and Germany, to screen *Big Brother*, the sensational new reality show of 2000. But it was also doing more laudable things, such as airing Saira Shah's *Under the Veil*, about the Taliban's oppression of women in Afghanistan – and this some months before 9/11. Awards flooded in for *Faking It*, *The Great Plague* and *Banzai*. Unlike the BBC, one of Channel 4's problems was that it was no bigger than a medium-sized secondary school, and the ambitious Jackson had soon bounced up against its boundaries. It was never big enough to produce its own leaders, to allow creative people to move on and develop within the organisation.

Jackson had caught the eye of Barry Diller, a former Hollywood studio boss, who had set up the Fox Network for Rupert Murdoch. Diller now offered the high-flying Briton a senior post at USA Entertainment, which controlled three cable networks, a studio and a film arm. But the courtship that would culminate in this bold transatlantic venture took time and effort; and while it was going on, Jackson fell out comprehensively with his chairman, Vanni Treves.

Jackson had been recruited in 1997 by Treves's predecessor, Sir Michael Bishop, on a three-year contract, renewable annually after that. He and Treves had never hit it off. One was the consummate television ideas man, a spotter of trends and talent, the other an urbane City lawyer, a stickler for process and professional management. The shrewd and emollient Barry Cox found himself holding the ring between the two. Cox, a friend and former neighbour of Tony and Cherie Blair from their Hackney days, had been a member of the LWT cadre around John Birt and, like Greg Dyke, had made a small fortune from share options associated with the LWT franchise renewal in 1991. After LWT was taken over by Granada, he became Director of the ITV Companies Association and was made Deputy Chairman of Channel 4 in 1998.

He became aware of the tension between the Chairman and Chief Executive soon after he arrived, when Treves asked him if he would he be prepared to fire Jackson. 'If we had to', Cox replied cautiously.[8] Halfway through 2000, Treves began to be more outspoken. 'I never saw that Vanni and Michael fell out over the direction of the channel', Cox insists. 'It seemed a matter of personality [. . .] The crux of it was that Jackson wasn't the Chief Executive that Vanni expected.'[9] For his part, Jackson viewed Treves as ignorant of television and unwilling to learn. He said, 'Vanni [had] very little sympathy for or real interest in Channel 4's purpose [. . .] We had very little in common.'[10] The two were polite to each other but icy, and there was no trust.

By early 2001, word reached Jackson's colleagues that he was trying to tie down a job in the USA, and it was observed that he seized the chance to visit New York whenever he could. In April, Peter Bazalgette joined the Board,[11] and Jackson confided in him. They were old friends, and both lived in Notting Hill, where from time to time they would walk around the communal garden behind Bazalgette's magnificent house and discuss the big decisions that Jackson faced. It was a hallmark of Jackson's style to seek advice and chew over decisions with others in the industry – another source of tension with Treves, who thought chief executives should set policy and boldly strike out in the direction they wanted others to follow; in other words, they should be decisive leaders.

Bazalgette's appointment was, to some extent, an anomaly because it brought Endemol, about to become the channel's biggest supplier, within the inner sanctum, at a time when it was pressing for value pricing of programmes – fixed prices for popular strands. The channel's former practice had been to base payments on a detailed breakdown of costs plus a profit margin and a production fee. Value pricing was closer to the system negotiated by agents for screen stars, and it meant that if there were competition between channels for a format, the price would rise, as in an auction – which is exactly what happened with *Big Brother*. Bazalgette offered to withdraw from board meetings if anything was discussed in which he had a direct involvement, but this never occurred. The 2002 annual report recorded that he had no say in commissioning programmes. He was, however, the last Channel 4 director to be recruited from the independent sector, a decision that Ofcom encouraged.

Treves would sit down with Jackson regularly to try to talk things over, but his chief executive refused to confide in him about his long-term ambitions and gave no information about when he intended to leave or what he was looking around for. The Chairman became frustrated with his dithering. 'I wasn't at all sorry when Jackson left', he said. 'I was pleased [. . .] He wouldn't tell us when or what he was going to do or how much notice he would give. We were prepared to negotiate: we wouldn't have held people to contract.'[12]

This uncertainty over Jackson's future diverted the mind of the Board from what should have been their main concern: the swift deterioration in the company's finances. Jackson had a loyal secretary who built a cordon of steel around him, shielding him even from urgent calls from the Chairman. 'We were deeply frustrated', Treves recalls. 'We thought of firing him.'[13] They were deterred from such extreme action during the first half of 2001 because ratings remained solid and the awards kept rolling in. Nor was it obvious that if he left they could replace him with someone better. After basking in the glow of the previous year's Caribbean summer cricket coverage, Treves had written in the 2000 annual report that the place was 'brimming with creative energy.'

It was all building up to a classic Channel 4 bad exit. Bazalgette was at Alan Yentob's country house in Somerset for Sunday lunch in July when Jackson, also a guest, took him for a walk through the wet grass in the orchard and confided that he was going to resign and take the job in America. He asked Bazalgette whether he had considered applying for his job. 'The thought never crossed my mind', says Bazalgette. 'I wasn't sure I wanted to do it.'[14] Treves first heard of Jackson's decision on television.

He didn't call me to tell me first. I rang him up, and he said the story had been leaked – Michael doesn't do contrition. It didn't matter terribly. Michael Jackson cared about the channel in terms of Michael Jackson [. . .] It was unacceptable, but we were relieved – it was a problem sorted.[15]

Jackson's departure was confirmed on 23 July through a press release, and he formally left on 31 October.

The year continued on its grim course. Television advertising fell by 10 per cent in the year – described in the ITC annual report as the 'greatest unforeseen shock' of all. Channel 4's income sank by around 5 per cent, from £652 million to £619 million. By itself, this did not amount to a catastrophe, but it came at a time when, as Miller had warned, the losses from 4Ventures mounted to £65 million, creating the channel's first-ever pre-tax loss, of £28.2 million. Its income was back to its 1999 level, but by now it had more dependants to support. The programme budget was held at the previous year's level of £423 million. It was the start of a long period of advertising stagnation until 2006, when there was a structural shift in spending towards the Internet.

During 2001, Granada completed its purchase of United News and Media and bought Border Television. The ITV companies were being gobbled up into ever larger units, and the logical outcome – that they would all eventually merge under a single owner – frightened Channel 4. Terrestrial broadcasters still took 80 per cent of all viewing, but this was the year of the introduction of the personal video recorder, Sky Plus, which allowed people to watch programmes when they wanted, and to skip the commercials.

But even in this dark year, Channel 4's share of total television advertising rose to 23.5 per cent from 22 per cent: in other words, it was faring better than ITV. Audience share held at 10 per cent, only slightly lower than the figure Jackson had inherited from Grade. To tide it over the shortfall, the channel needed to raise a syndicated loan of £50 million, the first time it had raised money since building its new headquarters.

As the Jackson era ended in a slow fade, David Scott had to hold the channel together. He made immediate cuts of 20 per cent, removing £20 million from the overheads and 100 from the payroll – principally by not filling vacancies – and laid out a plan to bring the channel back into profit in 2002. The crisis tainted Jackson's legacy, and he did it further damage in an ill-judged farewell speech to politicians and opinion-formers on 31 October 2001, when he delivered the New Statesman Annual Media Lecture at the Banqueting House in Whitehall – from which Charles I had walked out to his execution before a chastened crowd in 1649.

Jackson's speech was unreported by the press at the time and not distributed to media correspondents. The tone was set by the opening sentence: 'Tomorrow I fly to New York to take up a new job as Chief Executive of USA Entertainment.' It was the speech of a man leaving for a new life, casting off the parochial debates of Britain before heading for the quintessential land of media. The opening minutes, dealing with the way he had modernised Channel 4, were well received, but the final third was greeted with appalled silence. It was an expansion of his central thesis that public-service broadcasting was a battle standard that broadcasters no longer had to rally to because it had become 'the ju-ju stick of British broadcasting – a redundant piece of voodoo.' He was thinking the unthinkable and, at that period in broadcasting history, saying the unsayable. He described giving a presentation to 1,000 media workers in their twenties.

> As soon as I used public-service broadcasting as a watchword I'd lost them. Blank faces all round. I was stunned. Had they never read their Asa Briggs? Had they never been to a MacTaggart lecture? Well, it seems not. And it seems as though public-service broadcasting is another shibboleth whose time has come. It's a term you never hear during the day-to-day practice of making television: you only hear it when people make speeches [. . .]
>
> We might regret it, but people are no longer enthused by the altruism of public-service broadcasting. Instead, they demand good programmes, channels and websites, as defined by them. That's the reality of modern media in Britain. An optimistic approach might be to say that public-service broadcasting has been a victim of its own success – it has written its own death warrant. Because people are now much freer, better educated, not pushed to the side of their own lives any more, the paternal impulse seems embarrassing and inappropriate.[16]

So, the person who had run Channel 4 as a hybrid commercial and public service for the past four years did not have faith in its founding tenets. David Puttnam said, 'His thinking was fragmented. The last third of the speech was utterly incoherent. I remember sitting there with [Lord] Andrew MacIntosh, and we were looking at each other thinking this guy was off his trolley: thank goodness he is going, he has completely misunderstood British broadcasting.'[17] Treves was even more outraged: 'I was incandescent. It struck me as traitorous.'[18]

Jackson – who was actually reprising a contribution he had made to a Downing Street seminar – was putting his finger on something important. A generation of viewers and television producers brought up in a multichannel environment were largely indifferent to public-service television's aspirations to educate and inform that had shaped Jeremy Isaacs. He later explained,

I said 'public' no longer seemed appropriate because Channel 4's great strength is the mixture of public and private. Service? It sounded patronising, like something invented by Joseph Chamberlain. And 'broadcasting' didn't sum up the complexity of a multi-platform digital age. My point was that we needed a better language in order to sustain public support for a mixed public/private broadcasting system.[19]

These are good points. But, like King Charles more than 350 years earlier – also charged with being a traitor – Jackson had fatally misjudged the prevailing mood. What would have won an A+ star as an essay on a university media-studies course went down like a primed hand grenade in the grandeur of the Banqueting House. Jackson's lack of communications skills, and the coterie of advisers who had helped frame his speech, had let him down – and might well have prevented him from being considered later on as a potential director general, or creative leader, of the BBC.

Yet, his achievements should not be underestimated. In some respects, he remains the closest any chief executive has come to filling the shoes of Jeremy Isaacs. Where Isaacs had inspiration and courage, Jackson had his nose to the wind and a handle on the digital future. He had been there at the birth in 1980 and understood how Channel 4 had been conceived by people rooted in the 1960s, hungering for a variety of freedoms – and how it had to keep being reinvented. He poured huge amounts of intellectual and creative energy into rethinking Channel 4, transforming the scope of its activities. Where Isaacs had communications skills and charisma, Jackson was a shyer, quiet figure; yet, people listened to his suggestions with respect and attention and yearned for him to endorse their ideas. They hung on his words for critical insights into their programmes, the one or two thoughts that might transform something from a good to a great idea. They followed his advice. But, again like Isaacs, he lacked conventional executive skills and would probably have benefited from several more years running BBC Television before being pitchforked into managing a channel of his own. Crucially, despite the restraining influence of David Scott, which was not, in the end, entirely effective, there was nobody around with the feline *savoir faire* of Justin Dukes to balance and understand him.

Many creative people loved working with Jackson because he encouraged risk-taking and had a relaxed attitude to spending, and he absolutely believed in the multi-platform expansion. There was a time when he invited anyone in the channel to come to him direct with ideas, however unconventional: Sara Ramsden and Dan Chambers proposed a female erotica channel. He had a firm view about television's relationship with the world and really did believe that the term 'public-service broadcasting' had been drained of meaning. He loathed the concept of making worthy programmes on behalf of minorities, but he backed the interesting and the bold and ensured that much of Channel 4's output was refreshed.

Even Treves concedes that he was a consummate television professional:

> Under Jackson, we held on to market share, we had a lot of success-
> ful new programming – *Queer as Folk* was brilliant, seminal – and we
> spent a ton of money on new ventures which didn't work [. . .]
>
> We didn't do anything that was catastrophic, but the tide turned
> against us. On the production side, producers got bigger and stronger,
> and the balance shifted inexorably against us. We could do nothing
> about that, except try to identify and cultivate new producers and to
> nurture them. The big guys were dealing with us on level terms. That
> old sense of affinity with the channel, even of obligation, dissipated as
> time went on. Ali G – we thought we had made him, but he ran away
> fast. That happened a lot.[20]

Said Barry Cox:

> I still have a lot of time for Michael Jackson's strategy. It was aiming
> at the right things [. . .] but he didn't have the executive grip to make
> things work. There were internal tensions. He had a laid-back attitude
> to internal matters and the financial crisis that broke. It was only after-
> wards I realised he had failed to control in-fighting between his various
> barons.[21]

Peter Bazalgette agrees: 'At the end of the day, Michael Jackson did them a very good turn, even if that meant employing 100 too many people.'[22] He was instrumental in setting up E4 and Film4, which remain at the core of Channel 4's multichannel offering. And under Jackson, the percentage of imported American programmes and films on the channel went down to 26 per cent of the annual output from the 42.1 per cent he inherited from Grade, and they cost a more modest 18 per cent of the programme budget.

● ● ● ●

When it came to replacing Jackson, the channel turned yet again to the headhunter Gill Carrick. Peter Fincham, now a multimillionaire after selling his production company Talkback, was on the shortlist but judged not very impressive this time around. Also interviewed were Jana Bennett, Dawn Airey and Rupert Gavin. Barry Cox recalled that the Labour peer Waheed Alli, whose Planet 24 company was now owned by Carlton, gave a magnificent presentation but was thought to be too much of an egotist, not a team player. Treves encouraged the channel's executives on the Board, Tim Gardam and David Scott, to interview the candidates – an unusual procedure given that they would be working for the successful one. 'I wanted advice from the senior people I respected', he explained, 'and secondly I thought it would encourage strong candidates to come forward and apply if they had the opportunity to talk to them. It was very open and worthwhile.'[23]

Peter Bazalgette went through an exploratory, rather stilted interview but withdrew. He had accrued bonuses of £600,000 which the channel could not match, and he would have to pay them back to Endemol if he left. After he had decided not to take it further, he bumped into Treves at a party at the National Portrait Gallery, and Treves asked him to go on to the Selection Committee instead, which he thought strange, and he declined. By the time the also-rans had been eliminated, the process had dragged on for weeks, but finally the Board narrowed it down to two: the BBC's Mark Thompson and Michael Lynton, an American who ran the European and international arms of AOL Time Warner.

Cox said, 'The star of the selection process was Michael Lynton. He is very charming, a wonderful speaker, he clearly understands managing creatives, he has a lovely east-coast accent – he was superb and we were all very keen.'[24] Lynton was once described by the *New Yorker* as a man with 'rather sad Al Pacino eyes, a broad mouth, looks less like an executive than a post-adolescent character actor.' Educated at the International School in The Hague, then at Harvard, he had written a dissertation on E.M. Forster, taken an MBA, worked on Wall Street and chaired Penguin Books. To Channel 4's directors, he looked like the man to take them to the new world of new media, which they simply did not understand. 'They were grasping at this digital chimera', said Bazalgette.[25]

The downside was he appeared to know very little about British television and Channel 4 programmes, although the Board discovered that the BBC had got very close to appointing him instead of Greg Dyke as Director General in 1999. Robin Miller was very keen on him, and so was Tim Gardam, worried about working for Thompson, a former BBC rival. Treves said, 'It was an extraordinary run-off. You can't imagine two more different but talented people than those two. Lynton is a man of very strong intellect and I thought he would bring a breadth of vision, and was sufficiently close to the British way of life to understand it.'[26] But before he was formally offered the job, he pulled out, because his mother was ill in New York and he did not want to move to London. Meanwhile, Thompson, hearing that he was not the first choice, had also made a strategic withdrawal from the contest, and for a time it seemed as if the whole process would have to begin again.

John Cummins, the media consultant, had a Christmas party at his offices in Golden Square in Soho two days before the decisive 10 December board meeting. As they left together, David Scott asked Bazalgette if he would re-enter the race, but he declined again. At the meeting of the Appointments Board, which preceded the main Board, several non-executive directors, not knowing that Lynton had pulled out, assumed Treves would announce his appointment there and then, and they were disconcerted when he broke the bad news, fearing months of drift at a channel that urgently needed a sense of direction. David Scott, with Vanni Treves's reluctant agreement, telephoned Mark Thompson to urge him to attend the interview.

> He told me that he could not, as he had just issued a press release an-
> nouncing that he was not a candidate. I urged him to see if he could
> retrieve that press release and held on the phone whilst he sought to see
> if that were possible. Fortunately it was, and he retrieved it.[27]

They decided on a fresh approach to him. Barry Cox took over the chair and the subsequent full board meeting, which continued at Treves's office at Macfarlanes, in the City of London.

The two men met at teatime that same afternoon in the marbled reception area of the Goring Hotel, the family-run establishment close to Buckingham Palace. Thompson accepted. Once again, as had happened with Michael Grade and with Michael Jackson, the Chairman had been big-game hunting at the BBC and bagged a trophy, even if this one was the second choice. He returned to the board meeting with the news, adding that Thompson had asked for the announcement to be delayed for twenty-four hours so he could tell the BBC.

The Board agreed, if asked, to say that nothing had been decided, but there was no chance of stifling the gossip because Belinda Giles, an independent producer, happened to enter the hotel just as Treves and Thompson were shaking hands. She was in the process of making a programme for David Lloyd, the channel's current-affairs controller and immediately telephoned him with the news.[28] Andrew Brann, the Secretary to the Board, was walking back to the office after the meeting and met a commissioning editor, who asked him if there had been any developments. When he took the agreed line, he was told that the word was already out that Thompson had the job.[29]

With his BBC gardening leave and then a family death, Thompson's actual arrival was delayed until March 2002. This meant that, at a critical time, almost a year had gone by without an authoritative chief executive's hand on the tiller, and the unpleasant task of cutting jobs fell to Scott. Treves, though, was much relieved.

> When Mark was hired, it was a breath of fresh air. He was excellent – he
> couldn't have been better. We developed very quickly what I regarded
> as a near-perfect working relationship. He kept me closely informed of
> anything going on of importance or difficulty. There were no surprises.
> If I didn't hear from him that meant nothing was going on. We saw
> things the same way.[30]

Thompson's strategy, when he finally did assume control, was to cut costs by another 10 per cent, on top of the 20 per cent that Scott had implemented five months earlier, primarily through more job losses, and to refocus resources and energy on the main Channel 4. He finally cancelled *Brookside* – he has never had a problem ruthlessly cancelling programmes – and unleashed what he called, in his subsequent MacTaggart Lecture, the biggest creative reinvention of Channel 4 in its history, recapturing, as he saw it, 'the spirit of adventure and courage of Jeremy Isaacs.'

Jackson, the departing leader, naturally resented this interpretation of history. 'It was the kind of thing they teach you at business school: you rubbish the past in order to promote the future. There was a sense that he claimed to have inherited a huge problem, so he could show how easily he'd dug out of it.'[31]

Jackson was right to the extent that Thompson took over a channel that was already in the throes of radical change, much of it forced by outside events but some due to his creative leadership.

Until 2000 and the rise of *Big Brother*, it had relied historically on raising more advertising revenue from impacts among upmarket viewers rather than the sixteen- to thirty-four-year-old young adults. In 1997, the revenue split was 50 per cent ABC1s, 40 per cent young adults and 10 per cent light viewers. But *Big Brother* changed all that, because it attracted a young, principally female audience, with the ratio changing around, so half of the commercial impacts came from young people. It was what the advertisers wanted. It meant that those upmarket viewers who had long been the channel's mainstay were no longer dominant. This group contained opinion-formers, the people who ran Britain. Soon they would start to show their resentment.[32]

22

Thompson's vaulting ambition

● ● ● ●

Channel 4's twentieth anniversary in 2002 was barely celebrated. To hold a high-profile media event would have been an embarrassment for a broadcaster slashing costs and cancelling its longest-running soap opera. They were handing out redundancy notices, not flutes of champagne. Mark Thompson had decided to tackle the crisis with a back-to-basics policy, making the main Channel 4 and its programmes his priorities. It was a somewhat perverse decision, seeing that this was the start of a three-year period of radical change in the industry, with Freeview taking off as a poor man's alternative to Sky and the rapid spread of broadband internet beginning to make a reality of video on demand, after years of hype.

Absorbed in a process of retrenchment and retreat, Thompson and the Board were slow to grasp the scale of the second phase of new media because they felt vulnerable and wanted to build up a cushion of cash for protection. They also failed to take the measure of the new communications regulator, Ofcom, which, in reviewing the state of public-service television, would judge that Channel 4 had not successfully adapted its content to new media. Vanni Treves, the Chairman, later conceded that he and his colleagues had been overwhelmed by the number of opportunities for new-media ventures and could not decide between them. 'We felt constrained by the fact that our job was to protect and promote the main channel. There was always a critical diffidence about going down routes that were untested and were not entirely consistent with what we were meant to do.'[1]

Channel 4 was wedded to a digital-channel strategy devised in 1997 by Michael Jackson, who felt that the way to get noticed was to create themed new services exploiting key strengths. E4 was initially driven by acquiring pay rights to *Friends* and *ER*. FilmFour, meanwhile, traded on its reputation for backing low-budget British movies but was masquerading 'as a premium film channel without a premium product', as one board member put it.[2] In 2002, it began developing More4, around its factual programmes.

Then Freeview happened. ITV Digital, the pay digital terrestrial service, went into administration in March 2002, having lost the battle with BSkyB. It had cost its backers, Carlton and Granada, £1 billion, and Channel 4 was estimated to be losing £60 million in revenue because of its demise. It had given away set-top boxes and grossly overpaid for football rights without ensuring that the technology worked properly to provide acceptable picture quality.[3] Greg Dyke, Director General of the BBC, hatched an audacious rescue that recycled the proposition as Freeview. The flaw in the technology was fixed, and the BBC, together with Crown Castle – which owned the masts and transmitters – won the licence handed back by ITV Digital in July 2002.

The simple pitch was to persuade people to buy a cheap receiver and, if necessary, to upgrade their aerial, in order to receive about thirty channels without taking out a scary monthly subscription or defacing their homes with a dish. It did not take long for many former multichannel sceptics to realise that this was a bargain. But for a broadcaster like Channel 4, shaped by a decade of Sky's supremacy and struggling with a weak advertising market, switching tack was potentially painful. It would have required cleansing the palate of previous truisms and adjusting to the fact that the market had changed.

Within two years, Freeview was a big success, adopted by 4 million homes, rising to 8 million by 2007 to overtake BSkyB's network. A BBC-dominated invention, it had the effect of buying time for all terrestrial broadcasters. Their share of viewing held up far better in Freeview homes than in Sky Digital homes because there was less choice. Dyke also decided to use the muscle of the BBC and not renew an encryption deal with the BSkyB platform, facing down the opposition from owners of sports rights and films. But Channel 4 turned down the chance to back Freeview and take up Dyke's offer of two extra cheap slots – a costly mistake (and one also made by ITV), as slots would trade for £12 million three years later.[4]

Thompson and the Board initially said that E4 and FilmFour would not work on Freeview because they were subscription services, and they still wanted a pay platform. Instead, the commercial supremo Rob Woodward threw his energies into renegotiating improved terms with BSkyB, which bore fruit in 2004, and into finding a partner for the feeble pay-film channel, which he failed to do. Separately, despite fierce lobbying by Channel 4, the weakened Carlton and Granada were then allowed by the Government to merge into ITV plc, which drew all the regional franchises across England and Wales into one company. The merger was given the green light in October 2003 after extensive scrutiny from the Competition Commission. It meant that ITV could sell its advertising through a single sales force, controlling 52 per cent of the total television market, with the restraint that Ofcom would ensure that it did not use that powerful position to drive up the price of advertising as audiences fell.

In parallel, the system of regulation was overhauled through the Communications Act of July 2003 to apply the liberal economic licensing regimes of telecoms and the Internet to broadcasting. The Act also allowed foreign – i.e., non-European – takeovers of British television companies and the potential merger of Channel Five with BSkyB, an additional worry for Channel 4 because it would have meant that the two could buy programme rights together. The appraisals of the old ITC, with its system of informal warnings before resorting to censures, sanctions and fines, was replaced by annual statements of programme policy and performance reviews conducted after the event. There had been an almost maternal affection for Channel 4 within the ITC because it was, in effect, their baby. The harder-headed Ofcom would be strictly evidence-based and would operate to a very different tempo.

At first, Channel 4 found the terms of the new legislation relatively benign, the more so since nobody raised the spectre of privatisation. Initial debates centred on ITV and its commitment to quality news and information, and it seemed that Channel 4 was small enough, once again, to fly under the political radar. To its satisfaction, it won a reworded remit, dropping the specific obligation to cater for minority tastes and interests not served by ITV and replacing it with more general duties to be creative, to innovate, experiment and appeal to a culturally diverse society.[5]

At the time, this was barely remarked on, until evidence began to mount that the channel was drifting towards a more predictable and commercial schedule. Charles Allen, Chief Executive of ITV, became alarmed as Channel 4 began to compete with his network head-on in the evening peak time, in particular by extending and moving *Big Brother* to 9 p.m. After stealing Richard and Judy in 2001, it swooped on Paul O'Grady, and in autumn 2005 placed *Deal or No Deal* hosted by Noel Edmonds against ITV's children's programmes, which had to be moved as a result. Channel 4's original purpose as complementary to ITV was now a folk memory. But the complaints missed the point that the channel's public-service remit had always been loose, from Jeremy Isaacs' days onwards, for fear it would inhibit innovation. Back in 1996, Michael Grade had been stung when a leading ITV executive dubbed it Channel Three and a Half.[6]

The principal licence requirements, expressed in hours per week for education, news, current affairs, religion and multicultural programming, had always been exceeded, as had the tougher quotas on the percentage of originated and regionally sourced programmes set in 1997. But tests of originality and innovation were harder to devise: the ITC often seemed to work on the principle of subjective opinion and totting up industry awards, and no alternative mechanism was contained in the revised licence. The defence for a mixed schedule had always been that of cross subsidy; cheap programmes such as *Countdown* helping to pay the bills for the likes of *Channel 4 News*.

David Puttnam, who chaired an unusual parliamentary scrutiny committee to pick through the communications legislation during 2002 and helped smooth the revised remit through said:

> It [the revised remit] took away the distraction of catering for minority audiences. There was a likelihood that minorities would be well served by digital channels, so that element of the remit was increasingly inappropriate for a broadly based channel. But there was no attempt to take the foot off the gas. The aim was to make sure programmes were at the cutting edge.[7]

The rewritten licence also allowed the channel a new borrowing limit of £200 million to fund acquisitions or joint ventures, though in the event it remained unused.

● ● ● ●

When the forty-four-year-old Thompson finally arrived, in March 2002, he sported a fashionable auburn stubble and wore loud checked shirts without a tie, as if consciously trying to shake off the staid BBC image. He told the Board of the importance of focusing on the creative culture of Channel 4 and impressing on junior commissioners and independents the need for innovation, creativity and risk-taking.[8]

But he found Horseferry Road a tense place, lacking team spirit, with the different departments seemingly pulling in opposite directions, principally 4Ventures and Channel 4 itself. Many felt that he saw the job simply as a stepping-stone to his ambition – fulfilled sooner than he would then have guessed – to succeed Greg Dyke as Director General of the BBC. Commercial experience would burnish his credentials. A skilled broadcaster, with the ability to dissect an editorial dilemma and make a cogent case in a crisis, he had risen confidently through the BBC ranks throughout the 1980s and 1990s and now had to prove that he was chief-executive material.

Thompson's first impression was that he had arrived at an organisation in a state of shock amounting to paralysis after an exhausting year that had profoundly shaken its confidence.

> I was really surprised that Channel 4 had no in-house strategy. In the BBC there is very basic sense that we are operating with a strategic map: we all have a working model of what the BBC is trying to do. BSkyB also has a very firm strategy. That didn't exist at Channel 4. When I opened the cupboard at Channel 4 there was nothing there. Michael Grade had run it on targeting sixteen-to-thirty-fours, and ABC1s, and buying American programmes. I needed four or five years to build up a strategy.

There was a sense that E4 had leached all the energy out of the main Channel 4. David Scott was in a very dejected state, Tim Gardam [. . .] hated what the channel had become. Andy Barnes in advertising was suicidal. We were worried we would go bust. What we did was quite brutal.[9]

His first objective was to try to stop the losses at 4Ventures. He almost halved the marketing budget from £29 million to £17 million in 2003 and began to get a growth plan together. Commercially, *Big Brother* was at a high water mark but, as Barnes was already pointing out, the problem with its success was that it created the perception of Channel 4 as being a big channel for ten weeks of the year and a small channel for the other forty-two.[10]

Thompson confirmed the purchase of the terrestrial rights to *The Simpsons*, finalised in February 2002. It was needed to shore up the early evening happy hour and to bolster defences against multichannel competition. He also recommitted Channel 4 to more drama series such as *Teachers* and *No Angels*, a policy laid out by Jackson which had drifted significantly off course under Gardam. For some time, the screenwriter Paul Abbott had tried to write about his feckless family upbringing on a council estate in Burnley with no parents in charge, but he failed to turn it into a workable drama until Thompson and Tessa Ross, the Head of Drama, encouraged him to try again.[11] *Shameless* made its debut in January 2004, attracting an audience of 2.6 million, signalling the end of the channel's long hunt for at least one home-produced drama series able to run for years.

At the Edinburgh Television Festival in August 2002, Thompson gave the MacTaggart Lecture, entitled 'Television's Creative Deficit'. 'Right now we're trying to approach the Channel 4 schedule as if we are launching an entirely new channel', he said. In fact, the biggest problem was that £40 million had been taken away from programmes during the 2001 panic, and restoring the cash from cutting overheads took time. He said he and the Government would be looking at ways of underpinning and guaranteeing the channel's core programme budget in future years, but he stopped short of asking for a slice of the BBC licence fee, though he did describe the corporation as wallowing in a jacuzzi of cash. Thompson had assured his board that summer that he would not be making any proposal to ask for a government handout or a return to the funding formula. Nor did he see a problem before the middle of the decade. But this was the start of a long and muddled pitch for government concessions.

A wave of further redundancies began in September as staff dropped from 1,158 to 857.[12] As part of the cuts, he closed the multicultural department under Jasmin Anwar and compensated by obliging all commissioners to reflect Britain's diversity. The channel's own staffing reflected this objective, with 9.6 per cent coming from ethnic minorities, although such staff didn't necessarily have access to the purse strings. Sue Woodford, the channel's first Multicultural Commissioner and the wife of the Labour peer Lord Hollick, went to see Thompson to protest at the closure of the department, but he was unmovable.[13] The talk internally was of making retrenchments in sport and soap opera; there was debate about how long test-match cricket was sustainable, especially once its champion, David Brook, had left in autumn 2002.

When Controller of BBC2, Thompson had backed an ambitious young chef named Jamie Oliver, who upset the BBC in 2001 by appearing in Sainsbury's commercials. Channel 4 took him up for the successful *Jamie's Kitchen*, in which he tried to mould a band of unemployed youngsters into disciplined restaurant chefs and staff. It led to an even more popular follow-up, *Jamie's School Dinners*, in 2005, described as a near-perfect public-service programme because it fostered a huge debate, outlawed turkey twizzlers from school menus and forced a change in government policy.

Another breakthrough was *Operatunity*, commissioned by Jan Younghusband in 2001 and reaching the screen in February 2003. Although it cost only £900,000, it was the channel's most important arts programme for years, based on the possibility that a potential Pavarotti could be discovered driving a bus. 'I had to see how to make the live arts exciting on television', said Younghusband.[14] The two operatic talents it uncovered were Jane Gilchrist, a Tesco checkout operator, and Denise Leigh, a visually impaired housewife, who were cast in a performance of *Rigoletto* with English National Opera – the channel's first series on opera since *Harry Enfield's Guide to Opera* a decade earlier.

The series came from one of the channel's original suppliers, Diverse Productions, who followed it up with *Musicality*, casting a range of performers in the musical *Chicago*, which attracted a larger following of younger viewers and was an inspiration for the two popular BBC series in which Andrew Lloyd Webber held public talent contests to find stars for musical revivals – *How Do You Solve a Problem Like Maria?* (originally offered to Channel 4 but turned down) and *Any Dream Will Do*, as well as ITV's *Grease Is the Word*. Younghusband also got backing from Jackson and Gardam for *The Death of Klinghoffer*, a specially commissioned opera set on a Mediterranean cruise ship hijacked by Palestinian terrorists. Based on a true story, this extraordinary John Adams piece cost £1.7 million, of which the channel put up £1.5 million. Thompson proudly held a special screening at the Barbican in 2003, and the film was selected for the Sundance Festival in America. Oddly, Channel 4 had moved back to the 1980s Isaacs model of being a patron of the arts. The problem was that special events needed to be balanced with more regular arts series, and Channel Five began to steal a march with its gallery tours of great exhibitions.

An ambitious filmed opera was all very well, though, but there was still resentment over the rough treatment handed out to FilmFour Productions. At issue was whether the closure during 2002 was so brutal that good ideas were lost. Some were, including the successful cult film, *Shaun of the Dead* (2004). Tessa Ross, who was asked to take over the rump of FilmFour with a reduced budget of £10 million a year, said: 'Film projects with perhaps four years of development were thrown out of the window and the writers and directors took them elsewhere. With the seed corn gone, there was nothing in development. And they had optioned some fantastic material.'[15]

An unrepentant Thompson points out that he saved Channel 4's involvement in *Touching the Void* (2003), the Spanish-language *The Motorcycle Diaries* (2004) and *The Last King of Scotland* (2006), which won an Oscar in 2006. He believes he made two mistakes during his two years as Chief Executive, of which FilmFour was not one.

> The first was new media. I was painfully aware that Channel 4 didn't have anything more compelling than the services [twenty-four-hour webcams, etc.] around *Big Brother*. I should have put a bit more heat on that area. The penny had dropped, I had my conversion, but then I was gone.[16]

Andy Grumbridge, the Managing Editor of Channel 4's Interactive Division, confirms this: 'The mood at Channel 4 was to hunker down [. . .] At that stage we were not core to strategic development.'[17]

Thompson's second big mistake was not to put E4 onto Freeview, because he wanted to maintain it as a subscription channel.

> I thought there was no question about it. At the BBC we like having the UKTV channels, we like to understand the subscription and advertising markets. This was deep in my head. Spot advertising was iffy. Surely some position in pay was sensible? This is the thinking that led me to backing the wrong horse over Freeview.[18]

It was a nightmare trying to run an advertising-funded business in 2002–3. A small recovery in 2002 and the cut in overheads allowed the programme budget to be restored by 7.5 per cent to £430 million, but then 2003 turned sticky. E4 was performing better than expected by 2002, and taking it free to air would lose between £20 million and £30 million a year from subscription income. 'We'd had a near death experience and we were pretty shaky. But if I had my time again I would probably be braver, and take E4 free to air.'[19]

One of those who suggested putting E4 on to Freeview to Thompson was Stephen Carter, the new Chief Executive of the regulator Ofcom, just installed in a smart new building on the Thames. The personable former Chief Executive of the advertising agency J. Walter Thompson, rebuilding his career after a failed stint with cable company NTL, led an intellectually energetic cadre of economists, including Ed Richards, a former BBC strategist who had helped frame the Communications

Act while an adviser to the Prime Minister. Aided by Tim Suter and Robin Foster, they made a formidable team to mount a far-reaching three-stage review of how to maintain and strengthen public-service broadcasting in the years ahead. When it was launched in October 2003, nobody was fully prepared for the torch it shone into the nooks and crannies of the industry or how the slogan 'Knowledge is power' would translate into reality.

The report would not be published until February 2005, but in advance of it, Thompson and the Board decided to lobby against the idea that was gaining ground in some circles that Channel 4 should be charged a market price for use of the broadcasting spectrum – for which ITV paid but which Channel 4 was allowed to use for nothing. To support his case, Thompson predicted that his channel faced a potential shortfall of £100 million, but Ofcom never accepted this figure, which it called 'slippery' and looked as though it had been plucked from thin air. Both the Regulator and the Government were convinced that Thompson was crying wolf – a belief reinforced when the channel funded a temporary Soho House club at the Edinburgh Television Festival in 2005 and 2006 and served oysters rather than the conventional canapés. More solid evidence that Thompson had been exaggerating his plight came after he left the channel: it rebuilt its cash balances to more than £120 million by 2004, and by 2006 was earning £692 million in advertising income, £130 million more than predicted back in 2002.

Also under way as Thompson took over was a review of the programme-supply market undertaken by the ITC in response to pressure from the Producers Alliance for Cinema and Television (PACT), the independent producers' organisation. Chaired by Eileen Gallagher, PACT had gained the ear of the Department of Culture, Media and Sport, which oversaw a shift in the balance of power between the broadcasters and independent companies under new codes of practice drawn up by Ofcom. From the end of 2003, broadcasters would buy licences for the programmes they commissioned and paid for, with 85 per cent of the secondary rights remaining with the producers, a neat reversal of the previous deal. The objective was to encourage the growth of fewer, stronger production companies and the export of successful programme formats, such as *Supernanny* (from Ricochet, a fast-growing independent), and *Wife Swap,* which is exactly what happened. The independents won the opportunity to build up real assets, instead of being the cost-plus producers they had been since the start of Channel 4. A number built up sizeable businesses and either amalgamated, accepted takeover offers or floated on the stock exchange.

The biggest negative impact was on Channel 4, which estimates that the ruling cost it £10 million of profit each year as the role of its distributor, Channel 4 International, evaporated. Thompson was accused of not lobbying hard enough to fight the change or at least win some compensation, but he argues that the cause was lost when, in 2003, Greg Dyke tactlessly remarked to the Parliamentary Culture, Media and Sports Committee that the BBC was not there to make independents rich.

> That was a catastrophic remark. The BBC then missed its 25 per cent independent quota, and that was appalling. Channel 4's position was undermined by the BBC, which was on the back foot, and PACT was able to drive a hard deal. In his dark moments Luke Johnson [who became the channel's next chairman] thinks I caved in because I knew I was coming back to the BBC and the deal with PACT would undermine Channel 4. It's not true.[20]

Although he was clearly worried about whether the channel could remain financially viable on its own,[21] Thompson maintained his refusal to lobby for a slice of the BBC licence fee. Again, his critics thought it was because he knew he was going back there, although his defence is that he did not want the channel's freedom curtailed by taking public money – he knew at first hand the scrutiny the BBC worked under. His most significant decision was to back a radical idea, a potential merger of Channel 4 with Channel Five, which the Board cautiously agreed to explore during 2003. He then wanted to seek trust status for Channel 4, along the lines of the Scott Trust, which owned the *Guardian* newspaper, and transfer into it the original shares, which had passed from the old IBA to Channel 4 in 1992.

The theory was that the enlarged company would support the loss-making public-service side of Channel 4. They could merge their two advertising sales forces, together representing around a third of the market, to compete more effectively against ITV and could rationally organise their digital channels as a suite of complementary niche services. There had long been vague ideas that the two channels had a future together. In 1985, when the spare frequencies for a fifth television service were identified, it was thought possible that Channel 4 might run it. The 1988 Broadcasting White Paper had suggested that one of the three options for Channel 4 might be a joint operation with Five. Before the fifth channel was eventually launched in 1997, Greg Dyke, Chairman of the winning consortium, offered Channel 4 a stake in it, but the Board turned him down, with the result that the two channels competed expensively for imported programmes.

The first conversations with a view to reviving the idea took place in April 2003. Thompson, David Scott and Rob Woodward attended a dinner with Five's shareholders, including Clive Hollick, who controlled a 35-per-cent stake.[22] Hollick, indeed, had been thinking of the possibility of such a merger for some time and had approached Richard Hooper and Stephen Carter of Ofcom to find out whether the Regulator would have any objections.[23] Says Carter, 'It was not our place to say to a Channel Five shareholder that a merger of Five and Channel 4 is something we would block. At most we would indicate that it clearly presented issues.'[24]

John Newbigin, a former adviser to the Labour Party leader Neil Kinnock and now a lobbyist for Channel 4, had breakfast with Hollick at the Labour Party conference in September. 'His pitch was that the only way these two channels would survive was to get together', Newbigin recalls.[25] He argued that Channel 4 could be run much more efficiently and commercially and generate profits of £150 million to £200 million. 'Clive's huge enthusiasm for it was not something I had been previously aware of.'[26] Thompson could see clearly that there would be considerable operational benefits.

> Suppose Channel 4 cancelled *Big Brother* – it could move to Channel Five. Even if something is fading or creatively on the way out, it can turn up against you as incoming fire on another channel: that's the nightmare. With a second channel you could send it there. Then *Home and Away* might appeal to *Hollyoaks* viewers on Channel 4. The notion of a bigger ecology is tempting: you can do an awful lot with two terrestrial channels, combined with an idea of trying to get a little media group together [. . .] The idea was to broaden our commercial base, so cross-subsidising the public-service broadcasting side to shore up Channel 4.[27]

It fell to Jonathan Thompson, Channel 4's Director of Strategy, to prepare the ground during the autumn of 2003. He believes that the plans for both the merger and the trust could have got further if the case had been made more carefully and convincingly. According to Newbigin, the problem was that, although the commercial benefits were clear, insufficient thought had been given to the organisation and structure. There were talks with Gordon Brown's adviser, former investment banker Shriti Vadera. Thompson was firing off a series of internal papers to the Treasury. A recipient of one Channel 4 missive rang Newbigin to say, 'It's so economically illiterate I've put it in the waste-paper bin.'[28]

David Scott was concerned that after merger, Channel Five's shareholders would lobby to change Channel 4's statutory corporation structure so that Five's shareholders could ultimately own the whole joint operation. He believed any relationship with Channel Five could only emerge if Channel 4 first became a trust, which would not be vulnerable to this sort of destabilisation. But any such change of structure would require government agreement and legislation.

Every two years, the most senior executives in broadcasting spend three days discussing the future of the industry in King's College, Cambridge, at a conference organised by the Royal Television Society. By the time of the September 2003 gathering, almost half the population had access to some form of multichannel television, and the proposed merger of Granada and Carlton was a racing certainty. The conference theme, 'The End Game', looked forward to 2010 when the analogue signal would be switched off, leaving digital as the only game in town. Spectrum Strategy Consulting, led by Janice Hughes, an engaging Cambridge economist, prepared five scenarios in an exercise created to stimulate debate. Channel 4 emerged as a serious loser in all but one of her five models, winning only if the BBC's licence fee was top-sliced by around a fifth in 2010 and most of the money handed to the channel. In all the other scenarios, it lost alarming chunks of audiences and advertising.[29]

If ITV were to become a purely commercial network, ditching its public-service remit and reinvesting half the savings in entertainment programming, Channel 4's slice of the advertising cake would fall by a quarter, squeezed as it was between BSkyB with its soaring subscriptions, the BBC with a generous licence fee and an unfettered ITV. Thompson was sympathetic to the basic analysis but delivered a spirited criticism of the Spectrum model because it assumed he and Channel Five – the other big loser – would do nothing to react. Channel Five's Chief Executive, Jane Lighting, was more upbeat, speculating, correctly, that the growing success of Freeview would have the effect of limiting competition.

This was followed by a platform debate between the four men who had served as Chief Executive of Channel 4, with Jeremy Isaacs and Michael Grade vying to see who could sport the more garish socks. Michael Jackson, who looked uncomfortable, said the threat to the channel was exaggerated. 'Despite new media, people still have a pyschological desire for the collective experience that television is uniquely placed to serve', he said. Thompson observed the issue for all of them when running the channel had been how to meet the commercial pressures but leave room for some non-commercial decisions. 'None of us has run Channel 4 to maximise revenue, profit or audience share.'[30]

When privatisation was raised, Grade, who had safely shepherded the channel through two previous threats, said there was no point to it: Channel 4 would simply become a clone of ITV or Sky One. He added, 'The BBC is a natural partner for Channel 4.'[31]

Isaacs was against privatisation at any cost but suggested a Scott Trust formula might offer an alternative. 'To me, independence and the ability to make non-commercial decisions alongside commercial ones is what the channel is all about and would be lost if privatisation happened. I am not saying I would never consider Trust ownership.'[32]

From the floor, the merchant banker Anthony Fry predicted that privatisation would happen in the next five to ten years because the Treasury would not be able to resist it. The audience, asked to vote on the likelihood, was split fifty-fifty. At this stage, there was no political pressure to privatise. But Channel 4 was sending out confusing messages. The convention debates reinforced its sense of vulnerability.

In October, Thompson told the Board that the shareholders of Channel Five would like to see as wide as possible a collaboration with Channel 4 and that he would hold further discussions. Yet, according to Newbigin,

It became clearer and clearer that the only person who believed in it was Mark. The rest of us were having an extraordinary job selling it, because we didn't believe in it. He got pretty irritated. Mark can be quite forceful: he said it was the only game in town and we had to make it work.[33]

Robin Miller, the businessman on the Board, saw it as a sensible if unlikely solution, and Barry Cox recalls that they gave Thompson enough rope to have a go.

Ofcom's first material interaction with the channel was in July 2003, when it chose Vanni Treves's successor after winning the argument with the outgoing ITC as to which body should make the decision. Everyone agreed it was time for a change. Treves had served for six years, and there were concerns about the Board's grasp of issues, as Carter explains:

The Board then was a collection of talented individuals overseeing a core channel and a series of underperforming pay ventures and a film business going nowhere. The Board was at that point slightly a trophy board; it was a glamorous thing to be on. It was going to have to be more involved.[34]

The Selection Panel comprised the Ofcom Chairman Lord David Currie, Richard Hooper, Carter and an independent panel member, Anne Robinson (former Chairperson of the National Association of Pension Funds), with Gill Carrick again appointed to muster the candidates. When she produced her first shortlist, Carter complained that it was too predictable.

We at Ofcom said the world is becoming much more competitive and the channel is going to be facing significant financial and commercial pressures, and took the view Channel 4 should have a chairman with a completely fresh perspective – someone with commercial experience, but not necessarily broadcasting experience [. . .] We also needed someone with significant empathy with public-service broadcasting. We were not looking for someone who would want to privatise or sell the asset because, even though at that point we had not said Channel 4 should not be privatised, it was pretty clear to me, David and Ed Richards that was where the Public Service Broadcasting review was heading.[35]

So, Carrick came back with a fresh list, this time including Luke Johnson, an entrepreneur who had made a fortune from Pizza Express and who was the son of Paul Johnson, the polemical journalist who had dubbed Grade Britain's pornographer-in-chief. Luke Johnson had been a devoted Channel 4 viewer ever since he was

a medical student at Magdalen College, Oxford. David Currie and Robinson conducted the final interview with him at the Goring Hotel. Currie put to him that they
knew deal-making was in his blood, but what about the media? Johnson responded
by telling him to examine his family tree.

The final decision did not come for another week, during which word spread that
Penny Hughes, a former Coca-Cola executive, would be appointed. Johnson was
in the middle of a board meeting for a dentistry business he had invested in when
Currie's call came. Convinced that he would not get the job, he declined to take the
call; but ten minutes later, Currie came through again, convincing his personal assistant that the matter was urgent. Johnson took the call in the boardroom. When
Currie offered him the position, he rose quickly from his chair and said, 'Of course
I'll accept.'[36] The press reaction to his appointment took Johnson by surprise. There
was a barrage of sneering comment about a pizza man taking over a cultural icon.
People were flabbergasted. Sir Christopher Bland, Chairman of British Telecom and
a former Chairman of the BBC, told him, 'I can't think what they were doing. On the
other hand it might be the making of you.'[37]

But would it be the making of Channel 4, or its undoing? The Ofcom panel
were aware of his shortcomings, in particular that he was neither a diplomat nor a
charmer. Carter explained:

> We recommended Luke in the final analysis because he cared passion-
> ately about the brand and the business, and he wanted the job a lot. It
> wasn't a vanity job for him. He'd made a considerable amount of money,
> he was a renowned deal-maker, he watched the channel, he understood
> the product, he believed in what it did, he thought there was absolutely
> no case to privatise it as long as the owners of the investment made the
> necessary future investment [. . .] I wouldn't say we agreed with abso-
> lutely everything he said, but he had done his homework. We thought
> at the time he would be a very good contrast to Mark, who has many
> virtues but he is not a commercial animal, either instinctively or by
> experience.[38]

The brainy top Ofcom team felt assured that Thompson's status as a broadcaster
would compensate for any shortfall.

Johnson's first problem was that two days after his appointment, on 28 January 2004,
he faced losing his Chief Executive. With the publication of the devastating Hutton
Report into the BBC's reporting of the origins of the Iraq war, first the BBC Chairman
Gavyn Davies resigned, followed by the Director General, Greg Dyke, who telephoned
Thompson to give him advance warning that he was going and to urge him to return
to the BBC. The event provided the most dramatic episode in Jon Snow's career as

presenter of *Channel 4 News*, when Alastair Campbell stormed into the studios to give a live, unscheduled interview blasting the BBC. As soon as Johnson heard the news, he realised that Thompson might be tempted back and asked him about his intention. Says Thompson, 'From that moment, Luke was keeping a very watchful eye on me. We all knew what was at stake: it was a very momentous week.'[39]

On 19 February, *Broadcast* magazine reported Thompson as saying that he would not apply for the BBC job, and Thompson continued to develop his plans for a Channel 4/Channel Five merger. Johnson, anxious not to alienate his Chief Executive and give him a further incentive to leave, concealed the fact that he thought the merger was a bad idea. At Johnson's first board meeting, Thompson presented a discussion paper on its feasibility, and it was agreed that he would enter into more detailed discussions with Channel Five's main shareholders, get specialist legal advice on the trust process and, on the insistence of Ofcom, appoint financial advisers.[40]

The Board's deliberations were leaked to Janine Gibson of the *Guardian*, who rang Peter Bazalgette for confirmation. He declined to comment and rang the Chief Press Officer, Matt Baker, to tell him Gibson was about to break the story, which she did on 27 February. Johnson and Mark Thompson were furious. Johnson says that Thompson initially accused Bazalgette of leaking the story, which was not the case. He subsequently wrote to Bazalgette to clear this up – the leak was suspected to have come from elsewhere. Johnson warned the whole Board at the next meeting that there would be dire consequences if anything like it happened again.[41]

With the story out in the open, David Puttnam had lunch with Thompson on 4 March at the Quirinale, a quiet basement Italian restaurant near Parliament. 'He pitched me the Channel Five move', Puttnam recalls.

> I couldn't make head nor tail of it. I couldn't understand the rationale. I think the purpose of the lunch was to enlist me as a supporter but I dissed the idea. Then when I asked him what was he going to do about the BBC, he went on about how happy he was at Channel 4.[42]

Thompson then wrote an article for the *Guardian*, exploring a little on the trust and merger idea. On 18 March, Thompson met Richard Hooper, Stephen Carter and Ed Richard and took them through a board paper on the proposed merger. He returned to present the idea formally to the Ofcom content board twelve days later. Over the course of two hours, he argued that single channels could not survive in the modern world, that they needed to be in groups, that consolidation would be good for both sides. Channel 4 was absolutely on its own, and it made commercial sense to put a more formidable group together. 'My reading is that Mark and the team had an idea, not without merit, but an idea not fully worked through', says Carter.[43]

Hooper, chairing the Content Board, was more specific:

The problem facing Ofcom was terribly simple: that if Channels 4 and Five got together, then somewhere in the chain there would be dividends being paid, because shareholders don't invest in companies just for the fun of it [. . .] You are putting a non-profit distributing broadcaster together with a for-profit distributing commercial broadcaster, and therefore you could not square the circle that this will continue to be a true public-service broadcaster [. . .] You couldn't get around that. It seemed to destroy the very strength Channel 4 offered, and we never got an answer to that.[44]

Thompson also lobbied Tessa Jowell, but she did not believe the merger would materialise. She thought he was playing with it – not serious about it, just looking at the possibility.

In April, Thompson had to present the channel's annual report to the press, with rumours still rampant about his imminent defection to the BBC. When asked about it, he replied,

I have to say the whole issue of my contractual arrangements I regard as a private matter between me and Channel 4. I absolutely intend to stay at Channel 4 and deal with the uncertainty and challenging question of Channel 4's future. I don't intend to take a part in any process leading to any kind of recruitment at the BBC. I have the job I want.

Later that month, Michael Grade was appointed BBC Chairman, and his first priority was to find a Director General. Within a week of arriving, he had won his man over. Thompson insists he was reluctant to go:

The thing is, I loved Channel 4 and I didn't want to do this [BBC] job. Every emotional instinct was to stay at Channel 4 – it's a fantastic place, I loved the people, I loved its size, I thought we were distinctly turning a corner [. . .] This was shockingly bad timing for me. I still try to avoid Horseferry Road; I hate driving past. But if I was the right person to come back to the BBC, it seemed self-indulgent to take a personal view.[45]

He went for an interview on 19 May, and three days later, on the Friday, Grade told him the job was his. It was yet another bad exit, and Johnson was furious.

He didn't tell me. That's why I was so cross. I learnt about it on the news. It was one time I lost my temper with him. He had broken an undertaking back in February that he would tell me if he was called for an interview. He assured me. But I learnt about it when Kevin Lygo phoned me to tell me there was a press conference shortly to start at the BBC, to break the news [. . .] So I called him on his mobile. What I said was unprintable. I was very pleased to get hold of him on the mobile because if I had not let off steam to him I might have let off steam to a journalist [. . .] He's a good manager, Mark, but he's even better at his career management.[46]

Thompson's brief term at Channel 4 was disruptive. He started a big debate about Channel 4's future, casting doubt on its ability to remain independent, without properly preparing the ground or considering the downside, that by flirting with Channel Five the channel courted privatisation. On the programming side, he did back some edgy programming, from *The Autopsy* to illusionist Derren Brown's Russian roulette stunt, but he also doubled *Big Brother*'s output and was unnecessarily ruthless with FilmFour.

There was a haggle over holding him to gardening leave, then a decidedly cool farewell drinks in the boardroom, and that was that. 'That's this industry – you don't get unambitious shrinking violets in the media world do you?' Johnson observes.[47] Left in the lurch, he decided to act as Executive Chairman to hold the fort; and that would colour the course of events.

23

Two men with L plates

• • • •

On Friday, 22 May 2004, the day Mark Thompson walked out on Channel 4 to return to the BBC, a man with long sideburns, wearing a T-shirt and jeans, arrived at his home in the commuter village of Chaldon, Surrey, his laptop bag slung over his shoulder. A passer-by might have mistaken him for a successful country and western singer, but it was, in fact, Andy Duncan, the BBC's Marketing Director, who had overseen Thompson's press conference earlier in the day. 'Channel 4 . . .' he mused, as he loped the last few yards towards his front door, 'that would be the perfect job for me.'[1]

In seventeen years, this driven, casually dressed tyro had risen from a fast-track graduate trainee to become Unilever's UK Marketing Director, running its food businesses, which included margarine spreads, and then a senior executive in charge of a €4 billion sector of Unilever's food business in Europe. Now aged forty-one, he was the anthesis of the trendy, competitive men and women who ran the media industry. He revels in his modest roots. His father, a printer, is an Irish Protestant from Belfast and his mother a former secretary from Croydon. He was brought up on a housing estate in South Croydon with two sisters and went to Gilbert Scott Junior School in the middle of another estate. From there, he won a scholarship to Whitgift, a leading public school in Croydon, and he has never left the area: he and his entire extended family still live within three miles of each other.

'I had a fairly unremarkable upbringing. There is no background of great achievement in my family. I spent most of my time at Whitgift basically being a rebel, mucking about, doing lots of sport. Hockey, football, tennis.'[2] He started applying himself in the sixth form when he took business studies for A Level, then went to the University of Manchester's Institute of Science and Technology in 1981 and took a degree in management science. He is an evangelical Christian who believes in the efficacy of prayer and attends the modest Croham Road Baptist Church in Croydon. At the church's youth club, at the age of seventeen, he met Jocelyn, a designer and artist, and they were married there when he was twenty-four. Most of his best friends are people he grew up with, and he plays hockey and football with old schoolfriends.

After a year at NatWest's marketing department, followed by four months work-ing for disabled children in America, he made a trip to Calcutta in the summer of 1983 to look at the missionary work of Mother Theresa. 'I learnt more in that sum-mer than most years of my life. I was deeply shocked. Calcutta was worse then than now, just appalling. It gave me a perspective on life which I don't think I ever lost.'[3] He is, in short, an intense, focused, optimistic and pious man who smiles a lot and is completely lacking in show-business pzazz.

> I think of myself as down to earth: what you see is what you get. I am
> a great believer in balance, so for me home is always more important
> than work, and family and friends are a really important part of my life.
> I think you can get work out of proportion.[4]

With his commitment to family life, Duncan did not want to travel abroad a lot – an almost mandatory rite of passage to the top tier of Unilever. Instead, he decided to join the BBC, where along with marketing he also ran communications and audi-ence research, deciding which programmes were promoted on air – a power televi-sion producers understand. So his connection with television was mostly as a viewer, as an advertiser with Unilever and then as a marketing expert. He was not seeped in media culture. At the end of the working day at Broadcasting House, he would leave promptly and go home, not head for the Groucho Club or a screening at BAFTA, unless duty called.

'The marketing discipline was very similar to programme commissioning', he maintains. 'They are the same tribe. You are a guardian of the slot or the strand.'[5] In his three years at the BBC, Duncan had applied his Unilever experience of research-ing markets to providing the assurance for the leap to Freeview and the launch of its digital channels, including CBBC, cbeebies, BBC3 and BBC4.

His background had also moulded a stubborn character. When convinced he is right, Duncan does not waver and is not afraid to punch out the same message again and again.

A day or two after organising Thompson's debut press conference, Duncan rang his former boss Greg Dyke, whose sacking had created the vacancy that Thompson had now filled, and asked if he was a credible candidate for Channel 4's top job. Dyke did not try to deter him, so he consulted former colleagues at Unilever, where he had trained, and they, too, were moderately encouraging. Dyke had recruited him to professionalise the BBC's marketing, which he had done, as well as playing a leading role in the successful Freeview project. Although to outsiders he had no

obvious qualifications for leading a public-service broadcaster, Dyke was prepared
to give him a positive reference, as was Niall Fitzgerald, the former Chief Executive
of Unilever, now Chairman of Reuters.

Some days later, he received an approach from a headhunter, Jan Hall of Spencer
Stewart, asking whether he was interested in joining Vodafone. He turned her down
but discovered that she was also advising Luke Johnson about Thompson's replacement – a job for which his name had not yet figured on her radar. So he phoned her
and told her he would be interested in Channel 4.[6] That set the wheels in motion.
Dyke put in a word for him with Johnson, who had talked to several professional
broadcasters, including Jana Bennett, BBC Director of Television, and Channel Five's
Dawn Airey. Johnson invited Duncan for an interview, and a week later, on 2 July, his
appointment was announced.

It was a product of unusual circumstances. After losing Thompson, Luke Johnson
had decided to run the channel himself for a while – an irresistible opportunity to
learn how it really worked. He loved doing it, but his hands-on style quickly provoked
tensions. Ofcom looked on nervously as this energetic businessman took some short
cuts. His abrasive treatment of Peter Bazalgette over the leak of its talks with Channel Five was not the only clash with eminent directors – he also had a bumpy few
months with Lord Puttnam when he became Deputy Chairman in February 2006.[7]
Nor did he get along with David Scott, the loyal but conservative Deputy Chief Executive, who personified the history and traditions of the channel but who resolved
to leave in 2005.

Although he could be warm, Johnson could also be habitually brusque. He insisted on monthly board meetings and showered directors with information and
e-mails. At his first February board meeting, finding that a key policy paper had
been sent off before the Board had seen it, he issued a tart order: send it to us first,
or at least at the same time.[8] Between 2003 and 2006, there was a complete change of
non-executive directors, encouraged by Ofcom. At first, the emphasis was on enterprise and youth, with a later leavening of older public-service hands to appease the
Culture Secretary, Tessa Jowell.[9]

Johnson took charge because everyone told him of the dangers of drift, pointing
to the interregnum between Jackson and Thompson two years earlier. The entire
media industry was in a state of flux. The newly merged ITV was distracted and
haemorrhaging viewers, and the BBC was trying to regroup after the Hutton Report.
'It was not a time to mess around. I just did it. It was traumatic. Thompson was a very
formidable figure and to lose him was a blow. People were saying he was pretty irre-
placeable. So I cleared my desk.'[10] Stephen Carter, Chief Executive of Ofcom noted, 'It
was a tough gig. He held the ship steady. He was there three or four days a week.'[11]

Johnson decided that his priority was to retain the services of Kevin Lygo, the
Director of Television, hired back from Channel Five the year before to replace Tim

Gardam. Gardam's management style had spread fear and unhappiness among commissioners and the scheduling team, from which they were only just recovering by the summer of 2004.

For example, Dorothy Byrne, the Controller of News and Current Affairs, felt obliged to appeal to the Human Resources department after an especially ill-tempered exchange and made Gardam sign a letter promising not to shout at her or cause her 'psychological pain.'[12] Others were not so resilient and left – including the gifted Peter Grimsdale, who had played a key role in driving the channel's success in the 1990s and coordinating *Big Brother*'s expansion into a multimedia event.[13] One of Channel 4's most senior figures, Sara Ramsden, who moved to run Sky One in 2002 and chaired the Edinburgh Television Festival the following year, put on a discussion there about bullying, to ventilate a widespread issue in the television industry.[14]

Byrne's quarrels with Gardam had not only been about his manner towards her but also about what he was doing to her programmes, particularly *Dispatches*, which he cut and shifted around the schedules when he arrived in 2002. When Lygo replaced him, he resolved to restore current affairs to the heart of the prime-time schedule. 'Here was this bloke from entertainment bringing current affairs to the fore', said Byrne. 'I don't think people quite realise the extraordinary things Lygo has done. *Dispatches* went up from twenty-two to forty editions a year while *Unreported World*, a Michael Jackson invention, went from eight to twenty.'[15] In short, Lygo had put the programming team on the front foot again in most areas.

The Director of Television is a critical figure. Lygo and Johnson, both metropolitan sophisticates, hit it off at once, and in spring 2004, the Board felt able to increase the programme budget to its highest ever, £449 million, then add another £20 million for extras, including more episodes of *Shameless*, a fourth series of *Teachers* and the Friday entertainment, *Bo' Selecta*. Company profits had recovered to £45 million, three times the 2002 figure, and the cash cushion was back to £75 million. They both knew they had some strong and varied programmes in the pipeline from the gritty *Sex Traffic* that autumn to *Jamie's School Dinners* (a breakthrough in campaigning public-service television), *Green Wing*, *Sugar Rush* and *The Government Inspector* for 2005.

Although Johnson was enjoying his role as Acting Chief Executive, he clearly had to find a replacement for Thompson fairly soon. He met potential candidates on his own and formed a selection committee of Kevin Lygo, Rob Woodward, Barry Cox and Robin Miller. The June board meeting was told that there was a reasonably strong shortlist of seven, although at that stage Andy Duncan had not been interviewed. In the end, it came down to a choice between Duncan and Peter Fincham, whose team at Talkback had helped transform entertainment for Channel 4. Cox, the only one with practical experience of television, favoured Fincham but was outvoted.[16] Channel 4 thus passed up the chance to appoint one of its most successful suppliers, an under-stated impresario, and the BBC subsequently hired Fincham to run BBC1.

Johnson reflected later, 'I think Fincham would have been OK, but the job isn't about being a brilliant programme-maker – you have to handle a diverse and unusual group of stakeholders. The regulatory and political aspects of the job are not recognised.'[17] Johnson thought the ceaseless lobbying would have driven Fincham to distraction, although he did offer to make him a non-executive director as compensation. (Fincham turned it down because he was joining the BBC.) Johnson also thought that Fincham and Lygo were too similar and that Lygo could well take care of the creative side. 'We agreed Andy Duncan was a more interesting candidate', he said.[18]

Duncan had been awarded Marketeer of the Year twice, once at Unilever for outstanding business success, running a business significantly larger than Channel 4, and then at the BBC, where he had been responsible for the successful launch of Freeview, chairing the enterprise. But Duncan was the first chief executive who did not have a background in programmes. Jeremy Isaacs had been a master of current affairs and a passionate supporter of the arts; Michael Grade an enthusiastic patron of writers such as Alan Bleasdale . . . and Duncan had won an industry grand prix in 1998 for doubling the sales of SuperNoodles. In Johnson, Channel 4 already had a chairman who was younger and less experienced in public life than his two most successful predecessors, Lord Attenborough and Sir Michael Bishop. He had just found out that the regulated media sector was a tough place. Now he decided that the man for the job in this new climate was a commercially trained marketing man, not an editorial figure.

Duncan's appointment was a telling symptom of the new realities. When they heard about the appointment of this highly untypical media supremo, who many, including Fincham, had never heard of, several of Channel 4's programme commissioners went to the pub to chew it over. One raised this question: 'What happens when we have our Hutton moment?' With Mark Thompson and Tim Gardam, they had been spoilt for choice as to which passionately committed programme-maker would defend them against any similar assault from the Government, Ofcom or the press. That question was recalled in January 2007 as the *Celebrity Big Brother* row, the channel's Hutton moment, broke.

In Carter's eyes, Johnson had chosen well. 'He managed to recruit a surprising and refreshing choice without alienating Kevin Lygo or Andy Barnes [the Advertising Director], both critical to Channel 4's ability to compete.'[19] Duncan was expected to guide Channel 4's digital strategy and to sort out E4, FilmFour and the forthcoming More4. In his pitch for the job, he observed that the channel was facing bigger issues than it realised. At his opening press conference in July, he said, 'My role is to future-proof Channel 4 and transition it from being highly successful in an analogue world to one that could deliver that public purpose in a digital world.' In short, Duncan staked his colours to keeping Channel 4 as a public-service broadcaster from the start, a refreshing change from the approach of Mark Thompson, even if he failed to come up with a memorable sound bite.

Duncan saw his detachment from programmes as a strength.

> I came to Channel 4 with a very fresh perspective, without traditional baggage. I could see clearly the context and where it was going. Probably twenty years ago, to be Chief Executive of Channel 4, what mattered by a mile was programme experience. I brought a much more mixed and balanced toolbox, commercial and financial skills, the know-how to run and manage an organisation – how to deal with advertisers, the need for brand and marketing skills, a strategic perspective, communications, lobbying. I haven't got programming experience but [. . .] I have a natural empathy with commissioning editors.[20]

The problem was that his staff and his suppliers, around 300 independent producers, did not see it like this at all. Many were flummoxed by him. In television, however you dress it up, people are hunting for hits, new talent, new programmes: they know they transform fortunes. They appreciated Duncan's willingness to create and work with teams and involve people, but many of them also saw someone who did not understand the creative process they engaged with, and this was exacerbated with his drive, later, into radio. It was a visceral thing. Channel 4 is peopled by professionals who can price a programme as they watch. They know how many cameras are involved, how much the director was paid. They can identify ways to improve programmes and think up new ones.

A member of Duncan's most senior team said: 'At least 75 per cent of Channel 4's activity is essentially about taking advertising income and turning it into programmes. That's 75 per cent he knows nothing about.'

Isaacs, Grade and Jackson used to send out notes of praise, so highly cherished that commissioning editors would ring their producers to gloat when they arrived. Duncan did not do this. Between 2004 and 2006, he kept away from close involvement with programming, never seeming at ease with Lygo, and did not begin to interfere until the *Celebrity Big Brother* row in 2007. But Lygo, however much he wanted news and current affairs to count on screen, lacked the practical experience of Thompson and Gardam in this tough area. And he did not like making public speeches or putting himself forward.

For the moment, though, the programming seemed to be working well, and the insistent grumbles about *Big Brother* were shrugged off. In fact, both *Big Brother* and *Celebrity Big Brother* were extended, unwisely, in 2005, so by 2006 they occupied a third of the year. The dependence on Endemol, which made the programmes, increased in the autumn of 2005 with the arrival of the blockbuster hit, *Deal or No Deal.*

What Duncan found surprisingly difficult was to win back the Chief Executive's territory from his Chairman. Once he had sampled its attractions, Johnson found it hard to pull back into a traditional non-executive role. From 2004, the annual reports carried an interesting page on governance, listing the demarcation lines between the Chairman and his Chief Executive. Johnson's natural style was interventionist:

> I've been more involved, more intense: perhaps one or two times people might have felt I got too involved. But with changes taking place in the industry, now is not a bad time to have an engaged, enthusiastic chairman who does try to gee up the Board. It is better to step over the line than be semi-detached. I am sure there are times when they consider me a small pain in the arse, but if in doubt I say send out the papers, e-mail, keep directors informed.[21]

Johnson aimed to have stimulating board meetings. The Board took an early decision to invest in the struggling speech radio station, One Word, taking a controlling stake, and, with Duncan's agreement, earmarked expansion into digital radio, bidding with a high-powered Channel 4-run consortium for the second national licence in 2007, which was won on Friday 6 July. It would challenge the BBC with three stations, E4, Pure4 and Channel 4 Radio – news and speech. They made forays into spin-off magazines: *Grand Designs* worked, *4Homes* and *Popworld* did not. They also backed *Quiz Call*, a late-night interactive quiz reaping premium-rate phone-call money, through a subsidiary, Ostrich Media; but this was sold in October 2006 because it raised questions about Channel 4's brand and reputation. The plug was pulled months before the premium-phone-line scandal broke. 'We're well out', said Johnson. 'The lesson is, we can exit smartly.'[22]

Although Duncan had been Johnson's choice, there were tensions between the two men at the beginning. Duncan said,

> We don't agree about everything – Luke can be a brusque character at times – but by and large we had a common perspective on the big issues. It is entirely fair to say Luke had to settle into the role of non-executive chairman. Channel 4 is a relatively big organisation for Luke, whose background is in small to medium-sized organisations, when he's been the entrepreneur running it. I'm the other way around. Channel 4 compared to Unilever or the BBC is a very small organisation and relatively straightforward. We are joined at the hip: we either succeed and get the thing turned around together, or we don't.[23]

So, Johnson had to learn how to be a chairman of a public body, and Duncan had to learn how to be a broadcaster. From July 2004, there were two people wearing L plates at the top of Channel 4, but for two and a half years, they managed pretty well.

The first issue needing a decision was the mooted merger between Channel 4 and Channel Five. The Board had, by now, employed an investment bank, UBS Warburg, to advise them, and working groups started to look at the practicalities that summer. They debated complementary programme schedules, thinking of Channel 4 as the *Daily Telegraph* and Five as the downmarket *Daily Express*. Ofcom signalled a helpful change in rules, allowing the two channels' sales houses to combine without a merger, to compete with ITV, but neither side wanted that.[24]

The Treasury, which was rather perplexed by Channel 4's lobbying, opposed a move to a trust, which would have meant handing over ownership, tartly telling the channel it already enjoyed most of the benefits of trust status anyway. They doubted a merger could guarantee the integrity and independence of Channel 4's programmes and scheduling. Channel 4 was perceived as a strong brand, and most outsiders were unconvinced by its gloomy predictions and variety of messages about its need for assistance. Johnson had always had doubts about the project, which had essentially been Thompson's brainchild. As a businessman, he judged it a regressive move: Channel Five was another terrestrial channel under pressure, and merging with it would destroy the value of Channel 4 for a relatively modest saving in overheads. It would mean Channel 4 would never float or be sold at a proper auction.

Channel Five's shareholders, Lord Hollick and Gerhard Zeiler, Chief Executive of RTL, had different agendas and were disappointed when the merger did not happen. For Hollick, it was a question of the terms on which he made his exit, for an enlarged company would send up the value of his minority stake. For Zeiler, it was a strategic issue, a solution to being trapped with Channel Five, the smallest terrestrial network. The snag was that neither channel had any intention of ceding control to the other.

Johnson felt he could not kill the merger stone dead before his new Chief Executive examined it. Duncan carried out a proper business analysis, and on 13 November there was a tense lunch in a private room at One Aldwych, attended by Johnson, Duncan, Rob Woodward and, for Five, Chief Executive Jane Lighting, Hollick and RTL directors. By the time the bill arrived, the merger was off, even though Zeiler made a last-minute dash to see Duncan and Johnson in an attempt to revive it. His mission foundered as soon as he revealed that he had been thinking of an equal split in the equity, whereas Johnson was advocating eighty-twenty in Channel 4's favour. 'We had a building, net cash, a great brand – we were far more valuable than Five', he reasoned.[25]

On 15 November, the Board voted unanimously to withdraw from a deal that Johnson said made no sense in either cultural or commercial terms. He reflected, 'As a means to an end, to ensure independence, a trust needed to come about. But for certain Channel 4 would have ended up owned by RTL.'[26] Johnson and Duncan saw eye to eye on this, but the episode exposed a key issue, which the former Deputy Chairman Barry Cox had finally come to realise before he left: Channel 4 felt too small on its own, and even self-help moves such as expanding into radio were not enough. So it stepped up its lobbying for some kind of subsidy from the Government, without fully preparing for the demands that extra public support would impose – in other words, it would have to demonstrate its public-service credentials in modernised, measurable terms, not just talk about them. There was another danger arising from the lobbying. As Sir Michael Bishop had observed a decade before, privatisation can become an option when a public corporation seeks assistance from the public purse for investment in its future.

Duncan decided early on to change tack on digital channels. 'The launch of Freeview had changed the world, but Channel 4 was stuck in the old paradigm of pay', he judged.[27] He decided that the digital channels should be run from within the commissioning body, not as semi-detached offshoots, so as to benefit from spin-off programmes. So he put an early end to the split between the 4Ventures division, there to pursue new developments for profit, and commissioning for the main channel. This undermined Rob Woodward's mini-empire, and he left at the end of January 2005. He was shortly followed by Heather Rabbatts, who ran education within 4Ventures despite it being a core public-service duty. The channel's 'hard' educational programming for teenagers was in a bad state, and Managing Editor Janey Walker prepared the way for a complete revamp and migration online.

In May of that year, Duncan had made E4 free, so any viewers who installed Freeview could watch it, not just those paying for Sky and cable. That meant being totally reliant on advertising, but at this point the channel was benefiting from ITV's weakness and attracting about half of the advertising money being pulled from it. Now that it was in another 8 million homes, the audience doubled, and it became the channel most watched by people under thirty-four – easily beating Sky One, which was not on Freeview. The move reaped dividends as advertising rose from £38 million in 2004 to £58 million that year, almost covering costs, and then to £87 million in 2006 – exceeding the £63 million spent on programming.

This boosted confidence in More4, a service for upmarket viewers unveiled at the 2005 Edinburgh Television Festival.[28] Luke Johnson, Andy Duncan and Kevin Lygo were all there, and the channel had taken over an elegant house in Edinburgh's New Town area to recreate a temporary Soho House – a London club patronised by the media. Hospitality was lavished on favoured delegates all weekend. Duncan revised the More4 plan by raising its annual budget to £33 million, earmarking £18 million for original drama, documentaries and daily news presented by Sarah Smith, daughter of the former Labour leader John Smith. 'This won't be another digital repeats channel', the trio promised, 'but one that restores your faith in intelligent television.'

It would be the home of *The West Wing*, the American political serial that had been booted around the schedule, and it would have a link with FourDocs, a new broadband site for short films.

More4 was launched on 10 October 2005 after a teasing marketing campaign that involved inserting envelopes marked 'adults-only entertainment' into broadsheet newspapers. The launch programme was *A Very Social Secretary*, Alastair Beaton's romp about David Blunkett's affair with Kimberly Fortier, which had inspired a small wave of satirical political dramas. Blunkett's lawyer complained, giving the channel the extra publicity it thrived on.

E4's status was confirmed early in 2007 with the critical success of *Skins*, an edgy teenage drama. More4 was not so fortunate: while it marginally exceeded its target of upmarket viewers, its advertising income of £20 million was below expectations. The collapse in advertising during the autumn of 2006, coupled with the rising costs of *Big Brother*, *Deal or No Deal* and *Desperate Housewives*, created near panic as predictions for November and December fell through the floor. Back in January, the channel had hoped to earn an extra £50 million in advertising and sponsorship, but in the event, revenue went the other way at the main channel, falling by £37 million to £692 million. In what seemed like a re-run of 2001, some £40 million had to be swiftly taken out of the overall programme budget, leading to new series being cancelled or curtailed and a near freeze in commissioning. The sharp rise in the price of *Big Brother* and *Deal or No Deal* was a contributing factor as well.

More4's original strategy was quietly adjusted within a year. Some £3 million was cut from the £4 million remaining in its kitty for new commissions. By 2007, the budget for original programmes was hacked back to £5 million. It became primarily a repeats channel, running time-shifted *Dispatches* and *Grand Designs*. The most telling signal of distress was the delay of its second Alastair Beaton satire, *The Trial of Tony Blair*, which was pushed from autumn into January 2007 and promoted as a Channel 4 drama. More4 ran it first on a Tuesday, the main channel two days later.

In 2006, although the three digital channels together had effectively doubled the joint advertising income to £124 million, there was still a gap between that and their total cost of £144 million. Taken together, the family were not yet profit-earners, nine years after the digital adventure began with FilmFour, though they were pointing in the right direction. Early in 2007, Duncan applied to Ofcom for permission to start a Channel 4+1 service, a time-delayed main channel, in a move to boost sagging ratings, and this happened in August. He argued that would make the 7 p.m. *Channel 4 News*, shifted to 8 p.m., more widely viewed. He believed the company was better off with the digital channels going free, even with the unforeseen downturn in the advertising market in 2006. At least it had escaped the clutches of the pay-platform owner, BSkyB, now in a fierce scrap with Virgin Media.

He also restored the channel's marketing budget, which rose to a peak of £39.6 million in 2005, of which a third was spent on promoting the digital channels, before a £7-million cut was made in 2007.

The able Marketing Director Polly Cochrane put in train a complete, much-needed overhaul of Channel 4's screen identity organised by Brett Foraker, the Creative Director. These assembled the number 4 from images of pylons, rocks, Tokyo street signs and washing lines, and won a string of awards.

The channel ran various new-media trials during 2006 to test how people would respond to the prospect of downloading programmes for a small payment: the answer was that they were not keen. After tortuous negotiations, though, agreement had been reached with PACT on sharing revenue, and, in December 2006, Channel 4 was the first British broadcaster to start a video-on-demand service, called 4oD, with a choice of sixty hours a week of free catch-up programmes you may have missed and several thousand archived programmes for a fee. By May 2007, this new service had attracted 1 million users and supplied 20 million programmes to people with personal computers prepared to wait for the lengthy downloads. 'It was very important to move early and protect our rights position with the independents, so we were the people to exploit it, not them', Duncan said.[29] It also represented an attempt by the channel to show it was no longer lagging in the multimedia world. Both ITV.com and the BBC 1-Player launched similar services later that summer.

● ● ● ●

In January 2006, back in the terrestrial world, the channel threw a glitzy party to celebrate its successes, with a stand-up routine from its house satirist Rory Bremner. This is the point in the calendar when the key advertising deals are finalised for the year ahead. Channel 4 had enjoyed a successful 2005, with audiences and commercial impacts firm. Lygo had just infuriated ITV by luring away Paul O'Grady – who attended the party – even though this meant ruthlessly halving Richard and Judy's contract. *Celebrity Big Brother* had provided the bizarre spectacle of the left-wing politician George Galloway pretending to be a cat as he was cradled by the actress Rula Lenska.

One media buyer speculated to the press, 'Channel 4 is the new ITV. Channel 4 is stealing the crown both on screen and off screen. The biggest bullies on the block are now Channel 4.'[30] There were dissenting voices, though. One critic accused the channel of 'stuffing money down the backs of sofas' after it spent excessively on a new reality format from Endemol called *Space Cadets*, which pretended to prepare volunteers for a Russian space trip while holing them up on a set at Milton Keynes. It flopped.

There was an even more glamorous party that July to celebrate the reinvention as a free channel of FilmFour, which by then had just 300,000 paid subscribers. Ewan McGregor loyally dressed up as a tomato on Nelson's column to promote the move:

FilmFour had backed *Trainspotting*, which made him a star. It was not the same channel, though: its tone changed as it had to observe the 9 p.m. watershed and add lengthy advertising breaks. Its audience grew strongly at first, then fluctuated. But the overall effect of all these moves was to raise Channel 4's overall portfolio share of audiences from 10.5 per cent in 2004 to 11 per cent in 2005, then to 12.1 per cent in 2006.

In the first stage of its three-part public-service television review in 2004, Ofcom decided that Channel 4 was a vital force, that it should keep its not-for-profit status and not be privatised. The Regulator relaxed the rules on public-service content for ITV, deciding that Channel 4, as a publicly owned asset, was now the main source of competition to the BBC in terms of providing plurality. While there might be a case at some stage for assistance, Ofcom was unconvinced of the potential crisis and said that, ideally, Channel 4 should pursue a public-service remit based on commercial self-reliance.

But it began to take a harder look at the channel's programming mix and new-media performance, pricing its public-service programming as worth £160 million, out of its £460 million spending on all programmes, compared to ITV's £260 million on a programme budget approaching £1 billion. Looking across all the main channels, Ofcom concluded that there was a potential gap of some £300 million in public-service provision opening up as digital switch-over arrived, largely accounted for by ITV dropping unprofitable minority programmes. In November 2004, as Duncan was bedding in, Ofcom, in Stage 2 of its review, unveiled a big new idea – devised by senior partner Ed Richards – to fill this notional gap, called the Public Service Provider (PSP). It would use public funds and operate trustworthy information broadband services geared towards younger people. Channel 4 would be able to bid in an open contest to run it but would not automatically be chosen.

In envisaging the PSP, Richards had been stimulated by referring back to Channel 4's arrival as a breath of fresh air in 1982. Philip Graf, the Chairman of the Ofcom Content Board, said later that he thought a PSP would act as the same kind of explosive force for change and good. It should be a separate entity for the same reasons that Channel 4 was not created as a new division within ITV.[31]

Reporting in February 2005 with its final conclusions, Ofcom said that there was no obvious funding gap at Channel 4, but it would be kept under review. Carter said later there had been a lot of debate over the PSP because the obvious answer to the plurality question was Channel 4. It was a lot easier to divert public funds into something people knew, liked and respected. 'But you have to look at Channel 4's schedule at the time. This was not a reekingly public-service broadcaster.'[32] And that was the nub of the issue. Channel 4 was beginning to look and sound too commercial, even as it held out a begging bowl, though Duncan was beginning to focus his demands. Another problem, in Ofcom's eyes, was the fatal lack of investment in new media after 2001, which had not kept pace with its audience's tastes.

'I said to Andy when he was appointed that a personal criticism of Channel 4 is that if there was ever a television brand that should have seen the Internet coming, it was Channel 4', said Carter. 'And where was it? It was nowhere.'[33] The only saving grace, in his eyes, was *Big Brother*, which had become a multi-platform event. If the Government was going to intervene, and provide money through Ofcom for a PSP, why should it be a broadcaster that had missed the Internet?

> There are some people who say the PSP is only a policy stalking horse to get Channel 4 to raise its game, to recognise the online environment and get it to divert some of its funds and interest in that area. I can genuinely say that is not why we did it [. . .] but if it had that outcome would it be a bad thing? [. . .] Look at what the BBC did between 1997 and 2000 in building up an online presence, and look at what Channel 4 did. The answer is chalk and cheese.[34]

Ofcom's conclusions resulted in the channel lobbying harder, but on somewhat changed grounds, for help to replace its fading benefit, the free analogue broadcasting spectrum, especially as advertising suddenly collapsed. In response, Tessa Jowell and the Treasury questioned to what extent Channel 4 would put any gifts of new spectrum to run public services and to what extent to boost their commercial capacity. Jowell thought, on balance, that they were more concerned about their commercial viability than a slavish commitment to their programme remit. She did not want Channel 4 to become a blatantly commercial channel, of which there was no shortage.

In 21 June 2006, Andy Duncan made a speech at the Banqueting House, five years after Michael Jackson had announced the death of public-service broadcasting there. Duncan, with more than half an eye on Jowell and the Treasury, said the opposite was true. 'Far from being on its last legs, public-service television is the sturdiest bridge we have from the old analogue world of mass viewing to the consumer-led made-to-measure media.'[35] He said Channel 4 was as much a public asset as the BBC and now positioned it as a second great public-broadcasting corporation providing competition in news, film and now radio to the BBC. The catch was that the BBC was about to face much stiffer public value tests and regulation, as a quid pro quo for winning a new charter.

Channel 4 as a mini-BBC was certainly what the policy-makers wanted to hear, but the lecture did not have much wider impact. It was delivered on the eve of Carter's departure from Ofcom and at the start of a tough financial review of Channel 4 led by his successor Ed Richards, based on the premise that nobody knew whether to trust the channel's warnings of future poverty. Carter said that there was, strictly, no basis for this review in legislation: it had sprung from Channel 4's campaign. It was the first ever independent review of its operations since launch in 1982. For seasoned hands, who knew Channel 4's long history of fighting for its independence, the review spelt danger. It all depended on whether the assessment were true: Channel 4 could fall over a financial cliff edge. Johnson, for one, thought it was a good thing:

> It focused attention on the threats facing Channel 4. Ofcom would be seen as sufficiently unbiased that the report they make to Government will be taken seriously, and that's important. Channel 4 has managed to do better than expected in the last two to three years: that's probably a combination of luck and skill but it is unlikely to continue for ever, and if you look at the performance of Five or ITV they are materially worse.[36]

The following month, Charles Allen, the outgoing Chief Executive of ITV, gave the MacTaggart Lecture at the Edinburgh Television Festival and tore into Channel 4 for

> behaving like a twenty-five-year-old still living at home, dipping into Mum's purse even when it's got a fat pay cheque in its back pocket [...] Look at its afternoon schedule, quiz show, game show, chat show, cartoon, soap. Or its peak-time schedule, dominated by reality, lifestyle, US acquisitions and shock docs. When exactly did 'remit' become a four-letter word?

This witty speech, which mocked the forthcoming 'wank week' on the theme of masturbation, and its dubious educational programmes, effectively trumped Duncan's lecture and marked an abrupt change in the weather vane – even though Channel 4 was fêted as Channel of the Year by the festival. Duncan was not at Edinburgh, but Kevin Lygo and Luke Johnson were, and they responded by sulking rather than counter-attacking, a foretaste of the way they would bungle the forthcoming *Celebrity Big Brother* row in January. When Allen turned up at their Soho House, Johnson, the host, was surly.

In a final session the next day, Johnson, quizzed about the channel's future, refused to stamp on the notion of privatisation, saying there needed to be a full and frank debate. Ten years earlier, at the same festival, Michael Grade, Chief Executive of Channel 4, had made his dramatic heartfelt speech – 'Sorry folks, no jokes' – exposing the threat of privatisation by the dying Major Government and the need for concerted opposition.

Duncan had no convincing arguments to challenge Allen's caricature, no vision backed up by tough programme strategies to articulate when the praise to which it was accustomed, from journalists and MPs, if not from many of its original founders, suddenly dried up. Nor did he recognise what was evident to so many, including his Deputy Chairman, David Puttnam, that Ofcom's financial review would now inevitably take a hard look at Channel 4's programming, the remit would be linked to funding, and that it would be wise to take the initiative and work on redefining its public value rather than have an Ofcom-imposed corset. The channel had already commissioned Price Waterhouse to analyse its undoubted importance to the creative economy, as part of its response to the financial review. But the Board was not united on how to proceed in tackling the future, and Luke Johnson, at an October board meeting in Belfast, encouraged a frank 'think the unthinkable' debate of options among board members. Duncan remained committed to Channel 4 remaining as a public corporation throughout this, but thought the Ofcom process should be taken in two stages, with the debate about the programme remit coming at a second, later stage.

At a Royal Television Society conference on 14 September, stubbornly – maybe naively – Duncan stuck to his guns, that this was a welcome financial review, not a remit review, while also gloomily predicting further declines in the advertising market. Many in the audience believed he was painting himself into a corner, almost willing the worst to happen, to prove him right. In an unexpected twist of fate, Michael Grade defected from the chairmanship of the BBC in November and was appointed Executive Chairman of ITV, to take the helm of Channel 4's harshest industry critic. This did not dent its lobbying, though this now began to be carried out behind the scenes. Then, in January 2007, at the worst possible time, Channel 4's Hutton moment arrived with *Celebrity Big Brother*.

Mark Thompson's decision to engage in merger talks with Channel Five had prompted low-key rumblings and mutterings about privatisation for the first time since 1996. Engaging in a debate about Channel 4's future at a critical time of change and instability was always going to raise questions about its purpose, hybrid status and ownership. But the appointment of Johnson and Duncan had propelled Channel 4 further along a trajectory that was leading to privatisation being debated openly, because they had campaigned for public assistance, without effectively championing Channel 4's cultural importance or the importance of upholding its independence.

The messages had been muddled, as muddled as the channel's decision to become ever more dependent on *Big Brother* since 2005 (see Chapter 24). The outcome was as follows. On 20 June, just a week before Gordon Brown took over as Prime Minister, Tessa Jowell confirmed that the BBC would contribute a modest £14 million towards Channel 4's digital switch-over costs – a drop in the ocean when set against its financial anxieties, but a significant move. It would receive its first direct public subsidy from BBC licence payers. Far more important was the conclusion of the Ofcom review. It was time for a fundamental external examination of Channel 4, from its role and funding to its programming.

24

Big Brother

● ● ● ●

Big Brother arrived in Britain on 18 July 2000, promoted as a late-night experiment. After the introductory show at 9 p.m., it was pushed back to 11 p.m., the zone for brash new ideas. The format had been developed over the previous three and a half years by John de Mol, a workaholic former DJ turned television producer and burgeoning media tycoon, based in Holland. When it was put on there during the autumn of 1999, it gained instant attention from other broadcasters for transforming the fortunes of an ailing cable channel called Veronica. By the final programme, 70 per cent of the country's 15 million population were tuning in. The format spread rapidly to Germany, Spain, the USA and then Britain.

George Orwell, in his novel *1984*, had forecast a society in which everyone was watched at all times by the all-seeing Big Brother. In fact, the spread of CCTV cameras had almost created this level of surveillance. The technology for discreet recording, including ultra-sensitive tiny microphones, was now in place. De Mol's big idea was to base a show on observing a group of people for twenty-four hours a day, seven days a week, so the audience had the frisson of knowing it was real. Ten contestants were carefully selected to live in a controlled laboratory environment, cut off from contact with the outside world or media. Each day, the highlights would be edited into a narrative, as a living soap opera, and it was streamed live on the Internet – the first programme to be treated this way.

The inmates were almost never out of the spotlight. They wore a microphone all day, except when they were asleep or in the shower. They had a storeroom for food, open for an hour a day, and were given a weekly task to accomplish. At any time, they could be summoned to the so-called Diary Room by a disembodied Big Brother voice – actually that of the producer in charge on the day – which had to be obeyed. In the house, they had to cooperate, up to a point, with people who had been strangers before, and then to nominate two of the group for eviction every week, with the final decision going to viewers through a phone-in vote. The last survivor won a cash prize.

The Dutch house was equipped with single beds and one double bed, as well as plenty of alcohol, in the hope that some of the inmates would have sex. In the first series, that duly happened, albeit in a whispery way under a duvet, and this was accepted within Holland's permissive culture. Anxieties started to mount, though, when the European broadcaster RTL – part-owner of Veronica – bought the rights for their German RTL2 channel, for a first series starting in March 2000.

In Germany, it sparked opposition and disquiet: the use of barbed-wire fences, security lights and guards to keep people out fed fears that the producers were creating a prison camp, stirring war memories. There was a political row about whether the programme violated a clause in the constitution protecting human dignity. The 100-day run started only after a compromise by which the producers agreed to turn off the cameras for an hour to ensure some privacy, whether the housemates wanted it or not.

The show then spread to Spain as *Gran Hermano*, then to the USA, where President Bill Clinton attacked it for invading privacy, and by July it was in Britain. Peter Bazalgette, whose production company Bazal had joined with de Mol's Endemol in 1998, had acquired the British rights as a matter of course. The urbane ex-BBC producer was a textbook example of how, as Anthony Smith had predicted when Channel 4 was established, programme-makers would evolve into astute businessmen. When he saw an article in *The Times* about the sexual escapade in the Dutch version, he realised he was engaged in a race against time: if he did not sell the *Big Brother* format to a British broadcaster, copycat lookalikes would spring up.

Bazalgette would later see the staggering success of *Big Brother* as part of a flowering of global television formats in the late 1990s – others included *Who Wants to Be a Millionaire?* and *Survivor* – all making fortunes for their creators.[1] British viewers had already developed an appetite for fly-on-the-wall docusoaps, starting with *The Family* in 1974, observing a working-class family in Reading. Between 1996 and 2000, there was a glut of them, as learner drivers, hedonistic holiday-makers, builders, chalet girls and traffic wardens were staked out by camera crews. Channel 4 largely stood aside from this as it developed its own line in formatted reality – *Grand Designs*, *No Going Back* and *Faking It*.

Bazalgatte duly photocopied the *Times* article and sent it with a covering letter to four commercial companies – Channel 4, Channel Five, ITV and Sky One. At Sky One, Elisabeth Murdoch never replied. At ITV, David Liddiment discussed it with his Head of Factual Commissioning and turned it down: he later called it his Beatles moment. Channel Five offered a nightly prime-time slot and £3.5 million. Channel 4 bid £4.6 million, later topped up with an extra £500,000. This was less than the £6 million Endemol was seeking, but it was re-costed, and the deal accepted in January

2000. Bazalgette also received insistent calls from Alan Yentob, but he thought the programme would be emasculated on the BBC.

Its progress to Channel 4 was more complicated than this bald account suggests. The format was hawked around and rejected by several commissioners at the channel.[2] So, Bazalgette went to see Julia LeStage, a loquacious American who had joined in 1996 to perk up daytime programming, a protégé of Dawn Airey. LeStage had formed a bond with Bazalgette through the teatime show he supplied, *Pet Rescue*. A granddaughter of William Fulbright, the US senator and philanthropist, she lived in Oxford with her academic husband but prided herself on being a populist. Michael Jackson, who appreciated her zest, asked her to hunt for fresh things to perk up the evening schedule, so she initiated a two-hour ideas session with Bazalgette and watched the latest tape from the Dutch *Big Brother* house.[3]

She was so enthused that she and Bazalgette caught an early plane next day to see the production live in Amsterdam. She walked in to watch housemates brushing their teeth and was duly hooked. Rushing back to London with tapes, she showed them to Tim Gardam, the Director of Programmes.[4] 'Tim was very nervous', she recalls. 'He put me through the intellectual wringer for several weeks; but he was titillated – he got it.'[5] In fact, she returned to live in Boston before the first *Big Brother* was screened, but insists: 'I knew the monster I had created.'[6]

Jackson recognised that while Channel 4 was *Big Brother*'s natural home, it was by no means a foregone conclusion that it would be successful. 'It was very much Tim's decision', he says.

> For myself, there was no sense of 'Wow, this is going to be a huge success.' I said, 'Try it, but don't do it for too many weeks.' It was an experiment, and worrying: it was on every night of the week, so it would be an embarrassment if it were to fail.[7]

Gardam confirms this: 'When I commissioned *Big Brother*, Michael was rather aghast. He thought it would run for one series.'[8] Gardam accordingly adapted it to his taste, cutting it to a nine-week run of sixty-four rather than 100 days, with a snappy weekly eviction. At Endemol, a team of more than 200 was assembled at Three Mills Studio in East London: later it would move to a permanent site at Elstree. Davina McCall was hired to host it, and another early recruit was Brett Kahr, a senior lecturer in psychotherapy at Regent's College, London, who played a central role in selecting the housemates and drawing up a lengthy application form, to test suitability and stamina. The minimum age was raised from eighteen to twenty-one, but was lowered later. As *Big Brother* developed, the selection became more scientific, with psychometric testing.

Conrad Green, Series Editor of the first version, summed up the essence of the format in its early days:

> At the core of *Big Brother* there's a unique tension [. . .] You have this brilliantly formatted balance of power at the core of it, where I as a producer can only intervene a certain amount; where the people in the house can determine their fate only to a certain extent and the audience controls things, but not completely. So, there's this strange triangle of control which makes everyone feel they participate in it much more.[9]

Bazalgette put it more simply, that it was a riveting personality contest with the added spice for everyone of being able to take part. This may have been true at the beginning, but, as the format matured, the triangle became distorted as the production team became more powerful and manipulative.

Liz Warner, now in charge of factual features, decided the Dutch and German versions, with spare prison-camp settings, looked dreadful. Obsessive about style, she insisted the British house had a designer look even if it was skin deep. It was a circular set, with one-way mirrors looking onto the dining area, garden, living room, bedroom and bathroom – where the camera was positioned above the lavatory. The whole thing was a construct of a peepshow crossed with a fairground haunted house; in effect, a studio designed to eliminate any hiding places for its guinea pigs. Outside the set was a blacked-out circular corridor, where the production crew prowled silently in the gloom, voices never raised above a whisper. The responsibility of the producer on the day was to ensure that every shot from fifteen cameras, five manned at any one time, was logged, then pared down into a series of playlets.

The *Big Brother* website went live just two minutes before the first ten housemates walked in from their black-windowed Mercedes with the numberplates BIG BRO. The nightly edited version, shown at 11 p.m., won audiences of around 1 million, and Dan Chambers, the commissioner of science programmes now working on *Big Brother* full time, had a sinking feeling during the second week that it would flop. But it had started to generate enormous media interest as the tabloids competed to be the *Big Brother* newspaper, and a word-of-mouth effect was also building as the website became Britain's most popular, with 2.5 million page impressions a day.

'The moment we realised it was an extraordinary programme was when they took their clothes off and started rolling in the mud', Gardam recalls. 'They were totally unselfconscious. There was an innocence about it, entirely a feel-good show.'[10] The first of the many headline-making rows came on 17 August. Nick Bateman, a thirty-two-year-old City broker and former pupil of Gordonstoun School, was caught writing down names of people to nominate for eviction, in the hope of persuading the other housemates to gang up on his chosen victims. It was against the rules of the house to have a pencil and to conspire in this way, and Craig Phillips, twenty-eight, a builder from Liverpool, organised an informal trial.

The website crashed under the weight of 7.5 million hits, and the audience that night reached 5.8 million, rising to 6.9 million the following night, when Nick was evicted. The story was front-page news in every national newspaper except the *Financial Times*. The nightly instalments were quickly rescheduled to 10 p.m., and the final programme attracted 9.9 million, with 7.4 million voting in the final poll. Nick's nemesis Craig was the eventual winner, walking away with £70,000. No serious complaints were received by the Regulator, and none from the participants.

The ITC reported, 'There was wide debate as to whether it was exploitative or shed any true light on human nature. In general, it was recognised as a fresh and entertaining format that was highly addictive to its [for Channel 4] large audiences and prompted 185 million page impressions to the website.'[11] The first series attracted 26 per cent of the audience, more than double the usual for the channel, putting it on a par with ITV. Channel 4's share of all viewing that summer, in the weeks that *Big Brother* was screened, swelled to 11.6 per cent, compared with 10.7 per cent the previous year.

Even better, half the programme's viewers were in the sixteen-to-thirty-four age group, and six out of ten were female. A further 12 per cent were under sixteen, and, once addicted, they would grow up expecting *Big Brother* as a summer regular, Channel 4's alternative to Wimbledon. But it had a toxic effect on the over-fifty-fives, who shunned it like the plague. Right from the start, when it aired in John de Mol's homeland, hardly anyone over fifty could bring themselves to watch it, and it was completely cold-shouldered by the over-sixty-fives. That was its commercial beauty: it divided audiences, driving away the middle-aged and old – the key factor that made it so profitable from the start.

Channel 4 set itself up in 1993 to sell advertisers three groups of viewers: young adults, upmarket professionals and light viewers of television. *Big Brother*'s arrival coincided with a growing demand from advertisers for young audiences: its first sponsor was Southern Comfort, attempting to turn itself into a cool cocktail. The programme was perfect for any television channel seeking to bring down its average audience age and, in Channel 4's case, to enhance its reputation for catering to youth. It was the most talked-about programme for a decade, fulfilling the channel's remit of being innovative while giving expression to the multimedia age.

As the annual report put it, 'Beyond the numbers, *Big Brother* reinforced Channel 4's position as a pioneering broadcaster.' The *Guardian* agreed: '*Big Brother* has completed Channel 4's transformation from an eccentric outsider to a powerful pioneer at the heart of British broadcasting.' But it also introduced a potential fault line running through the channel's position as a hybrid public-service broadcaster. Opinion-formers and MPs tended to belong to the age group that was offended by the programme. For the moment, this did not matter, for with Tony Blair in power the channel would remain safe from privatisation. But when the question was raised again, as it inevitably would be, the very success of *Big Brother* would weaken the arguments against it.

Big Brother created a practical challenge for Channel 4, too. Most of their main evening programmes were delivered as tapes, well in advance. There had never been much live television after the news. *Big Brother* was a mixture of catch-ups, fast-edited overnight from the previous day's recordings, and live evictions. It required new ways of working. The commissioners, lawyers and technical-support staff moved to the site of the house to work alongside Endemol's people.

Gardam needed someone energetic, with sound judgement, to lead the operation, and he had taken a shine to Julian Bellamy, who was commissioning current affairs. In December 1998, when Gardam arrived as Director of Programmes, Bellamy had ordered a fast-turnaround documentary about office Christmas parties, to be delivered on the day of transmission. As the clock ticked towards the start, 10 p.m., he sent the first part to the channel's play-out suite. As Part 1 went out, he was called by the producer and told that Part 2 would not arrive on time, and another programme had to be inserted to fill the gap. From that day forward, there was a rule, the Bellamy Rule, that you cannot start broadcasting without being in possession of the full programme.

This chastening experience endeared him to Gardam, who asked him to take over *Big Brother* after the first series, when it was being extended to E4 as well as the main channel. He became closely identified with the programme and its extension into *Celebrity Big Brother*, as well as with E4, until 2005, when he was headhunted to run BBC3. He returned to Channel 4 in 2007.

'I was initially terrified, excited', he admits.

> It is extraordinary to be involved in a show that absolutely everyone you meet consumes massively and wants to talk to you about. It was like being a human water cooler for those weeks. You are involved in a programme which is genuinely a step change. I was at the helm of a moment in television history that was changing the culture.[12]

The launch of E4 in January 2001 meant new opportunities for *Big Brother 2*. There was an 'as live' feed for twenty-one hours a day, and viewers could choose which of four video feeds to watch – or watch them all at the same time. There were spin-off shows, led by *Big Brother's Little Brother*, presented by Dermot O'Leary. *Big Brother* enabled E4 to double its ratings. *The Times* said, 'The second series of Big Brother has been the most successful venture into interactive television.'

There was a lot of improvisation as the programme-makers worked out a framework for twenty-four-hour broadcasting. How would you ensure that the conversation was complying with broadcasting codes? Bellamy knew that journalists were watching the raw footage for slip-ups. This was the challenge facing Danny Cohen, another rising executive, who would follow Bellamy as Controller of E4. With the lawyers and compliance team, Cohen and Bellamy invented a system using a team of students with headphones listening to all the conversations. When someone swore or said something that might be libellous, they wrote it down, together with the time-frame code, so that it could be bleeped out or cut during the ten-minute time delay.[13]

The sharing with splinter channels was rapidly copied by the BBC with *Fame Academy*, then ITV's *I'm a Celebrity . . . Get Me Out of Here!*, and is now standard for big shows of this type. *Big Brother* formally became a multimedia event after a deal negotiated with Endemol in 2002, during the Mark Thompson era. It set the style for five years to 2007. The price doubled to around £12 million a year, but the price per hour remained the same at around £100,000. 'There was no thought of cancelling it during my time', says Thompson. 'The issue was the amount of airtime: we really did ramp up the amount by streaming it and offering it through different windows as well as E4. We had a very, very good deal with *Big Brother*: it was a fantastic moneyspinner.'[14]

Before the start of the third series in 2002, an experienced hand, the former Commissioning Editor Peter Grimsdale, was rehired and put in overall charge of marshalling the multi-platform event. '*Big Brother* had been a massive success, but internally it was a mess', said Grimsdale.

> In order to get it working you have to make cross-channel decisions and nine others need to know. It was like setting up a war room, with thirty-five to forty people, including specialists in handling press and sponsorship and an editorial steering group [. . .] We had to have a much more collaborative way of working.[15]

Bellamy soon realised he was in charge of a soap opera. In the third series, Jade Goody from Bermondsey was the big story. In her selection tape, this eighteen-year-old dental assistant was jumping up and down on her bed, saying, 'I'm crazy, I'm mucky.' There was a debate about whether she would be too much of an irritant, driving viewers to the off switch. But Bellamy believed it made one of the best castings in the programme's history. Jade was podgy, she thought chickpeas came from chickens, that East Anglia (or Angular, as she called it) was abroad, and she got drunk very quickly. In a game of strip poker, she went further than the rules demanded, taking off her G-string, though the footage was edited. The tabloids called her Miss Piggy.

'The national demonisation of Jade Goody [. . .] made me fear for the first time that a reality show will one day provoke a suicide', wrote Mark Lawson in the *Guardian*. Bellamy remembers, 'There was a moment when we were all beginning to get concerned about this runaway train. The point where I was getting worried was when the *Sun* did a front page, "Vote The Pig Out". But as people learnt more about Jade's deprived background, they began to warm to her. She had nursed a drug-addicted disabled mother and had an absent criminal father.[16] Brett Kahr was consulted after derogatory photos of her were published in the *Sun*, but he put the executives' minds at rest by telling them that Jade had a lot more resources within her than they thought. And he was right: she soon became a celebrity, famous for being famous. In 2006, she launched a perfume, hosted one of the channel's successful new entertainment programmes, *The Friday Night Project*, and appeared on *The Jonathan Ross Show*. Bellamy said,

> My view is really simple. They are adults. They are perfectly capable of making their own decisions whether they want to be in the show or not. To assume that somehow they are deemed responsible by society to vote for a government but not able to decide about being in a television show is a contradiction. But there are times you have to make tricky judgements about what to show.[17]

How much intimacy should be screened was about to be tested again. Gardam was on his way to work in a taxi when Grimsdale phoned him. They were viewing the rushes to decide how much to show of a sexual encounter under the sheets between Jade and P.J. Ellis, a law student. An edited version was sent down the line to Gardam, but an apparent mistake in switching the footage meant it was sent to 500 television screens around the Channel 4 building.

Gardam viewed it with a lawyer and asked for two small but important cuts. This caused huge dissent – the team at Elstree wanted to show their version – but Gardam, whose teenage daughter watched the show, had become increasingly disenchanted by the programme and insisted on drawing the line. 'The moment you show live sex on telly, you've gone', he explained. 'But everyone disagreed with me.'[18] *Big Brother 3* was darker and nastier than the other two, yet it was the most popular of all the series, attracting an average of 5.8 million viewers for a share of 28 per cent.

The fourth series was dubbed internally by Bellamy as *Back to Basics*. 'We wanted to recapture the sense that they were ordinary people inside the house. But we failed to recognise that the audience had moved on.'[19] A symptom of this was that one in four of the videos from people applying showed them naked, no doubt influenced by Jade's romps in the previous series. As it turned out, though, *Big Brother 4* was incurably dull, and audiences fell sharply. The format was treading water. Here was a moment when the old Channel 4 could have pulled out on creative grounds and planned for a series of replacements. But by now they could not take the commercial risk of *Big Brother* turning up against them, perhaps on Channel Five. Anyway, most of the commissioners were as addicted to the format as were its loyal viewers, although Gardam refused to be drawn on how long it would go on for.[20] The board minutes do not record any deep concerns about the ethics of *Big Brother*, yet the Chairman Vanni Treves, a dismayed critic of the show, insists:

> We did discuss it, more than once, at board level. At the time it started it was quite ground-breaking and nothing like as nauseating as it is now [. . .] I didn't try to bring it to an end when I was Chairman. Really, I was completely confused about how *Big Brother* fitted into our priorities. I remember sitting down with Tim Gardam asking why we were doing it, seeing that it was just not consistent with our values. He said we have to pay the grocery bills somehow.[21]

Thompson decided that *Big Brother* would need constant reinvention and manipulation. Part of the voyeuristic fun of the early days, watching people cleaning their teeth, had evaporated for good, and so had the audience's rush to vote. Peter Bazalgette had always said it was about trash heroes and pantomime villains, prepared to engage in a range of ever more bizarre tasks and antics. So, the lesson was applied as they picked housemates for *Big Brother 5*, but with near catastrophic results.

The Creative Director of the series, Philip Edgar-Jones, a former Junior Director on *The Word*, rejigged the house so it was a meaner environment. Three separate rows quickly blew up among housemates and degenerated into a riotous 'fight night.' Within minutes, the production team cut the live feed and sent in security guards to separate the contestants. There was also an allegation of racism, when a white housemate was angered by remarks made about her by an Afro-Caribbean. The Police were called, and for a few days it seemed possible they might shut the programme down, when they insisted that they needed to interview everyone in the house, some as potential law-breakers and others as witnesses. Finally, they relented and agreed to interview people as they were evicted. *Big Brother 5* was saved, although it did not escape censure from Ofcom.

There was more sex, this time under a table, and the show was extended for ten minutes to accommodate the excitement. This was when criticism became more voluble. John Humphrys, delivering the MacTaggart Lecture that August, said:

> The first time I watched *Big Brother* live there were two men lying on a bed and talking about women, or rather 'fucking women', and talking about their responses to them, or rather, 'my fucking stiffy'. My, how we've pushed back the boundaries of television. How proud we should be. This is people giving us their real thoughts.

He quoted Lord Reith's view that to apply broadcasting to the shoddy, the vulgar and the sensational would be a blasphemy against human nature. 'What did he know, patronising old toff?' asked Humphrys. 'You can hear the cash registers [. . .] every time there is a fumble beneath the bedsheets. It is a battle between people who are concerned about society and those whose overwhelming interest is simply to make programmes that make money.'[22]

That autumn, Anthony Smith, now President of Magdalen College, Oxford, entered the fray in an article in the *Daily Mail*. 'Channel 4 is becoming tawdry and repetitive. The whole enterprise, if it does not look back to its origins, is destined to slip into the hands of the privatisers.' But the channel did not look back. It seemed to have very little connection by now with its roots, or any memory of them. It extended *Big Brother 5* by an extra week, to ten weeks, and then upped it to ninety-three days in 2006. A new strand was added on E4, called *Big Brother's Big Mouth*, to debate the night's show. Most seriously, it started to rock ITV by moving the start times of the main *Big Brother* forward to 9 p.m., a direct attack on its advertising.

In the balmy summer of 2006, then, *Big Brother 7* was faced with the challenge of filling thirteen weeks. The housemates duly included some eye-catching characters, led by Peter Bennett, who has Tourette's Syndrome, a disability that happens to be telegenic – so telegenic that he went on to win. Yet, by Friday 11 August, a live eviction night, when small groups of young women trickled out of Elstree and Borehamwood station looking for the house (a ten-minute walk down the High Street), it was clear that the programme had overstepped the mark. The production team, in their barrack-style offices within the perimeter fence of Elstree Studios, appeared surprised that their latest ruse, to recall four already-evicted contestants and put one up for a return to the house, had created a stink.

Surely everyone knew the most important rule of all, that Big Brother can rewrite the rules at any time? But since viewers had already voted, via their premium-rate calls, to evict the quartet, the producers had contravened the principle of fair competition. Some 875,000 calls were made that night, at 38 pence a time, and the surplus was handed to charity. The Independent Committee for the Supervision of Standards of the Telephone Information Services (ICSTIS), the premium-phone-line regulator, delivered a rap on the knuckles.

It demonstrated how easy it was for the production team to assume an almost value-free stance, where the pressing concern, in what can be languid days and boring nights, was what would make the best show for the next evening, even if that included reintroducing controversial characters. It was about being creative, perking up the ratings by prodding the captive humans, who can be as somnolent as sleeping lions in the zoo. In this series, they also ran a golden-ticket competition: the ticket, concealed in the wrapper of a Kit Kat chocolate bar, allowed the winner entry into the house. There was widespread incredulity when it ended up in the hands of someone who had been turned down by the team as too boring after attending auditions around the country. The mild-mannered Executive Producer, Philip Edgar-Jones, said he was astounded.

Big Brother 7 survived these mini-scandals and attracted an average audience of 4.7 million. Channel 4's revenue for 2006 was secure.

In June 2005, Andy Duncan, the evangelical Christian who was now Chief Executive, gave a lecture to a Faithworks network. He said:

> I make no claims for *Big Brother* as social or moral education. First and foremost it's an entertainment show and a very important one for us commercially because it attracts young viewers. I can understand how the language and behaviour of those it features may often be at odds with those of an older generation. But look more closely. *Big Brother* winners are all role models in their way – because in the final analysis viewers choose people whose values they identify with and admire.

This was not an original thought. Duncan, as he acknowledged, was drawing on the defence devised by his predecessor, Mark Thompson. Moreover, with Director of Programmes Kevin Lygo, they were making the channel even more dependent on the format than it needed to be, by extending *Big Brother* and by introducing an annual dollop of *Celebrity Big Brother*.

In March 2001, in an example of collaboration with the BBC not seen since Dennis Potter's unloved *Karaoke and Cold Lazarus*, Comic Relief had run an eight-day *Celebrity Big Brother*, won by Jack Dee. Channel 4 screened daily highlights, and it was hugely successful. It then became a shorter, regular fixture on Channel 4, though it was moved from November to January. Highlights of early series included Germaine Greer walking out, accusing Big Brother of bullying, and Les Dennis sharing his depression after his wife left him.

By the third *Celebrity Big Brother*, in 2005, the creep was under way: it had expanded to eighteen days. In 2006, it ran from 5 to 27 January and was won by Chantelle Houghton, who, in a clever twist, was not a celebrity at all, just a pretty blonde woman. This was the series that featured the extraordinary exchange between George Galloway, Respect MP for Bethnal Green and Bow, and Rula Lenska, the actress in *Rock Follies*, where he pretended to be a cat and buried his head in her lap.

Celebrity Big Brother was a somewhat different programme from *Big Brother*. The audience was older – more than half were over thirty-five – and the demographics flatter, with more liberal readers of the *Guardian* enticed in. Many were unaccustomed to *Big Brother*'s potential crudity, its bad language, its addiction to antics rather than debate. They had little idea of who Jade Goody was. But they knew an ugly racist incident when they saw it.

25

Channel 4 at the crossroads

• • • •

The *Celebrity Big Brother* débâcle, coming at the very beginning of 2007, set the tone
for what would be a trying year for Channel 4 and possibly a critical one. It was scant
consolation that it was not the only television station whose values and credibility
were being called into question. There was a spate of scandals that spring and summer about quizzes making use of premium-rate phone lines, where the winner was
often chosen long before the lines had closed: the Richard and Judy programme was
among those implicated. Then the BBC came under fire for screening, as part of a
press launch, a piece of film edited so as to give the false impression that the Queen
had walked out of a photo-shoot in a huff, and Mark Thompson was forced into a
grovelling apology. Back on Channel 4, no sooner had the *Celebrity Big Brother* row
cooled than Gillian McKeith of *You Are What You Eat* was forced to drop the title
of 'Doctor'. It was further revealed that Gordon Ramsay had only pretended to have
caught sea bass for his cookery show and that *Born Survivor* Bear Grylls had defied
the wilderness by staying in luxury motels. What could the hapless viewer believe?

At the root of these lapses, trivial though some of them seemed, was a drift away
from Channel 4's core mandate to be innovative, culturally diverse and educative; and
it was unclear whether it could recover that original idealism and drive. In March,
the *Guardian* writer Stuart Jeffries posed the question, 'What Is the Point of Channel
4?' 'The programmes get tackier, the scandals get seamier', he wrote, as Vanessa Feltz
and Paul Daniels kicked off a celebrity version of *Wife Swap*.[1] The mandate or remit
was a sensitive point because over twenty-five years the channel had won the right to
operate on a loose rein, with the freedom to experiment. This had generally worked
when it repaid the trust with a range of fresh and worthwhile programming – notably but not only *Channel 4 News* – without making demands for public money. But
what if that trust was now being betrayed, even as it was begging for assistance?

It was against the background of such criticism that the issue of privatisation began to be debated again after a lull of ten years. Its proponents argued that since the channel had already become so commercial, it would not make that much difference were it obliged to operate on a profit-making basis. This time, it was noticeable how few of Channel 4's old allies rushed to nip the notion in the bud; but then the liberal elite were appalled by *Big Brother*, and young people, the channel's most identifiable bloc of fans, were not that politically involved. It was significant that the advertising industry was to emerge as the most fervent supporters of the status quo.[2]

Duncan and his colleagues did themselves no favours during Ofcom's investigation into the Shilpa–Jade row when they pointed out that the channel was always prone to controversy because its core values included 'making trouble, inspiring change and doing it first'.[3] These values were instilled into programme commissioners when they joined, but doing it first did not now seem to apply to some of its ageing programmes, while causing trouble for the sake of it was neither sensible nor public-spirited. All the same, the philosophy allowed the channel's executives to argue, rather speciously, that although *Celebrity Big Brother* had not set out to create a national debate about racism, 'there was undeniable public value in having the debate'.[4] This was like a man pleading that he had not intended to beat up his wife, but at least her plight had provided a rigorous test for the emergency services.

Unsurprisingly, that line of defence quickly crumbled. On 24 May, Ofcom published its adjudication, finding the channel guilty of serious editorial misjudgements, and, on the same day, the Board released the results of its own review, led by the Non-Executive Director Tony Hall, which came to even harsher conclusions. (The channel had originally planned to publish its own inquiry after, but the two were released together in the hope of minimising damage.) The Board review concluded that programme-makers had to ask in future not what they could get away with while ostensibly complying with the programming code – a skill the channel's lawyers had honed over the years – but exactly why they were testing the limits of acceptability. It recommended the appointment of a new senior editorial figure, a viewers' editor, to provide a detached perspective, and it formulated new rules of engagement for *Big Brother*, including a written policy on how the show would tackle seriously offensive language and behaviour. Endemol's producers were reined in with tighter lines of control, and the channel could be informed routinely of all controversial material. Duncan decided to restore a *Right to Reply*-style of programme in the autumn, so that viewers could once more have their say.

Five days before the start of *Big Brother 8*, Peter Bazalgette, the Creative Director of Endemol International, said he believed that the biggest danger the programme faced was of being emasculated – a favourite word of his – by too many controls.[5] It had to be free to be its freaky self. The new series was duly launched on 30 May after tussles over the final selection of housemates, amid a widespread air of apprehension. Mark

Thompson was not alone in believing it could be the last series – and many thought that, if it were not, the privatisation of Channel 4 would become a certainty.

The commissioners had instructed Endemol to make it light and amusing, stressing conversation rather than lewd antics, with no bullying or fighting. Kevin Lygo, who had been criticised for not being more decisive in his interventions over the Shilpa–Jade incident, removed himself from direct responsibility in March to take a more strategic programming role across all the company's channels. It was part of a restructuring of the whole commissioning area. Julian Bellamy arrived from BBC3 to take his place as Head of Channel 4 on 2 May: a hurried appointment without a formal selection process. Continuing the game of musical chairs, Danny Cohen, the cerebral head of E4 and factual entertainment – which included *Big Brother* – left to replace Bellamy at BBC3.

It was no surprise that Lygo and Cohen, the two closest to the shop-soiled programme, should seek an exit. Cohen, in any case, was getting married and said he wanted his life back.[6] Bellamy, a robust populist of thirty-five, who had made his name on *Big Brother 2–5*, was handed the task of squiring the channel through the year and bringing it new energy. Angela Jain, who had been part of the *Big Brother* team since 2004, was promoted to replace Cohen.

Almost inevitably, hers would be a baptism of fire, although *Big Brother 8* started peacefully enough. To begin with, it was an all-female household, and when Tom Utley, the querulous middle-aged *Daily Mail* columnist, wrote that he was quite liking the housemates because they were not the usual array of freaks, you could be sure it was not going to satisfy its most loyal audience: young women who enjoy extreme behaviour and, moreover, who like to watch young men. On 7 June, it seemed that the Shilpa–Jade affair was going to be played out again after one of the women casually referred to another as a 'nigger'. The offender was immediately ejected, forestalling any intervention by Ofcom and sending the audience figure up by 1 million. This time, Andy Duncan acquitted himself well in an interview on the *Today* programme and, overall, the handling of the affair showed that lessons had been learned since January.

However, the spurt of interest generated by the incident, and by some low-key sexual activity once men had been admitted to the sanctum, was no more than temporary. On 20 July, the *Times* reported that young viewers were 'evicting *Big Brother* from their homes' as evidence mounted that the bubble had burst. Audiences for its first fifty days were down overall by 17 per cent on the previous year, and, most significantly, more than a quarter of its young audience, the sixteen- to thirty-four-year-olds, had vanished.[7] It was no longer generating regular front-page splashes for the tabloids: only the *Sun*, *Star* and *Mirror* covered it at all regularly. The producers tried to spice up the second half, but to no avail. *Big Brother 8*'s audience was 18 per cent down overall, averaging 3.8 million. The final, on 31 August, largely ignored by the press, was eclipsed by the memorial service organised by Princes William and Harry to mark the tenth anniversary of Princess Diana's death.

Not much else seemed to be going right for the channel, either. Until now it had been unique among the terrestrial broadcasters in holding its audience share firm, at around 10 per cent, since 1993. But the numbers were being whittled away as 80 per cent of homes now had multichannel digital television, and the spread of YouTube and other compelling social-networking sites seduced its potential audience with computer-generated entertainment. Duncan pulled one last trick to delay the inevitable by introducing a time-shifted Channel 4+1 – a device until then used only by cable and satellite channels,[8] but Kevin Lygo, in overall charge of programming, confessed that he could not see ratings going in any other direction than down after this.[9]

At the March seasonal programme launch, he announced an end to overpaying for American imports. The third series of *Desperate Housewives* had ended with audiences down 18 per cent compared with series two,[10] meaning that it barely covered the £40 million total price tag for series 3 and 4. *ER*, by now an elderly import, performed weakly at 10 p.m. on Mondays, and *My Name is Earl*, replacing *Friends*, limped along. There had been high hopes for *Studio 60 on the Sunset Strip*, bought from Aaron Sorkin, the creator of *The West Wing*, but it flopped in America and the first and only series was assigned to More4.

The revival of *Shipwrecked* – another attempt to find alternative reality programmes to *Big Brother* – flopped, and a provocative documentary about climate change, *The Great Global Warming Swindle*, infuriated the scientific community, though in many ways its brazenly one-sided approach harked back to the channel's early opinionated years. A projected 'Wank Week' was cancelled after protests, but the commissioner of these late-night masturbation documentaries was promoted by Bellamy to run factual entertainment.

Returning series of *Grand Designs* and *Location, Location, Location* prevented audiences from disappearing too rapidly, as did Gordon Ramsay's *The F Word* and a second series of *How to Look Good Naked*. The channel swept the board at the 2006 British Comedy Awards, and two distinctive offerings – *Derren Brown: Trick or Treat* and *Peep Show* – returned on Friday nights, while the latest import, *Ugly Betty*, held its own. Another UK-made drama, *Cape Wrath*, was not so lucky, attracting just 1.1 million viewers. It continued to screen serious documentaries at 9 p.m., and *Dispatches* pursued its examination of radical Islam with *Undercover Mosque* and *Between the Mullahs and the Military*. None of these successes, though, could alleviate the air of foreboding that permeated the channel as a deceptively mild spring gave way to a stormy summer.

Lord Puttnam was at the Hay-on-Wye Literary Festival over the wet May bank holiday and spoke his mind: 'I am not proud of the *Big Brother* row', he told a reporter. 'I am not even proud of *Big Brother* – but it accounts for 15 per cent of the total revenue that keeps Channel 4 afloat.'[11] He added that the channel's remit would have to be changed and that a generation of commissioners and programme-makers needed checking, because they were no longer imbued with the sense of public-service broadcasting. He was expanding on his views about how to rebuild public trust in the honesty of television, which would become the overarching media issue of the year. 'I am all for the channel being challenging, even at times controversial. But you are effectively throwing the baby out with the bathwater if you seek to be simply challenging and controversial without being respected and trusted.'[12]

Anthony Smith had joined the debate by telling the *Guardian* that Channel 4 had lost its soul and was now run by people who did not understand its purpose. Copies of his anguished after-dinner speech to the elite Athenaeum Club in London, 'Has *Big Brother* Won?', were now being passed around like some secret counter-revolutionary document in a Communist dictatorship. It was a *cri de coeur* about the demise of an older culture of broadcasting, 'predicated upon the presence of a cadre of producers who were bringing something they felt of value to the public.'[13] He told the club members, 'The breaking down of public service has been taking place by slow accretion for decades. My detestation of *Big Brother* is, I think, rooted in the realisation that a whole system of values has been swept away.'[14]

At the same time, a faction within the channel was worried at the course of events and questioned the leadership of Andy Duncan, whose perceived failings they blamed on his lack of programme-making experience. Separately, there was criticism of the 'much of a muchness' leisure and lifestyle weekday programmes that now dominated the schedule between 8 p.m. and 10 p.m. Angus MacQueen, the newly appointed Head of Documentaries, said,

> I think Channel 4 has become very conservative. I watched all its output in September, before I joined, and it was like my old aunt giving me advice: how to live, eat, clean the house, bring up the kids, talk to my husband – middle-class norms, conservative with a small c. We have lost the multicultural, multidimensional impulse.[15]

He started to champion a return to the purer observational documentaries of the 1990s, some of which he had made, and a switch away from formats where people and events are engineered to fit the programme. Channel 4 was sorely in need of a series to restore its reputation, or a breakthrough campaigning hit such as *Jamie's School Dinners*.

More4's Peter Dale, a seasoned commissioner of serious documentaries, lobbied for Channel 4 to conduct a fundamental debate about its aims and values. Puttnam had wanted this too, and in early autumn 2006 had warned that the task should not be handed to Ofcom, which was already undertaking the first independent financial review of the channel. Duncan did start, and the issue of commencing a 'public value' process was discussed at a no-holds-barred board meeting held in Belfast in October 2006. The initial thinking was not put in the public domain.

This inconclusive internal debate was overtaken by the publication of Ofcom's financial review, conducted by the consultants LEK as a response to the channel's lobbying for financial help.[16] This little publicised document, released two days before the Easter bank holiday, in retrospect marks the point at which Channel 4 ceded control over its future. At Ofcom's insistence, the consultants had dug uncomfortably deep into the broadcaster's internal systems, and although the public account was heavily edited, it laid bare two key facts. It found proof that serious documentaries were in decline – down 25 per cent in five years – and spending on British-made original programming had been cut. Original production had fallen to 74 per cent of the main channel's evening programmes, from 81 per cent in 2000.

Spending on British programmes was down by 7 per cent since 2003, when adjusted for inflation, while the cost of imported programmes had gone up significantly, to swallow 22 per cent of the programme budget compared with 18 per cent in 2001. (*The Simpsons* accounted largely for this.) Duncan interpreted the report as supporting his view of Channel 4's future funding problems. 'This report makes clear that it is no longer a question of if Channel 4 needs new forms of public support but when.'[17]

It also proved the channel had indeed been drifting away from its public-service remit, whether through pressures from competition, decisions to play safe, or a mix of both. Ofcom said funding was not an issue: although Thompson had originally maintained that the channel could start losing money from 2008, Ofcom said it would not happen until 2010 or perhaps 2012. The view in the industry, expressed by the *Royal Television Society Journal* in May, was that Duncan had been crying wolf and was suffering 'a bad case of hypochondria.'[18]

The report painted a picture of a television station which, far from being in a desperate plight, was relatively prosperous in comparison with its rivals. Commercial success was still driven by its wooing of younger and wealthier viewers, the golden formula devised in Michael Grade's era. Ninety per cent of its income was based on a solid appeal to affluent ABC1s and young adults – more sixteen-to-thirty-fours watched Channel 4 than ITV, even though ITV's total audience was twice the size. But the period since 2000 had been tougher than the preceding two decades when all commercial television had surfed a wave of booming advertising. The review did not hold out much hope for the channel filling the revenue gap through new-media activities. It forecast profits for the digital channels eventually, but not enough to make up a shortfall on the main channel. There were ways of economising – cutting the marketing budget, controlling staff costs, which had grown rapidly in the advertising sales area, and selling its freehold headquarters – but the heart of the potential problem was that the whole Channel 4 set-up still relied on the health of the main channel.

Ofcom took the issue seriously because it regarded Channel 4 as an important balance to the BBC, and it had to advise the Government on future options. After publishing the LEK Report in April, the Regulator undertook its own analysis, a factual account of the remit delivery, which confirmed that there had been a loss of variety in programming. While Channel 4 was meeting and exceeding its licence targets, it had changed over time through an accretion of questionable decisions and commercial pressures, without anyone blowing the whistle. There had been a shift to more accessible and commercial educational output, and budgets for news, arts, current affairs and religion had been reduced or pegged. Sport and children's programming had declined, and it was the only channel to show more films in peak evening time. There was a big problem over education, one of its main obligations, where a new policy to attract teenagers was urgently being worked out.

As for innovation, the analysis proved that the channel was relying more on established hits, up 6 per cent over five years, while new programmes and series, which provide the hits of the future, were down an ominous 3.1 per cent. It was heavily reliant on a small number of programmes and factual entertainment from a handful of key suppliers, led by Endemol.[19] Ofcom decided that, since this drift had happened in relatively prosperous times, without being formally picked up, it needed new benchmarking measures to help the Board and management to focus on their delivery of public-service broadcasting.

Responding to the Ofcom study, the BBC and Channel Five said there was no case for intervention yet. Channel Five said it should look for creative solutions rather than outside intervention and seek salvation in its remit – to innovate and find new programmes. ITV, at this stage, withheld its comment from publication. Advertising and media agencies were protective. The IPA said, 'We believe in Channel 4's historic set-up [. . .] We see no benefit to the viewer in seeking to privatise it. It would compete with the mass market and lose much of its unique value.'[20]

A month later, on 1 May, the channel's annual report was published. Profit – or surplus, as they now preferred to call it – was down 70 per cent to £14.5 million. Luke Johnson kept up the pressure for assistance.

> Channel 4 now needs some modest attention from policy-makers [. . .] perhaps 3 per cent of the £3 billion BBC annual licence [. . .] In 2007, we will be unable to increase programme budgets in line with industry cost inflation, so inevitably our output will suffer somewhat. In coming years we will be forced to steadily reduce our output of public-service broadcasting and focus more and more of our schedule on strictly commercial shows unless we receive help in kind.[21]

Back in February, the week after *Celebrity Big Brother* ended, Duncan had a ninety-minute meeting with Gordon Brown, the Chancellor of the Exchequer and Prime Minister designate. They discussed a range of options, but Brown left Duncan with a strong sense that he thought Channel 4 should be held to its public purpose, providing plurality alongside the BBC. Duncan impressed on him the wider role it played in the creative economy, citing the Price Waterhouse study showing that it supported 22,000 jobs and provided a £2 billion boost to the national economy. It fostered talent and acted as an investment 'angel' for fifty new independents a year and stimulated regional production. 'My conversations suggest there's a very, very strong consensus behind Channel 4's public-service role and providing plurality', Duncan said afterwards.[22]

In March, Brown's media adviser, the economist Stuart Wood, arranged with independent producer Ron Ackerman of Diverse Productions for a seminar on Channel 4, attended by Danny Cohen. Wood seemed well aware of the channel's future financial problems. Then it was reported in May that Brown was toying with the idea of selling the channel to a commercial buyer. The story had been put about by a faction among Brown's Treasury advisers who sought to test the water, possibly to encourage a rethink in programme priorities.

Ofcom's financial review was followed up in June by a carefully argued and worded statement from Ed Richards, now seeking to work with Channel 4's board for better measurement and feedback. He said that sooner or later the channel would arrive at a crossroads. The financial review had posited two alternative routes: it could continue to be a purely commercially funded company, maintaining editorial and operational independence, or the public-service commitment could be maintained or strengthened and possibly extended to new services and channels, with public support if necessary. This second course would involve the more intense scrutiny that comes with public money – in other words, the loss of a degree of independence. After consulting the Government, Richards had decided the matter was so urgent that Ofcom would bring forward its next public-service broadcasting review to the autumn of 2007 and link it with separate studies of children's programmes and television news. It looked as if Ofcom was engaged in a process of tough love, to save Channel 4 from itself.

'Before our work', said Richards, 'there was no single, thorough independent review. The analysis is illuminating. We need a significant improvement in monitoring how the remit works. I shudder to think of Channel 4 ten years ago, the extent to which there was no real accountability or monitoring of what was going on.'[23] He argued that the world had changed.

> Once, the BBC just got on with things, what it did was public service. Channel 4, what it did was the remit. We have all got beyond that [. . .] When we started this work it was a financial review of Channel 4. Well, the fact is that when you do a financial review of Channel 4 you end up thinking about the remit and its delivery. It is inescapable – the two things are related.[24]

Ofcom asked the channel to come up with their view of how to be accountable by the early autumn. Richards was treading a fine line, trying to create the conditions for a frank discussion about an important public asset needing sympathetic treatment while avoiding too blatant an intervention in its management. He also threw doubt on the channel's historic cross-subsidy model by which it justified the use of commercial programmes to pay for worthier output. The model had, in effect, been invented by Jeremy Isaacs, with his 'means and ends' programmes to eke out a modest budget, then adapted by Michael Grade.

In a speech, long planned but hurriedly scheduled the next week, on 19 June, Andy Duncan announced a strategic review of the channel's public-service contribution, but gave listeners little detail or substance to chew over. The audience was packed with Channel 4 staffers: a number were openly saying that they were unhappy about taking public money and turning into a second-rank BBC.

The day following Duncan's speech, Tessa Jowell, the outgoing Secretary of State for Culture, Media and Sport, confirmed that Channel 4 would receive £14 million assistance from the BBC to cover its digital switch-over expenses. Jowell's successor, James Purnell, was strongly against privatisation and in favour of the channel remaining as a publicly owned asset. He agreed that the public-service review needed to be carried out urgently.

But there remained an opportunity of self-help through diversification. In July, a consortium in which Channel 4 was the controlling 55-per-cent shareholder won the licence for a second national digital-radio multiplex from Ofcom. It planned to launch three stations in 2008, hiring a staff of 100 and drawing on its own strong programmes, and to rent out the other seven stations for an annual income of between £1 million and £2 million a year apiece. This guarantee of revenue seemed a better model than its previous digital-channel launches, but the scale of recruitment raised eyebrows at a time when the channel's programme budget was under pressure. Later in the month, it dug into its reserves to pay £28 million for a half share in EMAP's music channels – The Box, Kerrang! and a coveted Freeview channel. This was the most significant diversification since the appointment of Luke Johnson as Chairman three and a half years earlier.

Taken together, these two moves dovetailed with Channel 4's ambitions to expand as a multimedia brand, onto all platforms, and to cater even better for young adults, through their favoured leisure pursuit of music. But, as with the modest award of BBC licence funds to pay for the costs of the digital switch-over, these were not deals that could transform the channel's fortunes. If anything, they demonstrated that there would be no quick fixes for Channel 4.

Conclusion

● ● ● ●

And that is the story so far. After twenty-five years, Channel 4 has arrived at a cross-roads, a point when its role is being reassessed. Questions abound. Does it still broadcast enough that is special to warrant its privileged position? Is it valued enough to qualify for more support in future? If the answer is yes, then how should it reform to better serve viewers, without losing its independent stance? If it needs fresh capital or investment, or subsidy, how can that best be provided? Well, the past can provide pointers to the future.

As the history shows, the channel has evolved enormously since 1982. Channel 4 began as a subsidised, quirky broadcaster owned by the Regulator, led by the charismatic Jeremy Isaacs, screening some experimental programmes that could only have been made for it, along with a lot of other things that padded out the afternoon and early evening. After a shaky start, it settled into its Charlotte Street groove, and the independent production sector it fostered roared into life and forced its way into the rest of broadcasting.

After surviving the tricky political battles of the late Thatcher years, Channel 4 avoided privatisation but was changed into a hybrid public corporation after 1993, without shareholders, taking control of its finances through the sale of its own advertising. This was a critical moment, and it was shepherded through by Michael Grade and his team.

Although technically the programme remit did not change, the schedule was sharpened up; it became more dependent on American imports, stripped programmes such as *Countdown* and expanded into breakfast and daytime. As it journeyed through the 1990s, it was commercialised, to the dismay of its purist founders, but was still recognisably different. It retains to this day the bonus of having no shareholders to service.

Under Michael Jackson from 1997 onwards, encouraged by the Blair Government, the channel began the long, faltering process of transformation from a single television channel into a multimedia brand. It still demonstrated innovation and had a wonderful cash bonanza when its payments to ITV ceased in 1999, which, to some extent, it squandered.

From 2002, it has been casting around for security while responding to competition by becoming increasingly dependent on factual entertainment, exemplified by the spread, until summer 2007, of *Big Brother* and its spin-offs. It still provides some ambitious documentaries, news, home-grown entertainment and arts events.

Throughout the years, it has demonstrated an institutional ability to adapt and thrive, as the media landscape around it utterly changed. To that extent, the history to date is largely a story of success: a small, tough, privileged channel holding its own, except in new media, until recently protective of its independence.

The history reminds us how the early founders of Channel 4 had been haunted about what would happen if, in what was still a restricted four-channel world, ITV turned around and attacked Channel 4 directly at birth, killing it off.

So, for the first seventeen years, the formative Isaacs and Grade eras, it was protected within a framework designed to prevent full-blooded competition. In a sense, ITV was the original Big Brother in the 1980s, paying for Channel 4 while selling its advertising, freeing the new channel to concentrate on being complementary with some programmes, catering for underserved minorities. From 1993, as profound changes began, the protection was greatly diluted, with the funding formula, under which ITV would have had to pay some of the shortfall if the channel hit hard times. The formula (and by now tattered relationship with ITV) ended in 1999, when Channel 4 welcomed the chance to become a free-standing broadcaster, still in public ownership. The funding formula was seen from the moment it began as a piece of rogue legislation because it was not fairly constructed and resulted in the grim annual ritual of cash being transferred over to ITV, never the other way, like an imperial tribute. But it is not impossible that some sort of modern safety net could be rethought and revived again, giving Channel 4's minority interest and unprofitable programmes respite. The question is, who would be made to underwrite it, and meet the call for funds? In 2003, Michael Grade made an interesting suggestion, that the channel could be linked to the BBC. But by September 2007, he had changed his mind about the channel he had twice helped save from privatisation. Now the Executive Chairman of ITV, he told the Royal Television Society's biennial convention in Cambridge that it would be preferable for Channel 4 to be privatised rather than compromise its independence with a government subsidy.

Although Channel 4 is expanding into a multimedia brand, it is a creative organisation and has worked best in the past when run by people with a deep understanding of the television industry, which is still its main activity. Jeremy Isaacs was the outstanding producer of his generation. Michael Grade surrounded himself with exceptional creative and commercial executives. The most pertinent demonstration of how to force through a programming overhaul – which Channel 4 in the summer of 2007 embarked on – was provided by Michael Jackson in 1997, when he funded a set of favoured producers to identify new stars, programmes, writers, directors and producers. But he also set in train a division of the organisation into the commercial 4Ventures and the old Channel 4, which threatened the broadcaster's focus on public service.

The exception was Mark Thompson, whose two-year stint was disruptive, raising the hare of merger with Channel Five and the spectre of the channel's financial precariousness without allowing the time to find answers. The Andy Duncan era, since 2004, has seen Channel 4 ditch merger, on the grounds that it made neither commercial nor cultural sense, embrace Freeview – breathing life into FilmFour and boosting E4 – and set a course for expansion into digital radio and music, whose outcome is uncertain. Between 2005 and 2006, it prospered as ITV weakened.

One problem is that much of the discussion since the huge financial shock of 2001, when Channel 4 ran up into its first ever loss, has been framed by an expectation of decline and the need to demonstrate the difficulties it faces in a tough advertising market, rather than the point of it all: the programmes.

This prolonged debate, so heavily focused on strategy rather than achievements and a mission to innovate, has helped create a negative, whinging environment. In short, Channel 4, the past master of marketing, got its mission and messages the wrong way round. It needed to ensure it was delivering a wide range of programmes of public value and catering for a range of viewers, not just the sixteen-to-thirty-fours, at best before, or at least while, it was begging for public assistance.

Peter Bazalgette observed in May,

> Having taken the view that everything is going to fail, the moment advertising rates fall a cheer goes up: this is a vindication. It's not good for morale. They've got into a rather nasty bind: good news is bad news and bad news is good news. And that is a very bad way to run an organisation. It informs a lot of the way they present themselves in public.[1]

Kevin Lygo agreed that the messages have been muddled.

> I think where we got it wrong, and I didn't see it at first, was that Andy, not surprisingly, has been too fixated on his conviction that it's all going to come to an end and we need help. I should have been made to go out and say – because Andy can't really do it and neither can Luke, and I feel guilty about this – that Channel 4 is such a marvellous thing [. . .] we

should have been shouting about the public-service remit and not saying 'We're doomed, we're doomed, the model is broke.' That is a confusing message, because there is a part of me that thinks, Do you know what, we are in show business, and if I come up with the hits, we will be fine.[2]

To some extent, Lygo corrected this at the Edinburgh Television Festival in a carefully planned speech that formally abandoned the channel's historic target of a 10-per-cent share of ratings, set originally by Isaacs. 'Much better to be an interesting channel at 8 per cent than a less interesting one at 10 per cent'.[3]

This is made possible because Channel 4's portfolio of digital channels is now sufficiently developed to make up for a shortfall in audiences. As well as starting a phased withdrawal from *Big Brother*, by moving out *Celebrity Big Brother* and offering a related programme on E4 (see Chapter 1), Lygo also said Channel 4 was dropping some tired factual programmes clogging up evenings at 8 p.m. and 9 p.m., including *You Are What You Eat*, *It's Me or the Dog*, *Selling Houses Abroad* and *Brat Camp*, to make space for new educational and documentary programmes, not just factual entertainment. It was practical proof that Channel 4 was rethinking its programme mix as part of the public-service review organised by Ofcom, which began in autumn of 2007 and the bargaining that would inevitably follow.

For Luke Johnson, there is no easy or fast financial solution to the longer-term funding gap.

> The challenge we face is that we have revenues short of £1 billion a year. Building alternative revenues of that sort of scale is really tough. [. . .] It isn't simply a matter of business, it's a matter of politics; the politics of the television and the media, where a huge number of vested interests lie [. . .] If the debate isn't had properly now, who knows how much influence we will have lost when it eventually is.[4]

There are optimistic pointers. Duncan says that the Board is now united behind him in seeking a settlement that underpins Channel 4's public-service role. And Channel 4 remains a strongly branded broadcaster with a unique appeal to young people, feeding their appetite for comedy and innovation, even as they tire of *Big Brother*. Tony Hall, who carried out the *Celebrity Big Brother* review, believes this appeal can be broadened to embrace more worthy strands, including youth-oriented arts and the holy grail of current affairs. It has other options to explore. It could modify its historic role as a publisher and produce some of its own programmes, as a means of building up a library to feed its digital channels, rather than simply buying the rights to two screenings. ITV2, 3 and 4 are more profitable than E4 because the parent, ITV, owns the catalogue. This is all the more pressing because the dominant part of the independent sector that Channel 4 was created to foster has become so powerful, like Frankenstein's monster, that the channel now risks being captured by its big suppliers.

The biggest suppliers have certainly succeeded in driving up the cost to the channel of their shows, under a system of value pricing. Most of the programmes that caused the major controversies of 2007, across all channels, were made by independents. In August, the channel decided to draw a line by pledging that 20 per cent of its funds would be spent with independent producers with modest turnovers, the baby 'Endemols' of the future. Ofcom's permission would be needed for this change, and the producer's trade body, PACT, have already lobbied against it. Michael Jackson, who pushed for the purchase of stakes in independents in 2000, sees it as a tempting option. To place this in context, Channel 4 is the only broadcaster of its size not to be in production.

Duncan believes that there is little political pressure for Channel 4 to be privatised and that a solution can be worked out. The obvious source of funds, if self-help and economies fail, would be to dip further into the BBC licence fee, which could be implemented at a break point halfway through the current ten-year charter in 2012. However, the BBC is struggling to live within a tough settlement.

Many people, including its founders, want Channel 4 to do well, despite its well-publicised lapses. They want it to return to its innovative, quirky, argumentative self. That outcome could flow from an adjusted Channel 4 model. If it gained an element of public funding alongside its advertising revenue, it would become even more of a strange hybrid. That would force it to become more accountable and open about its programming and its aims. It might be the very British compromise that this very British creation needs.

But we are now at the point where history ends, and futurology starts.

Notes

1 How Celebrity Big Brother changed Channel 4

1 *Royal Television Society Journal* September 2006, Channel 4 on the attack by Emily Bell.
2 There were 44,500 complaints to Ofcom, while Channel 4 was swamped.
3 Kevin Lygo, in interview, April 2007. The bronzes are depicted in an art history, D. Dinwiddie (ed.) (2003) *Portraits of the Masters: Bronze Sculptures of the Tibetan Buddhist Lineages*, Chicago, Ill.: Scrindia.
4 Channel 4's advertising income in 2006 was £680 million. That excludes E4, the revenue from phone calls, voting, downloads and sponsorship. Media agency Starcom estimated in 2006 that *Big Brother*'s total of twenty-one shows netted £165 million, 22 per cent of Channel 4's total advertising revenue; the company disputes this.
5 Kevin Lygo, in interview, March 2007.
6 David Puttnam, in interview with *Media Guardian*, June 2007. Channel 4 says its value is closer to 10 per cent.
7 David Puttnam, in interview, September 2006.
8 Luke Johnson, in interview, December 2006.
9 *Goldplated*, a drama series about the Cheshire set, was designed as a long-returning series, but had to be cancelled, while *Get Your Act Together with Harvey Goldsmith* was moved out of prime time after flopping. Even *Deal or No Deal* was weakening its hold.
10 Luke Johnson, in interview, December 2007.
11 *Deal or No Deal* had added 0.8 per cent to audience ratings, ensuring Channel 4 held close to its 10 per cent target.
12 Gordon Ramsay, in interview, December 2006.
13 Kevin Lygo, in interview, December 2006.
14 Kevin Lygo, in interview, December 2006.
15 Kevin Lygo, in interview, December 2006.
16 Kevin Lygo, in interview, December 2006.
17 Andy Duncan, press statement, Thursday, 18 January 2007 at Said Business School, Oxford, during the Oxford Media Convention.
18 Tessa Jowell, speaking to the press on Thursday, 18 January 2007 at the same venue.
19 Kevin Lygo, in interview, July 2007.

2 The long and winding road

1 Anthony Smith, in interview November 2006.
2 Anthony Smith, in interview, November 2006.
3 Anthony Smith, *Guardian*, 21 April 1972.
4 Smith, *Guardian*, 21 April 1972.
5 Anthony Smith, in interview, November 2006.
6 Smith, *Guardian*, 21 April 1972.

7   John Birt (2002) *John Birt: The Harder Path*, London: Little, Brown, p. 178.
8   Anthony Smith, in interview, November 2006.
9   Anthony Smith, in interview, November 2006.
10   Michael Darlow (2004) *Independents Struggle: The Programme Makers Who Took on the TV Establishment*, London: Quarto, p. 3.
11   Anthony Smith, in interview, November 2006.
12   Anthony Smith, in interview, November 2006.
13   Anthony Smith, in interview, November 2006.

3   Isaacs: maverick founder

1   Jeremy Isaacs (2007) *Look Me in the Eye: A Life in Television*, London: Abacus, p. 235.
2   Isaacs, *Look Me in the Eye*, p. 235.
3   MacTaggart Lecture, Signposting Television in the 1980s: The Fourth Channel, 1979.
4   MacTaggart Lecture.
5   Roger Graef, in interview, November 2006.
6   Roger Graef, in interview, November 2006.
7   Isaacs, *Look Me in the Eye*, p. 8.
8   Sir Denis Forman (1997) *Persona Granada: Memories of Sidney Bernstein and the Early Years of Independent Television*, London: André Deutsch.
9   Isaacs, *Look Me in the Eye*, p. 148.
10   This account is heavily based on the official history, Paul Bonner and Leslie Aston (2002) *Independent Television in Britain: New Developments in Independent Television 1981–92. Channel Four, TV-am, Cable and Satellite: Vol. 6*, Basingstoke: Palgrave Macmillan.
11   Speech, Royal Television Society Cambridge Convention, 14 September 1979.
12   Bonner and Aston, *Independent Television in Britain*, p. 12.
13   Anthony Smith, in interview, November 2006.
14   IBA (1980) 'The Fourth Channel: The Authority's Proposal', in Annual Report 1979/80, London: IBA.
15   Quoted in Bonner and Aston, *Independent Television in Britain*.
16   Anthony Smith, in interview, November 2006, recounting what the Board was told by Brian Tesler, who was called out of a board meeting to take a phone call from Willie Whitelaw over S4C.
17   Lord Attenborough, in interview, May 2007.
18   Lord Attenborough, in interview, May 2007.
19   Anthony Smith, in interview, November 2006.
20   Roger Graef, in interview, November 2006.
21   John Birt (2002) *John Birt: The Harder Path*, London: Little, Brown.
22   Lord Attenborough, in interview, May 2007.
23   Anthony Smith, in interview, November 2006.
24   Peter Catterall (1992) *The Making of Channel 4*, London: Frank Cass.
25   Catterall, *The Making of Channel 4*.
26   John Ranelagh, in interview, August 2006.
27   Lord Attenborough, in interview, May 2007.
28   Justin Dukes, in interview, March 2006.
29   Justin Dukes, in interview, March 2006.

30 Justin Dukes, in interview, March 2006.
31 Justin Dukes, in interview, March 2006.
32 Frank McGettigan, in interview, March 2006.

4 Godfather in the green Rolls Royce

1 Lord Attenborough, in interview, May 2007.
2 Jeremy Isaacs, in interview, December 2006.
3 Anthony Smith, in interview, November 2006.
4 Roger Graef, in interview, November 2006.

5 Miss No One from Nowhere joins Channel 4

1 *Guardian* article by Forgan.
2 Jeremy Isaacs (1989) *Storm Over Four: A Personal Account*, London: Weidenfeld & Nicolson, p. 38.
3 Paul Bonner and Leslie Aston (2002) *Independent Television in Britain: New Developments in Independent Television 1981–92. Channel Four, TV-am, Cable and Satellite: Vol. 6*, Basingstoke: Palgrave Macmillan, p. 39.
4 Isaacs, *Storm Over Four*, p. 39.
5 Liz Forgan, in interview, December 2006.
6 Liz Forgan, in interview, December 2006.
7 Jeremy Isaacs tribute at Naomi Sargant memorial, St John's, Smith Square, London SW1, January 2007.
8 Isaacs, Sargant memorial service.
9 Isaacs, Sargant memorial service.
10 Isaacs, Sargant memorial service.
11 Isaacs, Sargant memorial service.
12 Justin Dukes, in interview, March 2006.
13 Channel 4 board minutes, 27 March 1981.
14 Liz Forgan, in interview, December 2006.
15 Liz Forgan, in interview, December 2006.
16 Liz Forgan, in interview, December 2006.
17 Channel 4 board minutes, June 1981.
18 Nigel Stafford-Clark, in interview, July 2006.
19 Nigel Stafford-Clark, in interview, July 2006.
20 Nigel Stafford-Clark, in interview, July 2006.
21 Nigel Stafford-Clark, in interview, July 2006.
22 Sue Woodford, in interview, September 2006.
23 Sue Woodford, in interview, September 2006.
24 Sue Woodford, in interview, September 2006.
25 Sue Woodford, in interview, September 2006.
26 Channel 4 board minutes, July 1981.
27 Mike Bolland, in interview, September 2000.
28 Malcolm Gerrie, in interview, January 2007.

29 Malcolm Gerrie, in interview, January 2007.
30 Martin Lambie-Nairn (1997) *Brand Identity for Television: With Knobs On*, London: Phaidon.
31 Pam Masters, in interview, December 2006.
32 Pam Masters, in interview, December 2006.
33 Ann Harris, in interview, July 2006. Harris took the phone call from Korer that he had done the *Cheers* deal and needed a deal memo drawn up, which she duly wrote.
34 Ann Harris, in interview, July 2006.
35 Exchange of letters between Cecil Korer, Leslie Halliwell and Jeremy Isaacs over the purchase of *Cheers*, September 1982, Channel 4 archive.
36 Sir Richard Attenborough, Channel 4 board minutes, 20 October 1982. Attenborough said at the meeting that Equity's stand was 'entirely proper'.
37 Nigel Stafford-Clark, in interview, July 2006.
38 Isaacs, *Storm Over Four*, pp. 48–9.

6 Launch: a white-knuckle ride

1 The revenue potential of Channel 4, T.P. Barwise and A.S.C Ehrenberg Aske Research Ltd and The London Business School, ADMAP 1979.
2 Tim Simmons, in interview, July 2006.
3 Paul Coia, in interview, May 2006. He has preserved the original opening script from 2 November 1982.
4 Paul Coia, in interview, May 2006.
5 Mike Bolland, in interview, September 2006.
6 Mike Bolland, in interview, September 2006.
7 Jeremy Isaacs and Sue Stoessl, in a filmed presentation to advertisers, summer 1982.
8 Isaacs and Stoessl, presentation to advertisers.
9 John Ranelagh, in interview, August 2006.
10 Jeremy Isaacs (1989) *Storm Over Four: A Personal Account*, London: Weidenfeld & Nicolson, p. 49.
11 Isaacs, *Storm Over Four*, p. 49.
12 Mike Bolland, in interview, September 2006.
13 Pam Masters, in interview, December 2006.
14 Richard Whiteley (2000) *Himoff! The Memoirs of a TV Matinee Idle*, London: Orion.
15 Isaacs, *Storm Over Four*, p. 50.
16 Paul Coia, in interview, May 2006.
17 Tim Simmons, in interview, July 2006.
18 Dorothy Byrne, in interview, February 2007.
19 Channel 4 board minutes, January 1984.
20 Nick Fraser, in interview, July 2006.
21 Stephen Lambert (1982) *Channel 4: Television with a Difference?* London: BFI Publishing, p. 160.
22 Sue Stoessl, in interview, May 2006.
23 Nigel Stafford-Clark, in interview, July 2006.
24 Pam Masters, in interview, December 2006.
25 Paul Coia, in interview, May 2006; Jo Wright, working in presentation at Channel 4, in

interview, January 2006.

26   Channel 4 board minutes, 17 November 1982.
27   Channel 4 board minutes, 15 December 1982.
28   Channel 4 board minutes, 15 December 1982.
29   Nigel Stafford-Clark, in interview, July 2006.
30   Nigel Stafford-Clark, in interview, July 2006.
31   Ann Harris, in interview, May 2006.
32   John Ranelagh, in interview, August 2006.
33   Roger Graef, in interview, November 2006.
34   Channel 4 board minutes, 18 January.
35   Jeremy Isaacs, in interview, December 2006.
36   David Rose, from a series of reports prepared by commissioning editors for the Berystede meeting in Ascot of 28–9 January 1983, when the criticism of Channel 4 was most intense.
37   Mike Bolland, report at the Berystede meeting.
38   Cecil Korer, report at the Berystede meeting.
39   Brian Tesler, interviewed in Paul Bonner and Leslie Aston (2002) *Independent Television in Britain: New Developments in Independent Television 1981–92. Channel Four, TV-am, Cable and Satellite: Vol. 6*, Basingstoke: Palgrave Macmillan.
40   Channel 4 board minutes, 16 March.

7 Disaster! Channel 4 News

1   Richard Lindley (2005) *And Finally . . .?: The News from ITN*, London: Politico's, p. 261.
2   Liz Forgan, in interview, December 2006.
3   Liz Forgan, in interview, December 2006.
4   Edward Stourton, in interview, February 2007.
5   John Birt and Peter Jay (1975) 'Can Television News Break the Understanding Barrier', *The Times*, February.
6   Liz Forgan, in interview, December 2006.
7   Quoted in Lindley, *And Finally . . .?*, p. 261.
8   Liz Forgan, in interview, December 2006.
9   Liz Forgan, in interview, December 2006.
10   Stewart Purvis, in interview, November 2006.
11   Liz Forgan, in interview, December 2006.
12   Liz Forgan, in interview, December 2006.
13   John Morrison, in interview, September 2006.
14   John Morrison, in interview, September 2006.
15   Trevor McDonald, in interview, January 2007.
16   Liz Forgan, in interview, December 2006.
17   Trevor McDonald, in interview, January 2007.
18   Trevor McDonald, in interview, January 2007.
19   Stewart Purvis, in interview, November 2006.
20   Liz Forgan, in interview, December 2006.
21   Liz Forgan, report to Berystede, Ascot conference, 28–9 January 1983.
22   Michael Crick, in interview, October 2006.

23 Trevor McDonald, in interview, January 2007.
24 Trevor McDonald, in interview, January 2007.
25 Derrik Mercer memo to Channel 4 News staff, spring 1983, preserved by John Morrison.
26 Derrik Mercer, memo, April and May 1983.
27 Channel 4 board minutes, 15 June 1983.
28 John Morrison, in interview, September 2006.
29 Stewart Purvis, in interview, November 2006.
30 Liz Forgan, in interview, December 2006.
31 Stewart Purvis, in interview, November 2006.
32 Stewart Purvis, in interview, November 2006.
33 Stewart Purvis, in interview, November 2006; Lord Attenborough, in interview, May 2007.
34 Stewart Purvis, in interview, November 2006.
35 Stewart Purvis, in interview, November 2006.
36 Michael Crick, in interview, October 2006.
37 Research into *Channel 4 News*, 1984, preserved by John Morrison.

8   Two tigers at the table

1 Liz Forgan, in interview, December 2006.
2 The Broadcasting Act (Section 4[f]) had a clause requiring 'due impartiality' in the handling of news, current affairs and public issues, and the IBA was, in law, the broadcaster responsible for output.
3 Channel 4 board minutes, 17 November 1982.
4 Jeremy Isaacs (1989) *Storm Over Four: A Personal Account*, London: Weidenfeld & Nicolson, p. 84.
5 Brian Tesler, Channel 4 board minutes, 20 July 1983.
6 Liz Forgan, in interview, December 2006.
7 David Graham, in interview, November 2006.
8 David Graham, in interview, November 2006.
9 David Graham, in interview, November 2006.
10 Steve Hewlett, in interview, March 2007.
11 Steve Hewlett, in interview, March 2007.
12 Channel 4 board minutes, 19 January 1983.
13 David Graham, in interview, November 2006.
14 Channel 4 archive.
15 Liz Forgan, in interview, December 2006.
16 Liz Forgan, in interview, December 2006.
17 Liz Forgan, in interview, December 2006.
18 Channel 4 board minutes, 16 February 1983.
19 Channel 4 board minutes, 16 February 1983.
20 Jeremy Isaacs, in interview, December 2006.
21 Channel 4 board minutes, 20 July 1983.
22 Jeremy Isaacs, in interview, December 2006.
23 Lord Attenborough, in interview, May 2007.

24   Jeremy Isaacs, in interview, December 2006.
25   Jeremy Isaacs, in interview, December 2006.
26   Lord Attenborough, in interview, May 2007.
27   Isaacs, *Storm Over Four*, p. 144.
28   Jeremy Isaacs, in interview, December 2006.
29   Peter Catterall (1992) *The Making of Channel 4*, London: Frank Cass, p. 11.
30   Jeremy Isaacs, in interview, December 2006.
31   Peter Williams, in interview, January 2007.
32   Claudia Milne, in interview, March 2007.
33   Isaacs, *Storm Over Four*, p. 144.

9   Calmer waters

1   Jeremy Isaacs, 'All at 4' note, 19 April 1983.
2   Mike Bolland, in interview, September 2006.
3   Mike Bolland, in interview, September 2006.
4   Justin Dukes, in interview, March 2006.
5   Roger Graef, in interview, September 2006.
6   Justin Dukes, in interview, March 2006.
7   Sue Stoessl, in interview, July 2006.
8   *Broadcast Magazine* Special Supplement October 1987.
9   Jeremy Isaacs, 'All at 4' note.
10   Channel board minutes, 19 December 1984.
11   Jeremy Isaacs, 'All at 4' note.
12   Jeremy Isaacs, in interview, December 2006.
13   Sir Richard Attenborough was Chairman of the BFI, 1981–92; Anthony Smith Channel 4 Board Member, 1980–4 and Director of the BFI, 1979–88; Jeremy Isaacs Governor of the BFI, 1979–81.

10   Likely lads flourish as Isaacs leaves

1   Alan Marke, in interview, November 2006.
2   Alan Marke, in interview, November 2006.
3   Mike Bolland, in interview, September 2006.
4   Mike Bolland, in interview, September 2006.
5   Malcolm Gerrie interview, *Sounds*, 2 May 1987.
6   Jane Hewland, in interview, May 2006.
7   Jane Hewland, in interview, May 2006.
8   Jane Hewland, in interview, May 2006.
9   Charlie Parsons, in interview, July 2006.
10   Channel 4 archive, exchange of letters.
11   Stephen Garrett, in interview, March 2007.
12   Jane Hewland, in interview, May 2006.
13   *The Mirror*, 8 May 1999.
14   Channel 4 archive, February 1991.

15   Channel 4 archive, February 1991.

16   Sue Stoessl, in interview, July 2006.

17   Channel 4 board minutes, 22 July 1986.

18   Channel 4 board minutes, 22 July 1986.

19   Channel 4 board minutes, November 1986.

20   Channel 4 board minutes, November 1986.

21   *The House*, a BBC2 observational documentary about Royal Covent Garden in 1995 exposed his style of management.

22   John Ranelagh, in interview, August 2006.

23   Lord Attenborough, in interview, May 2007.

24   David Docherty (1988) *Keeping Faith? Channel 4 and Its Audience* (Broadcasting Research Unit Monograph), London: John Libbey & Co. The study could not be found in the otherwise well-ordered Channel 4 archive.

25   Docherty, *Keeping Faith*.

26   Docherty, *Keeping Faith*.

27   Docherty, *Keeping Faith*.

28   John Ranelagh, in interview, August 2006.

29   Docherty, *Keeping Faith*.

11   Dark horse makes the Grade

1   Channel 4 board minutes, 28 April 1987.

2   Liz Forgan, in interview, December 2006.

3   Channel 4 Annual Report, 1987.

4   Sir George Russell, in interview, October 2005, April 2006.

5   Raymond Snoddy, *Financial Times*, 11 September 1987.

6   Justin Dukes, in interview, March 2006.

7   Anthony Smith, in interview, November 2006.

8   Will Wyatt (2003) *The Fun Factory: A Life in the BBC*, London: Aurum Press.

9   Michael Grade (1999) *It Seemed Like a Good Idea at the Time*, London: Macmillan, p. 258.

10   Wyatt, *The Fun Factory*.

11   Grade, *It Seemed Like a Good Idea at the Time*, p. 282.

12   Grade, *It Seemed Like a Good Idea at the Time*, p. 282.

13   Justin Dukes, in interview, March 2006.

14   Paul Bonner and Leslie Aston (2002) *Independent Television in Britain: New Developments in Independent Television 1981–92. Channel Four, TV-am, Cable and Satellite: Vol. 6*, Basingstoke: Palgrave Macmillan.

15   Lord Attenborough, in interview, May 2007.

16   Lord Attenborough, in interview, May 2007.

17   Channel 4 board minutes, 17 November 1987.

18   Maggie Brown, the *Independent* media section.

19   Press conference, 17 November 1987.

20   Jeremy Isaacs (1989) *Storm Over Four: A Personal Account*, London: Weidenfeld & Nicolson.

21   Grade, *It Seemed Like a Good Idea at the Time*, p. 289.

22   Grade, *It Seemed Like a Good Idea at the Time*, p. 291.

23   Anthony Smith, in interview, November 2006.
24   Jeremy Isaacs, 'All at 4' note.
25   Grade, *It Seemed Like a Good Idea at the Time*, p. 292.
26   Peter Catterall (1992) *The Making of Channel 4*, London: Frank Cass, pp. 160–1.
27   Channel 4 board minutes, 25 January 1988.
28   David Scott, in interview, October 2006.
29   *Royal Television Society Journal*, October 1991.
30   Channel 4 Accounts, 31 March 1988, p. 40.

12   Breakfast with handcuffs

 1   Channel 4 board minutes, 29 March 1989. On 1 January 1993, it became a self-governing corporation, financed by advertising.
 2   Paul Bonner and Leslie Aston (2002) *Independent Television in Britain: New Developments in Independent Television 1981–92. Channel Four, TV-am, Cable and Satellite: Vol. 6*, Basingstoke: Palgrave Macmillan, p. 254.
 3   Those leaving included Pam Masters, Ellis Griffiths, Sue Stoessl, Michael Kustow and Naomi Sargant. Later, David Rose retired.
 4   John Willis, in interview, December 2006.
 5   John Willis, in interview, December 2006.
 6   John Willis, in interview, December 2006. Factual 9 p.m. slots would start at around £150,000 in 2007.
 7   Peter Moore, in interview, December 2006.
 8   Peter Moore, in interview, December 2006.
 9   Nick Broomfield would remain a presence at the channel, praising it in 2007 for fully funding *Ghosts*, his drama documentary about the cockle-pickers of Morecambe Bay.
10   Phil Grabsky, in interview, November 2006. He founded the independent Seventh Art Production Company.
11   Alan Marke, in interview, October 2006.
12   Alan Marke, in interview, October 2006.
13   Alan Marke, in interview, October 2006.
14   Channel 4 archive. The version transmitted did include Farrell, voiced over. Channel 4 tried to imply in its publicity that the programme had been held up by the banning order. David Glencross, Chief Executive of the ITC pointed out this was not true.
15   The current Horseferry Road site was bought for £23.5 million in June 1990, after an agonised internal debate, though the Marco Polo Building on Battersea Bridge, available after BSB collapsed, was checked out.
16   Roger Graef article, *Independent*, 28 August 1991.
17   The new licence required seven hours of education weekly, one of religion, four of current affairs, 25 per cent independent production, 50 per cent European. There had been no attempt to alter the remit, to offer a suitable proportion of matter calculated to appeal to tastes and interests not generally catered for by Channel 3: that innovation and experiment in the form and content of these programmes are encouraged, and generally that Channel 4 is given a distinctive character of its own.
18   Channel 4 board minutes, 24 September 1991.
19   Channel 4 archive, 18 September 1991.

20   *Royal Television Society Journal*, October 1991.
21   Bose, Mihir (1992) *Michael Grade: Screening the Image*, London: Virgin, p. 264.
22   *Royal Television Society Journal*, October 1991.
23   Bonner and Aston, *Independent Television in Britain*, p. 293.
24   Andrew Davidson (1992) *Under the Hammer: The Inside Story of the 1991 ITV Franchise Battle*, London: Heinemann.
25   Liz Forgan, in interview, December 2006.
26   Liz Forgan, in interview, December 2006.
27   John Willis, in interview, December 2006.
28   Duncan Gray, in interview, October 2006.

13   The golden formula

1   Stewart Butterfield, in interview, February 2006.
2   Stewart Butterfield, in interview, February 2006.
3   Stewart Butterfield, in interview, February 2006.
4   Stewart Butterfield, in interview, February 2006.
5   Andy Barnes, in interview, May 2006.
6   Andy Barnes, in interview, May 2006.
7   Andy Barnes, in interview, May 2006.
8   Sue Stoessl, in interview, July 2006.
9   Andy Barnes, in interview, May 2006.
10   Andy Barnes, in interview, May 2006.
11   Andy Barnes, in interview, May 2006.
12   Andy Barnes, in interview, May 2006.
13   Andy Barnes, in interview, May 2006.
14   Channel 4 board minutes, 15 December 1992.
15   Stewart Butterfield, in interview, February 2006.
16   Channel 4 Annual Report 1993.
17   Stewart Butterfield, in interview, February 2006.
18   Stewart Butterfield, in interview, February 2006.
19   Liz Forgan, in interview, December 2006.
20   Stewart Butterfield, in interview, February 2006.
21   Stewart Butterfield, in interview, February 2006.
22   Stewart Butterfield, in interview, February 2006.
23   Andy Barnes, in interview, May 2006.

14   Britain's Pornographer-in-Chief?

1   The *Daily Mail*, 8 June 1995.
2   Channel 4 board minutes, 12 June 1995.
3   Channel 4 board minutes, 12 June 1995.
4   Duncan Gray, in interview, September 2006.
5   David Stevenson, in interview, December 2006.
6   Andrew Newman, in interview, February 2007.

7 Duncan Gray, in interview, September 2006.
8 Duncan Gray, in interview, September 2006.
9 Duncan Gray, in interview, September 2006.
10 A letter to Channel 4, 8 March 1995, Channel 4 archive.
11 Duncan Gray, in interview, September 2006.
12 Channel 4 archive.
13 Scott Inquiry into *The Word*, Channel 4 archive.
14 Scott Inquiry into *The Word*, Channel 4 archive.
15 Scott Inquiry into *The Word*, Channel 4 archive.
16 Scott Inquiry into *The Word*, Channel 4 archive.
17 Scott Inquiry into *The Word*, Channel 4 archive.
18 Scott Inquiry into *The Word*, Channel 4 archive.
19 Channel 4 archive.
20 Channel 4 archive.
21 Scott Inquiry into *The Word*, Channel 4 archive.
22 Channel 4 archive.
23 Channel 4 board minutes, 24 April 1995.
24 Channel 4 archive.
25 John Willis, in interview, December 2006.
26 David Stevenson, in interview, January 2006.
27 Maggie Brown, *Guardian* media section, 9 December 1996.
28 David Stevenson, in interview, January 2006.
29 Chairman's statement, Channel 4 annual report, 1995.

15 Drama! GBH, Potter, Film on Four

1 Michael Palin was initially cast as Michael Murray because Robert Lindsay was not available. But he then became available so Palin ceded the role and took the persecuted headmaster's part instead.
2 Peter Ansorge, in interview, January 2007.
3 Alan Bleasdale, letter, 10 March 1991.
4 Peter Ansorge, in interview, January 2007.
5 Peter Ansorge, in interview, January 2007.
6 Robert Lindsay, in interview, January 2007.
7 Peter Ansorge, in interview, January 2007.
8 Peter Ansorge, in interview, January 2007.
9 Peter Ansorge, in interview, January 2007.
10 Dennis Potter, MacTaggart Lecture, August 1993.
11 Letter from Michael Grade, 8 August 1994, Channel 4 archive.
12 Peter Ansorge, in interview, January 2007.
13 John Willis, in interview, December 2006.
14 Liz Forgan, in interview, December 2006.
15 Liz Forgan, in interview, December 2006.
16 Douglas Rae, in interview, December 2006.
17 Peter Ansorge, in interview, January 2007.
18 *Brookside* file, Channel 4 archive.

19 *Brookside* file, Channel 4 archive.
20 Peter Ansorge, in interview, January 2007.
21 Paul Marquess, in interview, February 2007.
22 David Aukin, in interview, December 2006.
23 David Aukin, in interview, December 2006.
24 David Aukin, in interview, December 2006.
25 David Aukin, in interview, December 2006.
26 David Aukin, in interview, December 2006.
27 David Aukin, in interview, December 2006.
28 David Aukin, in interview, December 2006.
29 David Aukin, in interview, December 2006.

16 Whitehall warriors fight privatisation

1   Sir Michael Bishop, in interview, March and May 2006.
2   Sir Michael Bishop, in interview, March and May 2006.
3   Sir Michael Bishop, in interview, March and May 2006.
4   Channel 4 archive.
5   Memo, 17 July 1996, Channel 4 archive.
6   Sir Michael Bishop, in interview, March and May 2006.
7   Letter to John Major, Prime Minister, from Sir Michael Bishop, 28 June 1996, Channel 4 archive.
8   Sir Michael Bishop, in interview, March and May 2006.
9   Channel 4 archive.
10 Note of meeting, Channel 4 archive.
11 Channel 4 archive.
12 Channel 4 archive.
13 Channel 4 archive.
14 Sir Michael Bishop, in interview, March and May 2006.
15 Channel 4 archive.
16 Channel 4 archive.
17 Channel 4 archive.
18 Channel 4 archive.
19 Channel 4 archive.
20 Channel 4 archive.
21 Channel 4 archive.
22 Channel 4 paper, November 1996.
23 Channel 4 archive.
24 Sir Michael Bishop, in interview, March and May 2006.
25 Sir Michael Bishop, in interview, March and May 2006.
26 Channel 4 archive.
27 Letter from Tony Blair, Leader of the Labour Party, to Michael Grade, 16 July 1996, Channel 4 archive.
28 Sir Michael Bishop, in interview, March and May 2006.
29 Chris Smith, in interview, August 2006.
30 Sir Michael Bishop, interview with Maggie Brown, *Guardian* media section, January 1998.

17 Lexus man arrives

1   Andrew Newman, in interview, February 2007.
2   Peter Fincham, in interview, December 2006.
3   Channel 4 board minutes, 27 January 2007.
4   Dan Chambers, in interview, January 2007. Chambers was Director of Programmes, Channel Five, 2003–6.
5   David Scott, in interview, October 2006.
6   In 1996, turnover passed the half-billion mark at £518 million; operating profit before payment to ITV was £134.3 million; ratings were 10.7 per cent. In the four years since 1993, it eliminated the price discount inherited from ITV on its advertising, leading to substantial revenue growth.
7   Sir Jeremy Isaacs, in interview, December 2006.
8   Graham Smith, in interview, July 2006.
9   These figures are for 1998, the first year of Jackson's era, but such is the time lag in television that the schedules were devised the year before.
10 John Willis, in interview, December 2006.
11 John Willis, in interview, December 2006.
12 John Willis, in interview, December 2006.
13 David Plowright, in interview (by phone), May 2006. He died that August.
14 Michael Jackson, in interview, August 2006.
15 Will Wyatt (2003) *The Fun Factory: A Life in the BBC*, London: Aurum, p. 302.
16 Richard Eyre, in interview, November 2006. Eyre told Nigel Walmsley, a former Capital Radio director now running Carlton Television, and this led to him going on instead to run the ITV Network and apply for the director generalship of the BBC in 1999. A further irony is that Mark Thompson and Andy Duncan are both devout Christians.
17 Andy Barnes, in interview, May 2006.
18 John Willis, in interview, December 2006.
19 Chris Smith, in interview, August 2006.
20 Chris Smith, in interview, August 2006.
21 Chris Smith, in interview, August 2006.
22 Chris Smith, in interview, August 2006.
23 Interview with David Puttnam, September 2006, confirmed by Chris Smith. In the event, Puttnam did not become Vice Chairman of the BBC.
24 Vanni Treves, in interview, December 2006.
25 Vanni Treves, in interview, December 2006.
26 Vanni Treves, in interview, December 2006.
27 Vanni Treves, in interview, December 2006.
28 Vanni Treves, in interview, December 2006.
29 David Scott, in interview, October 2006.
30 Vanni Treves, in interview, December 2006.
31 Vanni Treves, in interview, December 2006.
32 Vanni Treves, in interview, December 2006.

18   New things in the air

1   Jon Snow, in interview, January 2007.
2   Stewart Purvis, in interview, November 2006.
3   Michael Jackson, Chief Executive's report, 'Open to Ideas', November 1997, Channel 4 archive.
4   Jackson, 'Open to Ideas'.
5   Jackson, 'Open to Ideas'.
6   Jackson, 'Open to Ideas'. In 2007, Kamal Ahmed was Executive Editor of the *Observer*.
7   Stewart Purvis, in interview, November 2006.
8   Stewart Purvis, in interview, November 2006.
9   Jon Snow, in interview, January 2007. Sara Nathan embarked on a new direction. She became a member of the Radio Authority, then a member of the first Ofcom Board, 2002–7, and Deputy Chair of the Ofcom content board. She continues to have a distinguished public career.
10 Michael Jackson, in interview, August 2006.
11 Channel 4 board minutes, January 1998.
12 Stewart Purvis, in interview, November 2006.
13 Jon Snow, in interview, January 2007.
14 Jon Snow, in interview, January 2007.
15 Tim Gardam, Director of Programmes, 'Core Channel Programme Strategy', 25 April 2000.
16 Gardam, 'Core Channel Programme Strategy'.
17 Peter Moore, in interview, November 2006.
18 Michael Jackson, in interview, August 2006.
19 Michael Jackson, in interview, August 2006.
20 Michael Jackson, in interview, August 2006.
21 Michael Jackson, in interview, August 2006.
22 Michael Jackson, in interview, August 2006.
23 Jules Oldroyd, in interview, March 2007.
24 Michael Jackson, in interview, August 2006.
25 Jules Oldroyd, in interview, March 2007.
26 Michael Jackson, in interview, August 2006.
27 David Scott, in interview, October 2006.
28 Michael Jackson, in interview, August 2006.
29 Michael Jackson, in interview, August 2006.
30 Caroline Leddy, Andrew Newman, Sue Murphy and Cheryl Taylor.
31 Kevin Lygo, in interview, December 2006.
32 Geoff Atkinson, in interview, July 2006.
33 Peter Fincham, in interview, December 2006.
34 Peter Fincham, in interview, December 2006.
35 Peter Fincham, in interview, December 2006.
36 Peter Fincham, in interview, December 2006.
37 Peter Fincham, in interview, December 2006.
38 Andrew Newman, in interview, February 2007.
39 Peter Fincham, in interview, December 2006.

40 Graham Norton, in interview, January 2007.
41 Graham Norton, in interview, January 2007.
42 Graham Norton, in interview, January 2007.
43 Michael Jackson, in interview, August 2006.
44 Russell T. Davies, in interview, March 2007.
45 Russell T. Davies, in interview, March 2007.
46 Russell T. Davies, in interview, March 2007.
47 Michael Jackson, in interview, August 2006.

19 Spending spree

1   Channel 4 board minutes, 19 June 1998.
2   Channel 4 was granted half of Digital 3 and 4 multiplexes and required to build digital terrestrial television transmitters. It had promised Chris Smith, Culture Secretary, a FilmFour channel under the agreement negotiated in 1997 to scrap the funding formula.
3   David Scott, in interview, October 2006.
4   Tom Sykes, in interview, September 2006.
5   Channel 4 board minutes, 9 April 2001. The policy was clearly falling apart.
6   David Scott, in interview, October 2006.
7   The Board of 8 July 2002 was told that the cost of films to Channel 4 were 'generous' by market standards. With 'hindsight was it seen as an overstated cost.' In other words, FilmFour Productions had been more subsidised than the losses suggested.
8   David Scott, in interview, October 2006.
9   Michael Jackson, Royal Television Society, Cambridge Convention, September 2003.
10 Michael Jackson, Royal Television Society, Cambridge Convention, September 2003.
11 The deal cost £117 million and expired at the end of 2000. The average cost per hour was £20,000, but a lot was simply unused.
12 David Scott, in interview, October 2006.
13 June Dromgoole, in interview, April 2007.
14 June Dromgoole, in interview, April 2007.
15 David Scott, in interview, October 2006.
16 The total figure was reported to be £124 million, and part of it was swiftly written off in 2000. The West Wing was delayed a year, its theme of quasi-realistic presidential politics was feared too boring for British tastes.
17 The total outlay in 2001 was £66.7 million, of which £11.7 million went on marketing. FilmFour Channels cost £23.6 million.
18 Channel 4 board minutes, 28 February 2000.
19 Tom Sykes, in interview, September 2006.
20 David Scott, in interview, October 2006.
21 Tom Sykes, in interview, September 2006.
22 Correspondence from Elstein in Channel 4 archive.
23 Channel 4 board meeting, 28 February 2000. The Board did not meet in August or January and had only seven or eight meetings a year.
24 John Newbigin, in interview, December 2006.
25 Tom Sykes, in interview, September 2006.

26 Michael Jackson, in interview, August 2006.
27 David Scott, in interview, October 2006.

20 The wall of leisure

1 Daisy Goodwin, in interview, May 2007.
2 Channel 4 Qualitative Research 2006. The *Grand Designs* audience is 54 per cent ABC1s, 57 per cent female, with 37 per cent aged thirty-seven to fifty-four, 36 per cent over fifty-five.
3 *Location, Location, Location* launched with a 1.8 million audience, an 8.8 per cent share, and was then tried out as a substitute for *Brookside*.
4 Ben Frow interview, *Media Guardian*, 31 March 2003.
5 Ben Frow interview, *Media Guardian*, 31 March 2003.
6 Ben Frow interview, *Media Guardian*, 31 March 2003.
7 Memo to commissioning heads, 'The Way Ahead', October 2002.
8 Jeremy Gibson, the BBC's Controller of Documentaries, was also considered for the post. Gardam formally arrived in December 1998 because David Elstein, Chief Executive of Five, held him to his contract. Gardam's direct boss Dawn Airey's sole concern was to ascertain his salary, to check that she was not being underpaid. Then she was sweetness and light.
9 Dan Chambers, in interview, January 2007.
10 Tim Gardam, in interview, January and February 2007.
11 Tim Gardam, in interview, January and February 2007.
12 Tim Gardam, letter preserved by David Stevenson.
13 Memo to commissioning heads, 'The Way Ahead', October 2002.
14 Memo to commissioning heads, 'The Way Ahead', October 2002.
15 Memo to commissioning heads, 'The Way Ahead', October 2002.
16 The channel ran a number of series with sexually provocative titles. *Private Parts* attracted 3.97 million at 10 p.m., a 22.5 per cent share. Commissioning editor Simon Andreae also broke new ground with *Anatomy of Desire*, which included a fetishist who liked to be nailed to a cross and a man whose testicles were inflated with two litres of saline. Other series in this vein included *Animal Passions*, *Beyond Love* and *Anatomy of Disgust*.
17 Dorothy Byrne, in interview, January 2007.
18 Lambert owned up in 2007 to editing footage of the Queen to make it appear she had walked out of a photo shoot with Annie Leibovitz. The débâcle also affected the standing of Peter Fincham, runner-up for the Chief Executive of Channel 4 job, who, as Controller of BBC1, had played the edited footage to journalists.
19 Tim Gardam, in interview, January and February 2007.
20 Amanda Ross, in interview, January 2007.
21 Amanda Ross, in interview, January 2007.
22 Amanda Ross, in interview, January 2007.
23 Amanda Ross, in interview, January 2007.
24 Peter Bazalgette, appointed April 2001–May 2004, was the last independent producer who would sit on the Channel 4 Board.
25 Amanda Ross, in interview, January 2007.

26 Sue Carroll, *Mirror*, 4 August 1999.
27 Tim Gardam, in interview, January and February 2007.
28 Director of Programmes Report to Channel 4 Board, 17 April 2000.
29 Director of Programmes Report to Channel 4 Board, 17 April 2000.
30 Rosemary Newell, in interview, January 2007.
31 Channel 4 archive.
32 An early list of the sports covered included archery, Australian rugby league, Australian Rules football, badminton, baseball, billiards, bowls, amateur boxing, canoeing, climbing, cricket, croquet, curling, cycling, diving, dressage, fencing, Gaelic football, golf, gymnastics, handball, handicapped sport, judo, lacrosse, netball, polo, rowing, shooting, show jumping, sumo wrestling, swimming, tennis, volleyball, water polo, amateur wrestling and yachting. In cooperation with ITV, it had covered athletics, racing, skating and snooker. It added the Tour de France in 1985, kaddadi, American football and then Italian football under Michael Grade.
33 Michael Jackson, in interview, August 2006.

21 Caught out by 9/11

1 'Implementing the Strategy: Structural and Organisational Implications', board paper, Channel 4 archive.
2 Vanni Treves had wanted Robin Miller as his deputy but was talked into having Barry Cox as a balance instead, in the wholesale change of board under Labour.
3 Robin Miller, Channel 4 board minutes, 11 December 2000.
4 Barry Cox, in interview, April 2007.
5 Tim Gardam, in interview, January and February 2007.
6 ITC Annual Report 2001. In 1997, the there was a 6-per-cent growth in advertising; for 1998 and 1999 it was 5 per cent, then in 2000 it was 11 per cent. The three main channels – ITV, Channel 4 and Five – saw £323 million disappear in 2001, 10 per cent of the total. For Channel 4, revenue fell by a more reasonable 5 per cent.
7 Channel 4 board minutes, 24 May 2001.
8 Barry Cox, in interview, April 2007.
9 Barry Cox, in interview, April 2007.
10 Michael Jackson, in interview, August 2006.
11 Peter Bazalgette, at this point, was Chairman of Endemol UK and a director of Brighter Pictures, Victoria Real and Zeppotron, the subsidiaries supplying Channel 4 with *Big Brother* and new-media extensions. He was a non-executive director, 2001–4.
12 Vanni Treves, in interview, December 2006.
13 Vanni Treves, in interview, December 2006. Interestingly, when Jackson finally did leave, Treves wrote in his leaving book, '3 out of 3! The Channel owes you a great deal as does the public interest. You have been a remarkable chief executive' (Michael Jackson, in interview, July 2007).
14 Peter Bazalgette, in interview, May 2007.
15 Vanni Treves, in interview, December 2006.
16 New Statesman Annual Media Lecture, Banqueting Hall, Whitehall, 31 October 2001.
17 David Puttnam, in interview, September 2006.
18 Vanni Treves, in interview, December 2006.

19 Michael Jackson, in interview, August 2006.
20 Vanni Treves, in interview, December 2006.
21 Barry Cox, in interview, April 2007.
22 Peter Bazalgette, in interview, May 2007.
23 Vanni Treves, in interview, December 2006.
24 Barry Cox, in interview, April 2007.
25 Peter Bazalgette, in interview, May 2007.
26 Vanni Treves, in interview, December 2006.
27 David Scott, written account, August 2007.
28 Belinda Giles, in interview, January 2007.
29 Andrew Brann, in interview, October 2006.
30 Vanni Treves, in interview, December 2006.
31 Michael Jackson, in interview, August 2006.
32 *Big Brother* generated the extra sixteen-to-thirty-four commercial impacts post-2000. The channel's weighting towards young adults suddenly jumped in 2000 from an index of 134 to 140. (Channel 4 Annual Report, 2000).

22 Thompson's vaulting ambition

1 Vanni Treves, in interview, December 2006. He had raised the Equitable chairmanship with the DCMS before taking it on.
2 Channel 4 board minutes, 28 October 2002. (Rob Woodward.)
3 Greg Dyke (2004) *Greg Dyke: Inside Story*, London: HarperCollins.
4 The other key architects were Carolyn Fairbairn, BBC Director of Strategy and Andy Duncan, Director of Marketing, with their teams.
5 The remit now set out the role: 'The provision of a broad range of high quality and other programmes which, in particular demonstrates innovation, experiment and creativity in the form and content of programmes; appeals to the tastes and interests of a culturally diverse society makes a significant contribution to meeting the need [. . .] for programmes of an educational nature, and other programmes of an educative value; exhibits a distinctive character.'
6 Steve Morrison, Chief Operating Officer of Granada Media Group, called for a stronger remit in 1996, in a speech called 'The Privatisation of Channel 4' at the Edinburgh Television Festival.
7 David Puttnam, in interview, September 2006.
8 Channel 4 board minutes, 25 March 2002.
9 Mark Thompson, in interview, March 2007.
10 Channel 4 board minutes, 28 October 2002.
11 Paul Abbott, in interview, December 2006.
12 Under a five-year financial plan, staff at Channel 4 were 596 and 261 in 4Ventures. Overheads were chopped back from £108 million to £72 million.
13 Sue Woodford, in interview, September 2006.
14 Jan Younghusband, in interview, May 2007.
15 Tessa Ross, in interview, April 2007.
16 Mark Thompson, in interview, March 2007.
17 Andy Grumbridge, in interview, July 2006.

18 Mark Thompson, in interview, March 2007.

19 It had a 16 per cent share of sixteen-to-thirty-fours in multichannel homes by 2003, up from 11 per cent, aided by E4.

20 Mark Thompson, in interview, March 2007.

21 Mark Thompson strategy paper, 14 July 2003.

22 Five's shareholders were RTL and United Business Media, chaired by Lord Clive Hollick, with a minority 35 per cent.

23 Richard Hooper, in interview, September 2006. Hooper had served on the United News and Media board. Hollick had sold his ITV franchises for £1.7 billion the height of the market in 2001.

24 Stephen Carter, in interview, July 2006.

25 John Newbigin, in interview, October 2006.

26 John Newbigin, in interview, October 2006.

27 Mark Thompson, in interview, March 2007.

28 John Newbigin, in interview, October 2006.

29 *Royal Television Society Journal*, October 2003.

30 *Royal Television Society Journal*, October 2003.

31 *Royal Television Society Journal*, October 2003. By the Royal Television Society convention in 2007, Michael Grade, now Executive Chairman of ITV, had changed his mind again, saying that privatisation for Channel 4 was preferable to taking a subsidy and losing its independence.

32 *Royal Television Society Journal*, October 2003.

33 John Newbigin, in interview, October 2006.

34 Stephen Carter, in interview, July 2006.

35 Stephen Carter, in interview, July 2006.

36 Luke Johnson, in interview, December 2006.

37 Luke Johnson, in interview, December 2006.

38 Stephen Carter, in interview, July 2006.

39 Mark Thompson, in interview, March 2007.

40 Luke Johnson, in interview, December 2006.

41 Luke Johnson and Peter Bazalgette, in correspondence, August 2007.

42 David Puttnam, in interview, September 2006.

43 Stephen Carter, in interview, July 2006.

44 Richard Hooper, in interview, September 2006.

45 Mark Thompson, in interview, March 2007.

46 Luke Johnson, in interview, December 2006.

47 Luke Johnson, in interview, December 2006.

23 Two men with L plates

1 Andy Duncan, in interview, December 2006.

2 Andy Duncan, in interview, December 2006.

3 Andy Duncan, in interview, December 2006.

4 Andy Duncan, in interview, December 2006.

5 Andy Duncan, in interview, December 2006.

6 Andy Duncan, in interview, December 2006.

7　David Puttnam, in interview, September 2006.

8　Channel 4 board minutes, 23 February 2004. It was the public-service review paper for Ofcom.

9　Johnson totally reconstructed the Board, with Karren Brady, Managing Director of Birmingham Football Club and Andy Mollett, Director of EMI, both appointed July 2004; Tony Hall, Chief Executive of the Royal Opera House, former Chief Executive BBC News (April 2005); Stephen Hill, former Chief Executive the *Financial Times* and founding partner 3i Quoted Private Equity Advisers (January 2006); Lord Puttnam, Deputy Chairman and Martha Lane-Fox, Founder lastminute.com (February 2006). The retired directors included Peter Bazalgette (Channel 4's Corporate Governance Report 2002 stated: 'Specifically, Peter Bazalgette plays no part in commissioning programmes'), Ian Ritchie, Andrew Graham, Robin Miller, Barry Cox and executives David Scott and Rob Woodward.

10　Luke Johnson, in interview, December 2006.

11　Stephen Carter, in interview, July 2006.

12　Dorothy Byrne, in interview, January 2007.

13　Peter Grimsdale, in interview, January 2007.

14　Sara Ramsden, in interview, May 2006.

15　Dorothy Byrne, in interview, January 2007.

16　Barry Cox, in interview, April 2007.

17　Luke Johnson, in interview, December 2006.

18　Luke Johnson, in interview, December 2006.

19　Stephen Carter, in interview, July 2006.

20　Andy Duncan, in interview, December 2006.

21　Luke Johnson, in interview, December 2006.

22　Luke Johnson, in interview, December 2006.

23　Andy Duncan, in interview, January 2007.

24　Ofcom removed an ex-ante piece of competition regulation inherited from the ITC that prevented the Channel 4 and Five sales houses aggregating.

25　Luke Johnson, in interview, December 2006.

26　Luke Johnson, in interview, December 2006.

27　Andy Duncan, in interview, January 2007.

28　More4 press release, August 2005.

29　Andy Duncan, in interview, January 2007.

30　The *Observer*, 22 January 2006.

31　Philip Graf, *Royal Television Society Journal*, September 2006.

32　Stephen Carter, in interview, July 2006.

33　Stephen Carter, in interview, July 2006.

34　Stephen Carter, in interview, July 2006.

35　Andy Duncan, The New Statesman Media Lecture, 'Maximising Public Value in the "Now" Media World', 21 June 2006.

36　Luke Johnson, in interview, December 2006.

24 Big Brother

1   Peter Bazalgette (2005) *Billion Dollar Game: How Three Men Risked It All and Changed the Face of TV*, London: Little, Brown.
2   Michael Jackson, in interview, August 2006.
3   Julia LeStage, in interview, January 2007.
4   Tim Gardam, in interview, January and February 2007.
5   Julia LeStage, in interview, October 2000.
6   Julia LeStage, in interview, October 2000.
7   Michael Jackson, in interview, August 2006.
8   Tim Gardam, interview, *Guardian*, July 2003.
9   Quoted in Matt Wells, *Guardian*, 3 November 2001.
10 Tim Gardam, in interview, January and February 2007.
11 ITC Annual Report, 2000.
12 Julian Bellamy, in interview, December 2006.
13 Danny Cohen, in interview, March 2007.
14 Mark Thompson, in interview, April 2007.
15 Peter Grimsdale, in interview, November 2006.
16 Neil Simpson (2005) *Jade's World: The Inside Story of Britain's Best-Loved Celebrity*, London: John Blake.
17 Julian Bellamy, in interview, December 2006.
18 Tim Gardam, in interview, January and February 2007.
19 Julian Bellamy, in interview, December 2006.
20 Tim Gardam, interview, *Guardian*, July 2003.
21 Vanni Treves, in interview, December 2006.
22 John Humphrys, 'First, Do No Harm', MacTaggart Lecture, 2004.

25 Channel 4 at the crossroads

1   'What's the Point of Channel 4?', *Guardian* G2, 22 March 2007.
2   Submissions by the IPA and others to the Ofcom Financial Review of Channel 4, May 2007.
3   Ofcom's Content-Sanctions Committee adjudication in the fifth series of *Celebrity Big Brother*, paras 4.9 and 4.10, published 24 May 1007.
4   Ofcom, *Celebrity Big Brother* adjudication.
5   Peter Bazalgette, in interview, May 2007.
6   Danny Cohen, in interview, March 2007.
7   By day forty-eight (of ninety-three) of *Big Brother 8*, the number of sixteen-to-thirty-fours watching had fallen from 1.9 million in 2006 to 1.4 million. Half a million had turned off. Amongst ABC1s, the drop was 20 per cent, or 355,000 people.
8   Introduced in the summer of 2007, Channel 4+1 was expected to regain up to 1 per cent of lost audience share.
9   Kevin Lygo, in interview, April 2007.
10 It averaged an audience of 2.6 million on Channel 4. The E4 repeats raised the total audience to 3.4 million, down 27 per cent.

11 David Puttnam, *Media Guardian*, 31 May 2007.

12 'How to Rebuild Public Trust', interview with Steve Clarke, *Royal Television Society Journal*, May 2007.

13 Anthony Smith, 'Has Big Brother Won?', speech to the Athenaeum, 6 March 2007.

14 Smith, 'Has Big Brother Won?'

15 Angus MacQueen, in interview, April 2007.

16 LEK analysis of Channel 4's finances going back over the previous five years, covering business plans, management accounts and future projections.

17 Channel 4 press release, 4 April 2007.

18 Article by Steve Hewlett, *Royal Television Society Journal*, forthcoming.

19 The top six super indies by spend are Endemol, Lime Pictures (*Hollyoaks*, part of All3Media), RDF, Olga TV (*The New Paul O'Grady Show*), At It Productions (*4Music Presents*) and Cactus (*Richard & Judy*).

20 Submissions by the IPA and others to the Ofcom Financial Review of Channel 4, May 2007.

21 Luke Johnson, Chairman's Introduction, Channel 4 Annual Report and Accounts, 2006.

22 Andy Duncan, in interview, February 2007.

23 Ed Richards, Ofcom press briefing, 14 June 2007.

24 Ed Richards, Ofcom press briefing.

Conclusion

1 Peter Bazalgette, in interview, May 2007.

2 Kevin Lygo, in interview, April 2007.

3 Kevin Lygo, speech to the Edinburgh Television Festival, 24 August 2007.

4 Luke Johnson, in interview, December 2006.

Index